THE EMERGENCE OF SYMBOLS

Cognition and Communication in Infancy

LANGUAGE, THOUGHT, AND CULTURE: *Advances in the*
Study of Cognition

Under the Editorship of: E. A. HAMMEL

DEPARTMENT OF ANTHROPOLOGY
UNIVERSITY OF CALIFORNIA
BERKELEY

THE EMERGENCE OF SYMBOLS

Cognition and Communication in Infancy

ELIZABETH BATES
Department of Psychology
University of Colorado
Boulder, Colorado

with the collaboration of

LAURA BENIGNI   LUIGIA CAMAIONI
INGE BRETHERTON   VIRGINIA VOLTERRA

VICKI CARLSON   KARLANA CARPEN   MARCIA ROSSER

ACADEMIC PRESS   New York   San Francisco   London   1979
A Subsidiary of Harcourt Brace Jovanovich, Publishers

ACADEMIC PRESS, INC.
111 Fifth Avenue, New York, New York 10003

United Kingdom Edition published by
ACADEMIC PRESS, INC. (LONDON) LTD.
24/28 Oval Road, London NW1 7DX

Library of Congress Cataloging in Publication Data
Main entry under title:

The emergence of symbols.

 (Language, thought, and culture)
 Bibliography: p.
 1. Infant psychology. 2. Cognition in children.
3. Children――Language. 4. Symbolism (Psychology)
I. Bates, Elizabeth. [DNLM: 1. Cognition――In
infancy and childhood. 2. Communication――In
infancy and childhood. 3. Language development.
4. Psycholinguistics. WS105.5.C8 E53]
BF723.I6E44 155.4'22   78―20040
ISBN 0―12―081540―0

*This book is women's work. We dedicate it to our mothers,
the women who got us interested in language in the first place.*

CONTENTS

PREFACE

We are investigating some very old themes in this book: the nature and origin of symbols, the interdependence of language and thought, parallels between ontogeny and phylogeny. The human infants who are the focus of our study are presented against a patchwork quilt of ideas from philosophy (ranging from Aristotle to Peirce and Wittgenstein), from psychology (particularly Piaget and Werner), plus some threads from Darwin, evolutionary theory, and modern regulatory biology. The data representing our own additions to this conceptual set are new and interesting. We have examined the emergence of symbols in language and in action, in a sample of 25 infants followed longitudinally from 9 to 13 months of age (plus a subsample studied once more at 19 months). In addition, the infants and their mothers provided us with considerable data concerning a network of communicative and cognitive developments that seem to bear a close structural relationship to the symbolic capacity itself, for example, tool use, imitation, and preverbal gesture.

This work is part of a fairly widespread effort in psycholinguistics in the past few years to seek out some possible prerequisites to language. Notice, however, that we have avoided talking about the "cause" or "explanation" for the emergence of symbols. One of our goals in this volume is to clarify some of the conceptual and methodological issues involved in the search for prerequisites to language. We have relied entirely on qualitative descriptions of behavior, interviews with mothers, and correlational analyses of the data yielded by both techniques. There is no reason to apologize for any of these methods, but we must be very clear about their limitations. In Chapter 1 we discuss the distinction between homology (behaviors with a shared structural base) and analogy (behaviors that are independent but similar adaptations to problems with a similar structure) in the study of linguistic and nonlinguistic developments. Emphasis is placed on the kinds of data that are necessary to establish claims of homology, and the kinds of causal inferences that are involved in such claims. In Chapter 2 conceptual and operational definitions are offered for such controversial terms as "intention," "convention," and "symbolic" versus "nonsymbolic" behavior. In Chapters 3 and 6 we discuss the limits and advantages of the correlational method as applied in our own research.

All of this care in labeling and packaging is necessary precisely because so many controversial issues are involved, for example, the role of gesture in language development, relations between language and tool use in ontogeny and phylogeny, the nature of the mother–child relationship and its role in cognitive and linguistic development. We have permitted ourselves the luxury of broad speculations based on biological theory, setting up analogies that (according to some of our friendlier critics) border on science fiction without the Orwellian flair. However, our results have implications for several new lines of research. Even though correlations are never a conclusive demonstration of cause, the correlations presented here give some indication of where to look next for some possible causes of language evolution and normal language development. We have introduced some notions concerning "threshold levels" in the component skills underlying language, that is, the amount of each capacity that is necessary for critical interactions to take place, leading to the emergence of a new and qualitatively different capacity for symbols. In other words, the location of prerequisites, or capacities that contribute to language development, is only a first step. If we can develop precise, graded measures of these capacities we may also be able to determine how much of a particular skill is necessary for language development to occur under normal circumstances. This threshold notion may also have implications for the diagnosis and treatment of language disorders that involve specific linguistic and nonlinguistic deficits. In addition, this approach has some implications for comparative research on cognitive development in nonhuman primates, that is, phylogenetic neighbors who have some of the machinery necessary for language development, but apparently not enough.

In sum, we are suggesting an approach that goes beyond the identification of prerequisites to language, to a more precise study of (*a*) requisite levels within these prerequisite skills and (*b*) the kinds of interactions among components that are possible at each level of cognitive development leading up to the emergence of symbols. Take, for example, the old evolutionary theme of the relationship between language and tool use. Does this purported relationship have any bearing on language development in ontogeny? If so, how much understanding of tool use does an infant have at the point where he discovers that things have names? Why should these two aspects of infant behavior be related at all? Can we explain the link within a conceptual model of symbol structure, or must we rest at the level of correlation? At the very least, the results presented here raise a new set of questions about the old issue of symbol development, and suggest some starting points for exploring those questions.

ACKNOWLEDGMENTS

This work represents a collaboration in the fullest sense of the term. In Chapters 3–6, the first author is the writer and the investigator with greatest responsibility for the final interpretation given to the data. Otherwise, alphabetical order is maintained and should be taken to mean full partnership at every level. There is one exception: Inge Bretherton must be credited for all the statistical analyses, since she assumed primary responsibility for managing several miles (or kilometers) of computer output. Chapters 1, 2, and 7 represent my own meanderings toward the close of the project, and have been kept separate from team authorship primarily to insure that responsibility is clarified. There are some passages in those chapters where the group reaction was one of detached amusement and tolerance. If they are to be blamed, it should be for their permissiveness and not for the consistent and high quality intellectual support and criticism that they have provided for many years. My own peculiar headship on the title page reflects page counts and nothing more. The research itself was entirely a team effort and a remarkably pleasant experience.

The data reported in Chapters 3–6 were collected by a team of sensitive and devoted research assistants who worked with us for months without pay before grant funds were available: Vicki Carlson, Dorothy Holloway, Jocelyn Javitz, Dorothy Poulsen, Marcia Rosser, Glenn Wasek, Domenico Maiolo, Valeria Venza, and Anna Zaccagnini. Karlana Carpen and Cecilia Shore also put in long hours helping in the final preparation of the manuscript. During the data collection period, equipment and tapes were provided by the Institute of Psychology, National Council of Research (CNR) in Rome, and by an NIMH Biomedical Research Grant to the University of Colorado. During the phases of transcription, data analysis, and writing, support was provided by NSF Grant #BNS57617624 at the University of Colorado, and by CNR in Rome, with supplementary assistance from the University of Colorado Council on Creative Research. In addition, grants from the Fulbright Foundation permitted Luigia Camaioni and Virginia Volterra to come to the United States to collaborate on later phases of the project.

Many of the ideas presented in Chapters 1, 2, and 7 grew out of a graduate seminar on language origins at the University of California at Berkeley, during my year as a visiting assistant professor in 1976–1977. I am especially grateful to my friend and coteacher in that course, Dan Slobin, and to the students who contributed so much to a long series of lively discussions: Chris Chiarello, Jeffrey Chubb, Jane Edwards, Mary Erbaugh, Sue Gal, Meredith Hoffman, Terry Jacobsen, John Kingston, Beth Ann O'Connell, Martha Platt, Henry Thompson, Jeanne van Osten, Robert van Valen, and Tony Woodbury. We are also grateful to several colleagues who took the time to read and criticize earlier versions of these chapters: Eve Clark, Veronica Fabian, Howard Gardner, Jerome Kagan, Brian MacWhinney, Michael Maratsos, Domenico Parisi, Steve Reznick, and Dan Slobin.

Finally, infinite thanks to the 25 children and their parents who taught us so much.

                                                                      Elizabeth Bates

Chapter 1
ON THE EVOLUTION AND DEVELOPMENT OF SYMBOLS[1]

Elizabeth Bates

Nature is a miser. She clothes her children in hand-me-downs, builds new machinery in makeshift fashion from sundry old parts, and saves genetic expenditures whenever she can by relying on high-probability world events to insure and stabilize outcomes. Looking at the beauty of her finished products, we often fail to see that they are held together with tape and safety pins. It is only when something goes wrong that we notice where the seams are. In this book we are looking at one of Nature's most interesting achievements, the construction of the capacity for symbols. Looking at the adult end of that development, we can be overwhelmed (narcissists that we are) at the complexity and perfection of a symbol-using mind. But if we trace this marvel to its beginning in human infancy, we will see that this particular work of art is a collage, put together out of a series of old parts that developed quite independently. This does not make the achievement any less wonderful. But it does begin to make it understandable.

If science proceeded in a linear fashion, this particular work on

[1] Portions of this chapter appear in E. Bates, "The Emergence of Symbols: Ontogeny and Phylogeny," in W. Collins (Ed.), *Proceedings from the 12th Minnesota Symposium in Child Development* (New Jersey: Erlbaum), in press.

1

symbol development would already be obsolete—and not simply because the question of the origin of symbols is an old one. Good questions like that are never fully answered; they merely get asked again in different ways. But the particular hypotheses and methods we have used to examine the onset of the symbolic capacity in infants were available long before we began to use them. In 1962, Piaget's book *La formation du symbol* was published in English under the title *Play, Dreams, and Imitation in Childhood*. In 1963, Werner and Kaplan published *Symbol Formation*. Both of these were seminal works by major figures in developmental psychology, with vast amounts of theory based on relatively scant observations. This seems like precisely the sort of situation that would inspire an important new line of research. The work we will report here, which began in 1972, owes a great deal to both these books in theme, in content, even in title. However, it is surprising that in the intervening 10 years these two major works had relatively little influence on developmental research. Why were Piaget and Werner so conspicuously ignored in the 1970s, at least with regard to their work on symbolization? I suspect that the answer has a lot to do with scientific fashion. It was also during the early 1960s that the new field of psycholinguistics burst forward, influenced in large measure by Chomsky (1957, 1965) and a general fascination with syntax. An important tenet of the early psycholinguistic movement was the uniqueness of language, a complex system that seemed unlike other aspects of cognition, acquired in accordance with an innate and highly specific developmental program (McNeill,1966). Just at that point in history, Piaget and Werner came into the American marketplace with theories stressing the integration of linguistic symbols with other aspects of symbolic functioning, and the gradual emergence of language from a network of nonlinguistic developments. This simply was not a message that people were ready to hear. Indeed, I remember reading *Symbol Formation* as a student in the middle 1960s, and finding it incomprehensible and largely irrelevant. When I returned to it again years later, I was amazed at how interesting the book had become while it had been sitting on my shelf all that time.

In the 1970s, the scientific atmosphere has changed markedly. The old question of language origins is again in vogue, and investigators are interested once again in the similarities between language and other cognitive systems. There are three converging developments underlying this shift. First, there has been a backlash against the Chomskian view that children are innately equipped with specific clues to the structure of language. In the early 1970s, several important theoretical papers appeared independently, all of them arguing against the autonomous syntax approach to child language (Bloom, 1973; Bruner, 1975a; Edwards, 1973; MacNamara, 1972; Ryan, 1974; Schlesinger, 1974; Sin-

clair, 1972; Slobin, 1973). None of these papers proposed a return to
Behaviorism or any other form of environmental determinism (cf. Katz
and Bever, 1976). The key theoretical point in 1960's research was
maintained: The child is viewed as a hypothesis tester, an active creator
of successive "theories" about his particular language. The difference
lies in the proposed source of the child's first hypotheses about language.
All of these authors argue that the first "clues" the child brings into
language acquisition are nonlinguistic in origin, derived from 2 prior
years of social interactions (Bruner, 1975a; Schaffer, 1977) and sensorimotor development as described by Piaget (1952, 1954, 1962). Similarly, the so-called functionalist approach to later grammatical development (Bates and MacWhinney,1978) holds that all surface forms are
acquired in the service of communicative functions. The range of possible forms that a language can take is strongly constrained by the range of
meanings that language must convey, interacting with the performance
constraints of the linear (i.e., one word at a time) speech channel. At
every level of language acquisition, from the discovery of symbols to the
use of complex embedded sentences, the child uses functions as his
guide to the acquisition of forms. The work reported in this book is very
much a part of the functionalist movement in psycholinguistics, and we
will have more to say about this general approach later. The point here is
that researchers are now interested in cognitive and social prerequisites
to language, and in nonlinguistic factors that contribute to linguistic
structure. This movement leads directly to the questions posed by Piaget
and by Werner and Kaplan regarding (*a*) the internal structure of
symbols and (*b*) parallels between linguistic and nonlinguistic symbolic
functioning.

   A second reason for renewed interest in the origins of symbols is the
excitement generated by research on the acquisition of language (or
something very languagelike) by nonhuman primates (Fouts,1973;
Gardner and Gardner,1974; Premack,1977; Rumbaugh and Gill,1977).
Above all, this research has challenged our belief in the uniqueness of
human language, suggesting that our symbol-using capacity is not as
discontinuous an evolution as we previously believed. The continuity
issue has led in turn to a definitional debate about when a particular
behavior is truly symbolic, when a particular type of communication can
be properly termed "language." Since many of the behaviors in question
are in fact only **partially** symbolic, we must ask what kinds of parts make
up a complete symbolic act. What are the preconditions for symbol use?
How many of those preconditions are met by chimpanzees?

   A third influence on current research comes from the study of language pathology. Part of the excitement in 1960s psycholinguistics came
from the field of neurolinguistics (Lenneberg,1967), in particular the

theory that the language capacity has its own specific neural wiring
which breaks down in brain-damaged children and adults in various
forms of the syndrome called "aphasia." However, despite years of
research on this question, it is still not entirely clear that aphasia is a
language-specific syndrome, or that "the" language area is entirely responsible for the breakdown in communicative competence (van Lancker, 1975). After 30 years of studying aphasics, Wepman (1977) has
concluded that aphasia is a syndrome reflecting a more general pattern
of cognitive impairment, manifest in both linguistic and certain specific
nonlinguistic behaviors. Research on different types of language impairment in children also suggests that a variety of cognitive and social
factors are involved (e.g., Johnston and Ramstad, 1977; Leonard, in
press). In addition, a peculiar phenomenon has recently been added to
the problem of defining language and language deficiency. It is apparently the case that autistic and aphasic children who do **not** acquire
speech in the usual fashion **can** acquire American Sign Language (e.g.,
Baron, Isensee, and Davis,1977; Bonvillian and Nelson,1978), as well as
several other forms of symbolic communication, e.g., the Premack plastic
chip system originally used with chimpanzees (Premack,1977). This
suggests that these children are impaired in some specific **aspect** of
language. Again, we are faced with discerning the internal structure of
symbols, to determine which subcomponents have been selectively impaired in different types of language dysfunction. In some cases the
"missing part" may not look very much like language at all.

All three of these trends are documented in the proceedings of the
1975 New York Academy of Sciences Conference on the Origins of
Language and Speech (Harnad, Steklis, and Lancaster,1977). In the
diverse areas of research represented in these proceedings, we see the
emergence of a cooperative effort, a comparative methodology for peel-
ing apart the different components that make up the language capacity.
Within the study of normal children, comparisons can be made between
language development and parallel (perhaps yoked) developments in
other domains. In comparisons across species, we can identify patterns
of cognitive abilities that seem to be associated with different degrees of
success in acquiring languagelike behavior. In language pathology, different syndromes of language dysfunction can be examined for the
involvement of various nonlinguistic factors. This book represents our
efforts to apply a part of this cooperative research program, examining
the emergence of symbols in normal infants through a comparison of
linguistic and nonlinguistic developments.

We are focusing on the period between 9 and 13 months of age in
normal children. This brief but important period in human ontogeny
includes two critical moments in the dawning of human communication

through symbols: (*a*) the onset of communicative intentions and conventional signals and (*b*) the emergence of symbols and the discovery that things have names. In the next chapter, we will describe these "moments" in more detail, developing a set of working definitions for "intention," "convention," and "symbol," and a model of the internal structure of symbols. The rest of the book will then be devoted to describing patterns of nonlinguistic development that accompany the emergence of symbols from 9 to 13 months. Before launching into that enterprise, however, we must deal with some prior questions:

1. What do we mean by "prerequisites" to language? What kind of a model of language–thought relations does this imply?
2. How does the identification of prerequisites to symbolic functioning "explain" the changes that take place from 9 to 13 months? In short, what model of causation have we assumed here?
3. How do we justify our belief that this set of developments in ontogeny has anything to do with the evolution of language in our species? Why do we believe that this is biological research at all?

On the Nature of Prerequisites

So far we have used the terms "cognitive" and "social prerequisites" as though their meanings were self-evident. Indeed, when we began our first study of infant communication (Bates, Camaioni, and Volterra, 1975), we thought we knew precisely what we were looking for. Upon closer examination, however, it became clear that there are a variety of models for the interdependence of language, cognition, and social development. In an earlier paper on this issue, we came to the conclusion (only slightly tongue in cheek) that there are over 30,000 possible models for the three-way relationship uniting language, cognitive and social developments (Bates, Benigni, Bretherton, Camaioni, and Volterra, 1977). Proponents can be found for just about every one of these positions. And while some approaches differ only in their academic interest, many of them lead to distinct empirical tests.

We do not intend to review 30,000 models here. We do, however, feel that the field would be in less of a muddle if researchers clarified their stand on what is, after all, nothing other than the classical debate on the relationship between language and thought. First, let us clarify some prior terms. Throughout this chapter we have used some rather general terms like "systems," "domains," and "structures." Obviously we are assuming from the outset that there is something identifiable as "language," which is conceptually and empirically separable from something else called "cognition" or "thought," which is in turn distinct from another thing called "social development" or "social interaction." What level are we talking about? At least four are possible. First, we could be discussing language as an entity apart from the human beings who use it. Second, we could be discussing some sort of physiological substrate, a "hardware" system that exists "inside" individuals. Third, we could be using terms like "system" to describe a set of observable behaviors, without making inferences about underlying structures. However, in this book we will use these terms in a fourth sense. **By "systems," "domains," or "structures," we are referring to some sort of software package, a "program" that an individual child or adult "has," which permits generation of behaviors that are externally identifiable as "linguistic," "cognitive," or "social."** In discussing the interdependence of systems, we are trying to determine whether there are indeed three separate programs corresponding to the three behavioral domains, or whether the three apparently separate domains in some sense share the same underlying structural principles. Obviously such an enterprise involves extensive inference from observable behaviors to hypothetical underlying programs. However, we do not share the Behaviorist view that such inference is inherently "unscientific." It is simply hard to do without making a mistake.

Furthermore, in raising the issue of interdependence of systems, we of course assume from the outset that these systems **interact.** Language is indeed acquired by and large in a social situation, fulfilling social goals and expressing cognitive content. I do not think anyone would deny that. But interaction and interdependence are not the same thing. **In our search for prerequisites to language, we are talking about a developmental dependence such that one system requires input from another in order to derive or build its structure.** We are suggesting that there is a Great Borrowing going on, in which language is viewed as a parasitic system that builds its structure by raiding the software packages of prior or parallel cognitive capacities.

In looking for prerequisites to language, investigators generally start with a qualitative analysis—essentially the observation that certain linguistic and nonlinguistic structures "look alike," or seem to belong together on logical grounds. The spate of theoretical papers cited earlier all posed various candidates for cognitive or social prerequisites to language on such qualitative grounds. For example, the Schaffer volume contains several papers arguing that turn-taking and rhythmic patterning in early mother–infant interaction is a sort of protodialogue that leads directly into language. From a cognitive perspective, Bloom (1973) argues that the sensorimotor achievement of object permanence (i.e., knowledge that an object is permanent in time and space despite changes in features, visual accessibility, etc.) might be a prerequisite for the capacity to name substantive objects and events. In our earlier work (Bates, Camaioni, and Volterra, 1975) we argued that social instrumentality (using humans as agents to obtain objects, or using objects as instruments to obtain adult attention in showing, pointing, etc.) involves the same structures that are required for nonsocial tool use (e.g., using a stick to rake in a toy). However, such qualitative observations are not sufficient to establish that two behavioral systems are related. In going beyond qualitative similarity to establish interdependence, the psychologist finds himself in a position parallel to that faced by ethologists, paleontologists, archeologists, historical linguists—any scientist who must infer common origins for two strikingly similar species, languages, shards of pottery, etc. For example, duck feet and fins of fish share common features of webbing. One possible reason for this structural similarity might be that ducks descended from fish ancestors, preserving the webbing intact. Alternatively, perhaps both ducks and fish descend from some third ancestral stock, a protospecies that lent protowebbing to fish and to ducks in separate branchings. There is also a third possibility. Ducks and fish may not be related at all, at least not in any branching recent and/or powerful enough to explain the featural detail of webbing. Instead, webbing may be an efficient, task-constrained, independently evolved "solution" to locomotion through water. Of course there are other possible solutions to the water problem, for example, some sort of jet-propelled movement. The fact that ducks and fish both hit upon the same webbing solution probably does relate to a more general type of shared inheritance (i.e., selection acting upon existing appendages or membranes originally evolved for other purposes). But this rather general piece of shared origins is a necessary but insufficient explanation for the striking featural details of webbing. The coincidental solution achieved by ducks and fish required the intervention of common task constraints interacting with the capacity to evolve and elaborate appendages.

The same three options apply for ethologists tracing the origins of markedly similar behavior patterns between two species. For example, Eibl-Eibesfeldt (1970) describes a highly similar drinking pattern found in two types of grouse. On the basis of other morphological features, zoologists believed that the relations between these two species was fairly remote. Yet the specificity and detail of this odd drinking pattern suggested a more recent relationship, either a direct descendance of one grouse from the other, or descendance from some common ancestor. In the end, the relationship turned out to be one of analogy, the only efficient solution to drinking in arid ground with a particular type of beak. In "analogy," the same solution is independently evolved by two species in response to similar task constraints. In "homology," two species share the same characteristic due to origins in some common genetic stock. In the case of the sand grouse, the possession of a particular type of long beak (a predisposing factor for the drinking pattern) is homologous between the two species. But the evolution of the drinking pattern itself is analogous.

The same homology–analogy problem confronts any researcher who seeks to reconstruct the history of human cultures, including language. Why do several languages share the same phonetic feature? Because of branching from a common ancestral language? Or because, given certain other properties of these languages, the articulatory system dictates certain phonetic combinations and precludes others? In archeology, are certain types of architecture the result of cultural transmission from one area to another? Or are they the result of general engineering principles applied independently to similar types of locally available materials? A parallel problem confronts those of us who seek to reconstruct the ontogenetic development of structures like those involved in language. On the one hand, we may believe that certain combinations of skills are inevitable, given the task constraints of language. On the other hand, why do certain linguistic and nonlinguistic skills fit together so well? What is responsible for what appears to be a striking qualitative similarity or compatibility in structure? There is one notable difference between ontogenetic and phylogenetic reconstruction. In historical studies (phylogenetic and/or "ethnogenetic"), parallels are set up **between** individuals (individual organisms, species, cultures, languages, etc.). In ontogenetic studies, parallels are set up **within** the same individuals, between different structures (organs, behavior systems, etc.). Obviously, then, in ontogenetic studies any two behavioral systems are homologous at some level, if only because they are housed in the same body. However, is the homology shared by two structures sufficient to explain the detailed similarities that we observe in these two forms? For example, can a homology as remote as general intelligence explain the resemblance between social and nonsocial tool use? Probably not. If not, the structures may be similar because of one of three situations:

1. "Homology through direct causation," in which one structure (e.g., nonsocial tool use) is a necessary (though perhaps insufficient) input to communicative development.
2. "Homology through shared origins," in which social and nonsocial

tool use emerge from some third source, perhaps a specific bit of underlying "software" that we can infer only from a set of related behaviors.

3. "Analogy through common task constraints," in which social and nonsocial tool use "look alike" because the respective tasks require independent but structurally similar solutions.

These different models require different kinds of developmental data. For example, researchers espousing homology through direct causation must demonstrate **sequencing** (e.g., that the development of nonsocial tool use always precedes intentional communication) and that no child will develop intentional signalling without showing at least minimal competence in nonsocial tool use. In addition, there should also be significant positive **correlations** between tool use and communicative development across a sample of children, since the child who develops tool use earlier and at higher levels should have an advantage in the development of social signals. Finally, **training** in tool use might be expected to enhance communicative development; however, training in communication should have no effect on tool use. In other words, transfer from one domain to another should be **unidirectional** within the direct causal model.

Researchers arguing for homology through shared origins or shared "software" would also predict significant positive correlations between these two skills across a sample of children. In other words, the child who develops the requisite underlying structure early is likely to apply that structure earlier than other children in both social and nonsocial situations. Furthermore, we would also expect training to work within this homology model, since any experience which enhances the underlying base should spill over into any domain that depends on that base. In other words, transfer from one domain to another should be **bidirectional** within the shared origins model. Finally, in the shared origins model we would have no reason to predict particular sequences of development, at least not for homologous developments at roughly equivalent levels of difficulty. If social and nonsocial tool use are related only because they share underlying cognitive structures, then there is no logical reason why the two should emerge in any particular order. One is not the "cause" of the other. If we do find regular sequencing between the two domains, it may be because of some factor extrinsic to their structural relationship. For example, social tool use may emerge earlier than nonsocial tool use because a child has more experience in operating on human agents. Alternatively, nonsocial tool use might emerge earlier because social applications of the same underlying capacity also require some additional experiences and/or capacities that are not yet available. In Piagetian terms, the time lag between these two kinds of instrumentality may be viewed as a "horizontal decalage" (Piaget, 1970).

The two homology models also have different implications for work with abnormal children. In general, both models would predict patterns of correlation that are the mirror image of those observed with normals. That is, behaviors that are present when language is present in normals should be absent when language is absent in abnormals. Hence with either a direct causal or a shared base model of homology, we might expect tool use and communication to be impaired simultaneously in abnormal children. The differences between the two homology models relate more to diagnosis and therapy with individuals, rather than to correlations across groups.

With regard to diagnosis, both models can be used to describe problems of "blockage" in some types of language impairment. For example, suppose we have a subset of children who do demonstrate appropriate levels of skill in tool use and still do not manifest corresponding levels in communication. This situation can be handled within a direct causal model, if we assume that tool use is necessary but not sufficient for the development of communication. In such instances, we must conclude (*a*) that some other prerequisite to intentional signaling has failed to develop (a competence explanation) or (*b*) that some third factor is blocking or inhibiting the transfer from tool use to communication (a performance explanation). However, with a direct causal model we would never expect the reverse situation, e.g., a child who manifests appropriate levels in communication but fails on tool use tasks. By contrast, a shared origins model can handle "blockage" in either direction: there may be children with criterial levels of tool use who still do not engage in intentional signalling, and vice-versa.

Within a shared base model, we must assume that when **either** capacity is present, the necessary cognitive substrate is there. If other structures dependent on this substrate fail to develop, it must be that (*a*) some other prerequisite for the deficient system is missing (a competence explanation) or (*b*) some other factor is inhibiting or blocking the use of the cognitive substrate of some domains (a performance explanation). In other words, the direct causal model permits blockage in one direction only. The shared base model can handle blockage in either direction. Note that the theoretical notion of "blockage" **assumes** one of these two models of interdependence. If the two domains actually have nothing to do with one another (i.e., are structurally independent), then the whole concept becomes meaningless. This is not a trivial issue, since in principle a blockage approach to diagnosis involves some strong claims about the kind of intervention that is appropriate, i.e., some form of "accessing" or "deblocking" an available structure rather than training the skill from scratch. In practice, deblocking and training may often turn out to look pretty much the same. If we took these models seriously, however, the therapist should be doing very different things—basically the difference between "teaching" and "facilitating recall."

A second implication of these two models concerns the nature of training approaches within therapeutic settings (as opposed to accessing or deblocking). In a direct causal model, we would propose unidirectional training programs, for example, from tool use to communication but not vice versa. In a shared base model, training can be bidirectional. Hence therapy programs would involve doing anything that could be expected to build up the underlying cognitive base.

If we fail to demonstrate correlation (in normals and/or in abnormals), training effects, or necessary sequencing between two hypothetically related structures, we are left only with our qualitative impression of similarity. This does not mean that we must deny our own perceptions, pretending that the parallel is not there. However, if there is no evidence for a relationship between two skills **within the child,** then we must conclude that the common structure exists **within the tasks.** In other words, the failure to demonstrate homology leaves us, by default, with the weaker claim of analogy. Task similarity can be expected, under some circumstances, to create correlations based on remote homologies like IQ, since problems with similar structure and levels of difficulty might require the same amount of general problem-solving ability. So our correlational evidence should include comparisons across abilities at similar levels of difficulty, demonstrating stronger relationships for homologous abilities than for analogous skills. Even so, correlational studies alone cannot fully differentiate homology from analogy. The strongest possible demonstration of homology is a training study demonstrating transfer from one task domain to another. Given the enormous methodological problems involved in training studies, we have decided in our own research to use the correlational method, as a first step toward narrowing down the set of possible prerequisites to language. Despite all the problems of interpretation that correlations pose, this approach is an advance over observational studies with small samples (including our own—Bates, Camaioni, and Volterra, 1975) that base claims of homology entirely upon qualitative similarities between linguistic and nonlinguistic behaviors.

The homology–analogy issue is also relevant to the growing literature on early mother–infant interaction (see Lewis and Rosenblum, 1977, and Schaffer, 1977, for reviews). Most of these studies are detailed microanalyses of postural symmetry, rhythms, and synchrony in vocalization, eye gaze, etc., suggesting that from the first few weeks of life mother and child are "calibrated" to one another in intricate patterns of turn-taking and "protodialogue." These are interesting in themselves, telling us a great deal about the early social predispositions and skills of human infants. However, many of these researchers are also convinced that these early patterns prepare the child for later developments in language (e.g., Bruner, 1977). In other words, the suggestion has been made that language and early dyadic interactions are homologous, within a direct causal model. While this is certainly a plausible hypothesis, we still do not have enough evidence to refute an analogy interpretation. The similarities in pattern between early and later dyadic exchange may be due simply to the structure of two-party interactions, demanding similar but independent solutions in turn-taking, average pause times, etc. Because the microanalytic techniques involved in this research are so time consuming, it has not been possible so far to set up longitudinal studies with samples large enough to permit correlational analyses. However, in the absence of such information we cannot distinguish between homology and analogy. Schaffer (1977) addresses this issue directly in the following passage:

> Under the circumstances it is not surprising to find a tendency to resort to argument based on analogy—no more. Developmental continuity therefore remains an assumption. At any rate let us be clear that there are at least three senses in which one may talk of continuity: first with regard to the *functions* of communication (the wish to obtain certain objects, to affect the other person's behavior, and so on); second with regard to the *constituent skills* required for communication (such as intentionality, role alternation, etc.); and third, with regard to the *situation* in which communication occurs. The last can be particularly misleading: vocal turn-taking, for instance . . . may be found in quite early interactions, providing them with the "mature" appearance of later verbal exchanges, and yet this may be brought about entirely by the mother's skill at inserting her vocalizations at appropriate moments into the child's sequence of vocal activity. The continuity, that is, is in this instance inherent in the dyadic situation and does not refer to a constitutent skill of the child's [pp. 14–15].

Table 1.1 summarizes the empirical consequences of these three models for prerequisites to language. Our own position on cognitive prerequisites to symbolic communication is the second, homology through shared underlying "software." This model predicts correlations and training effects. It does not predict particular sequences of development between cognitive and communicative behaviors, at least not within roughly equivalent levels. As we shall see later, our data do in fact support a model that permits correlated linguistic and nonlinguistic

TABLE 1.1
Empirical Consequences of Three Models of Language-Thought Relations

	Normals			Abnormals		
	Sequencing between domains	Correlations between domains	Training effects	Mirror-image correlations	Potential for "blockage"	Training effects
I. Direct causal model	+	+	Unidirectional	+	Unidirectional	Unidirectional
II. Homology through shared base	Optional	+	Bidirectional	+	Bidirectional	Bidirectional
III. Analogy	Optional	None (Except for general IQ, etc.)	None	None (Except for general IQ, etc.)	None	None

structures to emerge in either order within a developmental stage. The direct causal model for language–thought relations is often attributed to Piaget (see MacNamara, 1972). However, Moore and Harris (1977) cite a statement by Piaget (in the preface to Ferreiro, 1971) explicitly comparing the two homology models and predicting the success of the shared base approach. So, for those who do Piagetian research by exegesis, suffice it to say that (at least in this case) our approach to language–thought relations is orthodox.

To summarize, we have defined "prerequisite" as a structure in one system that provides necessary input to the structure of a second system. Hence the prerequisites to language that we are discussing here are not behavioral manifestations or performance in object permanence tasks, tool use, social interaction, etc. Rather, we propose that structural relationships between language and nonlinguistic capacities exist at the level of underlying software that permits various behaviors to occur. The key term here is "permits"—a different type of causality than the pulling–pushing kind that is usually involved in scientific explanations. This brings us to the second issue, a clarification of what we mean when we "explain" the emergence of symbols by locating prerequisite skills.

On the Nature of Explanation in
the Search for Prerequisites

Scientists occasionally mean very different things when they say they have "explained" a phenomenon. Our task in this section is to present the philosophy of science that guides this work, in particular the kind of causal model that we assume in the search for prerequisites to language.

First of all, we assume that all "explanation" is basically a "description" of a given phenomenon at some new level. Different levels of description satisfy different criteria for defining "cause." In the old Aristotelian framework, there are four types of cause, each corresponding to a different type of description: efficient, material, final, and formal. Let us examine these one at a time, to determine the peculiar type of causation that is involved in the identification and description of prerequisite structures.

Efficient causality—the sine qua non of Western science—is the dynamic, push-from-behind type of cause that we usually seek to explain, for example, why a book has fallen from a table. As Hume pointed out long ago, efficient causes are antecedent conditions that are reliably followed by particular consequences, for example, my arm shoving the book to the table's edge with maximal force. There may be more than one efficient cause acting in a given situation. If John throws a rock through a window and the window breaks, the rock is an instrumental efficient cause of the break. Its force as it hits the window is a proximal efficient cause. John's arm movement applying that force is a distal efficient cause. In evolutionary theory, natural selection is conceived as a distal efficient cause, operating on intervening causes involved in reproduction, geographic and behavioral isolation, and so forth. Within psychology, the Behaviorist era in many cases involved a search for efficient causal mechanisms as explanations of behavior, in particular environmental events that reliably produce (i.e., are followed by) those behaviors. As we shall see shortly, the whole issue of motivation and goals provided problems for this approach to psychological explanation by bringing in an entirely different level of causal analysis. Suffice it to say at this point that, in the search for prerequisites to language, we are not looking for efficient causes that push symbolic communication into existence.

A second type of causality is material: The material conditions that are necessary but insufficient for an event to take place (e.g., the presence of a rock in John's vicinity prior to the throwing act). To offer another example, if I bake a cake, the material causes for the cake are eggs, sugar, flour, etc. The efficient causes include stirring, heat, etc. Several philosophers of science have noted the "reductionist fallacy" in psychology (e.g., Koestler and Smythises, 1970), the tendency for behavioral scientists to believe that they have explained a class of behaviors if they have located the neural substrate involved in the production of those behaviors. When we discover, for example, that some aspect of language seems to involve an area in the left temporal lobe of most adults, at most we have located a material cause for language. That area has to be there for language to happen, just as sugar and flour have to be there for a cake to happen. In our research we are trying to identify software rather than hardware, that is, the operations, procedures, algorithms, etc., that the child has available to carry out certain behaviors and solve particular problems. While there is presumably some neural base (and, leading up to that, a genetic base) for such capacities, our task in this research is **not** to locate material causes for the symbolic capacity.

A third aspect of causal analysis is the location of final causes. Final causation is the goal-directed, pull-from-the-front aspect of a given situation. For the Jesuit scholars who taught me philosophy, much was made of the Will of God as the Final Cause for all world events—a possible historical reason why twentieth-century scientists have tried to expunge final causal explanations from the scientific method. In the decades of American Behaviorism, the debate over the role of reinforcement can be summarized as an argument between those who believed in final causality (e.g., the rat's goal in pressing the lever) versus those who would reduce reinforcement to the efficient causal level as a distal cause operating on a hypothetical proximal cause called "drive." Similarly, much of the struggle between Darwin and his opponents in the early history of evolutionary theory involved Darwin's view of efficient causal principles in natural selection, versus those who suggested a general final-causal force or movement toward "higher" forms of life. More recently, computer technology and modern cognitive science have conspired to reintroduce at least one kind of final causality into the roster of respectable explanatory variables: the goal of the individual organism, as it can be represented in a "software analysis" of the animal's behavior. Now that we can point to goals in a machine, Tolman's "radical" view that the rat expects to be rewarded has become commonplace. In this research, we are looking for relationships between language and nonlinguistic skills that go beyond shared motivation. Our hypothesis will be that certain developments are correlated across a sample of normal children because of some common rule or structural principle in the child which permits transfer from one task to another. However, an alternative interpretation of the same correlations could be made in final causal terms: Across a sample of children, some infants do well on linguistic and nonlinguistic measures and some children do poorly because the two measures require similar levels and types of motivation. Hence a timid and reluctant child would perform poorly, where a highly social child would do well on both tasks. We will return to this issue later in Chapter 3, when we deal with the issue of interpreting patterns of correlation.

The fourth and perhaps most ignored aspect of causality is formal causality: the principles or laws that govern the range of possible outcomes in a given situation.[2] In the rock-throwing example, these include the laws of trajectories, force, tension, etc., that constrain (or permit, or dictate) a broken window outcome. In the cake-baking example, formal causality places limits on the form that the material ingredients can take

---

[2] Readers familiar with Aristotle's formulations may find our interpretation of formal causality somewhat at odds with classical definitions. By formal cause, Aristotle was referring to the pure forms or essences that inhere in existing entities (e.g., the potential statue that is inherent in the stone). Within Aristotle's metaphysical theory, however, it is important to note that the theory of essences was the closest he came to an approximation of mathematical and natural physical laws as we know them now. Hence we have adopted a modern interpretation of the theory of essences, i.e., the forms that are possible solutions to classes of constraints regardless of the material embodying those constraints.

under certain conditions of stirring, heat, etc. The heat itself is an efficient cause. The principles of thermodynamics that govern heat are formal causes.

Formal causal explanations are not limited to the extraction and/or application of physical laws. They also include the discovery and use of logico-mathematical laws—precisely the kinds of laws, I would argue, that underlie the hierarchical organization and sequencing that is described in Piaget's theory of cognitive development. Biological explanations are usually at the efficient or material level. However, in a 1917 classic *On Growth and Form,* D'Arcy Thompson sets forth a wide array of examples of formal constraints and task-determined solutions in biology, solutions that are inevitable given certain genetic and environmental starting points. Many of Thompson's examples involve the laws of form constraining the interactions of spheres, splashes and drops, spikules and spirals. To illustrate, what does it mean to "explain" the roundness of form of a soap bubble? The efficient causes—wind frothing the water, or a little boy blowing a pipe—explain why the event took place when it did, but not the form of the solution. The material causes—air, water, soap—certainly do not contain "roundness" as an inherent aspect of their structure, although they must be able to participate in or permit roundness if the bubble is to happen. If there is a final cause in this situation (e.g., the little boy's goal in blowing bubbles), it still cannot explain the spherical outcome. In formal causal terms, the reason why soap bubbles are round is that roundness is the only possible solution to achieving maximum volume with minimum surface. Hence the "explanation" for roundness is task determined, a formally constrained solution to a problem.

Let us take a simple human example of such task-determined inevitability. It is a universal fact of human cultures that people eat with their hands—sometimes with an intervening fork or chopstick, but certainly never with the feet, nor with head movements in a trough. Do we want to argue that handfeeding is innate? Yes, of course we do. But there is no need to invoke a specific genetic mechanism for eating with the hands. Given the task of eating (biologically insured beyond a doubt), and the anatomical and neural organization of hands, the solution of handfeeding is so probable that no further genetic baggage is necessary for the outcome to be assured. Nor does handfeeding have to be "learned" (i.e., observed in conspecifics and/or trained and rewarded in the young). The solution is not determined directly by either genes or environment—or even, for that matter, by some simpleminded interactionism of the black + white = grey variety. Instead, the form of the solution is determined by the interaction of **three** sources of structure: genes, environment, and the critical structure of the task. Genes and environment provide material and efficient causal inputs to the solution; the task structure produces the rest of the solution via the operation of logico-mathematical formal causal principles.

Thompson also offers illustrations beyond the level of the single sphere, to outcomes governed by the possible interactions of spheres. If spheres are packed together with relatively constant pressure from all sides, the emerging solution will be a set of three-dimensional hexagonal structures, (i.e., a rhombic dodecahedron). At one level, this principle guarantees certain regularities of cell interaction in the formation of membranes. At another level, the same principle can be used to explain the regularity and beauty of beehives. No individual bee need embody the hexagonal "blueprint" of his hive. Instead, all the individual bee needs is a relatively simple "local" principle: to pack wax by burrowing his little hemispheric head in it. If enough bees with round heads do enough packing from a variety of directions, a hexagonal three-dimensional structure will emerge at the interface.

Parallel arguments can be made about the development of grammar in children. In a paper discussing the functionalist approach to child grammar, Bates and MacWhinney (1978) suggest that the human child arrives at hypotheses about his language through an interaction of a common set of cognitive structures (the first semantic and pragmatic meanings) and the powerful task constraints imposed by the linear ordering of the acoustic–articulatory speech channel. How does one map (or decode) messages that are essentially nonlinear in this peculiar one-at-a-time fashion? The sequence of steps children go through in deriving grammar, and the variety of hypotheses found in children between and within language communities, suggest that what has been selected for in our species is a flexible construction process, rather than a preformed set of structures. Given the strong converging constraints on the forms that grammar can take (performance constraints in Chomsky's sense of the term), Nature can bank on the laws of form to direct a solution out of simpler local principles.

In Piaget's theory (see *Structuralism*, 1971, and *Genetic Epistemology*, 1970), formal causal principles play a critical role in the development of cognitive structures. His notions of disequilibrium and equilibration involve a movement toward stability among cognitive structures during the solution of tasks—not unlike the movement of soap bubbles toward roundness under the constraint to achieve maximum volume with minimum surface. Piaget does not take the empiricist position that certain structures reside in the environment and are copied by the child; nor does he believe in the maturationist view that cognitive structures are "preformed" or laid down quite specifically in genetic instructions. Instead, Piaget takes the so-called "constructivist" view that many outcomes in cognitive development are "inevitable" rather than "innate" (see Piaget's critique of Chomsky in *Structuralism*, p. 81). However, if Piaget were to stop at task analysis in his argument about the origins of logic, the theory would amount to the analogy approach discussed earlier in this chapter. **Piaget's theory goes beyond the description of task constraints to a homology model, in which the child's solutions to a set of similar tasks become internalized, i.e., embodied in the form of rules or principles that can be applied to new tasks without going through the whole construction process all over again.** Hence, formally constrained task structure becomes cognitive structure through a sort of "congealing" of solutions. The child would never make such progress without certain material and efficient causal conditions that permit him to solve the problem in the first place. However, he would also never progress through the stages of logical development without the contribution of laws of form and task structure. Piaget has left it to other researchers to locate the material and efficient conditions of cognitive development. He has restricted himself to a description of cognition at the formal causal level.

We have taken an approach similar to Piaget's in this book. The kinds of relationships we are seeking between language and nonlinguistic systems are relationships between such cognitive structures, congealed solutions to tasks, underlying rules or capacities for engaging in tasks. We will argue that certain behaviors are correlated because the "software" that is needed to carry out those behaviors is the same. **Hence our research will "explain" the emergence of symbols by description at the formal causal level: We will describe commonalities in tasks, and by the correlational method attempt to demonstrate that these task structures have been internalized by the child in the form of procedures, rules, capacities, etc.**

On Evolutionary Theory and the Biology of Symbols

The major issue we are addressing in this book is the interdependence between linguistic and nonlinguistic factors during the emergence of the symbolic capacity. This question is logically independent of the nature–nurture issue in language development. However, the view that language is structurally derived from other systems is identified by some of its opponents with the empiricist or "learning theory" tradition in American psychology. Chomsky (1977) made this case explicitly in a recent address to the American Speech and Hearing Association. Inveighing against both American Behaviorism and what he termed the "incomprehensible" Piagetian view of cognitively based language, Chomsky stated:

> No one would suggest that a child "learns" to grow an arm, or to reach puberty. . . . And yet, it has been claimed that the same child "learns" the structural principles that underlie the human capacity for language . . . which should properly be viewed as a mental organ equivalent in many respects to other organs of the body.

This accusation of empiricism may be validly applied to some modern exponents of linguistic functionalism, perhaps most notably those who stress the contribution of maternal speech style to the child's acquisition of language (see Snow and Ferguson, 1977, for reviews). However, the view of language as a derived system is not "inherently" antibiological. In fact, we will argue that the capacity to derive or construct the symbolic function out of preexisting skills is part of the genetic makeup of our species. The purpose of this section is to place our interdependence model within the framework of recent evolutionary theory. We want to demonstrate that Nature builds many new systems out of old parts, and selects for organisms that can carry out the same reconstruction process ontogenetically, jerrybuilding the same new machines from the same old parts in a highly reliable fashion. Human language may be just such a jerrybuilt system, with human infants "discovering" and elaborating their capacity for symbolic communication by a route similar to the one that led our ancestors into language.

This section will contain three central arguments about a possible ontogenetic and phylogenetic model of language origins:

1. "Phylogenetic routes": Nature tends to build new systems out of available old parts.
2. "Ontogenetic routes": Once a new system emerges, it must be transmitted in some fashion from one generation to another. This transmission can be insured in two ways. On the one hand, the reconstruction of the system can be guaranteed directly through strong genetic control. Alternatively, Nature may make high probability bets that old genotypes, confronted with new but heavily constrained tasks, need very little new genetic control to fall into the most efficient solutions to those tasks. The result may be a situation in which individuals repeat the same construction process that led to the new system in the first place. In other words, ontogeny may at least partially recapitulate phylogeny.
3. "Heterochrony": Recent discoveries concerning the role of regu-

latory genes in ontogeny have provided some possible mechanisms for the evolution of new systems from old parts, in a fashion that creates parallels between phylogeny and ontogeny. Language may have evolved through "heterochrony," or changes in the timing and growth curves for old capacities. The emergence of symbols in human children may reflect the resulting interaction of old parts in the creation of a new system.

Phylogenetic Routes: New Systems from Old Parts

Stephen Gould's book, *Ever Since Darwin* (1977), contains a series of essays about the evolution of complex and highly adaptive systems. One of his major points regards the selection for new structures and functions out of fortuitous combinations of preexisting genetic material, in a clumsy fashion that would not appeal to a Clockmaker God:

> The theory of natural selection would never have replaced the doctrine of divine creation if evident admirable design pervaded all organisms. Darwin understood this, and he focused on features that would be out of place in a world constructed by perfect wisdom. . . . Darwin even wrote an entire book on orchids to argue that the structures evolved to insure fertilization by insects are jerrybuilt of available parts used by ancestors for other purposes. Orchids are Rube Goldberg machines; a perfect engineer would certainly have come up with something better [p. 94].

Gould argues further that the evolutionary Rube Goldberg principle applies even to the most highly specialized and "perfect" adaptations. He offers the example of the freshwater mussel *Lampsilis*, which possesses mounted upon its rear end a striking replica of a fish, complete with tail and eyespot. This "fish" serves the function of attracting real fish to the rear area, whereupon the clam releases a spray of eggs, a significant number of which will lodge in the gill slots of the marauder—an ideal location for growth, one that has become essential to the survival of the species. The fish decoy is so well designed for its purpose that it actually undulates in a fishlike swimming motion.

Gould notes that such perfect adaptation has historically presented a serious challenge to Darwin's theory of natural selection. The adaptive value of the evolutionary finished product is obvious. But such a complex product must, according to Darwinian theory, have emerged gradually:

> Natural selection has a constructive role in Darwin's system; it builds gradually, through a sequence of intermediate stages, by bringing together in sequential fashion elements that seem to have meaning only as parts of a final product. But how can a series of reasonable intermediate steps be constructed? Of what value could the first tiny step toward an eye be to its possessor? The dung-mimicking insect is well protected, but can there be any edge in looking only 5 percent like a turd [p. 101]?

The solution that is offered is Darwin's theory of "preadaptation." According to the doctrine of preadaptation, the components that will eventually fall together to serve a specialized new function first evolve separately in the service of completely different, prior functions. Those imperfect intermediate steps toward the new function are, then, maintained by the adaptive value they serve in an old system. In the case of *Lampsilis,* there is evidence from related species to suggest that the fish decoy evolved from a dark, ribbonlike rear membrane that was used to aereate the larvae and/or to keep them suspended in water after release. This membrane, in the service of its old function, moved in a flapping motion that fortuitously resembles the swimming movements of a fish. This movement must have led in turn to an intermediate stage of double function, attracting live fish and resulting in the increased viability of the larvae who lodge in the gill slots. Once the new function was established via fish mimicry through movement, further selection on that function may have "shaped" the decoy to mimic fish by shape and pattern as well.

Gould offers a series of other examples of preadaptation, old parts that are used in infant–parent relations, in courtship, and in aggression appeasement between same-sex adults. An important point for all these cases is that radical, almost discontinuous change in function can be brought about by much smaller alterations in form. New systems are "bought" phylogenetically at relatively little genetic cost.

Ontogenetic Routes: Genetic Determination versus Task Determination

The Rube Goldberg approach to evolution explains how new inventions are selected phylogenetically out of existing genetic materials. Small, continuous changes in the underlying genetic substrate can bring about radical, discontinuous changes in genetic expression, by making new functions possible and placing the animal in a new task domain. Hence new products can be bought with only a small amount of genetic expenditure to put old parts together. Just how **much** genetic expenditure is necessary, however, to insure that the same new discovery is transmitted from one generation to another? It may be that *Lampsilis* initially derived its fish from an undulating membrane. It is not necessarily the case that successive generations of *Lampsilis* repeat the same sequence. In other words, phylogenetic construction routes may be independent of ontogenetic sequences.

However, if the constraints of a new task domain are strong enough, Nature may not have to invest a great deal of genetic currency to insure that each generation combines old material in the same new ways. She may, instead, use the same construction routes in ontogeny that were used in phylogeny. Take the example of the zigzag courtship dance of Tinbergen's stickleback fish (Pelkwijk and Tinbergen, 1937). Faced with a complex behavior, universal to sticklebacks and highly stereotyped in form, we might want to conclude, a priori, that the dance is an innate "behavioral organ" of that species, highly specialized and predetermined in form. And in a way we would be right. However, there is more than one way for a complex outcome to be innate. One way is through some sort of strong, direct predetermination—the kind that the layman associates with the word "innate." A stickleback zigzag could be the result of specific genetic instructions that could be paraphrased as follows:

> Under Internal Arousal State C, proceed by moving in a rightward direction at approximately 45 degrees from midline for 1 ± 0.33 seconds. Then shift 90 degrees in the leftward direction and move for 1 ± 0.33 seconds. Then shift rightward 90 degrees . . .

A mechanical stickleback would probably have to be built with just such an internal program, embodied at the level of gears and springs. However, through a series of experiments Tinbergen determined that the biological stickleback organizes his dance somewhat differently. His zigzag behavior is produced by some mechanism that holds the approach system and the avoidance system at competing levels of arousal. As the male fish nears, his approach system is temporarily closed down by signals from the female, permitting the avoidance system to emerge. As he retreats, the level of avoidance decreases and the approach system reemerges. Hence he changes course back toward approach. Nature did not need to build in a whole new wiring system to produce zigzag dancing. Instead, a mechanism for holding two old systems in balance was sufficient to produce the zigzag "solution." The unique perceptual pattern produced by this dance was in turn available to serve a new function, as a signal to the female that can heighten her arousal and increase the likelihood of reproduction. This discovery in turn provided a selective advantage for males with "locked" approach and avoidance drives. In short, Nature was able to buy a new system at relatively little genetic cost. The most important point for our purposes is that the same old parts that were used in phylogeny are still used in the construction of the zigzag in individual fish. As Tinbergen demonstrated, if the approach or avoidance component is tampered with slightly, the whole behavior falls apart. The dance is certainly an innate "behavioral organ" of the stickleback. But it is innate in a different way than we usually associate with theories of biological determinism—that is, in a probabilistic or indirect fashion. Two primitive systems are set in conflict, and one solution inevitably emerges. Like the handfeeding example in humans noted in the previous section, we have a case in which innate material and efficient conditions interact with formal causal principles to produce predictable results.

There are, then, two ways to transmit phylogenetic discoveries in the ontogeny of individual organisms. The new system may require a great deal of heavy genetic underwriting, so that the old construction route leaves few traces in ontogeny. Or, instead, the same solutions may be rediscovered from one generation to another with just a few indirect genetic "clues" or predispositions. These predispositions have their effect by guaranteeing that the animal will enter into situations with particular task demands which are likely to produce certain high-probability solutions.

The two alternative routes to stable outcomes are not peculiar to the evolution of behavior systems. They apply at every level of organization from the molecular to the cellular to the interaction of organs and organisms. Not surprisingly, in every area of bioloy we find the same debate between proponents of "hard" versus "soft" determinism. For example, Gottlieb (1971) has reviewed a debate in embryology between the "predeterminist" view that genetic structure unidirectionally determines both form and function, versus the "probabilistic determinism" view that form and function influence one another bidirectionally. In this book, we will present a functionalist or probabilistic view of the emergence of symbols. We suggest that the symbolic function in humans, like the zigzag dance in stickleback fish, is constructed in individual organisms out of "old parts," cognitive and communicative developments that are only indirectly related to language. Because some of the components are "preadapted" in the service of nonlinguistic and perhaps noncommunicative functions, their role in language development may not be obvious. However, if one of the old components is disturbed or delayed, the new system may fail to appear. Furthermore, children who advance rapidly in the development of prerequisite components should begin to use symbols earlier than other children. In other words, we suggest that the strategies summarized in Table 1.1 for establishing a homology approach to language thought relations form a program of biological research, aimed at uncovering the old parts that make up the symbolic capacity. We are definitively not reopening a nature–nurture debate on the development of language. Rather, this is a sort of nature–nature debate, on the different ways that a given outcome can be innate.

Heterochrony: How Parallels between Ontogeny and Phylogeny Come About

To summarize so far, we have proposed that the symbolic capacity emerged phylogenetically from a combination of cognitive and communicative capacities that were preadapted in the service of other functions. Second, we suggest that the transmission of this new system from one generation to another involves probabilistic determinism: Formal causal constraints of tasks interact with material and efficient causal aspects of biology to insure the orchestration of old capacities within the symbolic function. Implicit in this second argument is the view that the emergence of symbols requires relatively little genetic underwriting: a discontinuous development which resulted from small and continuous changes in the genetic substrate.

We are verging on the old theory that ontogeny recapitulates phylogeny. Wasn't that view discredited a long time ago? According to Gould (*Ontogeny and Phylogeny,* 1977b), only one version of recapitulation theory has been discredited. A strong case can still be made for parallels between ontogeny and phylogeny within modern genetics and evolutionary theory. The new approach to recapitulation involves the concept of "heterochrony": selection for new outcomes through changes in the timing and growth curves of preexisting genetic material. The theory of heterochrony is related to recent discoveries in genetics concerning the role of regulatory genes. This approach is important for our purposes because it provides a plausible explanation for the development of a complex new outcome like the human capacity for symbols from a set of preexisting cognitive capacities, with relatively little genetic change. Since we are going to draw on the concept of heterochrony later in this volume, it is worth our time to briefly "recapitulate" Gould's history of recapitulation, leading up to modern regulatory biology.

According to Gould, the history or recapitulation theory (i.e., the notion that individual development within a species repeats the sequence of ancestral forms of that species) can be dated back to pre-Socratic speculation. In modern times, the notion of recapitulation is a theme that runs throughout the history of evolutionary theory and the concept of natural selection. The best-known proponent of recapitulation was Haeckel (1892), who claimed that the development of the individual organism (particularly in utero) involves a repetition of the series of forms taken by **adult** ancestors—that is, fish to amphibian to primitive mammal to primate. Note that this sequence was not viewed as a mere by-product of natural selection. Instead, recapitulation was seen as a final causal mechanism, a biological law (the so-called "biogenetic principle") governing the forward movement of evolution. The law of recapitulation involves a process Haeckel termed "palingenesis": The old sequence of features is maintained by succeeding species, but new features are added on. Palingenesis in turn involved two processes: terminal addition and acceleration. Terminal addition refers to the tendency for new features to be added to the end of an inherited ontogenetic sequence. If this process alone were operating, the lifespan of successive species would have to increase indefinitely as new features were added. The second process, acceleration, insures that this will not happen. As new features are added, it was believed that the earlier sequence was compressed, or accelerated backward in ontogeny. Hence the adult fish stage occurs during the embryonic phase of a higher species' individual development. Exceptions to palengenesis were obvious even during Haeckel's time, with cases in which the larvae of more recent species exhibit new features not present in ancestral adults, and then go on to repeat the rest of a familiar developmental sequence. The process that generates these exceptions was termed "cenogenesis," or the addition of new features somewhere in the ontogenetic sequence other than the terminal position. Cenogenesis became necessary when, under exceptional circumstances, the juvenile of a given species required new adaptations unique to that stage of development in order to survive into adulthood. The exceptions produced by cenogenesis were not viewed as refutations of recapitulation theory, but rather as infrequent but annoying obfuscations of the evolutionary record written in individual development. Haeckel believed that examples produced by this ancillary process were usually recognizable, and that the "smokescreen" could be removed to permit observation of the more general process of recapitulation.

Note that for Haeckel, recapitulation of ancestral forms is not insured by any here-and-now adaptive properties of those forms. Rather, the general process of repetition is viewed as a biological axiom on a par with natural selection. The entire ontogenetic sequence is in a sense vestigial, like our wisdom teeth or appendix, a leftover that hangs around simply because there is no adaptive reason to get rid of it. This sort of vestigial recapitulation is very different from the functional recapitulation we hinted at earlier, where a construction sequence is repeated in ontogeny because it is the only **viable** way to get from here to there. Haeckel's version of recapitulation theory eventually withered away, according to Gould, because of the advent of experimental embryology and the rediscovery of Mendelian genetics. Haeckel's theory could not be proven wrong, insofar as the "fudge factor" of cenogenesis permitted explanation of any exceptions to the notions of terminal addition and acceleration. But this "law" lost its force as an explanatory principle when attention turned to the microlevel, to the efficient causes or actual mechanics of embryology and genetics. Prior to this withering away, however, Gould notes that a stunning counterposition explaining many of the facts of recapitulation had already been offered by von Baer (1828). Von Baer argues that the observable phenomena of recapitulation were actually the mere by-products of a very different kind of principle, the principle of increasing differentiation in development. All organisms develop from a relatively homogeneous state to a more complex, heterogeneous, and specialized endpoint. In that sense, the **embryonic** stages of a higher species tend to recapitulate the **embryonic** stages of its ancestors up to the point where the new species branches off to differentiate its own special features. Unlike Haeckel's vestigial recapitulation, this is functional recapitulation, in which species repeat the fetal stages of their ancestors because it is the only logically possible way to go from a homogeneous to a highly differentiated state. Von Baer was ignored during Haeckel's heyday. Later, when interest in recapitulation ebbed for other reasons, von Baer's principle was dragged out of the archives to explain that loss of interest.

Gould argues that many of the undeniable phenomena of recapitulation can indeed be explained by von Baer's principle. There are also other reasons for the pervasiveness of recapitulation, particularly the phenomena that justified the belief in terminal addition: If new changes are introduced at very early stages in ontogeny, the consequences for later stages are accumulative and the potential for disaster is enormous. More often than not, if the early stages are tampered with, it is likely that a nonviable organism will result. The later a change is introduced, the more likely it is to remain in the gene pool. However, Gould documents a large number of striking parallels between ontogeny and phylogeny that cannot be explained either by the principle of differentiation or by the viability of late changes. Many of these examples suggest that versions of ancestral traits and sequences of features have been **actively** selected in particular species, for specific adaptive functions. Furthermore, recapitulation is not the only type of parallel that can be found between ontogeny and phylogeny. In recapitulation, the new species repeats an old sequence and then goes on to add something else (perhaps something as simple as a larger version of the old endpoint—a tendency for increased growth in successive generations referred to as Cope's law). A reverse process, called "paedomorphosis," is also quite frequent in the evolutionary record. In paedomorphosis, a new species maintains in its **adult** form a feature or set of features that characterized the **juvenile** stages of its ancestors. The result is a very different kind of adult, and the juvenile features may serve a quite different function in adult circumstances.

Gould suggests two mechanisms which operate to produce either recapitulation or paedomorphosis: acceleration of growth, and retardation of growth. Retardation of puberty, with the rest of somatic growth remaining constant, produces a result termed "hypermorphosis." This is a particular type of recapitulation in which the new species goes through all the ontogenetic sequences experienced by its ancestors, but then goes through an additional phase of growth before sexual maturity truncates development. The resulting species is generally identical in form to the parent species, but much larger; hence hypermorphosis through retardation of puberty provides an explanation for the pervasive evolutionary fact described by Cope's law (i.e., the tendency for the offspring of successful species to be larger than their parents). Acceleration of puberty has very different effects, a type of paedomorphosis termed "progenesis" in which development is truncated by sexual maturity before the adult stages are reached. The result is essentially a sexually mature larva, a grownup infant capable of reproducing other individuals with the same growth patterns. Both these processes involve changes in the timing of puberty with somatic growth remaining constant. Gould notes that the opposite process is also possible, with retiming of somatic growth relative to a constant onset time for puberty. If somatic growth is accelerated while puberty remains constant, then the result is recapitulation of the ancestral ontogenesis plus addition of a new prepubescent stage. On the other hand, if somatic growth is retarded while puberty begins at more or less the same time, we have a particular type of paedomorphosis termed "neoteny." Here too the result is an adult with juvenile features. To offer just one example, the evolutionary history of domestic dogs and cats supposedly has involved selection by neoteny, so that the submissive features and the attachment formations of dog and cat juveniles are extended into adulthood—resulting in the behavior patterns of "pets," something no self-respecting jungle adult would put up with.

This process of natural selection through changes in developmental timing is called "heterochrony." This principle is important in modern evolutionary theory for several reasons. First of all, the striking parallels that are found between ontogeny and phylogeny in many species have been liberated from Haeckel's law, and incorporated within modern genetics and the orthodox theory of natural selection. As Gould notes, these parallels have been hard to ignore since pre-Socratic times; it is to our benefit that it is once again "respectable" to study these parallels scientifically. Secondly, the principle of heterochrony offers a solution to the problem of genetic variability versus discontinuous evolution. If the only sources of genetic variation were introduction of new structure (through genetic combination and mutation), it would be very difficult to explain many large and seemingly discontinuous changes in the evolutionary record. There simply has not been sufficient genetic time for many of those developments to take place under the operation of mutation and combination through mating. Heterochrony explains how a seemingly major change can be introduced by rearranging old genetic material. We just examined four types of heterochrony: acceleration and retardation of puberty, and acceleration and retardation of somatic growth. If these processes operated only at the level of the whole organism, we would still have an ample source of phenotypic variability. However, it is also possible for acceleration and retardation to operate on one or more **aspects** of organismic development. For example, Gould devotes considerable space to the "dissociability" of size and shape in development, and the varying consequences of retiming one with respect to the other in the histories of several species.

A third reason why the principle of heterochrony is gaining importance in evolutionary theory is that a genetic mechanism has been found to explain how such retiming takes place. Until recently, attention has been focused almost exclusively on structural genes, the DNA "xerox originals" that are responsible for protein synthesis and hence the growth and patterning of living matter. There is, however, another type of gene, the so-called regulator gene. Regulator genes do not directly contribute protein structure. Instead, they are the stage managers of development, determining the onset times and sequencing of protein synthesis among the structural genes. A change in the regulator genes may result in a reorchestration of the entire gene complex; hence enormous phenotypic results can be obtained by a very small genetic change. If Nature wanted to produce new machinery out of old parts, it is possible that a small investment in the regulator genes may be the only genetic expenditure that is required.

There is also ample reason to believe that the principle of heterochrony may be the major determinant in the evolution of the hominid line. Gould cites a list of over 20 features compiled by Bolk (1926), in which *Homo sapiens* in its adult form can be said to resemble the juvenile form of other primates. Examples include the straight profile and weak brow ridges, the bulbous and large cranium relative to body size, and the ventral pointing of the vaginal canal in adult human females. Any one of these juvenile features might have very different consequences in an adult. For example, the ventral orientation of the vaginal canal means that mounting is more efficiently accomplished from the front rather than the back. This change in turn would probably have required a change in the signaling system prior to mating (see Morgan, 1972, for some interesting speculations in this regard). The most important consequences, however, probably involved the prolonged and helpless infancy of our species. One result would be the necessity for a prolonged and intricate attachment bond uniting parent and child, a system which may in turn have affected social organization as a whole. Another consequence could be that the period of infant neural plasticity was prolonged; curiosity and a marked capacity for learning—characteristic only of the juvenile stages in many other mammals—would grow beyond their usual levels, and perhaps remain in adulthood. Gould suggests that the extension of primate infancy into adulthood may be the primary mechanism underlying the evolution of human culture.

If heterochrony (in particular neoteny, or selection for juvenile characteristics in the adult animal through somatic retardation) has played a larger role in human evolution than the introduction of new features, we might expect that the difference between man and other primates resides primarily in the regulatory genes rather than structural genes. Recent evidence suggests that this is precisely the case. King and Wilson (1975) have assessed the "genetic distance" between man and chimpanzee using a variety of techniques for examining similarity and dissimilarity in structural genes. On all of their measures, man and chimpanzee are more than 99% genetically identical—more alike than sister species of Drosophila (fruitflies who differ from one another in phenotype far less than we differ from the chimp). How can such massive behavioral and morphological differences result from a genetic blueprint that is virtually identical for both species? King and Wilson conclude that the phenotypic differences between man and chimpanzees must involve regulator genes, resulting in differential timing and sequencing of the same old parts.

In our view, these recent discoveries strongly support the theory that the human Language Acquisition Device (McNeill, 1966) evolved through a recombination of preexisting capacities into a novel configuration. The argument can be summarized as follows:

1. Language can be viewed as a new machine created out of various cognitive and social components that evolved initially in the service of completely different functions.
2. This construction process probably came about through heterochrony, or changes in the growth patterns of one or more cognitive–social capacities. We can infer that at some point in history, these "old parts" reached a new quantitative level that permitted qualitatively new interactions, including the emergence of symbols.
3. The orchestration of these components into new combinations may have required the intervention of formal causes, task constraints that contribute much of the structure of the eventual linguistic–symbolic outcome.
4. If the evolution of language involved changes in the regulatory genes, and considerable interaction with task constraints, then it is likely that the process is at least partially repeated in the ontogeny of individual language users.
5. At least some forms of language deficiency may result from a deficit in one or more of the nonlinguistic components that underlie the capacity for symbols.

These arguments do not mean, as some psychologists have suggested, that the difference between signing chimps like Washoe and normal human children is quantitative and trivial. The difference may be quantitative, involving relative proportions of skills available at varying times in development. But the difference is hardly trivial. Heterochrony may have operated by producing quantitative adjustments of particular, dissociable cognitive skills. The result would be a new configuration of capacities, which in turn could result in the enormous qualitative difference between man and his nearest neighbors. In short, quantitative changes in the material and efficient causal substrate may have placed human children in a completely new ballpark, a set of cognitive and communicative tasks which in turn lead the child into a new set of solutions. We will return to the concept of heterochrony in Chapter 7, to discuss our findings concerning capacities that correlate with the emergence of symbols.

In the next chapter, we will report on some early findings that led to this research, and to the hypothesis that the symbolic capacity has an internal structure comprised of some older and perhaps simpler cognitive and communicative components. We will present a simple model of the internal structure of symbols, based on theories by Piaget (1962), Werner and Kaplan (1963), and Charles Sanders Peirce (1932). The next four chapters will report on different aspects of our findings: correlations between cognitive and communicative measures (Chapter 3); qualitative analyses of symbols in language and in action (Chapter 4); correlations between our cognitive–communicative measures and social developments in mother–child attachment (Chapter 5); a small follow-up study of some of our children at 19 months of age (Chapter 6). In the last chapter, we will return to the evolutionary themes outlined here as a guide for future work.

Chapter 2
INTENTIONS, CONVENTIONS, AND SYMBOLS

Elizabeth Bates

Two Moments in the Dawn of Language

We have spent a lot of time watching infants from 9 to 13 months of age. I suppose that whenever one stares at a phenomenon long enough, it can begin to take on cosmic importance—the deepest workings of the universe unfolding in an infant's smile. And yet—all qualifications aside—as we continue to stare we still believe that this brief period in human ontogeny reflects not one but two critical moments in the dawning of human communication through symbols: (*a*) the onset of communicative intentions and conventional signals and (*b*) the emergence of symbols and the discovery that things have names. In the next few pages, I will describe in fairly general terms the behaviors that comprise these two developmental moments, based on findings from our first longitudinal study with three infants (Bates, Camaioni, and Volterra, 1975), as well as research by several other investigators (Bruner, 1975a; Carter, 1974; Dore, 1975; Lock, 1976; Sugarman, 1977). This brief description will lead to (*a*) some working definitions of "intention," "convention," and "symbol," and (*b*) a summary of the kinds of behaviors that permit us to impute these hoary philosophical structures to 1-year-old children.

The rest of the chapter will then be devoted to a model (in the most charitable sense of the term) of the internal structure of symbols, based on a synthesis of work by Peirce (1932), Piaget (1962), and Werner and Kaplan (1963).

Conventions and Intentions

The First Moment—the onset of communicative intentions and conventional signaling—occurs around 9–10 months of age for most infants. Prior to that time, communication certainly takes place. The infant cries, or reaches toward his goal, and the adult interprets the child's desires and intervenes to meet them. But does the child realize **as he emits his signals** that they will serve a communicative purpose? Are the cries and reaches aimed at the adult listener, or at the goal itself? Obviously from a phylogenetic perspective the infant's cry was selected for its communicative value. Ask any parent who has tried to ignore that cry at 3 o'clock in the morning. But we have reason to believe that in the first 9 months of life this behavior is, from the infant's point of view, merely a built-in reaction to a particular internal state. In other words, prior to 9 months we suggest that communication is efficiently caused, but not finally caused in the Aristotelian sense outlined earlier. Consider the following simple experiment. The infant is placed at Point A, facing the goal out of his reach at Point B. The human being who will eventually obtain the goal for this child is placed at right angles at Point C, out of the child's line of visual regard from A to B.

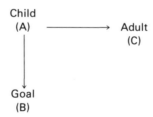

Prior to 8–9 months, the child will reach, fuss, perhaps cry in the direction of B. If he is sufficiently unhappy, he may cease his efforts altogether and turn to C for comfort. But he typically does **not**, while reaching toward the goal, turn to look (expectantly?) at the adult.

Around 9 months this pattern changes in three clear ways. First, the child begins to alternate eye contact between the goal (B) and the adult (C) **while he emits his signal.** At this point, it is difficult to avoid the inference that the child sees some relationship among the goal, the adult, and the signal. This does not mean that all intentional communication involves shifting eye contact. In fact, this pattern of alternating eye contact often becomes **less** frequent in the next few weeks as the child becomes more confident that his signals work. As communicative development continues, the child is likely to check for feedback from the adult primarily when his signals have failed, or their fate is in some way uncertain. Note that we are not **defining** intentionality in terms of eye contact and checks for feedback. However, we require these behaviors as **evidence** that the child is aware of the effects that his signals will have as he emits them.

A second change involves sequencing and substitution of signals. Prior to 9 months, any change in crying, fussing, etc., seems to be contingent upon changes in the availability of the goal itself. After 9 months the child will augment, add, or substitute signals contingent upon changes in adult behavior toward the goal. Hence we can infer that these behaviors are aimed at the adult agent rather than the goal–object itself. This pattern is illustrated in the following example from Bates, Camaioni, and Volterra (1975):

> Marta is unable to open a small purse, and places it in front of her father's hand (which is resting on the floor). F does nothing, so M puts the purse in his hand and utters a series of small sounds, looking at F. F still does not react, and M insists, pointing to the purse and whining. F asks, "What do I have to do?" M again points to the purse, looks at F, and makes a series of small sounds. Finally, F touches the purse clasp and simultaneously says, "Should I open it?" Marta nods sharply [p. 219].

A third change involves the form of the individual signals. For example, a reach-and-grasp motion may become abbreviated into a short open-shut intention movement that is apparently aimed at the adult listener rather than the goal. Similarly, grunts, effort sounds, and other fussing noises may become "ritualized" into shorter, more regular sounds that shift in volume depending upon the action of the adult.

What we have described so far are the first intentional uses of human agents as a means to a nonsocial goal—a behavior that we have termed the "protoimperative." In the same period we also witness the use of nonsocial means to a social goal, in this case the goal of sharing adult attention toward some referent. These behaviors have been called "protodeclaratives." We do **not** mean to suggest that infants have no social goals until 9 months. Much younger infants smile, laugh, and clearly enjoy prolonged social interactions. If a game ceases, the younger infant may fuss or shake his arms to make it start again. However, around 9 months some important new elements enter into the child's efforts to initiate or continue social interaction. He begins to give or show objects, with no discernible goal other than to obtain adult attention. The same kinds of evidence that permitted us to infer intentional commands also lead to the conclusion that the protodeclarative is an intentional communication. The child alternates eye contact between the referent–object and the adult. He augments, adds, or substitutes signals until his display has been recognized (by a laugh, a nod, an "mm-hmm," or some appropriate comment). And the form of these declarative signals becomes increasingly ritualized, resulting after a few weeks in clear-cut pointing and various deictic sounds.

We will define intentional communication as "signaling behavior in which the sender is aware a priori of the effect that a signal will have on his listener, and he persists in that behavior until the effect is obtained or failure is clearly indicated." The behavioral evidence that permits us to infer the presence of communicative intentions include (a) alternations in eye contact between the goal and the intended listener, (b) augmentations, additions, and substitutions of signals until the goal has been obtained, and (c) changes in the form of the signal toward abbreviated and/or exaggerated patterns that are appropriate **only** for achieving a communicative goal.

This third type of evidence, the "ritualization" of signals, also permits us to infer that the child recognizes the "conventional" aspect of communication. Austin (1963) described the "illocutionary force" or conventional purpose of speech acts as the effect that is planned or intended by the speaker, and recognized as such by both speaker and listener. These include conventional speech acts such as promising, pronouncing man and wife, christening, and commanding. The "perlocutionary" aspect of speech acts includes, by contrast, side effects that may or may not have been intended by the speaker, but in any case are not part of the public, conventional purpose of that speech act. For example, by promising to drive carefully I may or may not convince you to lend me your car. The act of promising is illocutionary. The act of persuasion is perlocutionary. The crucial factor distinguishing illocution from perlocution is the public, conventional nature of the act, a status insured by the community of speakers who use particular classes of utterances for an agreed upon purpose. The community that unites a 9-month-old and his caretakers is a small one. Nevertheless, particular gestures and sounds can be said to attain an illocutionary or conventional force in that small community. Both child and parent come to know the purpose of a subset of signals.

We will define "conventions" as "sounds or gestures whose form and function are agreed upon and recognized by both parent and child." Conventional signals are the by-product of the fact that the child now intends for his signals to have a communicative effect. Hence he eventually hits upon the best and most reliable behaviors for achieving intended effects. The process by which behaviors like reaching, fussing, and grasping become "ritualized" (i.e., abbreviated and/or exaggerated in form) is, in our view, nothing other than the process of "conventionalization." We infer the presence of communicative conventions from two aspects of behavior. First, the **form** of the signals changes in shape, toward a stable, agreed upon version. Second, the signals are used **regularly** and predictably within certain communicative situations.

Note that in the definitions provided here, conventions do not necessarily have to be arbitrary in form. They can be derived from functionally based behaviors. However, it is certainly true that once a child begins using arbitrary signals—signals that he could not possibly have discovered without observing them in the social world—we have particularly clear evidence that he recognizes and uses conventions. Indeed, around 9–10 months when functionally based behaviors are "conventionalized" into signals, we also find the children incorporating new conventions directly, via imitation of adults in social games. This is the period where pattycake, waving byebye, and other "bravure" appear in the child's repertoire. One of our favorites in Bates, Camaioni, and Volterra (1975) was the raised-fist gesture that Carlotta acquired in this period, in response to the adult shout *Compagni!* (i.e., "comrades!"). Dressed in a tiny red sweater, she was a social success with this gesture at a variety of Roman occasions. Other children develop much more idiosyncratic gestures, private conventions that arise in games between parent and child. Children and parents vary tremendously in the extent and richness of these ritual exchanges. However, in all of the investigations of this phenomenon carried out to date, the process always begins around 9 months of age. It is as though the idea of intentional, conventional signaling required some underlying developments that are simply not ready before that time.

We now have some idea what those underlying developments might be. What we have described here is the development of two types of social tool use: in person-to-object sequences (the protoimperative) and object-to-person sequences (the protodeclarative). Not surprisingly, this same period also contains the beginning of nonsocial tool use, in object-to-object, means–end sequences. For example, unlike younger infants, the 9-month-old who cannot reach a toy resting on a cloth support will pull the cloth toward him and then take the toy. Piaget (1954) has referred to this period in cognitive development as Sensorimotor Stage 5, the onset of "tertiary circular reactions" and "the invention of novel means to familiar ends." Piaget predicts a parallel between social and nonsocial developments in Stage 5, with the "externalization of causality" extended to both social and nonsocial causes. We confirmed this developmental coincidence in our first study (Bates, Camaioni, and Volterra, 1975). In an independent investigation, Sugarman (1973) also reported similar onset times for imperative signaling and Stage 5 tool use. More recently, Harding and Golinkoff (1977) have reported significant correlations in a sample of 46 infants between Stage 5 causal behaviors and the onset of conventionalized request vocalizations. We will report further evidence supporting the relationship between communication and causal development in Chapter 3. For present purposes, it is sufficient to note that the relatively sudden onset of intentional, conventional communication around 9 months seems to be related to some other developments in learning how to get things done in the world.

To summarize, we can infer the onset of intentionality from at least three types of evidence: changes in eye contact and checks for feedback, alterations in signaling until the goal is reached, and changes in the shape of signals toward a form that is appropriate only for communication. We can infer that the child recognizes the conventional nature of signals from a move toward stability in the form of signals, regularity of use in communicative routines, and the adoption of arbitrary behaviors that could only have been derived through imitation in social games.

Symbols and Symbolic Communication

The kind of conventionalized communication that we observe at 10 months of age is still not symbolic communication in any standard use of the word "symbol." The Second Moment in the dawning stages of language is the discovery that things have names, a discovery that most children in our research achieve by 13 months of age. During the 9–13-month period, the child's repertoire of conventions—both vocal and gestural—is expanding and becoming increasingly stable. Still, there is an important distinction between the appropriate use of a convention in a familiar game or problem-solving sequence, and the realization that the convention is a "symbolic vehicle" that "names," "stands for," or "evokes" a particular element in that situation. **Conventional communication is not symbolic communication until we can infer that the child has objectified the vehicle–referent relationship to some extent, realizing that the vehicle (i.e., the symbol) can be substituted for its referent for certain purposes, at the same time realizing that the symbol is not the same thing as its referent.** It is the particular use of a convention to evoke, recognize, or stand for its referent that makes that conventional use a truly symbolic act.

We have already specified the behaviors that we use to infer "intention" and "convention." It is much more difficult to specify the set of behaviors that lead us to infer a truly symbolic awareness of the relationship between a conventional behavior (vehicle) and its referent. It is probably easier to offer a series of examples, ranging along a continuum from conventional procedures that are used at appropriate points in a game, to the kinds of referential acts or procedures that we can comfortably call "naming." Let us start with vocal gestures, where the transition into naming is most clear. Around 9–10 months, when we observe conventionalized reaching, grunting, giving, etc., some of the children in the sample developed very clear and consistent vocal gestures that were used systematically in request or showing sequences. For example, Carlotta (Bates, Camaioni, and Volterra, 1975) used the sound *na-na* in requesting anything whatsoever, from food to company (for a similar example see Carter, 1974). Although *na-na* has no unique referent object or class of objects, we could of course conclude that this wordlike sound encodes or means "I want X." However, we would have to extend the same semantic analysis to all the other conventions used in the same request act (e.g., pointing, reaching, whining). The vocal gesture— although it sounds more like a word—is functionally equivalent to all the other request gestures. We have every reason to believe that is it cognitively equivalent as well.

Other examples come still closer to "true words," without actually deserving the status of names. There is Shvachkin's example (in Ferguson and Slobin, 1973) of the word "kitty" used by his daughter after throwing her toy kitten out of the crib, at the point at which her father is supposed to put the toy back in the crib. The vocal gesture "kitty" functions here as a procedure used at a conventional point in a particular game. It is not used in any other context to refer to the cat. Similarly, our own subject Carlotta used the word *bam* while knocking over toys, but in no other context. Another subject Marta used the sound *da* (Italian for "give") while giving or taking objects. However, like Carlotta's *bam*, Marta's *da* existed for weeks only as a procedure during a game, at fixed points of occurrence. These wordlike sounds were not used to describe ongoing sequences by other participants, to demand the initiation of a *bam* or *da* game. Many similar examples of what we have termed "nonreferential" or "prereferential" words have been offered by other researchers. To the extent that these uses are contextbound, they seem to belong to the context as a whole rather than to the referent in the peculiar way that names can be said to "belong to" or identify referents.

In Carlotta, a subtle change took place in *bam* around 12–13 months of age. In one observation, she sat among her toys unoccupied for a brief moment, said the word *bam,* and then turned to bang on her toy piano. The temporal separation of the vocal gesture from its proper point in the activity with which it was linked gives the first clue that *bam* signifies or stands for the act of banging. As described by Werner and Kaplan in *Symbol Formation* (1963), such behavior is truly symbolic activity, wherein the vehicle is differentiated from its referent though simultaneously standing for, suggesting, or evoking its referent. Around this same time, Carlotta began to produce referential acts that we can more comfortably call naming. *Mao-mao* was a sound made in the presence of cats in a variety of contexts. Similarly, *woo-woo* was used in the presence of dogs (including the sound of a dog barking outside), and so forth. Once this process began, the repertoire of animal sounds expanded to a considerable list. At this point, it seems fair to conclude that for Carlotta, things have names.

Our inference that the child has some grasp of vehicle–referent relations in his vocal productions is based, then, on a slow process of decontextualization, in which the word procedure is used not in a single multifaceted game, but in a variety of contexts linked by the presence or involvement of a particular referent for that word. Unquestionably, this last development in word games has enormous qualitative consequences for language acquisition and for cognitive activity in general. However, we do not see the discovery of naming as a discontinuous leap. In naming, words are still procedures or activities with certain contextual rules of use. But the rules of the game have changed. What we have here is a developmental version of Wittgenstein's theory of meaning as a language game (Wittgenstein, 1958), except that now a major point of the game is to recognize or identify a referent (i.e., "What I do with this object is I make this noise . . .").

The same decontextualization that takes place in production between 9 and 13 months can also be seen in language comprehension. By 9 months, many of our subjects understood two or three utterances such as *no, Where's Daddy?,* or *Where's your belly button?* The child showed evidence of comprehension by obeying the command, or looking in a particular, well-established place for the referent. For example, many children responded early on to *Where's Daddy?* by looking toward the outside entrance where fathers typically appear and disappear at set points in the day. By 13 months, comprehension of the same words now included goal-directed searches in a variety of places, including evidence for some memory of the place where the referent last disappeared. Also, in games like *Where's your nose?,* the *nose* portion of the question was recognized and appropriately acted upon in a variety of slots, e.g., *Where's Mama's nose?, Where's sister's nose?* We would certainly hesitate to call this sort of frame–slot comprehension "syntax." However, it does provide evidence of a gradual "freeing-up" of the verbal and nonverbal contexts within which a given word-scheme can occur, so that the domain to which the word refers is much more like a naming range. *Nose* applies to a variety of noses, and not to a particular game of touching one's own nose. Things have names at 13 months, in comprehension as well as production.

Recall that at 9 months of age some of the first conventionalized or abbreviated signals were derived from what were initially goal-oriented behaviors (e.g., reaching and fussing). Once the ritualization process began, however, new procedures were taken directly from adult behaviors in game sequences via imitation (e.g., *byebye* and *pattycake*). The same is true for the shift at 13 months. While some of the referential words are derived from earlier, nonreferential uses of the same sound (e.g., Carlotta's *bam*), once the idea of naming is established, new names come into the child's repertoire without passing through the same lengthy process of decontextualization. Still, whenever we have sufficient history of a word in comprehension and/or production (e.g., Gruendel, 1977; Nelson, 1977), there does seem to be a period of tinkering with the contextual range of use. Typically, the context is first overly narrow from the adult perspective (e.g., *kitty* in the Shvachkin example), and may then become overly wide, leading to overextensions such as applying the word *kitty* to all furry animals. The same process of contextual widening and narrowing also goes on in adult word acquisition (e.g., Werner and Kaplan, 1963). What we are most interested in here, however, is the **first** stage in which the contextual range for word use permits us to infer that the child understands what names are. In particular, we are interested in the developments that accompany the discovery of symbols in speech.

Just as the shift toward communicative tool use at 9 months was accompanied by parallel nonsocial developments, the shift into symbolic or referential communication at 13 months was also accompanied by parallel developments in nonsocial activities. First of all, naming acts occur both inside and outside of communicative schemes. Some of the first naming acts occur within the already established imperative frames (still accompanied by pointing, reaching, etc.) or in the declarative bids for shared attention to objects (also accompanied by previously established protodeclarative gestures). However, naming also occurred in solitary play, as objects were noticed and recognized prior to use in some further activity. Apparently the naming game serves both a cognitive and a social function from its first appearance by 13 months of age. Premack (1977) reports similar solitary naming behaviors in his chimpanzee's play with plastic chip symbols, and Gardner and Gardner (1974) have also reported naming without a communicative function in the chimpanzee Washoe's use of American Sign Language. If we can extrapolate at all from patterns of naming in child and chimpanzee, we can conclude that the recognitory or identifying function of symbols is at least as important in phylogeny and ontogeny as their function in communication.

It is also around 13 months that we witness the earliest evidence for nonverbal symbolic activity in play. Here too the recognitory function of symbolic activity is in evidence. Brief and tenuous "pretend" activities begin around this age: The child places a toy telephone receiver against his ear, stirs in a bowl with a spoon, puts a doll's shoe up against a doll's foot. In these schemes, the object is "recognized" by carrying out an activity typically associated with that object. **An activity need not be conventional, arbitrary, and/or imitated for it to serve that identifying function.** However, it is easier for us as observers to recognize this kind of play when the child uses as his symbolic vehicle a stereotypic behavior that could only have been derived through observation and imitation of adult activities that are (probably) poorly understood.

Many researchers have noted the coincidence between the appearance of this behavior and the first recognizable words (e.g., Inhelder *et al.*, 1971; Nicholich, 1975; Sinclair, 1970). Escalona (1973), among others, has suggested that these gestural procedures should be considered a kind of enactive or motor naming. **If we consider the symbolic play gestures to be a form of naming, we can ask whether children use vocal and manual gestures to recognize, identify, or name the same set of objects, events, social games.** At the period in which symbols emerge, is there a bias toward the use of one modality for particular functions or meanings? Or is the 13-month-old symbol-using capacity essentially modality free? Part of the answer to this question will depend upon our model for the internal structure of symbols.

Toward a Model of Symbolic Activity

In the previous section, we described a series of behaviors leading up to the discovery of the language game of "naming," including both vocal naming, and gestural or "enactive" naming in symbolic play. The following working definition of "symbol" emerges from these behaviors:

The comprehension or use, inside or outside communicative situations, of a relationship between a sign and its referent, such that the sign is treated as belonging to and/or substitutable for its referent in a variety of contexts; at the same time the user is aware that the sign is separable from its referent, that is, not the same thing.

Clearly, there are a good many unanalyzed terms in this definition, in particular "aware," "substitutable," "sign," and "referent." When we must decide, with child or chimpanzee, whether a given activity is "symbolic," then further operational definition of these unanalyzed terms becomes critical. We will start with some criteria for recognizing "substitutability" and "awareness" in nonlinguistic symbolic activity. It will be quite clear that, under the application of these criteria, some behaviors are only "quasi-symbolic" or "presymbolic"—a result that may be uncomfortable for some philosophers, but perhaps inevitable if we are to take a diachronic perspective (in both ontogeny and phylogeny) on the emergence of symbols. Then we will turn to an examination of the nature of sign–referent relations in emerging symbol systems, distinguishing between "subjective" or "psychological" sign–referent relations (i.e., from the point of view of a 12-month-old) and "objective" relations between events that serve as vehicles and referents (i.e., from the point of view of Charles Sanders Peirce).

Substitution and Awareness

Note first of all that we have defined symbolic activity as behavior that can occur inside or outside communication. This approach is at odds with definitions of symbols as "interpersonal conventions used intentionally to convey meanings," a definition used by a number of language philosophers including Searle (1975), Grice (1975), and Langer (1962). In our infant research, intentional communication through conventional signals is viewed as a process that precedes, correlates with, and hence possibly contributes to the emergence of symbols. However, we believe that the symbolic function involves a further development, a separate capacity that is manifested in both communicative and noncommunicative behavior, greatly changing the form of each. Symbolic activity includes symbolic communication. However, symbolic activity may also include some private and often idiosyncratic behaviors.

In a seminar at Berkeley in 1976, Dan Slobin and I joined with a group of students in a session devoted to speculations about the origins of symbolic play. We reviewed the animal and human literature in search of anecdotes that would yield criteria for identifying "symboliclike" activity. In the primate literature, a number of anecdotes emerged that were striking primarily for their complete and humanlike imitative form. For example, Jolly (1972) reported an unpublished anecdote about Washoe, in which Washoe picked up her doll, filled the bathtub with water, dumped the doll in the tub, soaped it down, took it out, and dried it with a towel! Other examples were impressive insofar as they suggest the kind of aesthetic pleasure that humans take in symbolic objects. For example, Kellogg and Kellogg (1933) gave the following description of some chimpanzee behaviors with objects:

> On frequent occasions she would adorn herself with larger or heavier articles in the same manner. Thus she would sometimes place a blanket or piece of clothing over her shoulders and drag it around with her; she would put small branches containing foliage upon her back and similarly carry or trail them; or she would wrap herself in hanging tree moss or in rags by putting them behind her back and holding them with both hands in front. She would thereupon walk upright with a train following her wake, towards which she would gaze with a play smile, moving usually in a wide circle as she did so [p. 120].

What is it about these behaviors that makes them classifiable as "symbolic," other than the fact that they look like things that people do? In search of a more precise definition of "substitutability" and "awareness," we came up with the following criteria with corresponding human and nonhuman examples.

PARTIAL AND/OR RECOMBINATIVE EXECUTION OF BEHAVIORS

Within symbolic activity, in contrast to the activity for which it stands, the means is typically in discontinuation from the goal, and the sequence can be interrupted with certain parts exaggerated or recombined.

HUMAN CHILD "Donald . . . was also discovered at about the same age prancing back and forth across the room with his hands joined behind his back (in exaggerated imitation of his father's walk . . .) [from Kellogg and Kellogg, 1933, p. 138]."

NONHUMAN Play-fighting and play-mounting in the juveniles of many species.

SUBSTITUTABILITY OF ONE OR MORE OBJECTS FOR THE OBJECT USUALLY INVOLVED IN EXECUTION OF THE SCHEME

The animal or child carries out a given activity with an object that may resemble the appropriate object for that scheme to some extent, but is not appropriate for the completion and actual function of that act.

HUMAN CHILD "Pierre puts the handle of the broom on the doll's mouth, holding the doll in a nursing position. His expression and movement indicate that the broom handle represents a baby's bottle . . . [Sinclair, 1970, p. 123]."

NONHUMAN "Both infants (chimpanzees) . . . frequently substituted one instrument for another: in default of a pencil both Roody and Jone would attempt scratching paper with a nail, stick or even their fingernail . . . [Kohts, 1935, p. 530]."

also Cats chasing walnuts, spools, etc. with the movements typically observed in chasing insects or small animals.

SIGNS OF PLEASURE OR LACK OF SERIOUSNESS

The animal or child indicates that the symbolic activity is not the same thing as the real activity it represents or depicts by giving some signal (intentional or unintentional) expressing "playfulness."

HUMAN CHILD "Jacqueline . . . saw a cloth whose fringed edges vaguely recalled those of her pillow; she seized it, held a fold of it in her right hand, sucked the thumb of the same hand and lay down on her side **laughing hard.** She kept her eyes open, but blinked from time to time as if she were alluding to closed eyes [Piaget, 1962, p. 96; emphasis added]."

NONHUMAN "The initiator (chimpanzee) may approach another animal by walking or trotting towards him with a highly characteristic bounce to the gait; the head bounces up and down, his gaze may not be directed at the animal he approaches, he is often wearing the *playface*, and soft guttural exhalations may be audible (the playface is a special expression indicating playful intent in which only the lower teeth show . . .) [Morris, 1975, p. 235]."

also: "Cats and dogs both have preliminary play movements, play intention movements in fact, which consist of a half-crouch with fore-legs extended stiffly, combined with wide-open eyes and ears pulled forward . . . [Morris, 1975, p. 233]."

AWARENESS OF OBJECT SUBSTITUTION

The animal or child indicates his knowledge of the inappropriateness of the substitute object by "voluntarily" (i.e., in a goal-directed fashion) altering or eliminating any portion of the symbolic act that does not fit the substitute.

> HUMAN CHILD "On seeing a pillow, she got into the position for sleeping on her side, seizing the pillow with one hand and pressing it against her face. . . . But instead of miming the action half-seriously, she smiled broadly. . . . She remained in this position for a moment, then sat up delightedly [Piaget, 1962, p. 96]."
>
> NONHUMAN   "(The playface) appears to occur most often at the beginning of a playful interaction, the point at which it is most necessary to avoid being misunderstood. . . . If the other animal responds and takes up the chase, the tempo may quicken slightly and the playface becomes less evident (since it has served its function of letting the partner know the intent of this particular action) . . . [Morris, 1975, p. 235]."
>
> also: The cat playing chase-and-capture with a walnut or spool typically does not try to eat or bite the object.

Note that these examples illustrate different **aspects** of symbolic activity, each satisfying one or two of the criteria. Most examples in our survey, however, were missing one or more of the components in this operationalization of symbolic awareness and substitutability. Does this mean that the behaviors are not, then, symbolic? What do we do with behaviors that are "quasi-symbolic" or perhaps "presymbolic"? The fuzzy boundaries leading into productive symbolic activity may simply be a biological fact, a continuum with behaviors that fall somewhere in the middle, or just barely short of the endpoint. This observation does not, however, liberate us from the necessity of defining that endpoint in some detail. This is particularly true with regard to an analysis of sign–referent relationships. The rest of the chapter will be devoted to that issue.

Sign–Referent Relations

A complete situation of symbol use involves not two but four parts: the **objective, observable vehicle and its real world referent,** and the **subjective, psychological vehicle and its mental referent.** We will begin with a definition of the possible relations between objective vehicles and referents, following Peirce (1932). Then we will reconsider Peirce's classification from the perspective of a 12-month-old who must interpret and use objective vehicle–referent relations. A key theme will be the contrasts that can exist, in a given symbolic act, between objective versus subjective conventional acts (i.e., vehicles). This contrast will permit us to compare our view with those of Piaget, and of Werner and Kaplan. The purpose of this exercise is to develop a model of the internal structure of symbols, locating the cognitive "parts" that comprise this newly evolved machinery. If we can locate the seams and joints of symbolic structures, we will have made some progress toward understanding where symbols come from.

SIGN–REFERENT RELATIONS: PIERCE'S PROPOSAL

Within C. S. Peirce's multidimensional classification of signs, one classification pertains to the physical relationship between a sign and its referent. This is the division of sign–referent relations into "icon," "index," and "symbol," relationships that exist independently of a community. Recall the old philosophical question about a tree falling in the forest with no one there to hear it. Can it be said to make a sound? That of course depends on one's definition of "sound." A tree can at least be said to set up certain patterns or air waves, whether or not those waves strike someone's ears. There is at least "sound potential." Similarly, Peirce's description of icons, indices, and symbols refers to the "sign potential" of an objective relationship between two world objects or events.

An icon is a sign that is related to its referent by virtue of some actual physical resemblance between the two. For example, a drawing of a flame is an icon for fire insofar as the picture preserves some of the two-dimensional visual properties of fire. Signs can vary in their "degree of iconicity," that is, the number of attributes (or amount of a particular attribute) shared by vehicle and referent (Tversky, 1977). The implications for a community of sign users are that, if the group who have made use of the iconic sign–referent relation were to die off without a trace, the relationship could potentially be rediscovered and used by other knowers capable of noting the same physical resemblance. The greater the degree of iconicity, the greater the probability of rediscovery.

An index is a sign that is related to its referent by virtue of some literal physical participation in the referent object–event. For example, smoke indexes fire insofar as smoke is an event that is created by and hence consistently co-occurs with fire. It is less clear what degree of indexicality might mean in comparison with degree of iconicity. Presumably a sign could be more or less indexical to the degree that it consistently co-occurs with its referent. Here the quantity of indexicality would be measured in spatiotemporal terms rather than numbers of features or amount of a particular feature. The implications for a community of sign users are similar for indices and icons, in that if a community of knowers were to disappear without a trace, the index–referent relationship might well be discovered again independently by another group through experience with the same physical world. Here too, the greater the degree of indexicality, the greater the probability that the relationship will be rediscovered.

A "symbol" is a sign that is related to its referent **only** through the conventions agreed upon by a community of users. The relationship is truly arbitrary, in that there is no "natural" physical resemblance or participation between the two. The word "fire" stands for its referent because we have agreed to use those sounds in that particular way. The "degree of arbitrariness" in a sign–referent relationship is the inverse of the degree of iconicity and/or indexicality between the sign and referent. The implications for a community of sign users are that if a community of knowers were to disappear without a trace, the relationship could never be or would be unlikely to be rediscovered independently. As the degree of arbitrariness of a given sign–referent relationship approaches 100% (i.e., as the degree of iconicity and/or indexicality approaches zero), the probability that a given relationship will be discovered twice approaches zero.

I should note that Peirce did not discuss the probabilities of rediscovery in the rather literal quantitative terms provided here. He did, however, stress that these three classes are pure forms, whereas the real-world sign–referent relationships to which we apply this analysis are often likely to be mixtures of at least two types.

For example, because of their physical participation with their referents, indices are likely to contain certain iconic aspects as well. Smoke blows in the same direction as fire, and may increase in size proportionally with the size of the fire. A hoofprint of a deer is an index for the whole deer, but it bears an iconic relationship to the deer's hoof, as well as the direction the deer was taking.

In addition to the typical mix between icons and indices, there are also many sign–referent relations that contain degrees of arbitrariness mixed with either iconicity or indexicality. Although some theories of language origins and language processing have made too much of "sound symbolism" or onomatopaeia (see Stross, 1976, for a review), it is certainly true that some linguistic signs bear a partial iconic relationship to the thing or event they represent (e.g., "boom," "sneeze," "clank"). Such instances of easily recovered physical resemblance between acoustic sign and referent are, however, fairly rare. Indeed, this fact has been used by some writers in asserting the greater arbitrariness, and hence more "abstract" nature of speech over visual–gestural forms of communication like American Sign Language (ASL). Similarly, alphabetic writing systems have been proclaimed as more abstract and hence "higher" forms of writing than ideographic or hieroglyphic systems (Gleitman and Rozin, 1977). I will clarify my own opposition to this view later with regard to the comparison between language acquisition and other aspects of culture acquisition in normal children. With regard to the comparison between speech and ASL, and alphabetic versus hieroglyphic writing, the supposedly greater iconicity of the visual sign–referent relationship is often deceptive. For most ASL gestures, and for hieroglyphs in many sophisticated writing systems, we can perceive the iconicity between sign and referent only **after** we have been told the meaning of the sign (e.g., Frischberg, 1977). Many ASL signs and hieroglyphs do indeed begin as icons. However, these signs generally undergo a historical process of drift from iconicity to arbitrariness, due to pressures involved in ease and speed of articulation. Like the reach–fuss communications of our 9-month-old infants, the signals become increasingly abstract and conventionalized through use, preserving only the clean minimum lines necessary for unambiguous communication with group members (as opposed to outsiders).

In addition to this process of conventionalization across time, there is another type of arbitrariness that applies at the moment a given icon is first invented. Given the fact that we cannot exhaustively represent every feature of a referent in a given symbolic act, we must "select" some aspect of that object–event for depiction with an iconic sign. The selection process itself is often quite arbitrary, so that a knower who comes upon the sign much later cannot make the connection between the feature that is depicted, and the more complete object–event to which that feature belongs. For example, in ASL there is a sign that consists of a cross made on the upper arm between the elbow and shoulder. Informed that this sign is the ASL convention for nurse or paramedic, one can easily make the connection to an identifying red cross on a medic's sleeve. However, the likelihood of discovering that relationship without being told is very low. This type of iconic relationship, between a complex referent and a vehicle depicting some arbitrarily chosen aspect of that referent, has been termed a "metonymic" relationship.

These arguments about the arbitrariness of ASL signs pertain primarily to the probability of discovery of a relationship that is only remotely iconic. This does not mean, however, that—once we are told about the iconic bond between sign and referent—we make no use of that iconicity. As Brown (1977) has pointed out, the iconicity of certain ASL signs may be a mnemonic, an aid in either recalling or recognizing those signs after they are first presented. In Chapter 1 we noted a phenomenon that has been reported by several researchers (e.g., Bonvillian and Nelson, 1978), in which autistic or aphasic children who have been unable to acquire speech do make significant progress in the acquisition of ASL. Brown has suggested that the iconicity of certain ASL signs may be an aid to these children in acquiring language in the visual mode. He points out that, although many signs are indeed very remotely related to their referents, the signs that predominate in the vocabularies of these children (and, incidentally, in the vocabularies of signing chimpanzees) tend to be terms for "basic level objects" (Rosch, 1978). In contrast with more abstract meanings like people and week, basic level notions like chair and car tend to retain much more of their iconicity. In an experiment with normal hearing children, Brown taught a series of 8 such basic level signs. In one condition, the children received the ASL signs with their actual translations in English words. In another condition, the same signs and English meanings were scrambled so that any iconicity from sound to meaning was lost. Acquisition was significantly better in the group that had the iconic aid.

To summarize, the iconicity of ASL signs and hieroglyphs may be useful in remembering relationships **after** they have been pointed out. But the processes of historic drift toward arbitrariness of form, and metonymic processes in sign selection, have led to a situation in which the iconicity of signs is of very little use in discovery. Indeed, many dialects of gestural language are every bit as mutually unintelligible as spoken languages. The same is true for hieroglyphic writing systems. Hence the oft-cited contrast in arbitrariness between speech and manual language is deceptive. We will return to this point later, with regard to the acquisition of linguistic and nonlinguistic symbols in infants.

PEIRCE RECONSIDERED FROM AN INFANT'S POINT OF VIEW

So far I have discussed the "objective" relations that can exist between external, real-world events that serve as signs and referents. As adults, we have no difficulty grasping the distinction between icons and indices versus symbols, insofar as the former are "natural," the latter artificial and preserved through convention. However, the ability to distinguish the natural from the artificial is a fairly sophisticated acquisition. **I will argue here that the three types of objective vehicle–referent relations are related at first to only two kinds of subjective or psychological vehicle–referent relations, based on two kinds of psychological processes.** Iconicities are detected and acquired through perception of similarity; both indices and symbols are detected and acquired through a single process of perception of contiguity. The knowledge that indices and symbols are different is a very late development, and of no relevance to the acquisition of sign–referent relations by young infants.

Consider the point of view of a 12-month-old entering into a world of sign relations. The child's developing perceptual apparatus will presumably permit him to pick up iconic relationships as soon as he can attend to and compare a given perceptual feature or set of features across entities. Sensitivity to similarity is crucial to the recognition that a single object is the same at Time A and Time B despite apparent transformations in size and shape brought about by movements in space (i.e., size and shape constancy). Also, the perception of similarity is a critical process in the formation of natural categories uniting more than one object. In short, the recognition of iconic relationships—independent of their use in communication and/or representation—is a fundamental aspect of information processing. This does not necessarily mean that the detection of similarity is raw and immediate. Tversky (1977) and Goodman (1968) have pointed out that the statement that two entities are similar presupposes analysis into features and the selection of particular features for comparison. Goodman implies that this selection process may be so arbitrary as to render the whole concept of similarity useless as an explanatory variable. Tversky, on the other hand, believes that the analysis and weighting of features in similarity judgments is a lawful process that warrants further study. In either case, we could not conclude that perception of similarity is as simple and immediate as, say, perception of color. The child must learn about extraction, weighting, and comparison of features in analyzing similarities between objects and events. Nevertheless, this process is clearly distinguishable from the type of perception that underlies the detection of indexical and symbolic sign relations.

How does the child come to recognize indices? If he cannot find an iconic relationship that binds two events, he must simply perceive and remember that the two phenomena are always found together or in sequence (e.g., mother putting on her coat is an index of mother leaving). In other words, the process that underlies the acquisition of indices is the perception of "contiguity"—a process that is pervasive and undeniable, albeit somewhat unpopular in cognitive psychology. **What this means is that, from the perspective of a novice knower, objective indices and objective symbols are equally arbitrary kinds of sign–referent relations. And the process by which the two are acquired is identical.**

For both the 1-year-old and the adult, the relationship between the word "shoe" and the object it refers to is learned by association. The sounds are acquired as a game or procedure carried out in the presence of shoes and shoelike objects. But the relationship between shoes and the gesture of putting shoe to foot is probably just as arbitrary for a 1-year-old child as is the utterance of *shoe*. From the comfort of our adult perspective, we know that this gesture, unlike the sound, has a solid functional basis. Hence it is in fact participatory and indexical with its referent. But, then, you and I know a lot about the reasons for carrying out certain cultural acts (although, as I shall stress later, we know a lot less than is apparent at first glance). However, most of the gestural "naming" carried out by infants in our study involves acts whose functions are generally quite opaque from the child's point of view. Vocal gestures and manual gestures are things that one simply **does** in association with certain referent objects and events. Neither one of them looks like their referents; hence they are not icons. And if the reason for the natural participation is unknown to the child, then he cannot differentiate the objective index from the objective symbol. Human children are apparently equipped with a tendency to recognize, and, more importantly, to reproduce new acts that are quite arbitrary from their point of view, serving as signs purely by association with particular situations.

Of course, the tendency to store and later recognize arbitrary relations between events is an ability shared by many species. This is essentially the mechanism involved in classical conditioning, once believed to be the basis for the acquisition of virtually all knowledge about the world. However, much attention has been given in the recent animal learning literature to the difference between the conditionability of truly arbitrary relations versus relations that reflect some biologically constrained, natural "belongingness" (e.g., Hinde and Stevenson-Hinde, 1973; Schwartz, 1978; Seligman and Hager, 1972; Shettleworth, 1972). The best known examples of such prepared or biologically constrained learning are reported by Garcia and Koelling (1966). In a series of studies on taste aversion, Garcia and Koelling report that rats will connect nausea with food stimuli when the stimuli and the aversive experience are separated by up to 24 hours—despite the plethora of more contiguous but less appropriate stimuli that have intervened between the unconditioned stimulus and the conditioned stimulus. In his review of such phenomena, Schwartz has suggested that the number and range of truly arbitrary or unprepared relations that can be learned increases up the phylogenetic scale. This reverses the older view that the simplest and most basic mechanism is arbitrary learning, while "belongingness" is the product of a higher and more interpretive intelligence. Instead, according to Schwartz, the ability to pick up large numbers of arbitrary relations without analyzing or understanding the reason for the relationship can be viewed as **more** rather than **less** human.

Furthermore, in human symbolic processing the mere recognition of arbitrary sign–referent relations is carried one critical step further. We also **reproduce** the arbitrarily determined sign, with actions that bear an iconic relationship to that objective sign. This is essentially the mechanism of imitation. According to Piaget, such iconic reproductions or imitations are initially acquired in the presence of the sign–model. Later they can be executed in the absence of the model. The ability to call forth the actions used to imitate a sign is, according to Piaget, the basis of our capacity for representation (literally "re-presentation"), and as such is the basis for the internalized actions we call thought. Furthermore, the imitation need not always be fully expressed on the plane of action. The child does not have to literally act out the reproduction for it to serve a symbolic or "evocative" function. Merely by calling potential imitations into "mental readiness"—without actually executing the set of actions at the peripheral level—we can symbolize a given situation internally. Hence the "internal" sign is used to remind us of the whole referent situation, in the same way the objective sign initially reminded us of its referent. We use an **iconic** action (an internal or a literal external imitation) to remind us of an **arbitrary** relationship between the objective sign–model and its referent. In other words, a single symbolic act may involve a mixture of iconic and arbitrary relationships at different levels.

In fact, a given symbolic act can involve mixtures of all three types of relationships (iconic, arbitrary, and indexical) holding between different poles of the four-way relationship uniting the subjective or psychological vehicle, the subjective referent, the objective vehicle, and the objective referent. To illustrate these poles more carefully, let us take the example illustrated in Figure 2.1: A child uses the act of stirring in a circular

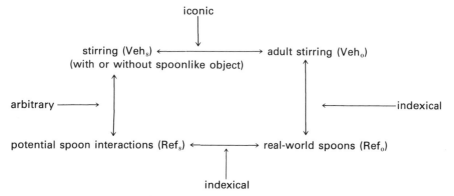

Figure 2.1. *Analysis of child "naming" a spoon or representing spoonness with a gesture of stirring in a circular motion.*

motion to gesturally "name" or recognize a spoon or spoonlike object. Note: We are **assuming** here, for purposes of analysis, that the child uses "stirring" as the vehicle to name "spoons" as the referent. This is the sort of inference that we typically draw with regard to children's naming behavior. The child could actually be using the stirring gesture to "name" food, or (for that matter) to "name" the action of stirring itself. In that case we would have to provide a different analysis. In Figure 2.1, however, we will assume that spoons are being "named," and that stirring is the gestural "name" that is being applied. Furthermore, in this particular instance we will assume that the child's stirring act is a deferred imitation of adult activities that are no longer physically present in the situation.

First of all, in this situation the "objective vehicle" (Veh_o) is the absent adult model of stirring, insofar as this is the aspect of "spoon events in the world" that the child has chosen to imitate in recognizing or naming something spoonlike.

Second, the "objective referent" (Ref_o) in this situation is the class of real-world spoons and spoon events. The objective referent is **not** just this particular spoonlike object. The child could have carried out the same symbolic act of naming with his empty hand in a stirring gesture, with no actual object in the situation to receive that action. In other words, by stirring with a spoon, a stick, or an empty hand the child is symbolizing or referring to "spoonness." And so it is external spoonness that is being represented.

Third, the "subjective vehicle" (Veh_s) is the child's own act of stirring, derived through imitation of real-world stirring (Veh_o). The subjective vehicle would be the same if the child were stirring with a real spoon, a stick, or other spoonlike object, or with his empty hand. As Piaget has stressed repeatedly, the symbol in this sort of gestural symbolic play is not the object assimilated by the symbol (e.g., the spoon or stick) but the act itself. Furthermore, the subjective vehicle would be the same even if the child did not act out the stirring gesture literally. The internalized stirring act and the literal externalized imitation of the stirring act are equivalent in their psychological role as subjective vehicles or symbols for naming, recognizing, evoking, representing "spoonness." Of course only the literal stirring act is available to us as observers. The child might be constructing mental symbols all over the place and we would not know about it. However, it is important to stress that from a Piagetian or a Wernerian perspective, the subjective vehicle is the "mental act" of calling up a particular action to stand for or represent some larger portion of the child's knowledge. (In Chapter 7 we will take up the issue of whether or not the imitation is actually carried out on the plane of action, and the role of internalized versus externalized imitations in symbolic activity.)

Finally the "subjective referent" (Ref_s) is the entire complex of potential interactions with spoons in the child's repertoire, the "action package" that comprises his knowledge of spoons.[1] In this case, the stirring act was selected out of this action package to serve as the symbol, the tip of an iceberg of action–knowledge about spoons.

Now let us turn to the relationships uniting the various poles in this four-way unit.

First of all, the objective stirring act (Veh_o) serves as a sign for external spoonness (Ref_o) by virtue of a real-world "indexical" relationship, insofar as the act and the object participate together in a functional relationship (i.e., stirring takes its form from the requirement of mixing ingredients with the spoon). However, since the child need not be aware of that function (he most probably is not), the indexical relationship between the objective vehicle and the objective referent is at this particular point cognitively irrelevant.

Second, the subjective vehicle (the child's own act of stirring) stands in "iconic" relation to the objective vehicle, insofar as it is an imitation of that vehicle. The better the imitation, the greater the degree of iconicity between the two vehicles. As a child corrects and improves his imitation (including deferred imitations), we can infer that he has perceived and used this iconicity, both in acquiring the subjective vehicle to begin with and in exercising the vehicle in play. In the instance examined here, we have specified that he "externalizes" or acts the Veh_s out literally. However, the relationship of the Veh_s to the Veh_o would be the same if the child had only **mentally** selected that act as a symbol for spoonness, that is, if he had "called up" that portion of the action program for interacting with spoons.

Third, the relationship between the subjective vehicle (the child's own stirring act) and the action–package that comprises the subjective referent is at this point in development an **arbitrary** relationship. The child does not know why the stirring act belongs to the complex of activities that are carried out with spoons. He merely recognizes that they do belong together, and uses that knowledge in reproducing stirring as a symbolic vehicle. Later on he may come to analyze and adjust the internal relations of his "spoon program." He may come to understand the reason for the circular stirring movement, (i.e., to mix the

---

[1] Piaget uses the word "action" in this regard to include voluntary perceptual acts like looking, scanning, listening, etc., as opposed to passive reception of sensory information. Hence the Ref_s includes perceptual knowledge of objects based on such voluntary perceptual acts.

ingredients together in a bowl). At this point the relationship of stirring (Veh$_s$) to the rest of the interactions with spoons that comprise "spoon meaning" (Ref$_s$) would become a subjective index. At the earlier stages, however, stirring belongs to and hence can stand for spoons primarily by virtue of association.

There is also a second type of arbitrariness involved in the relationship between the subjective referent and the subjective vehicle, one which would remain even if the indexical function of stirring were recognized. Why does the child choose **this particular** action to serve as symbol, and not one of the myriad other things he can do with spoons? How does one particular gesture come to have a more salient role as a "mental reminder" than another? It is of course possible that stirring is, for this child, the only thing he knows how to do with spoons. However, in his own nonimitative manipulations with objects we see him carry out a great many activities (e.g., banging, bringing to the mouth). So this hypothesis is unlikely. Perhaps the stirring gesture is a "better" symbol not because it is the only thing he can do with spoons, but **because it is the most unique activity associated with that object.** As such, it would function as a better identifier for that particular object and no other. Rosch (1978) defines the prototypic or defining member of a category as that member which contains the largest number of features shared by the members of that category, while at the same time involving the least overlap (i.e., smallest number of features) with other categories. Hence a robin is a "best exemplar" of the category "bird" because it has a maximal number of bird features, and a minimum of nonbird features. Ostriches are peripheral members of the category "bird" because they are missing a number of bird features, while at the same time they overlap with other animals in features like locomotion by running rather than flying. It is possible that symbol selection is guided by similar criteria, so that the child selects the "prototypic" activity associated with spoons—one that is regularly carried out with spoons, and very rarely carried out with any other object. Alternatively, some much less specific kind of salience (e.g., Odom, 1977) may be involved in symbol selection. The issue of "symbol selection" is, as far as I know, entirely unexplored in anyone's research. This is a process that should be distinguished from "symbol acquisition." Until we understand the selection process better, it appears that the selection of a particular scheme to represent or symbolize an action–package is essentially arbitrary. If so, this would be an example in infant symbolic activity of the sort of "metonymic relation" discussed earlier regarding the origins of signs in American Sign Language. In other words, both the criteria for symbol selection, and the nature of the symbol–referent relation may be arbitrary from the point of view of a 12-month-old.

Fourth and finally, the relationship between the subjective referent and the objective referent is essentially "indexical," insofar as these interactions were acquired in a series of actual physical transactions with spoons (motoric, visual, auditory, etc.). In Piaget's theory all thought is regarded as internalized action formed by assimilation and accommodation to an objective reality; hence all sensorimotor knowledge is presumably indexical in nature. This would mean, in Figure 2.1, that the child's spoon-defining actions and the spoon itself are joined by literal physical participation, and hence stand in an indexical relation. Of course, the physical form of objects and events will constrain the form of actions on those objects and events—just as fire constrains the size and direction of smoke. So the indices that comprise sensorimotor knowledge of the world will contain a mixture of iconicities, or isomorphic relations to real-world forms. Such mixtures are to be expected within Peirce's model.

Contrast the situation in Figure 2.1 with a second situation (in Figure 2.2) in which the same child utters the word "spoon" upon seeing a spoon or spoonlike object. Here the actual, objective, external vehicle–referent relationship is conventional and arbitrary. However, the rest of the matrix is identical to Figure 2.1. The relationship between the objective vehicle (the adult utterance "spoon") and the subjective vehicle

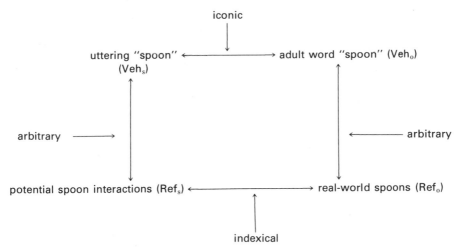

Figure 2.2. *Analysis of child "naming" a spoon or representing spoonness with uttering of the vocal gesture "spoon."*

(the child's approximation of the word "spoon") is iconic, insofar as it was derived by imitation. The relationship between the subjective vehicle (whether it is actually uttered, or merely called into readiness internally) and the subjective referent (the same complex of spoon-defining activities that served as Ref_s in Figure 2.1) is arbitrary, in that the sound-making procedure "spoon" has come to be associated with other games played with spoons entirely by situational contiguity. Finally, the relationship between the subjective referent and the objective referent is indexical, insofar as all sensorimotor action packages come to be organized around entities and events in the world through actual physical participation with those entitites (including voluntary perceptual acts—see footnote on p. 55).

In other words, at this stage in development, the three relationships relevant to cognitive processing are identical for the gestural and the vocal naming act. The only difference is in the real-world relationship (Veh_o–Ref_o), which is at this point unknown to the child. What makes the child choose the sound procedure versus the gestural procedure to "name" or recognize the object? Until we have a theory to predict and explain the process of symbol selection, we must conclude that the selection process is arbitrary. Hence in both examples the subjective vehicle–referent relationship is metonymic.

To summarize so far, Peirce's tripartite division of index, icon, and symbol describes objective vehicle–referent relations. From the perspective of the knower, at least the novice knower, there are only two processes for perceiving and acquiring sign–referent relations: Icons are mastered through perception of similarity; indices and symbols are mastered through perception of contiguity (i.e., by association). Hence both indices and symbols are equally arbitrary from the point of view of the knower. Our adult understanding of the distinction between index and symbol is based **not** on the evolution of some third knowing process, but rather on knowledge about the respective origins of symbols versus indices. We eventually come to understand that symbols are manufactured by other human beings, while indices are the by-products of certain functional relations. We may come to understand this simply by being told. Alternatively, we can eventually make this distinction by trial and error, discovering which relations are necessary and which relations are dissociable.

Why, then, should some ASL signs be easier to learn by virtue of their iconicity, as Brown (1977) has demonstrated? There is a clear difference between the recognitory gestures that arise in symbolic play (some of which are similar to ASL gestures) and gestural symbols that literally "depict" their referents. The stirring act is related to the meaning "spoon" by virtue of a functional relationship (which is opaque to the 1-year-old). However, **if the stirring motion were used as a gestural "verb," to stand for or evoke the class of stirring actions themselves, we would have an example of an iconic Veh_o–Ref_o relationship.** This situation is illustrated in Figure 2.3. Note that this situation of symbol use is fully iconic at all interstices, and hence fully transparent and "discoverable." Perception of similarity from a particular instance of stirring to the class of stirring acts is sufficient to acquire the entire structure. It is important to distinguish this sort of fully transparent iconic symbolic act from the kinds of gestural symbols described in Figure 2.1. Stirring to name spoons requires both perception of similarity (to carry out the Veh_s–Veh_o imitation) and perception of contiguity (to record the relation between stirring and spoons). Stirring to name stirring acts requires only the process of perception of similarity.

Sign languages like ASL can exploit both kinds of gestural relations, either by using signs that literally depict their referents (stirring to stand for stirring), or by using signs that depict an act conventionally associated with a referent (stirring to stand for spoons). However, the latter form of depiction will work only if there is **prior cultural knowledge** associating action and referent through contiguity. For a 1-year-old, the cultural conventions and the communicative conventions are being acquired at the same time. **It is no easier to acquire an arbitrary gesture than it is to acquire an arbitrary sound.** Indeed, there is strong developmental evidence that young children do not recognize the linguistic vehicle–referent relation as any more arbitrary or less indexical

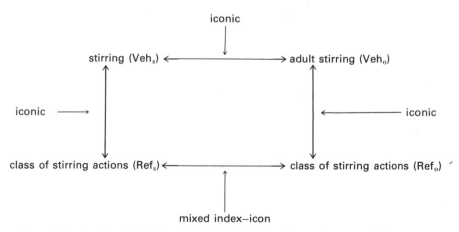

Figure 2.3. *Analysis of child "naming" the act of stirring by carrying out a stirring gesture.*

than any of the other little understood facts he has stored about the world. "Word realism" is a term that describes the belief of children as old as 5 years of age, that a name is an inherent part of the referent. The word "cow" is just as much a "feature" of cows as color, size, shape, horns, etc. Tanz (1978) interprets this tendency in young children as follows:

> "Word realism" describes children's tendency to treat names as inherent properties of objects. When questioned, children reveal a belief that if the name is changed, the object is also changed, and that name is held by virtue of the object's possessing various other of its properties. In other words, children who display word-realism speak as if referential words were icons and indexes rather than symbols. Although word-realism is a meta-linguistic orientation that is incorrect from our point of view, it could be regarded as having a certain amount of validity—as a description of the child's own initial language performance. In the child's early output, names are identical. They do not occur without their referents, and hence behave *like* attributes of the referents.
>
> It is impossible to imagine that the child arrives at word-realism by application of the same capacity for synthesis that enables him to gradually recognize various manifestations of an object as being the same object. By this account, word-realism is an overgeneralization of object constancy .

There is also evidence from Feldman and Shen (1971) that bilingual children, with greater experience in the detachability and interchangeability of labels, overcome this confusion between symbols and indices earlier than monolingual children, by around 4 years of age. By this time, however, much of language acquisition has proceeded on course without the mature realization that the sound–meaning relations of language are more arbitrary than most conventions.

There are many cases, however, in which even the adult fails to distinguish symbols and indices in cultural activities. Some cultural acts are viewed as "natural" relations, assumed to be as cosmically insured as the relationship between smoke and fire, when in fact the act and its result are joined only by social habit. We accept many cultural activities without questioning how or why they work, assuming indexicality. There simply is not time to "check out" the truly functional, indexical status of every sign–referent, means–end relationship that we use in everyday life. Complex technological societies would collapse under their own weight if all their participants were entirely scientific in coming to understand and use culture. Take the following trivial but true example. A woman for years observed her mother cook the Sunday ham by first removing the center bone, then placing the ham in the oven. Years later, when this woman began cooking hams for her own family, she proceeded in exactly the same fashion. On a visit to her daughter, the mother observed this process and asked in puzzlement why the center bone had to be removed. The daughter replied, "Why, that's how you always did it," to which the mother responded, "Yes, but in **my** oven that was the only way I could fit the damn thing in."

This example is illustrative, but not at all unusual. Stop for a moment and catalogue all the conventional activities you carry out in a single day, from brushing your teeth in the morning, turning your car key in the ignition, a thousand procedures that you carry out in interacting with and operating on a complex technological culture. You understand why you do them only to the extent that you recognize a contiguity between means and ends, antecedents and consequents. With the human capacity for imitation, we are not restricted merely to "recognizing" contiguous events and "expecting" certain results to follow certain signals. We can also "reproduce" such relationships, so that activities are used as means to ends even though, as far as we know, the means–end relationship is arbitrary. We reap the benefits of use, functioning adequately in the culture; meanwhile we can analyze at our leisure the relationship that permits the means to work. In a sense, then, imitation is a crucial component in what we might call the Culture Acquisition Device (CAD) or Culture Acquisition System (CAS) (a pun—with apologies to the author—upon McNeill, 1966).

Note that I have begun to discuss means–end relations and vehicle–referent relations in very much the same terms. I am making an assumption here that will be explicit for the rest of the book: **Means–end relations will be viewed as sign–referent relations incorporated within a problem–solving situation.** We are capable of observing and recording that X regularly follows or cooccurs with Y, or that X and Y look very much alike, without having to use that information in any way. At this point our knowledge of the relationship between X and Y is simply evocative; that is, X can remind us of Y because of either a similarity or a contiguity relationship. I may never make any **use** of that knowledge beyond this epistemic "knowing" use, to make predictions and/or explain events. However, if I am capable of **reproducing X** in some fashion, it is also in my power in some cases to **make Y happen.** In other words, it should be possible to use the X–Y relationship for control as well as prediction and explanation. Communication is one of the problem-solving situations that can be handled in this fashion: I reproduce or indicate X in order to evoke Y in my listener. There are other means–end situations to which the same thing applies. If the relationship is one of contiguity, I may be able in some cases to reproduce X and rest assured that Y will follow. If the relationship is one of similarity, I may be able to use X as a substitute for Y in certain instances. **The point is that**

vehicle–referent knowledge is potential means–end knowledge. This is not a new point. Indeed, the view of "sign–sign" or "sign–stimulus" relations as potential "means–end readiness" is the essence of Tolman's cognitive learning theory (Tolman, 1932). Tolman used this theory to explain, among other things, facts about incidental learning—that is, that animals can use behaviors as means to ends when they had merely observed relationships, in the absence of reinforcement.

Whether or not a vehicle–referent relationship is used in a means–end sequence, the link between the two can still be arbitrary. That is, I can "know what something is for" without knowing "how it works." Means to ends can be indexical (functioning adequately because of some real-world physical relationship) or arbitrary (functioning adequately only because of cultural conventions that insure the link). Both types of means–ends relations can be "acquired" through perception of contiguity, and "reproduced" through imitation.

How do we ever get beyond memorizing long lists of relations by brute force? Surely we eventually come to truly understand how things work. Earlier on I mentioned that, after a cultural means is acquired, we can analyze the means–end relationship at our leisure. What do I mean here by "analysis"?

There is ample evidence in all of cognitive and learning psychology to suggest that learning by association makes greater demands on memory than learning by similarity, and/or by extraction of general rules to account for classes of instances. There is, then, a constant psychological pressure to get rid of knowledge by contiguity alone. In the Peircian terms used here, by "analysis for understanding" we mean that subjectively arbitrary vehicle–referent relationships are broken down, examined, and replaced by subjective icons and indices whenever possible.

First, analysis into subjective indices will involve trial and error experience with the means–end relationship. By varying the means across situations and noting the results, I can determine which **aspects** of the means are really functionally related to the outcome. Some aspects will always be crucial, others will be optional and permit wide substitutions in the same action-frame, still others will be crucial only in certain applications of the scheme. We will pursue this argument further in Chapter 7 with regard to language development and the acquisition of grammar. I will argue there that the extraction of form classes in the construction of grammatical rules is essentially the product of playing with means, determining which linguistic means belong to the same functional slot.

A second type of analysis for understanding (one which undoubtedly goes on during indexical analysis as well) will be the discovery of underlying iconicities holding seemingly arbitrary vehicles and referents together. **In fact, we could argue that science is a process of discovering iconicities to "explain" contiguous events.** We "explain" the contiguity between smoke and fire by locating at the molecular level certain chemical structures that "fit" one another in lock and key fashion (i.e., a sort of deep structure iconicity). Two entities may respond to the same physical force because of some underlying similarity of weight, heat, chemical composition, etc. Hence those two entities move together in the world in regular and predictable ways when that force is presented. **In other words, many forms of scientific explanation can be summarized as demonstrations that objects–events are contiguous in space and/or in time because at some level those objects–events are the same.** If we **cannot** reduce a contiguous relation to some underlying iconicity, we must simply stop at that level, group similar contiguous relations together, and call that class of events a "law." However, the discovery of deeper iconicities or similarities seems to be in some way cognitively appealing, aesthetically preferable to a list of associations.

To summarize, Peirce's three-way classification of sign–referent relations (which become means–end relations when used toward some purpose) involves two basic psychological processes: perception of contiguity and perception of similarity. Insofar as any given relationship may at a particular moment be only partially analyzed, these two processes interact to create a continuum from arbitrariness to iconicity.

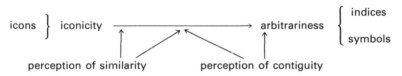

Points at mid continuum would represent relations to which both similarity and contiguity analysis are being applied. In Chapter 7, we will elaborate on the process by which linguistic forms move from one end of the continuum to another, including a discussion of individual differences in style of language acquisition as they relate to differential use of this continuum.

PIAGET AND WERNER AND KAPLAN RECONSIDERED

The model just presented is compatible in most respects with the traditional approaches to symbol structure presented by Piaget (1962) and by Werner and Kaplan (1963). There are, however, some clear differences in emphasis that should be made explicit before we apply this model to our own data.

Turning first to Piaget, there are three main differences between the approach used here and Piaget's position.

The first difference is merely terminological: In Peircian terms "signs" comprise the larger class, of which "symbols" are a subclass of signs involving arbitrary and conventional sign–referent relations. For Piaget, the words "symbol" and "symbolic function" refer to the larger class, while "signs" are defined as the subclass of symbol relations that are arbitrary and conventional. In other words, the use of the two terms "sign" and "symbol" is reversed between Piaget and Peirce. This difference is important only to the extent that it is misleading and confusing. We have chosen to use Peircian terminology here first of all because it is used by a wider range of investigators in the field of semiotics, and secondly because Peirce's terms lend themselves more readily to a comparison between subjective versus objective vehicle–referent relations.

The second difference is that, insofar as he discusses language at all, Piaget bows repeatedly to the classic philosophical distinction between the arbitrary and conventional nature of linguistic symbols, and the private and iconic nature of other symbols. Regarding the public–private distinction, I agree with Piaget that linguistic signs will have a particularly strong impact on subsequent cognitive development to the extent that they are used communicatively, and hence are a constant source of new information about the world. However, I do not agree (as should be clear by now) with the suggestion that linguistic signs are "more arbitrary" and "more abstract" than gestural symbols in any relevant way for early cognitive development. Indeed, I fail to see why Piaget believes that this traditional philosophic view is required by his own epistemology. He has clearly specified that all sensorimotor interactions with the world are essentially indexical in nature (the Ref_s–Ref_o relations discussed earlier). He has also pointed out that internal or mental signs are derived by the internalization of what were initially iconic, externally expressed imitations of things in the world (i.e., Veh_s–Veh_o relations). This is not restricted to social imitations of other human beings. Piaget also uses "imitation" in a looser sense, in discussing all forms of **static, content–dependent, highly accommodative "figurative" knowledge of objects** (see *Genetic Epistemology*, p. 14). We assimilate objects to the extent that we apply our previously acquired schemes to them, often deforming the object to make it fit that scheme (e.g., adjusting the nipple to fit the mouth). We accommodate to objects to the extent that we change our schemes to meet the feedback from the object (e.g., adjusting the mouth to fit the nipple). Much of our knowledge of physical objects, according to Piaget, comes from accommodations to their visual contours, kinaesthetic feedback, etc. As a result, our actions on the object take on an iconic, imitative relationship to that object (hence the mixed icon–index relations discussed earlier where participations with the object result in partial isomorphisms between object and action). What this means is that mental imagery consists of the internalized imitation of the visual, manual, and other action patterns carried out on the object in our first interactions with it. **It seems, then, that in his stress on iconicity and indexicality in sensorimotor knowing, there is nothing in Piaget's theory that requires a difference between the way we come to know words and how they are used, and the way we come to know anything else about the world.** The actual, objective nature of the Veh_o-Ref_o relationship does not participate in any crucial way in the initial stages of acquisition (i.e., Veh_s-Ref_s relations). I am left with an uncomfortable impasse regarding this issue. Either I have entirely failed to grasp why Piaget believes that linguistic signs are more arbitrary to the infant than other signs, or Piaget himself has made such a claim as a gratuitous bow to traditional European language philosophy. For the moment, I have the vanity to believe the latter.

The third difference between the analysis presented here and Piaget's position regards an emphasis on the difference between representation and symbolization. Throughout many of Piaget's works, these terms are used more or less interchangeably. I have come to believe, instead, that these are different albeit interacting aspects of symbolic activity. **"Re-presentation" is defined as the calling up of action patterns for interacting with an object in the absence of perceptual support from that object.** As such, the development of representation is related to memory for absent objects and their spatial locations, and to problems involved in the imitation of absent models. Representation is an important aspect of the development of the symbolic capacity, since the ability to call up action schemes in the absence of perceptual input is involved in the construction of "internalized" Veh_s-Ref_s relations. The ability to hold an internal scheme in consciousness is relevant to the ability to select one aspect of that internal array to serve as the "representative" or symbol of that array. However, the selection process itself is distinct from the ability to represent internal schemes at all. **Symbolization is defined here as the selection process, the choice of one aspect of a complex array to serve as the top of the iceberg, a light-weight mental token that can be substituted for the entire knowledge package for purposes of higher-order cognitive operations.** It is presumably easier to manipulate symbols mentally than to manipulate in one operation everything we know about the thing or event being symbolized, that is, the entire Ref_s, or mental file drawer full of possible object-defining interactions. Representation provides us with internal referents in the absence of "presentational" support from objective referents. Symbolization selects from those internal referents one portion for use in further processing. Representation creates mental wholes; symbolization selects parts to stand for the whole.

There are a couple of implications that follow from this distinction. First, insofar as symbolization is a selection process, early versions of symbolization can go on "presentationally" instead of "representationally." That is, the child can select a single action scheme to "name" an object or event in the full presence of that object–event. Very little representation may be required for such activity. The early stages of symbol development can be characterized by a gradual move from presentational to representational symbolization; this is the core of the process we have and will refer to as "decontextualization."

Second, representation is based on calling up a whole set of integrated action patterns—the whole mental file drawer of actions associated with a given external referent. As a result, representation itself is inherently "static," taking the whole set of patterns as a given, crucially tied to the imitative patterns involved in taking that knowledge in to begin with. Symbolization, on the other hand, is defined as selection from that action package for further use. As a result, symbolization is a more "flexible" or "dynamic" analytic tool, useful in breaking down wholes into parts that can enter into novel relationships. Hence symbolization bears a much less direct relationship to things as given in the external world; it is instead a transforming or operative aspect of mental processes. The respective roles of these two different aspects of symbol development should become clearer in later chapters (see in particular Chapters 4 and 7). While these distinctions are, in my view, implicit in Piaget (particularly with regard to the distinction between figurative and operative knowing), I do not believe that he has been sufficiently explicit about the role of this distinction in language development.

Turning now to Werner and Kaplan's (1963) theory of symbol formation, our model is really quite compatible with their approach in most respects. One important difference regards the issue of subjective iconicity in symbolic development. Werner and Kaplan apparently feel that **all** subjective or psychological vehicle–referent relations (regardless of the objective relation) are eventually translated into internal "icons." This is the essence of the rather mysterious process they refer to as "physiognomization of meaning." A word (or for that matter any other externally arbitrary symbol) is given meaning through setting up internal bodily postures and states of readiness that are in some indirect way isomorphic with the external referent. To illustrate this notion of internal states of readiness in knowing, consider the following exercise. Imagine to yourself a tree stump, in as much perceptual detail as you can manage. Now, without allowing the visual image to alter, think of that tree stump as something you are going to sit on at a picnic. Having established that particular "state of readiness," now switch your plans to a decision to use the tree stump as a table for your picnic. As rapidly as possible, switch back and forth between the two decisions (i.e., chair versus table). The internal sensation of change between states of readiness should illustrate what Werner and Kaplan mean by "physiognomization"—a reaction of the whole organism to the meaning of a given object. Werner and Kaplan also use the process of "word satiation" to illustrate this process. Say a word repeatedly, over and over (try "spoon"—since it is probably already close to satiation). After a while, even though we continue to "know" at some shallow level the relationship between sound and meaning, the word becomes naked sound. Some rich, global, internal merging of sound and meaning has been lost. For these authors, the internal iconicity set up between subjective vehicle and referent is the active, assimilative aspect of meaning, the process that distinguishes true symbolic behavior from simple associative knowing. They discuss at length, for example, the loss of meaning in schizophrenia as a loss not of sound–referent associations per se (i.e., subjectively arbitrary Veh_s–Ref_s relations), but of internal iconicity in the same relationship.

I am perfectly willing to accept the phenomena that Werner and Kaplan point out as support for such notions as "subjective iconicity." However, in the model presented here we do not require internal iconicity as part of the definition of symbolic activity. In our view, children can use action schemes as symbolizers for whole action-packages even though from their perspective the Veh_s–Ref_s relationship is entirely arbitrary. Just as Piaget places too much emphasis on the arbitrariness of language as opposed to other symbols, we believe that Werner and Kaplan place too much stress on the role of iconicity in linguistic and nonlinguistic symbols. From our perspective, much of symbol development involves a tension between arbitrariness and iconicity, as the two processes of perception of contiguity and perception of similarity interact in analyzing sign–referent relations.

The purpose of this section has been to locate some of the seams, joints, natural divisions in the internal structure of symbols—the various aspects of symbols where different cognitive capacities might have their effect. For example, imitation may be implicated in the formation of Veh_s–Veh_o relations without necessarily affecting understanding of the vehicle–referent relationship. By contrast, the kind of part–whole analysis involved in tool use might contribute to the process whereby arbitrary and contiguous vehicle–referent relations are broken down into underlying icons (i.e., similarities and complementarities at some level). In other words, imitation may involve analysis for reproduction; tool use involves analysis for understanding. A third area of sensorimotor development, object permanence, may bear an entirely different relationship to the emergence of symbols. Brown (1973) has suggested that object permanence should be implicated in the ability to "recognize" objects from partial cues (i.e., in partial hidings where a portion of the object is showing—a Stage 3 accomplishment in Piagetian terms). Certainly this basic level of object recognition will be required to use vocal or manual gestures to name objects. Second, Brown proposes that a later form of object permanence, "recall" in the absence of perceptual support, should be involved in the ability to talk about absent objects. In the Peircian framework presented here, these two aspects of object permanence may affect the process by which vehicles come to elicit referents, either presentationally or representationally.

The point of this exercise is that the symbolic capacity has an internal structure, with a set of components that can be related in different ways within and across developmental levels. Correlations between symbol development and other cognitive capacities may involve different aspects of this internal structure, i.e., specific rather than general homologies. This theme will be stressed throughout the book, in interpreting our correlational results. In Chapter 7, we will return once again to the Peircian framework and to the evolutionary concepts outlined in the last chapter, to see what we have learned about the "old parts" that make up the emerging capacity for symbol use.

Chapter 3

COGNITION AND COMMUNICATION FROM NINE TO THIRTEEN MONTHS: CORRELATIONAL FINDINGS

Elizabeth Bates
Laura Benigni
Inge Bretherton
Luigia Camaioni
Virginia Volterra

In Chapter 1, we discussed several models for the relationship between language and thought, relevant to the search for prerequisites to language. We proposed that, in the period that interests us here, the relationship between linguistic and nonlinguistic developments leading to the emergence of symbols is one of homology through shared structural bases. In other words, communicative and noncommunicative developments will be related to one another through shared "software" or underlying capacities that are required for both types of behaviors. Hence we would predict correlations among both developments. We would not expect to find particular sequences between communicative and noncommunicative behaviors at roughly equivalent levels of difficulty, since one is in no way the direct cause of the other.

In the same chapter, we also raised the issue of "deep" versus "local" homologies. Just how general are the software packages underlying related developments from 9 to 13 months? The orthodox Piagetian position can be characterized as a deep homology model. Piaget suggests that each substage of sensorimotor development is characterized by a common set of "operative structures." These are relatively content-free principles that govern behavior across a variety of domains, including object relations, knowledge of space and time, causal understanding, and imitation (Piaget, 1954). Indeed, the sensorimotor substages are each "defined" in terms of these general principles cutting across domains. A child may lag behind in one or more applications of these operative structures (i.e., "horizontal decalage"). Nevertheless, we would expect that a child who arrives at a structure early in one area will also be advanced in successive applications of that structure later on. In other words, within a large enough sample of children we would predict correlations across all domains of sensorimotor development.

A contrasting view is offered by several "neo-Piagetian" researchers, including Fischer (in press), Case (1978), Pascual-Leone (1972; see also Ammon, 1977, for a review), Klahr and Wallace (1976), and Moore and Meltzoff (1978). Though these researchers retain important aspects of Piaget's structural theory, they reject the notion of a single, unified stage cutting across domains. Instead, they have proposed that successive stages are reached **within** domains, each characterized by somewhat different structural principles reflecting the different characteristics of the tasks or problems that the child must solve in that content area. This is the approach that we have termed "local homology." According to this model, we would expect correlations only at points in development where different behaviors share "specific" structures. Hence language development might correlate with one or two areas at 11 months, with several very different kinds of activities at 13 months, and so forth. At each point, we should be able to specify the shared task constraints that result in this local "borrowing" of software.

In the longitudinal study presented in this chapter, we have administered a battery of communicative and cognitive measures to children between the ages of 9 and 13 months. In addition, we have a general measure of locomotor development that should permit us to determine whether our correlations reflect little more than some general factor of rate of maturation. If our communicative and cognitive measures are related across the board (assuming that we can rule out general maturation), there is some support for the orthodox "deep homology" approach to sensorimotor development. However, if we find consistent but specific patterns of correlation among particular cognitive and communicative measures, a local homology model would be preferable. The Piagetian measures that we are using here were developed and standardized by Uzgiris and Hunt (1975). It is probably worth noting at the outset that Uzgiris and Hunt report very low correlations among their various tests of sensorimotor development, suggesting something much more like a local homology model, with separate domains developing according to their own unique structural principles. If we replicate their findings, then we know precisely what to expect: a pattern of **specific** relationships between symbol development and various other aspects of cognition.

Given our earlier findings, we have some idea what specific relationships to expect, particularly with regard to causal developments at 9 months and the onset of communicative intentions. However, there are also a large number of hypotheses that have been put forth by other investigators regarding relationships between language and symbolic play, object permanence, imitation, and other aspects of sensorimotor development (e.g., Bloom, 1973; Edwards, 1973; MacNamara, 1972; Ryan, 1974). In addition, the progressions we have seen from preverbal to symbolic behavior suggest a causal relationship (at least of the formal causal sort outlined on page 16) that should result in cross-session correlations among early communicative developments and later aspects of symbolic activity.

Before proceeding with the methodology and results of our study, we should add a few caveats about correlational methods in general.

The first caveat regards the necessity of establishing a "pattern" of correlations in which some measures predict symbol development while others do not. If **all** of our measures were significantly related, we would know about as much as we would if **none** of our measures were correlated, since a wide variety of general factors like IQ, maturation, etc., could account for such nonspecific patterns.

Second, relationships between behaviors can emerge statistically only at points in which there is some variance among subjects concerning mastery of both structures. For example, it would be useless to examine the correlation between visual tracking and vocal communication in 9-month-olds, since all our subjects are already quite proficient at visual tracking at the beginning of the study. However, around 2–3 months of age, when visual tracking is something to be mastered, variance in that domain might be predictive of variance in some more sophisticated behavior months later. In this study, information on cognitive and communicative development is available only for the 9–13-month range. Hence, if we fail to find relationships between two variables in this period, we **cannot** conclude that these variables share no common structures or operations. Rather, we can only infer that shared structures between these domains do not contribute to individual differences in behavior between 9 and 13 months. There is an obvious sense in which a functioning heart and liver are also prerequisites to language. But since all our children will have those prerequisites by 9 months of age, this causal relationship will not show up in the correlational findings. Similarly, aspects of object permanence or manipulative play at 6 months of age may be important inputs to language development at 12 months. If we knew which children were the first to master those operations around 6 months, we might be able to predict who will be most precocious in language around 12 months. But we simply do not have that information. **We will find correlations only for behaviors that show significant variation among subjects in the 9–13-month range.** Hence whenever we report that Behavior X and Behavior Y are structurally unrelated, we mean that if there are structural relations between the two, these relations have no impact on behavior in this time period. This point may seem obvious, but we have found it necessary to make it many times to avoid misunderstanding of our findings.

A third point also concerns temporal patterns in correlation, in this case two models for the passage from primitive to more sophisticated forms of communication. Both models predict that the same children who begin using early forms of conventional signalling (e.g., requests with abbreviated reaching) will also be the first to use language. However, the first model predicts that when the more sophisticated forms come in, the primitive forms will drop out. In statistical terms, this would mean that the scores for certain request signals at 9 months will correlate with the scores for language at 13 months. However, **within** the 13-month session, the correlation between these more primitive requests and language should be either zero, or perhaps even negative (meaning that the less mature children use one form, while the more mature children use another). In other words, this model predicts that later behaviors will "supplant" earlier forms of communication. A second model would suggest instead that the children in this age range are simply expanding their repertoire. They may be led into more sophisticated signals by virtue of high frequency experience with earlier signals. But they continue to use signals at both levels, either alternating them within requests and declaratives, or using them all together to increase the likelihood of communicative success. In this model, we would expect positive correlations both across sessions and within sessions throughout the period being studied. In the discussion of results, we will refer to the first model as "Replacement," and to the second as "Expansion."

Finally, we are very aware of the difference between correlation and causation, and of the many factors that can be responsible even for a specific and consistent pattern of correlations. There are inherent weaknesses in the correlational method which will require that any strong conclusions drawn from our findings be validated with the use of alternative methods. At the end of this chapter, we will discuss supporting evidence in work comparing normal and abnormal language development, and in comparative research on sensorimotor development and symbolic activity in other primates.

Method

Subjects

The subjects were 25 infants, studied between the ages of $9\frac{1}{2}$ and $12\frac{1}{2}$ months. Twelve of the infants were Italians from the Rome area; 13 were Americans from Boulder, Colorado. Because of difficulties in locating subjects, we were unable to match the two samples for sex or birth order. Hence the American sample contains six males and seven females, with nine firstborns and four laterborns. The Italian sample contains five males and seven females, with six firstborns and six laterborns. All infants lived in middle-class families, in which one or both parents were educated beyond the high school level. Within both the Italian and the American samples, about a third of the mothers worked part-time outside the home. In these cases, children were cared for by a relative or regular babysitter. One potentially important difference between the two samples is that the Italian children were generally cared for by a relative. American children had less frequent contact with grandparents, aunts, etc., and were generally cared for by hired babysitters or neighbors in babysitting cooperatives.

Procedure

Each child was visited in the home four times, beginning at about $9\frac{1}{2}$ months. In addition, around the child's first birthday, he and his mother participated in a standardized observational session in our laboratories (in Rome and Boulder, respectively). The data for this laboratory session, a version of Ainsworth's Strange Situation for the assessment of the mother–child attachment relationship (Ainsworth and Wittig, 1969), will be described in Chapter 5.

The means and range of ages at each session were as follows:

$$
\begin{aligned}
&\text{Session A} \quad \overline{X} = 0;9(14) \quad \text{from} \quad 0;8(29) \text{ to } 0;9(28)\\
&\text{Session B} \quad \overline{X} = 0;10(16) \quad \text{from} \quad 0;10(3) \text{ to } 0;11(1)\\
&\text{Session C} \quad \overline{X} = 0;11(19) \quad \text{from} \quad 0;11(4) \text{ to } 1;0(2)\\
&\text{Session D} \quad \overline{X} = 1;0(21) \quad \text{from} \quad 1;0(3) \text{ to } 1;1(6)
\end{aligned}
$$

The home visits each lasted approximately 2 hours. Each session included cognitive testing, behavioral observation (with or without videotaping), and extensive interviews with the mother. Of the 13 experimenters involved in this project (the five authors and eight graduate assistants), there were two observers present at each session. One observer saw the same child regularly, while the other saw different infants from session to session. Testing, interviews, and observation were **not** counterbalanced in any formal sense. Rather, tasks were varied in order according to the child's level of interest. While this occasionally meant that items were skipped, we were also assured maximal motivation for the information that was obtained. In some cases, when a child was ill or in particularly poor humor, the session was interrupted and continued later in the same week.

Task Descriptions and Scoring

MATERNAL INTERVIEW

The standard interview with the mother was audiorecorded, and presented as informally as possible at convenient points throughout the visit. In the first session, questions included background information on the child's earlier social and sensorimotor developments. At later sessions, the interview concentrated more on communicative and symbolic behaviors since the last visit. Mothers were urged to provide anecdotal details, so that we might obtain as clear a record as possible for the contexts of early preverbal and verbal communication. The decision to classify a given anecdote as speech or prespeech, symbolic or nonsymbolic activity, etc., was made later by the experimenters. The mothers simply provided as much descriptive detail as possible. A checklist of interview items, with space for notes, was left with the mothers between sessions, to record their observations for the next interview.

The interview is summarized in Appendix 3.1. The questions were quite detailed, so that various levels of sophistication for any given behavior could be discerned. For example, the item for showing objects involved probes for whether the child merely extends forward something he already has in hand, or whether he characteristically looks for things in order to pick them up or show them. Similar breakdowns are available for giving, various forms of pointing and requests, the various contexts for language comprehension and production, and so forth. This level of detail was too fine grained for the correlational analysis, for two reasons. First, in many of the smaller categories entries were too few for use in a correlation matrix across all 25 children. Second, there are serious problems in the use of many dichotomous items (i.e., presence versus absence of behavior) in correlational research. Without extensive preselection of items, dichotomous data tend to produce a large number of spurious high or low correlations, based on the small amount of variance in the distribution of scores. For the correlational analysis, then, we combined the dichotomous entries into ordinal subscales within given classes of behaviors. For example, a child who reportedly only extended objects in hand but never looked around for objects in order to use them in showing, received a score for Showing of one point. If the same child also engaged in the more stable, planned forms of showing, he received a score of two points. This analysis was justified by the fact that, in the vast majority of cases, if the more sophisticated level of a given behavior was reported to be present, the earlier form was also present—a finding that confirmed the earlier research from which the various behaviors that make up the interview subscales were derived. Appendix 3.1 shows the various behaviors that make up the interview subscales, as well as items not included in the correlation matrix. After grouping into ordinal subscales, 10 interview scores were available for each child, for each session: Giving, Showing, Communicative Pointing, Ritual Requests, Number of Words Comprehended, Number of Non-referential Words Produced, Number of Referential Words Produced, Number of Combinatorial Play Schemes (e.g., stacking rings, building towers), Number of Symbolic Play Schemes (e.g., pretending to talk on the telephone, pretending to eat with empty utensils), and finally a measure of Level of Word Comprehension that distinguishes between comprehension only in routine places and games versus comprehension involving goal-directed search for objects and persons in new contexts.

The maternal interviews were coded twice, once by the experimenters responsible for the data collection (e.g., the American authors coded the American data) and once by the experimenters from the other sample (e.g., the Italian authors coded the American data). Differences between the two codings were resolved in joint meetings. During these meetings specific coding criteria were developed for each category of behavior to deal with questionable cases (these detailed criteria are summarized in Appendix 3.3). For a few remaining ambiguous cases a conservative standard was used. For example, a particular vocalization used regularly by a child, but in unclear contexts, was **not** classified as a word until its usage became clearer in later sessions.

OBSERVATIONAL MEASURES

At Sessions A and C ($9\frac{1}{2}$ and $11\frac{1}{2}$ months, respectively), records of the child's social and play behaviors were made on a home observation checklist, supplemented by narrative notes (see Appendix 3.2 for the checklist items). One of the rotating experimenters recorded, while the observer who regularly saw the child interviewed the mother or interacted with the infant. At sessions B and D ($10\frac{1}{2}$ and $12\frac{1}{2}$ months, respectively), a more structured videorecording supplemented these checklisted observations. Each videorecording, lasting about 15 minutes, included standard segments in which toys were given back and forth, or held out of the child's reach to elicit requests. Also included were play between mother and child in building towers, reading a book together, and playing with any of the toys from our battery. In addition, videorecords contain several minutes of each child playing alone with the test toys.

In both the Italian and the American samples, toys used included play telephones, a large rubber ball, dolls and stuffed animals, two or more small vehicles, toy eating utensils and a baby bottle, a long necklace, blocks and nesting cups, stacking rings, a slinky, a jumping jack, a jack-in-the-box, two mechanical wind-up toys, and the various items from the Uzgiris–Hunt Schemes Scale (e.g., tinfoil, cotton, a plastic flower, a doll's shoe).

The videorecords were transcribed as simple narrative descriptions, by five of the eight graduate assistants. The transcribers practiced separately on the same subset of tapes until they had achieved a similar level of descriptive detail. Where they occurred, disagreements consisted almost entirely of omissions rather than differential interpretations of the same behavior. After this practice phase, the assistants each took several of the tapes and transcribed them separately. (For a discussion of the level of detail in transcription used here, with examples, see Bates, Camaioni, and Volterra, 1975.)

The same checklist used by the assistants in the paper–pencil observations was also used for coding from the videotranscripts (see Appendix 3.2). These videotranscripts, observation records and narrative notes, were coded by the five authors at the same time that the interviews were coded. The same procedure described for the interview was followed, in that all the data were coded first by the authors responsible for data collection, then separately by the authors from the opposite sample. Differences were resolved in joint meetings, with specific criteria designed to cover questionable causes (these criteria are also summarized in Appendix 3.2).

As was the case for the interviews, the first round of coding yielded very fine-grained categorizations. In contrast with the interviews, the observations were in the form of frequency data rather than dichotomous "presence–absence" for a given behavior. However, in the short time span covered in each visit, behaviors tended to be very low frequency in many of the finer grained categories, too low to be of interest in a correlational analysis, and too infrequent to justify ordinal scaling. Hence we decided to collapse many of the smaller categories into single scores for frequency of giving, showing, communicative pointing, and so on. Second, we decided to use a relative frequency scale rather than absolute frequencies. In this scale, 0 = no manifestation of the behavior,

1 = one instance, 2 = more than one and less then five instances, 3 = more than five and less than ten, and so forth, in increasing increments of five. For the collapsed variables (e.g., all types of giving), this yielded a range of 0–5 within categories. There were two reasons for using relative frequencies. First, this decision normalized the data somewhat, reducing the impact of occasional cases in which, for example, mother and child became involved in a large number of repetitions of turn-taking in giving, showing off, etc., within a single game. Though these instances were interesting and amusing, they would have skewed the data enormously. Second, the videorecords permitted much more precise absolute frequency data than the observations by a single observer with a pencil. In the case of certain high frequency behaviors, the home observer often had to estimate. We felt that the use of a relative frequency scale would permit us to combine the film data with the observations in a more meaningful fashion.

The final combining of variables yielded 17 observation scores, for each child at each session. These were Showing Off (repeating a behavior that elicited adult laughter or comment), Ritualized Showing Off (e.g., initiating pattycake, peekaboo, waving byebye, etc.), Showing, Giving, Noncommunicative Pointing (examining objects with the index finger), Communicative Pointing (usually with arm outstretched and some effort to check for adult confirmation), Unritualized Requests (with whining or fussing only), Ritualized Requests (involving some sort of "conventionalized" sound or gesture), Unritualized Refusals, Ritualized Refusals (e.g., shaking the head "no," or use of a characteristic, conventional sound), Frequency of Word Comprehension, Frequency of Nonreferential Speech, Frequency of Referential Speech, Number of Referential Words, Frequency of Combinatorial Play, Frequency of Symbolic Play, and Number of Different Symbolic Play Schemes.

We should stress at this point that the interview scores and observation scores for the same behaviors reflect very different types of measurement, that is, level of sophistication versus frequency. This is actually a more conservative approach, in that if the two types of measures correlate with each other and show similar relationships to other variables, there is stronger converging evidence that the relationships are in some sense real rather than artifacts of particular measurement techniques.

COGNITIVE MEASURES

For the cognitive portion of the study, we administered items from the six Uzgiris and Hunt Ordinal Scales of Infant Development (Uzgiris and Hunt, 1975), including Object Permanence, Spatial Relations, Means–End Relations, Imitation, Schemes, and Operational Causality. In Session A we began each scale with the last item likely to be passed successfully by a 9-month-old child, dropping back to earlier items when a task proved too difficult. In subsequent sessions testing began with the last item that each child passed successfully at the previous session, and continued until the infant failed twice on an item, or refused to continue.

Of course, only a subset of the items within the various scales were relevant in the 9–13-month range. For example, the Object Permanence items of relevance all involved various types of object disappearance and reappearance, from covering the object partially with a single screen (an item passed correctly by all our children at Session A), to deducing the results of a single invisible displacement (the first of the Stage 6 representational items, passed successfully by most of the children in our study by the last session). In the Means–End scale, the relevant items began with pulling a cloth support to obtain an object—a task passed successfully by 60% of the children at our first session, and by all of them in subsequent sessions. The remaining Means–End items in this time period were elaborations of the support task (i.e., using more tenuous supports, like strings, or inventing the use of a stick as a tool in obtaining objects), with a final pair of additional items involving a small amount of foresight or representation in problem solving. The Spatial Relations Scale in the 9–13-month range is somewhat heterogeneous, involving use of detours in chasing a ball, and using gravity in several games including building towers. All the Operational Causality items of relevance here involved schemes that the child uses to set a moving display back into motion. The Imitation Scale in the 9–13-month range assigns scores for level of sophistication of imitation, from imitating an adult gesture or sound that is already in the child's repertoire, through imitations of increasingly novel and difficult visible models, to deferred imitations that take place at least 15 minutes after the model was presented. Finally, the Uzgiris-Hunt Schemes Scale in this age range begins with simple repetitive schemes with objects (e.g., banging, shaking, dropping), through exploratory manipulations of one object and combinations of two or more objects, to symbolic and/or socially appropriate schemes such as "pretend" eating with empty utensils, and finally to object naming as the top item in the scale.

In our study the Uzgiris–Hunt Method was modified in several ways. First, their scoring system requires two clear successes out of three trials on each item. Given the large set of measures used in this study, we found that children tired too rapidly when we insisted on this more conservative scoring system. Hence we decided to accept one clear dem-

onstration out of one to three trials as a successful pass. Two adminis-
trations of an item passed on the first trial were given only if the child
showed considerable interest, or if he failed on the subsequent item.

A second modification concerned the vocal and gestural imitation
tasks. Uzgiris and Hunt note that this scale is the most difficult to
administer, depending more than any other on fluctuating mood factors. This was markedly the case in our study. Hence we decided to train
mothers to administer the specific imitation items from the scale. They
tried these items in the week following each visit, and recorded their
results on a checklist that we left with them each month. The imitation
scores reported here are a composite derived according to the Uzgiris–
Hunt criteria from three data sources: the mother's report, our own
efforts to elicit imitation at each session, and spontaneous imitations by
the child at each session. The child was given a score for the highest level
of imitation demonstrated across these three measures, with the total
scale combining both vocal and gestural scores.

Third, although we administered the standard items from the Operational Causality scale, this task was not analyzed as a separate cognitive
measure. Within the age range considered here, the operational causality items all include scores for behaviors that overlap with other communicative measures in this study. For example, a child receives points
for giving a mechanical toy to the adult as a request to set that toy in
motion. Since this same behavior would also be recorded in our observational checklist for gestural communication, correlations between the
two measures would mean very little.

Finally, Uzgiris and Hunt use a single Schemes scale for modes of
playing and interacting with objects. This scale treats manipulative,
exploratory play as an ordinal step below primitive forms of symbolic or
"pretend" play, and also gives scores for naming objects. Since we were
interested in more detailed information about the development of the
symbolic function, manipulative or combinatorial play was analyzed
separately from symbolic play, and included **both** the maternal interview
and the observational play measures described above. We did, however,
use the same objects recommended by Uzgiris and Hunt for the Schemes
Scale.

To summarize, the scoring method used for Object Permanence,
Means–End Relations, and Spatial Relations was the one recommended
by Uzgiris and Hunt, modified so that children received the same score
for one clear success per item that Uzgiris and Hunt give for two
successes. The Imitation score used in our analyses was the composite
observation–interview score described above. Performance on Operational Causality items (e.g., giving the mechanical doll to the experi-

menter as a request to make it move again) was simply entered into the appropriate observational categories for communicative behaviors. The Schemes Scale was broken down into separate scores for the frequency and differentiation of symbolic and combinatorial play schemes, in both interviews and observations.

LOCOMOTION

A single score for locomotion was derived from both the maternal report and the observations. The ordinal scale for locomotion (described in Appendix 3.4) included items like pulling to a standing position with support, crawling, walking with and without support, and so on. Where there were differences between the interview and the observations (a very rare occurrence), the highest behavior reported or observed was the final score given.

Data Analysis

For both interview and observational variables, if over 60% of the subjects failed to demonstrate a given behavior at a given session, that category was excluded from the correlational analysis, to reduce the number of spuriously high or low correlations with large sets of zero entries. (Table 3.1, presenting the means and intersession correlations for the variables used, indicates which sessions for a given variable were excluded from the analysis because of over 60% zero entries.)

All correlations are Pearson Product–Moment correlations, with the variance due to Nationality (i.e., Italy versus U.S.) statistically removed. A preliminary correlational analysis indicated a large number of significant relationships between Nationality and many of the communicative and cognitive scores. Some of these effects may have been due to small differences in method, some to differences in birth order and sex in the two samples, and others are undoubtedly due to true cultural differences. If the focus of the study were cultural differences, we would have some difficulty in interpreting the data, given these confounds. However, since we were primarily interested in relationships between cognitive and communicative variables that are independent of culture, all subsequent analyses removed the effect of Nationality through partial correlation. When this was done, the number of significant correlations with birth order and sex was also reduced to chance levels. Hence we will report only the correlations among locomotor, communicative, and cognitive measures.

All correlations reported here are significant beyond the $p < 0.05$

level, $df = 22$ (i.e., beyond $+ 0.344$ for a one-tailed prediction in the positive direction). When the variables with too few entries (i.e., more than 60% zero scores) were removed, the total matrix included 36 interview scores, 60 observation scores, 16 cognitive scale scores, and 4 locomotor scores for each child. Both within and across sessions, this yields a total of 6903 possible relationships (removing duplications and correlations of each variable with itself in the same session). Obviously we cannot present each of these correlations in this report. The data must be described in terms of overall patterns. For example, we will discuss the relationship between Object Permanence at four sessions, and the various language measures at four sessions, in terms of the percentage of significant correlations obtained, out of the total number of correlations possible for this particular set of measures.

To reduce such a large number of correlations into more manageable units, the method of choice would be factor analysis. However, factor analysis can only be used when there are enough subjects to counterbalance the number of variables to be entered into the analysis. With only 25 subjects and 116 variables, this was clearly not the case in our study. Nevertheless, within both gesture and language it is possible to discern a network of variables that relate particularly strongly to one another. This fact in turn permits us to discuss the relationships of cognitive variables to these two respective networks, in a conceptual approximation to factor analysis. We will use the terms Gestural Complex and Language Complex to refer to such conceptual groupings of individual correlations.

Results and Discussion

We will begin with a brief look at developmental trends and intersession correlations **within** the various communicative and cognitive behaviors. After that, the results are divided into four sections: gestural development, language development, relationships between nonverbal and verbal communication, and cognitive measures in relation to both gesture and language.

Table 3.1 presents the mean scores at each session for the interview, observation, and cognitive variables. Not surprisingly, scores are increasing from session to session in virtually all categories. However, for many of the observational variables scores tend to be higher at Sessions B and D ($10\frac{1}{2}$ and $12\frac{1}{2}$ months, respectively) than at A and C ($9\frac{1}{2}$ and $11\frac{1}{2}$ months, respectively). This tendency is probably due to the fact that

TABLE 3.1

Mean Scores per Session and Session to Session Correlations (Pearson r's with Nationality Partialed Out)

Measures	Abbre-viations[a]	Session				Correlations[b]		
		A	B	C	D	A/B	B/C	C/D
Interview								
1. Gestural Communication								
Communicative Point	CPoint	–	0.9	1.2	1.7	–	0.66	0.69
Show	Show	–	0.7	1.4	1.5	–	0.39	0.84
Give	Give	–	1.0	1.9	2.2	–	0.53	0.74
Ritualized Request	RitReq	0.9	1.5	2.0	2.4	0.79	0.68	0.75
2. Language								
Comprehension Level	LComp	0.9	1.3	1.6	1.7	0.55	0.44	0.65
Number of Words Comprehended	#Comp	2.4	4.8	7.4	10.4	0.76	0.92	0.90
Nonreferential Words	NRefWd	0.9	2.4	3.5	4.8	0.65	0.83	0.90
Referential Words	RefWd	–	–	2.1	3.4	–	–	0.89
3. Play								
Symbolic Play Schemes	SymbPl	–	0.9	2.3	4.3	–	0.74	0.92
Combinatorial Play	CombPl	0.9	2.0	3.1	3.8	0.40	0.72	0.86
Observations								
1. Gestural Communication								
Noncommunicative Point	NCPoint	0.6	1.8	1.3	2.2	0.58	0.58	0.36
Communicative Point	CPoint	–	1.0	0.8	1.8	–	0.28	0.55
Show	Show	1.0	2.1	2.2	2.6	0.42	0.33	0.34
Give	Give	0.9	2.2	2.2	3.5	0.30	0.61	0.60
Nonritualized Request	NRitReq	0.7	3.4	0.9	2.6	0.03	-0.09	0.08
Ritualized Request	RitReq	1.0	2.1	2.0	3.3	-0.41	0.34	0.24
Nonritualized Refusal	NRitRef	0.8	2.2	0.8	2.0	0.01	-0.33	0.04
Ritualized Refusal	RitRef	–	0.9	–	0.7	–	–	–
Nonritualized Show-off	NRitShff	0.6	1.2	1.4	1.2	0.47	0.37	0.01
Ritualized Show-off	RitShff	0.4	1.1	0.6	1.0	-0.39	-0.07	-0.04
2. Language								
Comprehension	Comp	0.9	1.5	1.2	2.3	0.43	0.53	0.41
Babbling	Bab	1.2	3.0	1.0	3.4	-0.13	0.18	0.15
Nonreferential Words	NRefWd	–	0.9	0.8	1.6	–	0.42	0.23

(continued)

TABLE 3.1 (continued)

Measures	Abbre-viations[a]	Session A	B	C	D	Correlations[b] A/B	B/C	C/D
Number of Referential Words	#RefWd	-	1.2	1.0	2.5	-	0.92	0.81
Referential Words (Frequency)	FRefWd	-	0.5	-	1.5	-	-	-
3. Play								
Number of Symbolic Play Schemes	#SymbPl	-	1.4	2.3	3.2	-	0.21	0.13
Frequency of Symbolic Play Schemes	FSymbPl	-	1.1	1.4	2.7	-	0.23	0.15
Combinatorial Play	CombPl	1.4	2.5	2.5	3.0	0.24	0.37	0.23
4. Uzgiris-Hunt Scales								
Object Permanence	ObjP	6.0	7.6	8.2	10.0	0.55	0.52	0.49
Spatial Relations	Space	8.4	9.2	9.9	10.8	0.29	0.42	0.36
Means-End	Means	7.8	9.4	11.0	12.3	0.43	0.48	0.63
Imitation	Imit	1.0	1.9	2.6	2.8	0.47	0.25	0.19
5. Locomotion	Loco	5.1	5.8	6.7	7.8	0.70	0.63	0.58

[a]The abbreviations used in this table will be used in all subsequent tables. The reader should bear in mind that, except where indicated, the observational measures are frequency measures. The prefixes F and # were used for those few observation measures where both a frequency score and a qualitative score (number of different instances of the behavior) were obtained.

[b]for r = or > 0.344, df 22, $p < 0.05$ (one tailed)
for r = or > 0.472, df 22, $p < 0.01$ (one tailed)

videorecords were available for the B and D visits only. Apparently even a 15-minute structured videorecord, transcribed and analyzed carefully by several raters, provides more data than paper–pencil observations over a longer time span. This is particularly true for some of the more subtle behaviors. For example, in paper–pencil observations we noticed very few instances of symbolic play. In the videorecordings, it was easier to discern brief moments such as the child placing the toy telephone receiver against his ear. Furthermore, the same instance can be replayed several times and viewed by more than one observer when questionable instances arise.

Table 3.1 also reports the diagonal intersession correlations for each variable with itself (i.e., A–B, B–C, C–D). In general, the interview measures and the cognitive scales are more internally consistent from session to session than the observational measures. Indeed, for the interview variables 92% of the intersession correlations for each measure were significant and positive. Compare this with 54% significant stability for the cognitive scales, and 38% positive intersession correlations for the various observation measures with themselves. Recall that the observation scores are based on relative frequency data; both the Piagetian scales and the interview measures reflect progress from more primitive to more sophisticated levels of the same behavior. Ordinal measures clearly have a certain amount of stability built into them, since a child who receives a high score at one session almost invariably either stays at the same level or progresses at the next session. Maternal reports of regression within categories were very rare; observed regressions within the cognitive scales were also very infrequent. By contrast, the observation measures are particularly sensitive to fluctuating motivation levels from one session to another. For example, a child who does a great deal of giving or showing at one home visit may engage in far less of the same behavior at the next visit—even though his level of competence has not changed. Motivational factors obviously influence the cognitive scales as well. However, a child can be enticed to perform on an object permanence item once, whereas the decision to give his mother a toy once or ten times is largely up to him.

In general, however, interview and observational measures of the same behavior tend to support one another. Table 3.2 presents the percentage of agreement for reported versus observed presence of several types of play and communication; Table 3.3 presents correlations among some of the same variables, where there were a sufficient number of entries in both observations and interviews to permit correlational analysis. Although the correlations are low (averaging + 0.43), they do tend to be significant and in the predicted direction (i.e., 76% of the possible relationships are significant beyond + 0.344). Since these are very different types of measures, this convergence is encouraging. Discrepancies between the maternal reports and observations in Table 3.2 usually reflect situations in which the child fails to demonstrate a behavior reported by the mother. This does not necessarily mean, as Ingram (1975) has suggested, that mothers are poor observers. Rather, it seems likely that mothers have observed the child in consistent and natural contexts, and are more likely to have witnessed a given behavior than we are in our short visits. There were some instances, however, in which we observed behaviors that the mother claimed not to have seen before. This was often the case when a behavior such as pointing or symbolic play was just beginning to emerge.

TABLE 3.2
Percent Agreement on Presence-Absence of Behaviors in Interview versus Observation

		Session			
	Measure	A	B	C	D
1.	Gestural Communication				
	NCPoint	80%	76%	56%	72%
	CPoint	100%	88%	68%	72%
	Show	68%	68%	80%	88%
	Give	56%	80%	96%	88%
	RitReq	36%	80%	88%	100%
	RitRef	64%	48%	46%	44%
2.	Language				
	Comp	68%	72%	68%	88%
	RefWd	84%	76%	62%	72%
	NRefWd	80%	52%	68%	76%
3.	Play				
	CombPl	68%	88%	96%	96%
	SymbPl	72%	60%	76%	96%

A final point regards the differences among the four sessions. Out of the 6903 possible intersession and within-session correlations in this matrix, we would expect 345 or 5% positive nonredundant relationships simply by chance. In fact, the number of significant relationships obtained was well beyond this chance level. Both within and across sessions, 1312 correlations, or 19% of the matrix, were significant beyond $p < 0.05$. There was a tendency, however, for the relationships among variables to become stronger from the first through the fourth sessions. Within Session A, only about 7% of the within-session correlations were significant beyond $p < 0.05$. At B, 14% of the within-session matrix was significant, compared with 22% at C and 38% at D. The tendency for significant relationships to increase across time has been noted in many longitudinal studies. In this study, the trend is probably related to the fact that most of the relevant behaviors had just begun to appear at 9 months, and became both more frequent and more perceptible in the intervening months. Since the same increase in strength from A to D did **not** occur for the cognitive scales, the pattern is probably not due simply to practice effects or an increase in experimenter bias across time.

TABLE 3.3
Intercorrelations between Interview and Observation Measure

Measures		Session			
Interview	Observation	A	B	C	D
1. Gestural Communication					
CPoint χ	CPoint	--	0.60**	0.45*	0.47**
Show χ	Show	--	0.63**	0.41*	0.49*
Give χ	Give	--	0.62**	0.59**	0.63**
RitReq χ	RitReq	-0.19	0.42*	0.70**	0.11
2. Language					
LComp χ	Comp	0.15	0.45*	0.18	0.46*
#Comp χ	Comp	0.29	0.65**	0.47**	0.75**
NRefWd χ	NRefWd	--	0.38*	0.43*	0.24
RefWd χ	#RefWd	--	--	0.54**	0.71**
RefWd χ	FRefWd	--	--	--	0.56**
3. Play					
CombPl χ	CombPl	0.31	0.25	0.51**	0.43*
SymbPl χ	#SymbPl	--	0.35*	0.37*	0.62**
SymbPl χ	FSymbPl	--	0.39*	0.29	0.43*

$*p < 0.05$ (one tailed)
$**p < 0.01$ (one tailed)

Gestural Development

For the various categories of nonverbal communication, the same sequences noted in earlier research (Bates, Camaioni, and Volterra, 1975) were replicated with this larger sample. By the first session, most of the children were reported to "show off" (i.e., repeat or initiate schemes that have been successful in provoking adult laughter or comment). Giving and showing objects tended to emerge between the first and second sessions. Noncommunicative pointing (used in exploring objects up close) was present in some children from the first session, while communicative pointing did not appear until much later. Requests and refusals tended to become increasingly ritualized across the 9–13-month period. However, these temporal coincidences across children are not alone sufficient to establish a hypothesis of inter-dependence among nonverbal communicative behaviors. **In fact, the correlational**

results suggest that some of these behaviors are good predictors of one another, and that others are not.

The categories that are strongly related to one another, in both interviews and observations, are Showing, Giving, Communicative Pointing, and Ritual Requests. These eight measures are significantly correlated with one another in 165 out of 378 possible combinations across and within sessions, or 44% of the relevant matrix. We suggest, then, that these communicative behaviors form a sort of Gestural Complex, a network of relationships that are presumably based on some shared structure. The categories which do **not** relate to this Gestural Complex are Noncommunicative Pointing, both Ritualized and Unritualized Showing Off, Unritualized Requests, and both Ritualized and Unritualized Refusals. These measures correlate with one another in only 9 out of 231 possible nonredundant combinations, or 4%. Furthermore, the same measures correlate with Giving, Showing, Communicative Pointing, and Ritual Requests in 34 out of 616 possible relationships, or 6%. Table 3.4 lists the positive, significant correlations of the measures in the Gestural Complex, both to each other and to the weaker gestural variables.

By comparing the behaviors which do and do not relate to the Gestural Complex, we can achieve some insights into the nature of this particular communicative network. For example, the Unritualized Request category at Session B tends to correlate positively with other gestures; the same category actually correlates negatively in later sessions. This pattern suggests a Replacement model for the development of requests. In early sessions, even the more mature children carry out most of their requests with simple whining and fussing. By later sessions, the more sophisticated children tend to use conventionalized signals in requests; whining and fussing, by contrast, characterize communications by the less mature children. This suggests that Giving, Showing, Communicative Pointing, and Ritual Requests are probably related to one another through a factor that has something to do with the use of conventional signals, rather than a general tendency to communicate at all.

Another interesting comparison can be made between Communicative and Noncommunicative Pointing. These two variables are correlated significantly with one another in many cases, perhaps due to the fact that they share the same gestural form (i.e., use of the extended index finger). However, whereas Communicative Pointing does relate to Giving, Showing, and Ritual Requests, Noncommunicative Pointing clearly does not relate to the same behavioral network. By definition, this gesture shares the "form" of communicative pointing, but not the "func-

TABLE 3.4
Significant[a] Positive Correlations between Gestural Communication Measures

Session	Session A Int.	Session A Obs.	Session B Int.	Session B Obs.	Session C Int.	Session C Obs.	Session D Int.	Session D Obs.
Interview Communicative Point								
Session B	LComp 0.47		RitReq 0.53	NCPoint 0.43 CPoint 0.60 RitReq 0.40	CPoint 0.66	NCPoint 0.48 CPoint 0.36	CPoint 0.55	NCPoint 0.40
Session C	RitReq 0.39		CPoint 0.66 Show 0.46 Give 0.40 RitReq 0.45	CPoint 0.46 RitReq 0.41 NRitReq 0.46	RitReq 0.45	CPoint 0.46 RitReq 0.41	CPoint 0.69	RitRef 0.45
Session D	RitReq 0.43		CPoint 0.55 Give 0.53 RitReq 0.43	NCPoint 0.44 CPoint 0.57 NRitReq 0.34	CPoint 0.69	CPoint 0.50	RitReq 0.52	NCPoint 0.37 CPoint 0.47 Show 0.37 Give 0.42
Interview Show								
Session B			Give 0.56	Show 0.63 RitReq 0.38	CPoint 0.46 Show 0.39 Give 0.41 RitReq 0.37		Show 0.47 Give 0.49	Give 0.39 RitRef 0.40
Session C		Give 0.41	Show 0.39 Give 0.37	Show 0.37	Give 0.77	Show 0.41 Give 0.53 RitReq 0.39	Show 0.84 Give 0.75	CPoint 0.46 Show 0.60 Give 0.58 RitReq 0.41
Session D		Give 0.45	Show 0.47	Show 0.46 NRitReq 0.49	Show 0.84 Give 0.61 RitReq 0.37	Show 0.34 Give 0.50	Give 0.87	CPoint 0.41 Show 0.49 Give 0.47 NRitShff 0.39

Interview / Session							
Interview Give							
Session B	RitReq 0.41	Show 0.56 RitReq 0.49	CPoint Give 0.38 Give 0.62	CPoint Show 0.40 Show 0.37 Give 0.53 RitReq 0.40	CPoint Show 0.67 Show 0.54 Give 0.49 RitReq 0.45	CPoint Give 0.53 Give 0.37	CPoint 0.51 CPoint 0.38 Give 0.60 RitReq 0.55
Session C	Give 0.47	Show 0.41 Give 0.53	Give 0.49	CPoint Show 0.77 Give 0.44	Show 0.59	CPoint Show 0.61 Give 0.74	CPoint 0.50 CPoint Show 0.49
Session D	Give 0.49 NRitShff 0.37	Show 0.49 Give 0.37 NRitReq 0.45	Show 0.34 Give 0.38 NRitReq 0.45	CPoint Show 0.75 Give 0.74	Show 0.55	CPoint Show 0.87	CPoint 0.44 Show 0.50 Give 0.63 RitReq 0.43
Interview RitReq							
Session A		Give 0.41 RitReq 0.79	CPoint 0.39 RitReq 0.73	CPoint RitReq 0.43 RitReq 0.74	CPoint 0.43 RitReq 0.69		
Session B	RitReq 0.79	CPoint 0.53 Give 0.49	CPoint RitReq 0.42	CPoint 0.45 Give 0.68 RitReq 0.37	CPoint 0.44 Give 0.37 RitReq 0.60	CPoint 0.43 RitReq 0.56	
Session C	RitReq 0.73	Show 0.37 Give 0.40 RitReq 0.68	Show 0.37 NRitReq 0.44 RitReq 0.39	CPoint 0.45 Give 0.44 RitReq 0.70	CPoint 0.42 Give 0.44 RitReq 0.54	Show 0.37 RitReq 0.75	
Session D	RitReq 0.69 Show 0.45	RitReq 0.56	NRitReq 0.41	RitReq 0.75	CPoint 0.47 RitReq 0.53	CPoint 0.52 RitReq 0.53	CPoint 0.46 Show 0.39

(continued)

89

TABLE 3.4 (continued)

Session	Session A Int.	Session A Obs.	Session B Int.	Session B Obs.	Session C Int.	Session C Obs.	Session D Int.	Session D Obs.
Observation Communicative Point Session B		NCPoint 0.45	CPoint 0.60 Give 0.38	NCPoint 0.38	CPoint 0.46		CPoint 0.57	NCPoint 0.51 CPoint 0.35
Session C	RitReq 0.43		CPoint 0.36 Give 0.67 RitReq 0.44	NRitReq 0.35	CPoint 0.46 RitReq 0.42	Show 0.45 RitReq 0.51	CPoint 0.50 RitReq 0.47	CPoint 0.55 Show 0.41 Give 0.45 RitReq 0.49 RitRef 0.36
Session D			Give 0.51	CPoint 0.35	Show 0.46 Give 0.50	CPoint 0.55 Show 0.36	CPoint 0.47 Show 0.41 Give 0.44 RitReq 0.46	Show 0.60 Give 0.55 RitReq 0.48 NRitShff 0.54
Observation Show Session A				Show 0.42 RitReq 0.38			RitReq 0.45	
Session B		Show 0.42	Show 0.63		Show 0.37 RitReq 0.37		Show 0.46 Give 0.34	

Session							
Session C		Give 0.54	Give 0.39	Show 0.41	CPoint 0.45 Give 0.46 RitReq 0.40	Show 0.34	CPoint 0.36 RitReq 0.42 NRitShff 0.49
Session D	NRitShff 0.44 RitShff 0.57	Give 0.38	NRitReq 0.38	Show 0.60 Give 0.49	CPoint 0.41 Give 0.36 RitShff 0.39	CPoint 0.37 Show 0.49 Give 0.50 RitReq 0.39	CPoint 0.60 Give 0.60 RitReq 0.44 NRitShff 0.41
Observation Give							
Session A				Show 0.41 Give 0.47	NCPoint 0.45 Give 0.50	Show 0.45 Give 0.49	Give 0.51
Session B		Give 0.62	Give 0.49	Show 0.49 Give 0.61 RitReq 0.39	Give 0.38		Show 0.58 RitReq 0.49
Session C		Give 0.49 RitReq 0.37	Give 0.50	Show 0.53 Give 0.59 RitReq 0.54	Show 0.46 RitReq 0.50	Show 0.50 Give 0.55	Show 0.36 Give 0.60 RitReq 0.54
Session D		Show 0.39 Give 0.60	Give 0.51	Show 0.58 Give 0.76	CPoint 0.45 Give 0.60 RitReq 0.38	CPoint 0.42 Show 0.47 Give 0.63	CPoint 0.55 Show 0.60 NRitReq 0.37 RitReq 0.63

(continued)

TABLE 3.4 (continued)

Session	Session A Int.	Session A Obs.	Session B Int.	Session B Obs.	Session C Int.	Session C Obs.	Session D Int.	Session D Obs.
Observation Ritualized Request Session A		NRitReq 0.46						
Session B			CPoint 0.40 Show 0.38 RitReq 0.42	RitShff 0.39	CPoint 0.41 RitReq 0.39			
Session C	RitReq 0.47	NRitShff 0.35	Give 0.45 RitReq 0.60	Give 0.39 NRitReq 0.48	CPoint 0.41 Show 0.39 RitReq 0.70	CPoint 0.51 Show 0.40 Give 0.50	RitReq 0.53	Give 0.38
Session D			Give 0.55	Give 0.49	Show 0.41 Give 0.49	CPoint 0.49 Show 0.42 Give 0.54	Give 0.43	CPoint 0.48 Show 0.44 Give 0.63 NRitReq 0.49

[a] Pearson r correlations with Nationality partialed out (df 22) = or > 0.344, $p < 0.05$ (one tailed).

tion." This finding suggests that the variables in the gestural communicative network are related to one another via a structure that involves use of conventional forms for a communicative purpose.

A third comparison regards the difference between Ritualized and Unritualized Refusals. We have correlational results only for the observational scores for these variables; furthermore, Ritual Refusals were sufficiently frequent for entry into the matrix only at sessions B and D (the two videotaped sessions). Hence the findings for this communicative category are probably less reliable than those for other behaviors. However, a comparison of Ritual versus Unritualized Refusals lends some support to the suggestion that the gestural network is based on conventionalization of signals. The relationship of Ritual Refusals to Giving, Showing, and Communicative Pointing is nonsignificant, but almost always in the positive direction. However, Unritualized Refusals tend to be correlated **negatively** with other gestural variables. Out of 112 possible correlations between Ritualized Refusal and the other gestural behaviors, 80 are negative, with 10 of these negative beyond − 0.344. We suggest that the tendency to protest and fuss during home visits relates negatively to other forms of gestural communication, for fairly obvious reasons. However, the child who protests with conventional signals (i.e., shaking his head no) is probably more sophisticated in all forms of communication. Hence the tendency to use Ritual Refusals cancels out the general pattern of negative correlations between refusals and other forms of communication. Furthermore, this pattern lends some support to a Replacement model for the passage from Unritualized and Ritualized Refusals.

A final comparison can be made between both Ritualized and Unritualized Showing Off, and the other gestural variables. In contrast with refusals, both of these are positive social behaviors. Furthermore, Ritual Showing Off through waving byebye, playing pattycake, etc., should involve conventionalization of signals to at least the same degree as Giving, Showing, and Pointing. And yet these two categories seem to fall outside the network of relationships that we have referred to as the Gestural Complex. Table 3.1 suggests that these are both low frequency behaviors in the observations. For the interviews, the data were too sparse to permit use in the correlation matrix. Hence it may be that these two levels of Showing Off have not been measured well enough in this study to yield reliable findings. There is, however, another interpretation that suggests at the very least that these behaviors are worth further study. Showing Off always involves use of the child's own body as the "referent" in a communicative act. Giving, Showing, Communicative Pointing, and Requests always involve reference to some "external" object or event. It is possible, then, that the behaviors in the Gestural

Complex are related to one another via some factor that involves (*a*) a communicative function, (*b*) use of conventional signals, and (*c*) some sort of external reference.

A final point as regards the relationship between nonverbal communication and general locomotor development: Correlations among communicative variables would be of relatively little interest if they were simple epiphenomena of general physical and neural maturation. Insofar as the locomotor development scale is an adequate measure of physical maturation, we can conclude that the pattern of results in gestural communication is not an artifact of very general developmental factors. Locomotion correlated positively and significantly with the gestural measures in only 4 out of 200 possible relationships, or 2% of the matrix.

Language Development

The transitions in language development between 9 and 13 months noted in our earlier research (Bates, Camaioni, and Volterra, 1975) were replicated in this study as well. By the first session, most of the children were reported to understand at least one or two words, and many of the children showed such comprehension in the first observation session. However, the level of comprehension in the earliest stages was limited to understanding of words or phrases within set, highly specific routines. For example, a child asked *Where's Daddy?* in the first session would typically look toward the outside door, the garage, or some spot where fathers usually reappear. Only much later would the same child respond by seeking out his father in a variety of places. Within production, the first words both in interviews and observations were generally nonreferential words. For example, many children produced the sound *mama* as a general request sound used for any listener. Later on, the same sound would be used specifically to request help from mother, and/or to name mother. At this point, the word would be classified as referential. (See Chapter 4 for a more detailed discussion of these data.) Table 3.1 lists the mean language scores per category across the four sessions. By the end of the study, all but four of the children used sounds that could clearly be classified as referential, in **both** the interview and observations. For the interviews, the mean number of referential words in Session D was 4.3, ranging from 0 to 19. For the observations, the mean number of referential words for this last session was 2.5, ranging from 0 to 15. As noted in Table 3.3, there was reasonably good agreement between the maternal interviews and the observations regarding language development.

This sequence of developments, from comprehension to nonreferential speech acts to true naming, has been reported by other researchers as well (e.g., Greenfield and Smith, 1976). Many authors have concluded from such sequential data that comprehension not only **precedes** but also leads to, causes, or is in some sense interdependent with, production. Furthermore, within production, the speculation has been that nonreferential speech is a precursor to referential speech, emerging earlier but involving many of the same underlying structures. This sort of interdependence hypothesis requires correlational as well as sequential data. In this section, we are addressing two correlational questions:

1. Do the various linguistic measures share some common factor, both within and across sessions?
2. Do the later developments replace earlier developments? Or does language development in this period involve expansion of the repertoire (i.e., earlier forms do not drop out, but continue to correlate with later forms throughout the study)?

With regard to the first question, it is clear that most of the language measures in this study are strongly correlated with one another. There was a total of 9 language measures (3 comprehension measures, 5 production measures, and a single observational measure of noncommunicative babbling). Out of the total of 435 possible between- and within-session correlations for these variables, 191 or 44% of the matrix are significant beyond $p < 0.05$. Furthermore, this pattern is distributed across both the interviews and the observations.

Table 3.5 lists the significant, positive correlations of the nine language measures with one another. It is clear that some of the language variables are better predictors of this "network" than others. The weakest predictor by far is Babbling, correlating with other aspects of language in only 10% out of 110 possible relationships, or 9% of the relevant matrix. Note that this variable was by definition noncommunicative, involving consonant–vowel sounds produced by the child in the absence of any discernible communicative intent (e.g., while playing alone with a variety of toys, vocalizing cheerfully but apparently randomly). It is possible, then, that the network of relations uniting the other aspects of language is based on use of the acoustic–articulatory system in the service of some communicative function. At least within the 9–13-month range, Babbling involves the "form" of language, but not the "function." Hence it falls outside this Language Complex. This interpretation is similar to the one proposed earlier to explain the difference between communicative and noncommunicative pointing in relation to the Gestural Complex.

TABLE 3.5
Significant[a] Positive Correlations between Language Measures

Session	Session A Int.	Session A Obs.	Session B Int.	Session B Obs.	Session C Int.	Session C Obs.	Session D Int.	Session D Obs.
Interview Level of Comprehension	#Comp 0.65 NRefwd 0.43		LComp 0.55 #Comp 0.42	LComp 0.55				FRefwd 0.40
Session A								
Session B	LComp 0.55 #Comp 0.55		#Comp 0.61	Comp 0.46 NRefwd 0.41 #Refwd 0.38 FRefwd 0.43	LComp 0.44 #Comp 0.57 Refwd 0.40	Comp 0.34 #Refwd 0.38	#Comp 0.56 Refwd 0.38	Comp 0.45 #Refwd 0.38 FRefwd 0.58
Session C			LComp 0.44	Comp 0.53 NRefwd 0.35			LComp 0.65 #Comp 0.39	LComp 0.38 #Comp 0.40 FRefwd 0.38
Session D					LComp 0.65 #Comp 0.39		#Comp 0.45	Comp 0.46 NRefwd 0.40 FRefwd 0.35
Interview # of words Comprehended	LComp 0.65 NRefwd 0.43		LComp 0.55 #Comp 0.78	Comp 0.55 FRefwd 0.49	#Comp 0.68		#Comp 0.71 NRefwd 0.36	Comp 0.52 #Refwd 0.45 FRefwd 0.70
Session A								

(continued)

Session B	LComp 0.42 Comp 0.49 / #Comp 0.78	LComp 0.61, NRefwd 0.38 → Comp 0.65, #Refwd 0.38, FRefwd 0.55	#Comp 0.92, NRefwd 0.42 → Comp 0.48, NRefwd 0.35, #Refwd 0.48	#Comp 0.86, NRefwd 0.49 → Comp 0.64, Bab 0.41, #Refwd 0.47, FRefwd 0.63
Session C	#Comp 0.68 Comp 0.49	LComp 0.57, #Comp 0.92, NRefwd 0.43 → Comp 0.64, #Refwd 0.37, FRefwd 0.52	NRefwd 0.52 → Comp 0.47, #Refwd 0.43	LComp 0.39, #Comp 0.90, NRefwd 0.61 → Comp 0.72, Bab 0.39, #Refwd 0.42, FRefwd 0.64
Session D	#Comp 0.71 Comp 0.39	LComp 0.56, #Comp 0.86, NRefwd 0.43 → Comp 0.64, #Refwd 0.45, FRefwd 0.55	LComp 0.39, #Comp 0.90, NRefwd 0.50 → Comp 0.42, #Refwd 0.52	LComp 0.45, NRefwd 0.61, Refwd 0.37 → Comp 0.75, Bab 0.44, #Refwd 0.56, FRefwd 0.72
Interview Nonreferential Words **Session A**	LComp 0.43 / #Comp 0.43	NRefwd 0.65 → Comp 0.53, FRefwd 0.72	NRefwd 0.68	NRefwd 0.58, #Refwd 0.37 → #Refwd 0.37, FRefwd 0.52
Session B	NRefwd 0.65 Comp 0.46	#Comp 0.38 → Comp 0.57, NRefwd 0.38, #Refwd 0.74, FRefwd 0.82	#Comp 0.43, NRefwd 0.83, Refwd 0.60 → Comp 0.37, #Refwd 0.72	#Comp 0.43, NRefwd 0.78, Refwd 0.51 → Comp 0.46, #Refwd 0.72, FRefwd 0.65

TABLE 3.5 (continued)

Session	Session A Int.	Session A Obs.	Session B Int.	Session B Obs.	Session C Int.	Session C Obs.	Session D Int.	Session D Obs.
Session C	NRefwd 0.68	Comp 0.35	#Comp 0.42 NRefwd 0.83	Comp 0.56 NRefwd 0.43 #Refwd 0.47 FRefwd 0.74	#Comp 0.52 Refwd 0.44	NRefwd 0.43 #Refwd 0.45	#Comp 0.50 NRefwd 0.90	Comp 0.51 Bab 0.41 #Refwd 0.51 FRefwd 0.60
Session D	#Comp 0.36 NRefwd 0.58	Comp 0.39	#Comp 0.49 NRefwd 0.90	Comp 0.67 NRefwd 0.52 #Refwd 0.61 FRefwd 0.81	#Comp 0.61 NRefwd 0.90 Refwd 0.36	Comp 0.44 NRefwd 0.49 #Refwd 0.56	#Comp 0.61	Comp 0.52 Bab 0.49 #Refwd 0.55 FRefwd 0.66
Interview Referential Words Session C			LComp 0.40 NRefwd 0.60	#Refwd 0.60 FRefwd 0.41	NRefwd 0.44	#Refwd 0.54	NRefwd 0.36 Refwd 0.89	#Refwd 0.61 FRefwd 0.49
Session D			LComp 0.38 NRefwd 0.51	#Refwd 0.63	Refwd 0.89	#Refwd 0.59	#Comp 0.37	#Refwd 0.71 FRefwd 0.56
Observation Comprehension Session A			#Comp 0.49 NRefwd 0.46	Comp 0.43 #Refwd 0.37 FRefwd 0.38	#Comp 0.49 NRefwd 0.35	Comp 0.66 #Refwd 0.48	#Comp 0.39 NRefwd 0.39	Comp 0.42 #Refwd 0.36
Session B	#Comp 0.61 NRefwd 0.53	Comp 0.43	LComp 0.46 #Comp 0.64 NRefwd 0.57	NRefwd 0.49 #Refwd 0.54 FRefwd 0.75	LComp 0.53 #Comp 0.64 NRefwd 0.56	Comp 0.53 #Refwd 0.46	#Comp 0.64 NRefwd 0.67	Comp 0.52 #Refwd 0.47 FRefwd 0.72

Session C	Comp 0.66	LComp 0.34 #Comp 0.48 NRefwd 0.37	Comp 0.53 NRefwd 0.50 #Refwd 0.46 FRefwd 0.43	#Comp 0.47	#Refwd 0.47	#Comp 0.42 NRefwd 0.44
						Comp 0.41 #Refwd 0.37 FRefwd 0.35
Session D	#Comp 0.52 Comp 0.42	LComp 0.45 #Comp 0.64 NRefwd 0.46	Comp 0.52 #Refwd 0.37 FRefwd 0.45	LComp 0.38 #Comp 0.72 NRefwd 0.51	Comp 0.41 #Refwd 0.48	LComp 0.46 #Comp 0.75 NRefwd 0.52
						#Refwd 0.55 FRefwd 0.63
Observation Babbling						
Session A						Bab 0.39
Session B				NRefwd 0.54		
Session C						
Session D	Bab 0.39	#Comp 0.41	#Comp 0.39 NRefwd 0.41	NRefwd 0.43	#Comp 0.44 NRefwd 0.49	
Observation Nonreferential Words						
Session B	LComp 0.41 NRefwd 0.38	Comp 0.49 #Refwd 0.50 FRefwd 0.45	LComp 0.35 NRefwd 0.43	Comp 0.50 NRefwd 0.42	NRefwd 0.52	
Session C	#Comp 0.35	Bab 0.54 NRefwd 0.42 #Refwd 0.49 FRefwd 0.57	NRefwd 0.43	#Refwd 0.46	NRefwd 0.49	Bab 0.43
Session D	LComp 0.40	LComp 0.40			LComp 0.40	

(continued)

TABLE 3.5 (continued)

Session	Session A		Session B		Session C		Session D	
	Int.	Obs.	Int.	Obs.	Int.	Obs.	Int.	Obs.
Observation Number of Referential Words		Comp 0.37	LComp 0.38, #Comp 0.38, NRefwd 0.74	Comp 0.54, NRefwd 0.50, FRefwd 0.77	LComp 0.38, #Comp 0.37, NRefwd 0.47, Refwd 0.60	Comp 0.46, NRefwd 0.49, #Refwd 0.92	#Comp 0.45, NRefwd 0.61, Refwd 0.63	Comp 0.37, #Refwd 0.74, FRefwd 0.53
Session B		Comp 0.48	LComp 0.38, #Comp 0.48, NRefwd 0.72	Comp 0.46, #Refwd 0.92, FRefwd 0.71	#Comp 0.43, NRefwd 0.45, Refwd 0.54	Comp 0.47, NRefwd 0.46	#Comp 0.52, NRefwd 0.56, Refwd 0.59	Comp 0.48, #Refwd 0.82
Session C	#Comp 0.45, NRefwd 0.37	Comp 0.36	LComp 0.38, #Comp 0.47, NRefwd 0.72	Comp 0.47, #Refwd 0.74, FRefwd 0.67	#Comp 0.42, NRefwd 0.51, Refwd 0.61	Comp 0.42, #Refwd 0.82	#Comp 0.56, NRefwd 0.55, Refwd 0.71	Comp 0.55, FRefwd 0.79
Session D	#Comp 0.49, NRefwd 0.72	Comp 0.38	LComp 0.43, #Comp 0.55, NRefwd 0.82	Comp 0.75, NRefwd 0.45, #Refwd 0.77	#Comp 0.52, NRefwd 0.74, Refwd 0.41	Comp 0.43, NRefwd 0.51, #Refwd 0.71	#Comp 0.55, NRefwd 0.81, FRefwd 0.68	Comp 0.45, #Refwd 0.67, FRefwd 0.68
Observation Frequency of Referential Words	LComp 0.40, #Comp 0.70, NRefwd 0.52		LComp 0.58, #Comp 0.63, NRefwd 0.65	Comp 0.72, #Refwd 0.53, FRefwd 0.68	LComp 0.38, #Comp 0.64, NRefwd 0.60, Refwd 0.49	Comp 0.35, #Refwd 0.56	LComp 0.35, #Comp 0.72, NRefwd 0.66, Refwd 0.56	Comp 0.63, #Refwd 0.79
Session B								
Session D								

aPearson r correlations with Nationality partialed out $(df\ 22) =$ or > 0.344, $p < 0.05$ (one tailed)

Among the eight communicative language measures in the language complex (i.e., excluding babbling), the weakest correlations are with the interview measure of Comprehension Level (correlating with other language measures in 35% of the relevant matrix) and observational measures of Nonreferential Speech (correlated with other language measures in 25% of the possible instances). Within both comprehension and production, these measures involve subtle transitional moments, from context-bound to relatively context-free use of language. It is possible that these measures enter into fewer correlations because the behaviors themselves are inherently unstable. However, we suspect that the low level of correlation for these measures, in comparison with number and frequency of comprehension and referential naming, is due the relative difficulty of "assessing" the transitional behaviors. The best means of assessing gradual transitions in the contextual use of language is an intensive and thorough diary study, or a microanalysis of an individual case such as that described in Carter (1975, 1977). In our own study as well, the histories of individual words in individual children are far more interesting and convincing than the gross division into referential and nonreferential, particularly since the developmental changes in these words really reflect a continuum rather than a sharp change in categories. For a more detailed discussion of qualitative changes in language and symbolic play in these 25 children, see Chapter 4. For present purposes, the Comprehension Level and Nonreferential Production measures should be regarded as crude approximations of a very subtle set of developments.

Of the remaining language measures, the Relative **Frequency** of Comprehension in the observations, and the **Number** of Words Comprehended according to the interviews, together predict the other language measures in 54% of the possible instances. Similarly, Number of Referential Words (combining correlations for both the interview and the observations) predicts the rest of the language matrix in 43% of the 105 possible combinations. Finally, the strongest language measure is the Frequency of Referential Speech in the observations, correlating significantly in 81% of 58 possible relationships with other language measures.

To summarize so far, there is clear evidence that various measures of early verbal communication are in some way interdependent. Relationships are particularly strong for Referential as opposed to Nonreferential speech, and for simple counts of comprehension as opposed to the measure of Comprehension Level. A second question concerns the temporal patterns among these measures. Are later forms replacing earlier forms? Or are the children expanding their linguistic repertoire to include all the behaviors measured here, retaining both the more primitive and the more sophisticated forms throughout the 9–13-month period? As should be clear from Table 3.5, there is an increase across time in the relationships among the language measures. For example, nonreferential speech continues to correlate highly with referential speech toward the end of the study. This supports an Expansion as opposed to a Replacement model for language development from 9 to 13 months. We should stress, however, that within **particular** words, for example the shift from *mama* as request to *mama* as name, the pattern was typically one of Replacement. (See Chapter 4.) The pattern of correlations in Table 3.5 reflects the fact that the children who proceeded fastest to the use of referential speech were concomitantly adding **more** nonreferential forms to their vocabulary than the linguistically less mature children. In other words, the linguistically advanced children are making more frequent and differentiated use of **both** types of speech.

Finally, there are very few correlations between locomotor development and the various language measures (i.e., 15 out of 120 correlations, or 13% of the matrix). Furthermore, the correlations between language and locomotion are much lower than the correlations of the language measures with each other. It is, then, extremely unlikely that the relationships among various aspects of early language development are artifacts of general maturation.

The Relationship between Language and Gestural Development

A major hypothesis derived from our earlier work is that preverbal, gestural communicative schemes provide a framework for the early acquisition of language. Hence we would predict positive, significant correlations between gesture and language in the 9–13-month age range. In addition to this first prediction, there are three more specific questions that we can ask with these data:

1. Are some gestural schemes better predictors of language than others?
2. Does language replace gestural communication, or do the two types of communication correlate throughout the 9–13-month range?
3. Since the preverbal measures used here are essentially gestural "productions," will they correlate more strongly with language production than with language comprehension?

With regard to the more general question, we do have a large number of significant, positive correlations between language and gestural communication. Taking both the interview and the observation measures, at all sessions, there is a total of 1500 possible nonredundant correlations between language and gesture. Of these 314, or 21% of the matrix, are significant beyond $p < 0.05$. In general, there are fewer correlations **between** language and gesture than there are **within** the two respective domains. That is, the language-to-language relationships and the gesture-to-gesture relationships are generally higher than gesture–language correlations. This pattern is not surprising, and merely justifies our initial division of these variables into two separate domains. Table 3.6 lists the significant, positive correlations between specific language and gestural measures.

The first of our more specific questions regards **which** of the various gestural measures are the best predictors of language development. As noted in Table 3.6, overall the strongest relationships to language are with the eight measures (four interview, four observation) that make up the Gestural Complex: Giving, Showing, Communicative Pointing, and Ritual Requests. Of these, Communicative Pointing is by far the best predictor, relating to the eight language measures (excluding babbling) in 83 out of 156 possible cases, or 53% of the matrix. Compare this with a correlation rate of 32% for observed and reported giving, 27% for observed and reported showing, and 22% for observed and reported ritual requests. The particularly strong prediction rate for communicative pointing suggests that this gesture is related to language not only through a general factor of communication with conventional signals, but also through a more specific set of structures involved in the act of reference to external objects and events. In a sense, pointing is really a gestural, sensorimotor form of naming, with no function other than sharing reference with the listener.

To summarize so far, the gestural variables that are the best predictors of language are the variables that are also the best predictors of each other. There is one interesting exception, however. Whereas Ritual and Unritualized Showing Off, Ritual and Unritualized Refusals, and Unritualized Requests all correlate with language at close to chance levels, the observation measure of Noncommunicative Pointing predicts the eight communicative language measures in 30 out of 104 possible instances, or 29%. Recall that Noncommunicative Pointing was **not** related to gestural communication. Yet it **is** related to language. Werner and Kaplan (1963) have suggested that "pointing for self" is related to the development of "objects of contemplation." In particular, they believe that noncommunicative pointing facilitates the psychological distancing

TABLE 3.6
Significant[a] Positive Correlations between Gestural Communication and Language Measures

Session	Session A		Session B		Session C		Session D	
	Int.	Obs.	Int.	Obs.	Int.	Obs.	Int.	Obs.
Interview Comprehension Level			CPoint 0.47 Show 0.36 Give 0.42		CPoint 0.50		CPoint 0.61	
Session A			RitReq 0.53					
Session B	RitReq 0.38	Show 0.38	CPoint 0.39 Show 0.45 Give 0.54 RitReq 0.48	Show 0.35	CPoint 0.42 Show 0.38 Give 0.37 RitReq 0.39	CPoint 0.37 Show 0.61 Give 0.40 RitReq 0.45	CPoint 0.57 RitReq 0.44	CPoint 0.35 Give 0.45
Session C						Show 0.34		NCPoint 0.36 CPoint 0.46 Give 0.45

Session D			NCPoint 0.44		RitReq 0.36 NCPoint 0.35 CPoint 0.41 Give 0.44 NRitShff 0.40
Interview # of words Comprehended		CPoint 0.66 Show 0.51 Give 0.48	NCPoint 0.42 CPoint 0.38	CPoint 0.62	CPoint 0.55 CPoint 0.49 NCPoint 0.44 CPoint 0.42
Session A		RitReq 0.40			
Session B	RitReq 0.41	CPoint 0.71 Show 0.57 Give 0.43 RitReq 0.49	CPoint 0.59 Show 0.43 NRitReq 0.48 RitReq 0.42 NRitShff 0.38	CPoint 0.74 NCPoint 0.37 CPoint 0.45 RitReq 0.38	CPoint 0.55 RitReq 0.36 NCPoint 0.51 CPoint 0.38 Give 0.37 RitRef 0.41

(continued)

TABLE 3.6 (continued)

Session	Session A Int.	Session A Obs.	Session B Int.	Session B Obs.	Session C Int.	Session C Obs.	Session D Int.	Session D Obs.
Session C	RitReq 0.38	NRitShff 0.39	CPoint 0.52 Show 0.57 Give 0.51 RitReq 0.36	CPoint 0.66 Show 0.44 NRitReq 0.40	CPoint 0.59	NCPoint 0.37 CPoint 0.40	CPoint 0.53	NCPoint 0.61 CPoint 0.50 Give 0.49 RitReq 0.41 RitRef 0.39
Session D	RitReq 0.46	NRitShff 0.44	CPoint 0.57 Show 0.43 Give 0.50 RitReq 0.45	CPoint 0.64 NRitReq 0.42	CPoint 0.61 Give 0.35	CPoint 0.59 Show 0.36 RitReq 0.38	CPoint 0.61 RitReq 0.47	NCPoint 0.57 CPoint 0.68 Show 0.46 Give 0.50 RitReq 0.50 RitRef 0.43
Interview Nonreferential Words Session A			Give 0.41	RitRef 0.45		CPoint 0.39		NCPoint 0.43 CPoint 0.35 NRitShff 0.39

	C1	C2	C3	C4	C5	C6	C7
Session B		Give 0.50	CPoint 0.41 Give 0.43 RitRef 0.40		CPoint 0.41		NCPoint 0.46 CPoint 0.45
Session C	RitReq 0.56	Give 0.52	CPoint 0.38 Show 0.34 Give 0.49	RitReq 0.35	CPoint 0.47 Show 0.41		NCPoint 0.42 CPoint 0.50
Session D	RitReq 0.38	Give 0.44	CPoint 0.39 Show 0.44 Give 0.41	Show 0.35 Give 0.37	CPoint 0.51 Show 0.40	Show 0.43 Give 0.37	NCPoint 0.45 CPoint 0.61 Give 0.39 RitReq 0.41 RitRef 0.38
Interview Referential Words Session C	RitReq 0.35 Show 0.53	Give 0.41	Show 0.48	RitReq 0.37	Show 0.42 Give 0.43 RitReq 0.40	CPoint 0.43 RitReq 0.37	NCPoint 0.42

(continued)

TABLE 3.6 (continued)

Session	Session A Int.	Session A Obs.	Session B Int.	Session B Obs.	Session C Int.	Session C Obs.	Session D Int.	Session D Obs.
Session D		Show 0.35	Give 0.43	Show 0.36		NCPoint 0.38 CPoint 0.41 Show 0.38 Give 0.56 RitReq 0.44	CPoint 0.41 RitReq 0.36	NCPoint 0.36 Show 0.42
Observation Comprehension Session A			CPoint 0.56 Show 0.38	CPoint 0.53		NCPoint 0.36	CPoint 0.38	NCPoint 0.44
Session B			CPoint 0.52	NCPoint 0.36 CPoint 0.55 Show 0.35	CPoint 0.35	CPoint 0.48 Show 0.38	CPoint 0.38	NCPoint 0.63 CPoint 0.43 RitRef 0.40
Session C	Give 0.50 RitShff 0.35		CPoint 0.41		Show 0.36	Give 0.39	Show 0.44 Give 0.43	NCPoint 0.36

Session D	Give 0.35	CPoint 0.47 Show 0.35 Give 0.46	CPoint 0.42 NRitReq 0.50	CPoint 0.57 Give 0.43	CPoint 0.41	CPoint 0.55 Give 0.39	NCPoint 0.38 CPoint 0.51 Give 0.63 NRitReq 0.35 RitReq 0.63
Observation Babbling Session A					RitShff 0.43		Show 0.39 NRitReq 0.45 RitReq 0.38
Session B	RitReq 0.51	RitReq 0.42	RitReq 0.43 RitShff 0.41	CPoint 0.52 RitReq 0.72	CPoint 0.52 RitReq 0.63	RitReq 0.59	
Session C	Show 0.35		RitReq 0.40				
Session D		CPoint 0.44 Show 0.51 RitReq 0.35		CPoint 0.46 Show 0.37			CPoint 0.46 RitReq 0.50 RitRef 0.40

(continued)

TABLE 3.6 (continued)

Session	Session A Int.	Session A Obs.	Session B Int.	Session B Obs.	Session C Int.	Session C Obs.	Session D Int.	Session D Obs.
Observation Nonreferen-tial Words		Show 0.47		Show 0.48		Show 0.39	Show 0.39	
Session B								
Session C	RitReq 0.38			Show 0.51 NRitShff 0.35	RitReq 0.41	NRitShff 0.42 RitReq 0.50		
Session D		Give 0.36		Give 0.58	Show 0.44 Give 0.38	Show 0.37 Give 0.67 RitReq 0.36	Show 0.39 Give 0.45	Give 0.57 NRitReq 0.44 RitReq 0.51
Observation # of Refer-ential Words Session B				Show 0.40	Show 0.48	Give 0.40 RitReq 0.42	Show 0.42 Give 0.47	CPoint 0.44 Give 0.34

Table 1

Session						
Session C	Give 0.36	CPoint 0.36	Show 0.41	NCPoint 0.39, Give 0.37, RitReq 0.41	Show 0.34, Give 0.41	CPoint 0.36
Session D	Give 0.35	CPoint 0.43, Give 0.52, RitReq 0.35 ‖ NCPoint 0.35, NRitReq 0.39	CPoint 0.43	NCPoint 0.44, CPoint 0.63, Give 0.49, RitReq 0.45	CPoint 0.44, Give 0.39	NCPoint 0.38, CPoint 0.46, Show 0.38, Give 0.44, RitReq 0.44

Observation Frequency of Referential Words

Session						
Session B	Give 0.38	NCPoint 0.38, Show 0.37, Give 0.35, RitRef 0.35	Show 0.35	CPoint 0.46, Show 0.36	Show 0.41, Give 0.37	NCPoint 0.45, CPoint 0.52
Session D		CPoint 0.48, Show 0.50, Give 0.67 ‖ CPoint 0.36, NRitReq 0.35, RitRef 0.35	CPoint 0.49	CPoint 0.76, Show 0.51, RitRef 0.35	CPoint 0.53	NCPoint 0.54, CPoint 0.53, Show 0.34, Give 0.41, RitReq 0.49, RitRef 0.39

[a] Pearson r correlations with Nationality partialed out (df 22) = or > p. 344, $p < 0.05$ (one tailed)

of the knower from the known, a development that is supposedly critical for an understanding of the concept of reference. Our findings lend some support to this view. It may be that the language complex in our data reflects (*a*) communicative function, and (*b*) the use of conventional signals. Hence it relates to variables in the gestural complex. In addition, however, language involves a particularly clear understanding of the sign–referent relationship. Since communicative pointing involves both reference and communication, it predicts the language complex very strongly. Insofar as noncommunicative pointing involves reference without a communicative function, it relates to language but not to gestural communication.

A second question regards the time course for gesture–language relationships. Our data do not support a model of communicative development in which preverbal communication is replaced by language toward the end of the first year. In fact, the correlations between these two domains actually increase across time (see Table 3.6). We can conclude from this pattern that communicative development between 9 and 13 months of age involves expansion of the repertoire. Children who are advanced in early language development continue to support their communications with gestural schemes.

A final question pertains to the relationship between comprehension and production in gesture versus language. Insofar as the gestural measures in this study are in fact communicative productions, we might expect them to correlate more highly with linguistic production than with comprehension. This was not the case, however. Language comprehension correlated with gestural development at about the same level as referential speech, and at a slightly higher level than nonreferential speech. And the strong relationships between Communicative Pointing and comprehension were similar to those for pointing and production. We can conclude, then, that communicative gesture and language are related via some common base involving both communication and reference, regardless of whether the child is in the role as message sender or message receiver.

Cognition and Communication

Recall that there was a total of nine cognitive measures used in this study: Object Permanence, Means–End Relations, Spatial Relations, Imitation (combining gestural and vocal), and five play measures including Reported Number of Combinatorial Play Schemes, Observed Frequency of Combinatorial Play, Reported Number of Symbolic Play Schemes,

Observed Number of Symbolic Play Schemes, and, finally, Observed Frequency of Symbolic Play. Table 3.7 lists the significant positive correlations of these nine measures with each other, with locomotion, and with the gestural and language measures. In this section, we will begin with a brief examination of the relationships among the cognitive measures themselves. Then we will look at the correlations between the cognitive measures, and both verbal and gestural communication.

Regarding the relationships among cognitive variables, Uzgiris and Hunt (1975) report low, nonsignificant correlations among their six sensorimotor scales throughout the first 2 years of life, when the effect of chronological age is partialled out. As noted earlier, this finding contrasts with the traditional Piagetian view of sensorimotor development (i.e., Piaget, 1954), in which progress in all aspects of sensorimotor development is presumed to reflect a single set of underlying operative schemes that define the six sensorimotor stages in all domains (e.g., secondary circular reactions, tertiary circular reactions). According to this more orthodox view, we would expect significant correlations among the various aspects of sensorimotor development, even though there may be "decalages" of differences in relative onset times between domains. The Uzgiris and Hunt findings suggest, instead, that correlations across children are based on what we might term "local homologies," or specific underlying schemes that define a particular domain, rather than "deep homologies," or general operative schemes than cut across sensorimotor developments in various domains. The "local homology" or "skill-specific" approach to development has been put forward recently by several neo-Piagetian theorists, including Fischer (1978) and Pascual-Leone (1972), and stands in marked contrast with the orthodox Piagetian view.

Our findings with regard to the relations among cognitive measures tend to support the neo-Piagetian, local homology view. As indicated in Table 3.7, four of the cognitive measures—Object Permanence, Means–Ends, Spatial Relations, and Imitation—correlate with one another at close to chance levels. This finding replicates the results of Uzgiris and Hunt, even though we changed their procedures in administration and scoring for all four measures.

However, the play measures **do** correlate significantly with other aspects of cognitive development. First, the five play measures correlate significantly with one another in 61 out of 136 possible combinations, or 45% of the relevant matrix. Furthermore, the two Combinatorial measures predict the three Symbolic measures in 19 out of 48 possible combinations, a prediction rate of 40%. The correlations among the play measures are in no way surprising, and merely provide further justifica-

TABLE 3.7

Significant[a] Positive Correlations between Cognitive, Communicative, and Locomotion Measures

Session	Session A Int.	Session A Obs.	Session B Int.	Session B Obs.	Session C Int.	Session C Obs.	Session D Int.	Session D Obs.
Object Permanence Session A	CombPl 0.39		Give 0.36 LComp 0.34 CombPl 0.38	Give 0.36 NRitReq 0.35 CombPl 0.35 ObjP 0.55	CPoint 0.48	Give 0.42 CombPl 0.38 ObjP 0.45	CPoint 0.45	Give 0.56 Comp 0.51 NRefFwd 0.43 Space 0.48
Session B	CombPl C.55	ObjP 0.55	CPoint 0.42		CPoint 0.35	ObjP 0.51		NRitReq 0.39 ObjP 0.39
Session C	#Comp 0.36 CombPl 0.63	CombPl 0.34 ObjP 0.45 Means 0.39	LComp 0.43 CombPl 0.64 SymPl 0.46	NRitReq 0.42 ObjP 0.52	CPoint 0.50 RitReq 0.43 CombPl 0.53 SymbPl 0.47	CPoint 0.40 RitReq 0.48 CombPl 0.43 Imit 0.41 Loco 0.41	CPoint 0.47 NRitRef 0.45 CombPl 0.42 Symb 0.46	CPoint 0.35 NRitRef 0.42 RitRef 0.42 Comp 0.36 CombPl 0.36 #SymbPl 0.42 FSymbPl 0.38 ObjP 0.49 Loco 0.39
Session D	CombPl 0.48		CombPl 0.40	ObjP 0.39		ObjP 0.49		
Spatial Relations Session A		Bab 0.45			SymbPl 0.35	#SymbPl 0.40 Imit 0.37		CPoint 0.37 RitShff 0.36 Bab 0.36
Session B	Give	Give 0.49			Give 0.49	NCPoint 0.48	Give 0.45	Give 0.48

Session							
			LComp 0.53			LComp 0.52, RefWd 0.42	RitReq 0.38, Comp 0.45
Session C	RitReq 0.49	Loco 0.48	NRitReq 0.35, Space 0.42	#Comp 0.39	Give 0.53, Space 0.42	Show 0.36, Give 0.35	NCPoint 0.35, NRitShff **0.45**, FRefwd 0.35, Space 0.36
Session D	ObjP 0.48			Give 0.41, RitReq 0.51, LComp 0.36, SymbPl 0.41	Give 0.51, Space 0.36	Show 0.53, Give 0.53, RitReq 0.44	Give 0.54, NRitShff 0.36, NRefWd 0.43
Imitation Session A	RitReq 0.42, Bab 0.37, Means 0.37, Loco 0.43	CPoint 0.35, Bab 0.48, #SymPl 0.55, FSymbPl 0.36, Imit 0.47	NRefWd 0.37, RefWd 0.37, CombPl 0.35	CPoint 0.37, Give 0.37, RitReq 0.43, NRefWd 0.60	NRefWd 0.35, SymPl 0.43	RitRef 0.35, CombPl 0.42, FSymbPl 0.45, Imit 0.35, Loco 0.39	
Session B	Bab 0.38, CombPl 0.39, Imit 0.47, Loco 0.35			Give 0.39, NRefWd 0.44	Give 0.39, NRefWd 0.44		
Session C	CombPl 0.34, Space 0.37	LComp 0.35, CombPl 0.36, SymPl 0.53	CPoint 0.35, Bab 0.35, #RefWd 0.64, FRefwd 0.52	Show 0.38, Give 0.44, LComp 0.64, RefWd 0.48, SymPl 0.35	CPoint 0.38, Give 0.44, RitReq 0.64, NRitShff 0.36, NRefWd 0.47, #SymPl 0.35, FSymbPl 0.39, ObjP 0.41, Loco 0.48	Show 0.40, Give 0.55, #Comp 0.46, NRefWd 0.42, SymPl 0.37	CPoint 0.50, Give 0.46, RitReq 0.37, Comp 0.42, #RefWd 0.50, FRefwd 0.36, CombPl 0.43, #SymPl 0.38, FSymbPl 0.39, Loco 0.43

(continued)

TABLE 3.7 (continued)

Session	Session A Int.	Session A Obs.	Session B Int.	Session B Obs.	Session C Int.	Session C Obs.	Session D Int.	Session D Obs.
Session D		NRitShff 0.36 Imit 0.35		Give 0.45			CombPl 0.43	CPoint 0.41 Give 0.39 NRitShff 0.35 CombPl 0.40 #SymPl 0.47 FSymPl 0.37
Means-End Session A	LComp 0.36	Show 0.61 RitShff 0.40 Imit 0.37 Loco 0.45	Show 0.58 Give 0.47 RitReq 0.36 LComp 0.48 #Comp 0.42 NRefwd 0.36 CombPl 0.41 SymbPl 0.42	Show 0.49 NRitReq 0.41 RitReq 0.35 Bab 0.41 NRefwd 0.35 #Refwd 0.44 Means 0.43	CPoint 0.43 Show 0.65 Give 0.47 RitReq 0.61 #Comp 0.38 Refwd 0.63 CombPl 0.52 SymbPl 0.51	CPoint 0.40 Show 0.37 Give 0.46 RitReq 0.48 #Refwd 0.39 ObjP 0.39	CPoint 0.37 Show 0.58 Give 0.47 RitReq 0.51 #Comp 0.45 Refwd 0.56 CombPl 0.44 SymbPl 0.53	CPoint 0.48 Show 0.61 Give 0.37 NRitRef 0.37 Bab 0.39 #Refwd 0.43 FRefwd 0.44 CombPl 0.47 #SymPl 0.66 FSymPl 0.39 Means 0.37 Loco 0.35
Session B	RitReq 0.50	NRitShff 0.47 Means 0.43	RitReq 0.57 SymbPl 0.48	Bab 0.53 CombPl 0.35	RitReq 0.60 SymbPl 0.60 Means 0.48	RitReq 0.44 NRefwd 0.35 FSymPl 0.37	RitReq 0.49 SymbPl 0.50	Loco 0.46
Session C	RitReq 0.38	NRitShff 0.36 Loco 0.35		Bab 0.45 Means 0.48	RitReq 0.48	#SymPl 0.43	Refwd 0.40	Means 0.63 Loco 0.58
Session D		Bab 0.37 Means 0.37 Loco 0.71			NRefwd 0.35	NRefwd 0.37 Means 0.63	Show 0.41 NRefwd 0.40	Comp 0.37 CombPl 0.39 Loco 0.50

Interview Symbolic Play Schemes — Session B

F1	F2	F3	F4	F5	F6	F7	F8
RitReq 0.37	Means 0.42	RitReq 0.47	RitReq 0.37	Give 0.38	CPoint 0.47	CPoint 0.41	CPoint 0.55
LComp 0.36		LComp 0.45	Bab 0.48	RitReq 0.41	SymbPl 0.38	RitReq 0.58	Show 0.47
#Comp 0.52		#Comp **0.48**	#SymbPl 0.35	#Comp 0.43	ObjP 0.46	#Comp 0.58	Give 0.39
CombPl 0.57		CombPl 0.37	FSymbPl 0.39	SymbPl 0.74	Imit 0.53	SymbPl 0.69	Comp 0.37
			Means 0.48		Loco 0.56		CombPl 0.55
							Loco 0.45

Session C

F1	F2	F3	F4	F5	F6	F7
RitReq 0.48	Give 0.47	Bab 0.50	Give 0.50	CPoint 0.54	CPoint 0.39	CPoint 0.61
NRitShff 0.40	RitReq 0.52	CombPl 0.43	RitReq 0.64	Show 0.44	Show 0.70	Show 0.43
Space 0.35	CombPl 0.54	SymbPl 0.35	CombPl 0.40	Give 0.39	Give 0.46	Give 0.45
Means 0.51	**SymbPl** 0.74	Means 0.60		RitReq 0.57	RitReq 0.92	RitReq 0.50
				ObjP 0.47		Bab 0.49
				Imit 0.48		CombPl 0.44
				Loco 0.36		#SymbPl 0.53
						FSymbPl 0.38
						Space 0.41
						Loco 0.46

Session D

F1	F2	F3	F4	F5	F6	F7
RitReq 0.55	Give 0.45	Bab 0.49	Give 0.40	CPoint 0.60	RitReq 0.73	CPoint 0.67
CombPl 0.37	RitReq 0.44	CombPl 0.37	RitReq 0.56	Show 0.43	#Comp 0.50	Show 0.55
NRitShff 0.40	CombPl 0.59	#SymbPl 0.41	CombPl 0.41	RitReq 0.49		Give 0.42
Imit 0.53	SymbPl 0.69	Means 0.50	SymbPl 0.92	#SymbPl 0.41		RitReq 0.43
Means 0.43				ObjP 0.46		NRitShff 0.37
				Imit 0.37		Bab 0.49
						CombPl 0.55
						#SymbPl 0.62
						FSymPl 0.43
						Loco 0.38

Observation Freq. Symb. Play Schemes — Session B

F1	F2	F3	F4	F5	F6
RitReq 0.50	Give 0.35	NReFwd 0.57	CPoint 0.44	CPoint 0.39	CPoint 0.36
NRefFwd 0.53	NRefFwd 0.40	RefFwd 0.36	Show 0.40	RitReq 0.39	Bab **0.41**
Imit 0.36	SymbPl 0.39	SymbPl 0.35		NRefFwd 0.42	RefFwd 0.44
				SymbPl 0.41	CombPl 0.39
					FSymbPl 0.35

TABLE 3.7 (continued)

Session	Session A		Session B		Session C		Session D	
	Int.	Obs.	Int.	Obs.	Int.	Obs.	Int.	Obs.
Session C		Bab 0.34 CombPl 0.46	SymbPl 0.38	Means 0.37	Give 0.37 SymbPl 0.72	Imit 0.39 Loco 0.37		
Session D	NRefWd 0.36 CombPl 0.40	CombPl 0.37 Imit 0.42 Means 0.39	Give 0.68 LComp 0.35 NRefWd 0.43 RefWd 0.37 CombPl 0.41 SymbPl 0.35	Give 0.66	Show 0.41 Give 0.38 NRefWd 0.39 RefWd 0.40 CombPl 0.61 SymPl 0.38	CPoint 0.54 Show 0.55 Give 0.49 RitReq 0.46 CombPl 0.48 ObjP 0.38 Imit 0.39	RefWd 0.37 CombPl 0.50 SymbPl 0.43	CPoint 0.42 Show 0.41 Give 0.48 RitReq 0.43 #RefWd 0.45 FRefWd 0.41 CombPl 0.43 #SymbPl 0.68 Imit 0.37
Observation # of Symb. Play Schemes								
Session B	RitReq 0.59	Imit 0.55	RitReq 0.53 LComp 0.39 SymbPl 0.35	Show 0.38 RitReq 0.36 RitShff 0.40 Bab 0.59 FSymbPl 0.62	CPoint 0.36 RitReq 0.56 NRefWd 0.36	CPoint 0.43 RitReq 0.47 NRefWd 0.43 Loco 0.34	RitReq 0.44	Loco 0.34
Session C		Space 0.40	SymbPl 0.45		Give 0.35 SymbPl 0.37	RitShff 0.36 FSymbPl 0.72 Imit 0.35 Means 0.43 Loco 0.36	SymbPl 0.41	Show 0.43

Session								
Session D	NRefFwd 0.35 CombPl 0.38	Means 0.66	Give 0.58 LComp 0.37 NRefFwd 0.41 CombPl 0.68	Give 0.42 NRitReq 0.37 #RefWd 0.41 FRefFwd 0.41	Show 0.51 Give 0.42 NRefWd 0.41 RefWd 0.56 CombPl 0.65 SymbPl 0.53	CPoint 0.61 Show 0.45 Give 0.52 ObjP 0.42 Imit 0.38	CPoint 0.40 Show 0.46 Give 0.45 RitReq 0.41 #Comp 0.44 NRefWd 0.48 RefWd 0.52 CombPl 0.62 SymbPl 0.62	NCPoint 0.37 CPoint 0.73 Show 0.75 Give 0.60 NRitReq 0.35 RitReq 0.58 NRitRef 0.45 NRitShff 0.43 Comp 0.35 Bab 0.38 **NRefWd 0.41** #RefWd 0.58 **FRefFwd 0.53** **CombPl 0.60** FSymbPl 0.68 **Imit 0.47**
Interview **Combinatorial** **Play** **Session A**	#Comp 0.46	ObjP 0.39	RitReq 0.37 LComp 0.39 #Comp 0.50 CombPl 0.40 SymbPl 0.36	NRitReq 0.44 ObjP 0.55	CPoint 0.60 RitReq 0.40 #Comp 0.37	CPoint 0.61 RitReq 0.50 CombPl 0.40 ObjP 0.63	CPoint 0.39 RitReq 0.35 #Comp 0.43 SymbPl 0.37	Show 0.38 Give 0.49 NRitReq 0.40 RitReq 0.38 RitReq 0.41 Comp 0.42 #RefWd 0.36 FRefWd 0.41 CombPl 0.41 #SymbPl 0.38 FSymbPl 0.40 ObjP 0.48
Session B	CombPl 0.40	Bab 0.35 CombPl 0.37	Give 0.48 SymbPl 0.37	Give 0.35	Give 0.41 CombPl 0.73	CPoint 0.44 Give 0.40	CPoint 0.39 Give 0.36	CPoint 0.52 Show 0.58

(continued)

TABLE 3.7 (continued)

Session	Session A Int.	Session A Obs.	Session B Int.	Session B Obs.	Session C Int.	Session C Obs.	Session D Int.	Session D Obs.
		ObjP 0.38 Means 0.41			SymbPl 0.54	ObjP 0.64 Imit 0.36	RitReq 0.46 #Comp 0.41 RefWd 0.37 CombPl 0.58 SymbPl 0.59	Give 0.55 NRitReq 0.40 RitReq 0.43 NRitRef 0.56 RitRef 0.41 Comp 0.40 CombPl 0.55 #SymbPl 0.68 FSymbPl 0.41 ObjP 0.39
Session C		CombPl 0.44 Imit 0.35 Means 0.52	Give 0.58 LComp 0.39 NRefWd 0.35 RefWd 0.35 CombPl 0.73	Give 0.65 CombPl 0.38	Show 0.49 Give 0.63 RitReq 0.38 RefWd 0.45 SymbPl 0.40	CPoint 0.38 Give 0.59 #RefWd 0.48 CombPl 0.37 ObjP 0.51 0.53	CPoint 0.35 Give 0.54 RefWd 0.44 CombPl 0.86 SymbPl 0.41	CPoint 0.43 Show 0.48 Give 0.55 NRitReq 0.42 RitReq 0.35 NRitRef 0.47 NRefWd 0.38 #RefWd 0.45 CombPl 0.45 #SymbPl 0.65 FSymbPl 0.61
Session D		Means 0.44	Give 0.43 LComp 0.35 NRefWd 0.38 CombPl 0.58	Give 0.63 #RefWd 0.44	Show 0.38 Give 0.43 RefWd 0.48 CombPl 0.86	Give 0.47 RitReq 0.39 #RefWd 0.35 CombPl 0.42 ObjP 0.42	Give 0.49 RefWd 0.39	CPoint 0.37 Show 0.35 Give 0.49 NRitRef 0.44 NRefWd 0.37 #RefWd 0.42 CombPl 0.43 #SymbPl 0.62 FSymbPl 0.50 Imit 0.43

Observational Combinatorial Play

	RitReq 0.38	ObjP 0.35	CombPl 0.37	Imit 0.39	CombPl 0.44	Give 0.44	Give 0.37	FSymbPl 0.37
Session A						CombPl 0.39; FSymbPl 0.46; ObjP 0.34; Imit 0.34		
Session B	RitReq 0.54		Give 0.60; RitReq 0.50	Give 0.55; RitShff 0.45; Bab 0.37; Means 0.35	Give 0.57; RitReq 0.44; NRefWd 0.35; CombPl 0.38; SymbPl 0.43	CPoint 0.41; CombPl 0.37	RitReq 0.38; SymbPl 0.37	Give 0.41; Comp 0.41; #RefWd 0.57; FSymbPl 0.48
Session C	RitReq 0.44; LComp 0.43; CombPl 0.40	CombPl 0.39; ObjP 0.38	CPoint 0.40; Give 0.52; RitReq 0.59; LComp 0.41; NRefWd 0.36	Give 0.50; CombPl 0.37	CPoint 0.56; RitReq 0.39; CombPl 0.51	Give 0.45; RitReq 0.56; #RefWd 0.46; ObjP 0.43	CPoint 0.52; CombPl 0.42	Give 0.41; Comp 0.41; #RefWd 0.57; FSymbPl 0.48
Session D	RitReq 0.49; #Comp 0.41; NRefWd 0.41; CombPl 0.47	Imit 0.45; Means 0.47; Loco 0.36	Give 0.49; LComp 0.48; #Comp 0.55; NRefWd 0.45; CombPl 0.55; SymbPl 0.55	Give 0.41; Bab 0.38; RefWd 0.50; FSymbPl 0.39	CPoint 0.44; Give 0.51; RitReq 0.39; #Comp 0.61; NRefWd 0.60; CombPl 0.45; SymbPl 0.44	CPoint 0.55; ObjP 0.36; Imit 0.43	CPoint 0.46; Give 0.41; RitReq 0.48; #Comp 0.60; NRefWd 0.62; CombPl 0.43; SymbPl 0.55	CPoint 0.59; Show 0.53; Give 0.70; RitReq 0.40; Comp 0.56; Bab 0.40; #RefWd 0.41; FRefWd 0.44; #SymbPl 0.60; FSymbPl 0.43; Imit 0.40; Means 0.39

[a] Pearson r correlations with Nationality partialed out $(df\ 22) =$ or > 0.344, $p < 0.05$ (one tailed).

121

tion for Uzgiris and Hunt's decision to treat these aspects of play within the same scale. However, Uzgiris and Hunt did not find significant correlations between the Schemes Scale and other aspects of sensorimotor development. By contrast, we found a number of significant relationships, when the Schemes Scale is broken down into types of play. For example, Combinatorial Play (taking the interview and observational correlations together) relates to Object Permanence in 44% of the possible instances, compared with a 25% rate of significant correlation with Imitation, and a 19% rate with Means–End Relations. The three Symbolic Play Measures do **not** relate to Object Permanence beyond chance levels, but taken together they do predict Imitation in 30% of the possible correlations. Furthermore, Symbolic Play correlates with Means–End Relations in 28% of the possible relationships. The fact that Imitation and Means–Ends both relate to aspects of play is particularly interesting, since these two measures do **not** correlate significantly with one another. This point will be important further on, when we discuss the correlations between cognitive measures and language.

To summarize so far, there is no single Cognitive Complex that is in any way comparable to the Gestural Complex and Language Complex discussed earlier. In general, our findings replicate those of Uzgiris and Hunt, in which the various aspects of sensorimotor intelligence develop fairly independently across a large sample of children. However, when the Schemes Scale is broken down into more detailed information on frequency and differentiation of play schemes, relationships between play and other aspects of cognition do emerge.

Let us turn now to the correlations between cognitive and communicative variables. The actual correlations are listed in Table 3.7. Table 3.8 summarizes the **percentage** of significant, positive correlations out of the total number possible for the nine cognitive measures with (*a*) the 8 measures in the Gestural Complex (i.e., Giving, Showing, Communicative Pointing, and Ritual Requests), (*b*) the 6 gestural measures that fall outside the Gestural Complex, (*c*) Language Comprehension (3 measures), (*d*) Nonreferential Production (2 measures), (*e*) Referential Production (3 measures), and (*f*) all the language measures taken together, including Babbling (9 measures). Overall, it is clear that some cognitive measures are good predictors of communicative development, while others are not. Second, there are some differences in the way that particular cognitive scales relate to gesture versus language, and to language comprehension versus language production.

First of all, it is generally true that Object Permanence and Spatial Relations are poor predictors of communicative development, either gestural or verbal. With the variables in the Gestural Complex, these two

TABLE 3.8

Percentage of Significant Positive Correlations between Cognitive and Communicative Measures[a]

Cognitive measures	Gestures		Language			
	Gesture complex 8 measures 28 scores	Other gestures 6 measures 22 scores	Comprehension 3 measures 12 scores	Nonreferential words 2 measures 7 scores	Referential words 3 measures 7 scores	Total language (including Bab) 9 measures 30 scores
Uzgiris-Hunt Scales						
Object Permanence (Four scores)	13%	6%	10%	4%	0%	5%
Spatial Relations (Four scores)	15%	7%	10%	4%	7%	8%
Imitation (Four scores)	18%	5%	8%	21%	21%	17%
Means-End (Four scores)	26%	6%	13%	21%	25%	20%
Combinatorial Play						
Total (Eight scores)	37%	6%	20%	18%	32%	21%
Interview (Four scores)	41%	10%	21%	14%	46%	23%
Observation (Four scores)	31%	1%	19%	21%	18%	19%

(continued)

123

TABLE 3.8 (continued)

| Cognitive measures | Gestures | | Language | | | |
	Gesture complex 8 measures 28 scores	Other gestures 6 measures 22 scores	Comprehension 3 measures 12 scores	Nonreferential words 2 measures 7 scores	Referential words 3 measures 7 scores	Total language (including Bab) 9 measures 30 scores
Symbolic play Total (Nine scores)	34%	5%	10%	22%	21%	19%
Interview (Three scores)	46%	5%	25%	0%	0%	16%
Observation number of schemes (Three scores)	31%	11%	11%	33%	29%	21%
Observation frequency (Three scores)	24%	0%	3%	33%	33%	19%

[a] 5% = change frequency.

cognitive measures correlate at somewhat better than chance levels (i.e., 13% prediction rate for Object Permanence, 15% for Spatial Relations). However, both measures are extremely poor predictors of language, with a 5% rate of significant correlation between Object Permanence and the nine language measures, and 9% rate between Spatial Relations and language. Within the language measures, these two cognitive variables predict comprehension slightly better than production (i.e., 10% versus chance levels for production).

The cognitive measures which **do** predict both language and gesture are Means–Ends, Imitation, and the various aspects of Play. However, these measures differ somewhat in particular patterns of correlation. For example, Imitation predicts language and gesture equally well, around 18% for each. By contrast, all the other measures are much stronger predictors of the Gesture Complex than language overall. For measures in the Gesture Complex, the highest rates of correlation are with Combinatorial Play (averaging 37%) and Symbolic Play (averaging 34%), followed by Means–Ends (26%) and Imitation (18%). For language, on the other hand, these four aspects of cognition predict the nine language measures at roughly similar levels: Combinatorial Play 21%, Means–Ends 20%, Symbolic Play 19%, and Imitation 17%.

There are also some different patterns for language comprehension versus language production. Both Imitation and Means–Ends correlate much better with either nonreferential or referential production than they do with comprehension. Indeed, Imitation predicts comprehension at close to chance levels (i.e., 8%). For the Play measures, the patterns are more complicated, and vary depending on how play was assessed. For example, Interview Combinatorial Play is an excellent predictor of referential speech (46%), versus 14% for nonreferential speech and 21% for comprehension. Observed Combinatorial Play, however, correlates with all aspects of comprehension and production at roughly similar levels. Interview Symbolic Play correlates with comprehension very strongly (25%), while related to production at close to chance levels. But with the two Observed Symbolic Play measures taken either together or separately, the reverse holds, so that relationships are much stronger with either type of language production than they are with comprehension.

The interview play measures had been included to elicit richer anecdotal information about behaviors that are less likely to occur spontaneously in the home visits than some of the other cognitive scale items. However, if we are interested in comparing play with the Uzgiris–Hunt measures, the best estimates are probably the observational play scores, since these are subject to the same motivational factors, experimenter

effects, etc., as the other cognitive tests. Using the observational measures only, we can conclude (*a*) the best predictors of language production are the two types of play, in contrast with any of the other Uzgiris–
Hunt measures, and (*b*) of these two aspects of play, Combinatorial Play
predicts both comprehension and production, while Symbolic Play is
much more specifically involved with production.

To summarize so far, Object Permanence and Spatial Relations are
poor predictors of communicative development, particularly language.
Imitation and Means–End Relations are both reasonably good predictors of gestural and verbal communicative development—even though
these two cognitive scales are **not** good predictors of one another. This
suggests that Imitation and Means–Ends may interact with communicative development in different ways. Finally, the various play measures
are the strongest predictors of both gesture and language. While the
relationship of play to language is complex, and seems to depend at least
in part on how play is assessed, it does generally seem that Combinatorial
Play predicts **both** comprehension and production, while Symbolic Play
is more often related to production alone. It is possible, then, that the
two types of play are also interacting with different aspects of language
development. This interpretation seems still more likely if we also recall
that these two types of play correlated with other cognitive measures in
very different ways.

In general, then, our findings support a local homology model not
only for the relationships among the cognitive variables themselves, but
also for the relationships between cognition and communication. These
various measures seem to be related to one another via particular "sub-
sets" of schemes, rather than some single, general developmental factor.
This interpretation becomes still clearer if we turn to the temporal
patterns among the cognition—communication correlations. Recall that
in general the correlations among communicative measures tend to
increase across sessions. This same pattern does **not** hold for the cognitive measures. For example, most of the significant correlations between
Means–End Relations and communication are with the Means–Ends
scores at Session A. By contrast, for Imitation more of the significant
correlations occur with the Imitation score at the third session. Combinatorial Play predicts communicative development fairly evenly across
the 9–13-month time period. On the other hand, correlations with
Symbolic Play tend to be much stronger toward the end of the study.
Even Object Permanence, which generally showed very little relationship
with communicative development, does tend to correlate at higher than
chance levels at Session C. In other words, the relationships with these
cognitive scales are far from homogeneous. Nor are the relationships

among **all** scores simply increasing across time (a finding that might merely indicate practice effects for mothers, children, and experimenters alike). Rather, the relationships between communicative and cognitive variables probably involve particular structures or schemes. Hence correlations reach significance only at those sessions in which there is considerable variation among subjects on these "sensitive" items.

We could go back and reconstruct the particular items that are varying at these "sensitive" sessions for each cognitive scale. For example, at Session A—the most relevant session for Means–Ends and Communications—children are just beginning to master support relationships, e.g., the use of cloths and string in obtaining objects. However, given how little we know about the internal psychometrics of these scales, such an endeavor would probably be hopelessly ad hoc at this point. We suggest instead that future correlational research on cognition and communication be preceded by much more detailed and specific task analysis, permitting clear predictions about the possible local homologies or shared schemes that we expect to find in these behavioral domains. Such an approach might, for example, be useful in teasing out the differential influence of cognitive structures on language comprehension in comparison with language production.

One further point regards the relationship between cognition and locomotor development. As noted in Table 3.7, there is a tendency for the locomotor scale to correlate significantly with some of the cognitive measures, at some sessions. In other words, there is probably a motor component in sensorimotor development. However, since locomotion predicted both verbal and gestural development at close to random levels, it is unlikely that the pattern of relationships between cognitive and communicative measures is an artifact of general motor development. Furthermore, the fact that the cognitive scales are essentially unrelated to one another greatly diminishes the probability that the pattern of relationships observed here is due to a general cognitive developmental factor like IQ.

Conclusion

To summarize briefly, the correlational results for gestural development suggest that there is a Gestural Complex developing between 9 and 13 months, reflected in Giving, Showing, Communicative Pointing, and Ritual Requests. If we contrast the measures that do correlate with this complex with the measures that do not, it seems that the Gestural

Complex involves (*a*) the use of conventional signals with (*b*) communicative intent, and possibly (*c*) reference to some external object or event other than the child's own ability to "show off." In general, gestural development seems to involve expansion of the repertoire from 9 to 13 months. However, there is some evidence that more ritualized requests and refusals are replacing unritualized versions of those two functions.

Within language development, there is also a Language Complex emerging from 9 to 13 months, indicating some sort of interdependence between comprehension and both referential and nonreferential production. Furthermore, language development in this age range consists primarily of expanding the repertoire. In other words, referential speech is not yet replacing nonreferential speech. Babbling, or consonant–vowel vocalizations serving no discernible communicative function, is apparently unrelated to the network of relations involved in language development—even though babbling obviously involves use of the same acoustic–articulatory channel.

There is also some form of interdependence between language development and the measures that form the Gestural Complex. This relationship increases across sessions, suggesting that language is not replacing gestural communication. Instead, it is apparently the case that children who are particularly precocious in language are also continuing to exercise gestural schemes. The most likely interpretation of these results is not that preverbal development **causes** language, but rather that language and preverbal communication both rely on some common underlying capacity for communication via conventional signals. However, unlike the Gesture Complex, language measures also correlate with noncommunicative pointing, suggesting that verbal development requires additional capacities, possibly involving the establishment of sign–referent relationships.

Finally, the evidence concerning cognition and communication supports a "local homology" or "skill-specific" model of sensorimotor development. There are four reasons for this conclusion:

1. The cognitive measures—with the exception of play—are **not** good predictors of one another.
2. Some cognitive variables are good predictors of communicative development (i.e., imitation, tool use, and play); others clearly are not (i.e., object permanence and spatial relations).
3. For each of the cognitive measures, correlations with communicative development occur in very different temporal patterns, suggesting that the relationships with communication involve particular items at "sensitive" sessions.

4. There is a tendency for the cognitive scales to predict comprehension and production in somewhat different ways.

In general, correlational studies by other investigators tend to support our pattern of findings. With regard to the link between causal development and communication, Harding and Golinkoff (1977) report significant positive correlations between intentional vocalization and causal understanding in a sample of 46 9-month-old infants. This is particularly interesting to us, since their measures of causality were quite different from ours, involving understanding of agent–action sequences rather than the static means–end relations involved in tool use. The correlations that we have found among language, imitation, and symbolic play are also reported in a study by Nicholich (1975). With regard to object permanence, Corrigan (1975) also failed to find any correlations between language development (in this case, a measure of Mean Length of Utterance) and a modified version of the Uzgiris–Hunt Object Permanence Scale. Halpern and Aviezer (1976) do report correlations between object permanence and language—but at a much later stage than the one examined here, in the period in which verb–noun relations in two-word speech became predominant in the child's linguistic productions.

Further support for this pattern of relationships can be found in studies with various populations of language-deficient children. In this chapter we have described the set of skills that are present when language is present. An alternative approach is to examine the pattern of skills that are absent when language is absent. Snyder (1975) administered the Uzgiris–Hunt scales to a sample of 15 language-delayed and 15 normal children, with both groups at the one-word stage. While the two groups were equally proficient at object permanence, spatial relations and imitation, the language-delayed children were significantly lower in performance on the means–end scale. Curcio (1977) reports similar findings for mute autistic children. Several investigators (e.g., Inhelder, 1966; Johnston and Ramstad, 1977; Morehead and Ingram, 1973) have noted that language-delayed children perform badly on tasks involving representation and use of symbols. For example, in the Morehead and Ingram study the language-delayed children and the normals were both able to imitate and elaborate on a game of putting a doll in a doll's bed, covering it with a blanket. But only the normals would generalize this game to putting the doll in a shoe box, covering it with a sheet of paper. And yet this group of language-delayed children (also called "childhood aphasics"—see Leonard, in press) are within the normal range for their age levels in general tests of nonverbal intelligence. **Specific** patterns of language deficiency seem to involve *specific* patterns of nonlinguistic deficits—again supporting the local homology approach to relations between language and cognition.

With retarded children, the findings are less clear. Snyder and Wood (1978) find that object permanence and language are unrelated in Down's Syndrome children, while means–end relations do correlate with degree of language deficiency. By contrast, Moore, Clark, Mael, Dawson-Myers, Rajotte, and Stoel-Gammon (1977) report significant correlations between object permanence and mean length of utterance in a sample of five Down's Syndrome children, even when the effects of age and IQ are statistically removed. However, the two studies involved very different measures of object permanence. Snyder and Wood used the traditional Uzgiris–Hunt scale, in which the same object undergoes a series of very similar disappearances. Moore *et al.* used a specially designed scale involving specific changes in the features of the objects hidden, and a variety of different hiding procedures. Though the Uzgiris–Hunt measure seems to tap delayed memory or "recall," the Moore *et al.* scale involves aspects of object "recognition" after featural changes. Insofar as naming is a recognitory activity, it should not be surprising if naming is correlated with the skills involved in object recognition. Here too we find support for the local homology approach to language–thought relations.

The cognition–communication relations reported here also receive support from phylogenetic comparisons. Recent research on sensorimotor development in primates (e.g., Chevalier–Skolnikoff, 1977; Parker, 1977) has demonstrated that tool use, imitation, and symbolic play are very poorly developed in all the higher primates but man. By contrast, object permanence can be demonstrated in a variety of nonhuman primates, all the way through the capacity to deduce invisible displacements (the stage reached by most of our children when they began to use symbols in language and in play). It can be argued that object permanence and spatial relations are widespread and phylogenetically very old functions, compared with complex object manipulations and social imitation. Under certain circumstances, chimpanzees and other higher primates are indeed capable of these latter activities—but, then, under special circumstances they are also capable of symbolic communication. We suggest that the phylogenetically recent cognitive capacities involved in imitation and tool use are the same abilities that are integrally, "locally" involved in the ontogenetic development of intentional communication via conventional signals—and, in particular, language. This does not mean that these are the **only** capacities involved in language development. For example, some form of object

permanence—if only enough to recognize that an object is the same—
must be a prerequisite to the idea that objects have names. However, as
we noted earlier, this particular homology could not show up in the
individual variation among our subjects from 9 to 13 months. Indeed, a
capacity for object recognition was well established in all our 9-month-
olds at the beginning of the study. However, the kind of object permanence that is developing around the time that language begins does not
seem to affect language development at all. It seems likely that such
knowledge of objects and their positions in space was available in the
primate line for a very long time, without making any significant impact
on the development of the symbolic capacity. In Chapter 7 we will return
to the ontogeny–phylogeny theme to explore how tool use and imitation
relate to symbol development, while object permanence and spatial
relations do not. For present purposes, we merely want to point out that
correlations in normal children, comparisons with language-deficient
children, and comparative research across species all support the view
that the same set of nonlinguistic skills are involved in the emergence of
symbols, in language and in action.

One final caveat: We have made no claims whatsoever about the role
of environmental versus genetic factors in bringing about the set of
relationships observed here. Since the communicative variables showed
such weak relationships to general locomotor development, it is unlikely
that the patterns revealed in this study are reflections of general matura-
tional factors (i.e., remote homologies of a very uninteresting sort). Also,
given the difference in patterning among the cognitive variables, it is
unlikely that these results are artifacts of "general intelligence," or of
some fairly nonspecific environmental factor such as "good mothering."
It may well be that some "specific" style of mother–child interaction is
responsible for the particular relationships observed here (see Chapter
5). If certain cognitive and communicative variables are sensitive to the
same environmental events, we would have yet another demonstration
that those variables are structurally similar. Our hypotheses are at the
level of "software," formal causal constraints in tasks internalized within
the child in the form of cognitive structures or procedures. We are
making no causal claims at either the material (e.g., hardware) or the
efficient (e.g., environmental event) level.

Appendix 3.1

Maternal Interview

I. Gestural Communication   Age of Onset

1. Does baby use his index finger to point to things that he is look-
    ing at closely (demonstrate)? At things far away? Things that
    surprise him? Any special sounds or words he makes when he does
    this? Does he look around at you to see if you are looking too?
    Any special sounds or words he uses when pointing?
2. If baby is playing with a toy or object, does he ever reach out to
    show it to you? (Demonstrate showing gesture with extended arm.)
    When did this begin? Does he only show you things he is already
    playing with, or will he go pick things up to show them?
3. Does baby ever give you things? Put them in your hand or your lap?
    Will he only give you things he's already playing with, or does he
    go pick things up just to give them to you? Will he cross the room
    to give something?
4. What does baby do if he wants something? Go and get it himself?
    If he cannot reach it, what does he do? Move toward it? Reach?
    Cry? Agitate? Any special sounds he makes when he wants something?
    Whining? Does he point at it? Does he look at you as if he ex-
    pects you to get it? Does he have any words that he uses when he
    wants things? (Ask for very explicit examples.)
5. What does baby do if you are doing something he does not like?
    Giving something he does not want? Cry? Agitate? Grunt or make
    any characteristic sounds? Shake his head? Push away or hit at
    you? Does he ever say *no* or any other words of refusal? Any
    special gestures for saying "no"?
6. Does baby every "show off" or try to be funny? How does he act when
    people are laughing? Does he laugh too? Will he repeat something
    he was doing because people smile and laugh (give example if none
    are forthcoming, e.g., Carlotta and the raspberries).

II. Language Comprehension and Production

1. What does baby do when you say *no*? Does he understand? Hesitate?
    Stop what he is doing? Or then go on?
2. Do you think he understands any (other) word? If (Daddy) is in the
    room, and you ask *Where's Daddy,* what does he do? Does he look
    around? Point? Move toward the person or thing named? If you ask
    him or tell him to find someone or something that is not in the
    room, what does he do? Point? Go to the door or look toward the
    door? Does he get excited when you name food, people, or things
    that he likes? Does he get upset if he hears words he does not
    like (for example *byebye* or *night* when he does not want to go to
    bed)? If you are looking in a book or at toys will he touch or
    point to the things you name?
    (Here the interviewer should try to draw an exhaustive list of
    words the child supposedly understand, and all mother's recollect-
    ions on when and how these began.)
3. Does baby ever "pretend" to talk without real words? (Offer example
    of pseudolanguage strings.)

4. What does he do when he hears music? "Dance" in rhythm? Try to sing?

5. Does baby know any words? (Or, if words have been previously mentioned, ask *Does he know any other words?*) If you point or show him something and ask *What is this?,* can he answer? If relevant, list all the words baby produces and when he first produced them. Elicit anecdotal evidence as far as possible concerning the circumstances in which the first wordlike sounds were used, including information as to whether these changed in usage across time. Offer the example of the word *daddy* that some children first use to indicate all men, then just for the father.

III. Play and Imitation

1. When baby plays, does he ever try to build towers, for example, with two or more blocks? Does he put things inside containers and take them out again? Can he put rings on a stick? String beads? Anything else involving two objects?

2. Have you ever noticed when baby plays that he "pretends" that one object is another one? For example, that a stick is a spoon to feed himself or dolls? That a block is a car? Does he have any "pretend" games? (Probe for extensive anecdotes.)

3. Have you ever noticed that he imitates something he's seen the day before? Games other children were playing, or other interesting actions? (Give examples if necessary.)

4. Has he ever tried to "fool" you? (If no anecdotes forthcoming, give examples.)

5. Do you remember when he first imitated a sound you made? (example: open vowel *ah*)? A syllable (example: consonant repetition *baba - gaga*)? Has he imitated whole words after you said them? If so, when was the first time?

6. Does baby imitate gestures (for example, byebye, clapping hands)? Do you remember the first time he did this? Does he now produce the gestures spontaneously? Will he wave byebye when asked, etc.? Only if asked, or spontaneously?

7. Does he like to look at books or pictures? What does he do when he does? Do you look at them together?

Categories Used in Correlations Matrix

1. Communicative Pointing (Range 0-3)
   a. Points to object and looks at adult
   b. Points to object as request
   c. Points to faraway objects
2. Showing (Range 0-2)
   a. Shows object already in hand
   b. Picks up object to show
3. Giving (Range 0-3)
   a. Gives object already in hand
   b. Picks up object in order to give it
   c. Crosses room in order to give object
4. Ritual Request (Range 0-4)
   a. Requests with ritualized sound
   b. Requests with wordlike sound
   c. Requests by pointing
   d. Requests with ritual gesture (e.g., opening and closing hand)

5. Comprehension Level (Range 0-2)
    a.   Comprehends in context of familiar routine or place
    b.   Goal-oriented understanding
6. Comprehension, number of Words
    Number of words comprehended other than "no"
7. Nonreferential Words
    Number of different nonreferential words reported
8. Referential Words
    Number of different referential words reported
9. Combinatorial Play (Range 0-6)
    a.   Empties container
    b.   Fills container
    c.   Takes rings off stack
    d.   Puts rings on stack
    e.   Builds tower or nests
    f.   Other
10. Symbolic Play
    Number of different schemes used

Appendix 3.2

Home Observation Checklist

Child_____

Session _____

Age_____

Others Present _____

_____

Behavior   Comments

(Note frequency of occurrence)

Communicative Gestures

1. Pointing to Objects
   (within arm's reach and far away)
   a. Noncommunicative Pointing
      (points to object without looking
       at adult and in nonsocial context)
   b. Communicative Pointing
      (points at object and looks at adult
       or points at object in social context,
       e.g., sitting on adult's lap while jointly
       looking at a book)
2. Showing an Object (frequency score collapses a and b)
   a. Extends arm to show object already in hand
   b. Picks up object and shows it to adult immediately
3. Giving object (frequency score collapses a-c)
   a. Gives object already in hand
   b. Picks up object and gives it to adult immediately
   c. Crosses room to give object to adult
4. Request
   a. Nonritualized request
      (stretches hand toward object out of reach; whines or fusses while
      leaning toward object)
   b. Ritualized request
      (stretches hand toward object with ritual gesture, sound, or word;
      requests object by pointing to it; requests adult aid by giving
      object to adult)
5. Refusal
   a. Nonritualized Refusal
      (e.g., pulls away from adult, pushes adult's hand away, whines
      or fusses in protest)
   b. Ritualized Refusal
      (makes ritualized gesture such as shaking head)
6. Showing Off
   a. Nonritualized Showing Off
      (repeats or initiates idiosyncratic behavior which has provoked
      laughter or comment from adults)

    b.   Ritualized Showing Off
        (repeats or initiates ritualized behavior, e.g., peekaboo gesture,
        which has provoked laughter or comments from adults)

Language

1. Comprehension
    (any behaviors which indicate that the child has understood one or
    more words by an adult)
2. Babbling
    (any consonant-vowel vocalization)
3. Nonreferential Words
    (any sound consistently made in a particular context, such as saying
    ba with every act of giving)
4. Frequency of Referential Words
    (Naming of objects or persons, including making animal sounds like
    meeow when referent is not present; also use of conventional greeting
    words like *hi* and *bye*)
5. Number of Different Referential Words

Play

1. Combinatorial Play (correlation score collapses a-e)
    a. Empties or fills container
    b. Nests one or more objects inside one another
    c. Builds tower of one or more objects
    d. Puts rings on stack or takes rings off stack
    e. Other behavior in which child combines two or more pieces
        systematically
2. Symbolic Play (correlation score collapses a and b)
    a. Pretends, using an object appropriately (e.g., talking into a toy
        telephone)
    b. Uses one object as though it were something else (e.g., talking
        into a spoon as though it were a telephone)
3. Imitation (incorporated into Uzgiris-Hunt Scale)
    a. Imitates sound which he has just heard
    b. Imitates word which he has just heard
    c. Imitates gesture which he has just seen
    d. Imitates sound, word or gesture which has occurred at least
        5 minutes earlier·

Appendix 3.3

General Scoring Criteria

If the transcripts read "behavior continues for some time," "B repeats the behavior several times," or other such ill-defined numbers, then two entries are given for that behavior.

Levels of frequency:
$$0 = 0$$
$$1 = \text{one time only}$$
$$2 = \text{more than 1, less than 5}$$
$$3 = \text{from 5 to 9}$$
$$4 = 10 \text{ or more}$$

Scoring Criteria for Discrete Behaviors

Pointing: exploratory or communicative use of index fingers. The one exception is simply putting the index finger into a hole or corner simply as a function of the object (e.g., the telephone dial).

Showing: If the baby holds out the object to the mother in a request sequence (e.g., to make her play with the telephone) but the mother does not cooperate, then this sort of showing is counted as a request-give under requests, as a show under showing.

Giving: Defined as either putting an object in the adult's hand, putting the object in the adult's lap, or depositing the object directly in front of the adult or by his hand, or throwing it intentionally in his direction (as in playing ball). Differs from offering in that contact with the object is relinquished. Hence placing the object in the adult's hand without letting go is a show.

Naming: Animal noises with referent not present, or any other naming with referent not present, is counted as a word as long as the context (e.g., obeying an adult request, like *How does the cat go?*) makes it clear that this is not a babble.

Greeting words like *hi* or *ciao* will be counted as naming. If accompanied by the appropriate gesture, that gesture counts as a ritual gesture.

Showing
off: "Repeats showing off" is entered only if the exhibition is repeated immediately after it obtains adult laughter. Later uses of the same scheme to obtain attention count as "provokes." Initiation of traditional routines for obtaining attention counts as "provokes."

Requests: Simply pulling the adult's hand or fingers in the direct effort to take an object out of the hand is not a request. However, touching the adult hand and waiting, placing the adult's hand on some object to request setting that object in motion, or pulling at an empy hand in an effort to obtain something all counts as requests. Ritual request is entered if there is no functional connection between the adult hand and the goal (e.g., a baby who regularly tugs at the adult's empty hand as a signal). Request-gives are also entered under give. Word-like sound requests are also entered under performative word.

Request with performative word differs from ritual-grunt request by the presence of consonants or consonant-vowel combinations. A sound will count as a ritual grunt (vowel only) or wordlike sound (with consonant) only if it either occurs two or more times accompanying the same function, or if M or observer note at that point that this is a regular sound used by the baby for a restricted function range.

A reach for an object out of range counts as an unritualized request even if there is no evidence of looking in the adult's face. However, a reach to successfully take an object in range is not counted as a request. If the object is in range (e.g., when baby and M are sitting very close) but the baby simply reaches and waits for M to give it, this counts as a request.

Reaches are counted as ritual gestures if there are empty open-closing grasping motions, handwaving, or other arbitrary, nonfunctional hand movements. If the baby in frustration of not obtaining an object out of reach pounds on the floor or highchair this gesture is <u>not</u> counted as a request, ritual or otherwise.

Unritualized complaining noises not accompanied by any other gestural reaching, etc., are not counted as requests. A give is counted as a request-give under the following types of evidence: a context in which some action might logically be expected by the adult (e.g., mechanical doll has stopped, or B seems to want the adult to speak in the telephone), satis-faction on the baby's part when an act is carried out, complaints and insistence when then the act is not carried out, and com-ments by the adult interpreting the give as a request (e.g., *You want me to wind it again?*). If the baby gives and then takes immediately back, this is not bounted as a request tive.

Combinatorial
  play: Acts must be successful to be counted. Efforts to build towers
           without stacking at least one block on another, efforts to fill
           a container in which object does not make it into the container,
           etc., do not count.

Babbling: Consonants or consonant-vowel combinations. Aspirations
           (h sounds) are counted as vowel only. Y sounds (*ia-ia*) count
           as consonants.

Performative
  words: Two or more instances of the same sound to fill the same non-
           naming function, or assurance by parent that this sound is
           regularly used in the same function range.
           Hi or other greeting words are placed under naming other, as
           are *boom* and other clear-cut noises used in interacting and
           semi-naming of objects.

Ritual
  gestures: Arbitrary games, routines, other movements that the child is
             highly unlikely to have produced entirely out of his own

repertoire. Includes waving hello-goodbye, clapping hands, provoking or continuing games like peekaboo, ritual refusals with clear headshaking (as opposed to simply turning the head away), handshaking with adult.

If the adult initiates a game like a peekaboo, the child's first repetition is counted as "imitates gesture" and not as a spontaneous production of a ritual gesture. If the child continues the gesture later, after some interruption, it then counts as both a ritual gesture and as deferred imitation. Ritual gestures include idiosyncratic portions of games and routines.

Refusals: If there is a vocalization during a refusal, the act is counted as an unritualized refusal (33) unless the same sound occurs at least twice in the same function range. (Same criterion as for ritualized request sounds.)

Imitation: If there is a demonstration of symbolic play and the child immediately follows suit, this counts as imitation of gesture but not as symbolic play. If the child continues the game later, this counts as deferred imitation and also as symbolic play.

Decisions concerning whether the child is imitating or simply producing his own spontaneous behaviors must be made in individual instances, based on both the amount of time elapsing between adult act and child's act, and on the degree of similarity between the two. If the child, for example, makes a sound that is somewhat similar to an adult sound, but one that might also have occurred spontaneously as a babble, this is not counted as an imitation.

Pretend
play: Pretend play with appropriate objects does not include acts which are already present in the baby's repertoire as nonplay schemes with objects (e.g., shaking or throwing), even if that act is coincidentally appropriate to the object (e.g., shaking a bell, throwing a ball). Also, if the act is virtually demanded by the properties of the object, e.g., fingering the telephone dial, this is not counted as appropriate play, even if the act is coincidentally appropriate. If the baby places real or artifical food in his mouth, sucks on the baby bottle, engages in caressing with a human figure, these acts are not counted. If he "pretend" eats with playful, nonfunctional motions (e.g., saying *ahm*, scraping fork against toy plate, feeding the observer), this is counted — e.g., using the baby bottle to feed doll or observer, caressing the doll, etc., are counted.

If the adult requests a game but does not demonstrate, this is counted as symbolic play. If the adult demonstrates and the baby follows suit immediately, this first instance is counted as imitation only. Later, similar acts initiated by the child count as symbolic play and as deferred imitation. If the child uses two schemas with the same object, e.g., feeding the doll and then hugging the doll, this is counted as two instances of symbolic play.

Appendix 3.4

Locomotor Scale

Age of Onset

1. Sits without support   _____

2. Walks with support   _____

3. Crawls (on all fours)   _____

4. Sits down by himself from a nonsitting
    position:

        with support   _____

        without support   _____

5. Stands up by himself from a nonstanding
    position:

        with support   _____

        without support   _____

6. Walks without support   _____

7. Goes up and down stairs   _____

8. Walks on his toes   _____

9. Jumps on both legs   _____

10. Goes up stairs alternating feet   _____

11. Runs   _____

Chapter 4

FIRST WORDS IN LANGUAGE AND ACTION: A QUALITATIVE LOOK

Virginia Volterra
Elizabeth Bates
Laura Benigni
Inge Bretherton
Luigia Camaioni

In the last chapter, we presented correlational results supporting the view that (*a*) language development and symbolic play are strongly related developments across a variety of measures, and (*b*) language and symbolic play enter into similar patterns of correlation with various nonlinguistic behaviors. Although the correlational method is admittedly an imprecise tool, these data support our view (and of course Piaget's) that the symbolic capacity develops simultaneously in language and in action. Indeed, we have proposed that these two developments represent two forms of naming: vocal and gestural. In this chapter, we want to reexamine the same data from a more qualitative perspective. How similar is the "content" of vocal and gestural naming? What happens to first words in these two domains in imitation, comprehension, and production? Can we relate our findings for two kinds of naming to the existing literature on the nature of first words?

At this point we enter into the middle of a lively debate on the nature of first words, a question that has interested psychologists (and for that matter, even Darwin, 1971) since the first diary studies (e.g., Stern and Stern, 1907; Leopold, 1939–1949). However, when we consider the various positions that students of child language have taken on this matter, we find ourselves faced with a curious situation. Each investigator has collected a reasonable amount of data, and when we compare the content of the various corpora, there are remarkable parallels in what children talk about. And yet many of these researchers seem to have reached very different conclusions about the data, as evidenced in two recent reviews by Bowerman (1976) and Clark (1973). One reason for the apparent disagreements is that researchers have been asking different questions of what are, in many ways, the same findings. The image that comes to mind is a jigsaw puzzle: Various sections of the puzzle are complete, but we are missing a critical frame-piece. By examining the very first words in **two** domains, gestural and vocal, we hope to provide such a frame piece—a unified starting point that has helped us to put some of the pieces together.

In the first part of this chapter we will review the positions taken by various authors on the nature of first words, discussed in terms of six dichotomies that have dominated the recent literature. Second, we will return to our own data, describing the development of symbols in five areas: language imitation, language comprehension, language production, gestural imitation, and gestural production. Third, we will compare developments in these five areas, stressing the parallels in content that we have found between vocal and gestural naming. Finally, we will take these results back to the six issues outlined in the literature review, pointing out how these different questions converge in the earliest stages of symbol development.

Previous Research on First Words: Some Basic Dichotomies

We cannot pretend to present details from the many studies now available on first words. Instead, we will summarize six basic distinctions that investigators have used to characterize early language:

1. substantive words versus function words
2. perceptual versus functional features in word meaning
3. prototypes versus features in the organization of lexical categories
4. referential versus nonreferential use of words
5. referential versus combinatorial meanings in word use
6. referential versus expressive styles in individual children

Substantive Words versus Function Words

The distinction between substantive words and function words pertains to the content or meaning of early symbols. The distinction was introduced by Bloom (1973) in a study of her daughter Allison at the one-word stage. In Bloom's terms, substantives are those words which refer to classes of objects or events that are discriminated on the basis of their perceptual features or attributes. Function words, by contrast, encode relations among these perceptually distinguished objects and events. Typically, the substantive portion of early vocabularies is comprised of names of persons or objects: *dog, shoe, car,* etc. In Bloom's records, function words include examples like *there, no, gone, away, stop,* and *more.* According to Bloom, the earliest stages involve high-frequency use of function words, while substantives (in particular object names) tend to be used less frequently and to be substituted for one another with great facility. This distinction brings to mind the so-called "pivot–open" constructions in two-word speech described by several researchers in the early 1960s (Braine, 1963; Brown, Cazden, and Bellugi, 1969; Miller and Ervin-Tripp, 1964—discussed as "operator" versus "open"). However, the pivot–open analysis was based entirely on the relative frequencies of the two types of words, and their distribution in two-word speech. By contrast, the substantive–function dichotomy pertains to the meanings of words, and their use in one-word speech.

Bloom describes a developmental sequence in which high-frequency use of function terms is gradually replaced by a much higher proportion of substantives. She suggests that this sequence is connected with cognitive development, in particular the transition into Stage 6 (i.e., representational) object permanence. This analysis is not based on cognitive tests independent of language. However, at the age at which Piaget reports a transition into Stage 6, Allison began using names of objects frequently and consistently. (Note: This argument on the basis of age norms may explain the discrepancy between Bloom's theory and our findings.) Bloom defends this coincidence between language and cognitive development by arguing that object permanence involves knowledge of the stability of objects in time and space—an ability that should contribute to recognition and labeling of objects. This is essentially the same prediction that Brown (1973) made (see Chapter 2, page 50). However, Brown noted that such recognitory object permanence is in fact a Stage IV phenomenon, occurring on the average around 8 months of age. Hence this ability is available long before children begin to name objects. Bloom seems to have combined two different aspects of object permanence: recognitory understanding at Stage IV, and the Stage VI ability to represent or recall an absent object and deduce hidden displacements. As we noted in Chapter 3, why should memory for absent objects (i.e., recall) be required to name present objects (i.e., recognition)? Our data and that of Corrigan (1975), Snyder (1975), and Curcio

(1977) indicate that there is no correlation between Stage VI object permanence and the earliest stages of speech (i.e., presentational as opposed to representational symbolizing). Furthermore, as Bowerman (1976) has pointed out, the particular developmental pattern that Allison demonstrated has not been replicated in studies of other children. Bloom's proposed connection between the substantive–function word distinction and cognitive development remains to be demonstrated.

A distinction similar to substantive–function can be found in Sinclair (1970), who divides early words into "denominations" (similar to Bloom's substantives) and "action–judgments" (i.e., function words). Sinclair also traces this distinction to cognition, to the contrast between "figurative" (static, imitative) and "operative" (transformational) thought. In contrast with Bloom's analysis, however, these aspects of cognition are seen as parallel developments **within** stages rather than sequential developments **between** stages. According to Sinclair, figurative thought leads primarily to lexical acquisition, while operative thought contributes more to the relationship structures and transformations involved in syntax. In particular, action–judgments are viewed as primitive expressions of relations among objects that will eventually develop into base grammatical relations like subject–verb–object. Nicolich (1975) takes up this theme, clearly summarized in the following quotation:

> Syntactic knowledge is of the operative type. There is no reason to suppose that knowledge of the relationships between perceptual–conceptual objects arises full blown when it is expressed syntactically. It seems plausible that early observations of relationships, such as these, should be expressed by single words referring to a fusion of what will later be separable perceptual–conceptual objects with cognitively and syntactically specifiable relations between them. In this sense "more" said when a food has been finished and another serving desired can *represent* an undifferentiated fusion of the empty dish, available food, a person capable of providing food, the speaker, and the prior assumption that the dish was previously full. The relational nature of what might be represented by single words is apparent. However, it is not syntactic knowledge at this point. When all of these relationships are known to the child and syntactically expressed, it is obvious that the meaning would be based on operative knowledge rather than figurative knowledge. The order implied by syntax does not exist in objects or words, but in their relationships as constructed by the subject. . . . The type of reference suggested for action judgments would be naturally self-limiting. A small number of such words would be expected to be learned by the child, and they would be limited to the period of time when they are useful, that is before he learns syntax [pp. 33–34].

Nicolich's own research on this question was carried out with five children between 14 and 19 months of age. Her results contrast with

Bloom's developmental claims and support Sinclair's view that denominations and action judgments are parallel developments. The total "number" of action judgments used by her sample proved to be very restricted, only 13 different forms across all five subjects. In that respect Nicolich agrees with Bloom. The number of action judgments used by each child varied with the level of symbolic development as assessed through an analysis of symbolic play (to be discussed later). However, for these five children there was no sequence like Bloom's in which use of function words preceded use of substantives. To summarize, there is ample evidence for something like a substantive–function division in early language. It is not yet clear just what this division means.

Perceptual versus Functional Features

A second distinction in the literature regards the kinds of features that children use in acquiring lexical items, and in extending their use beyond the first exemplars. This argument has focused on the distinction between "perceptual" versus "functional features." Perceptual features pertain to invariant aspects of an object or event like shape, size, color, etc. Functional features involve things that can be done to the object, and/or dynamic changes in the object (e.g., rollability of balls). This dichotomy should not be confused with the substantive–function distinction discussed above. The previous distinction dealt with entities versus relations in early word meanings. This second debate concerns the "nature" of substantives or object–event words.

Are lexical categories formed, stored, and used in the form of static perceptual invariants, or dynamic functional properties of particular objects and events? Although Clark and Nelson are viewed by other writers as opponents with regard to the respective perceptual and functional positions, it is important to note here that these two investigators have converged considerably in their most recent statements about lexical development (Clark, 1977; Nelson, 1977a). The "debate" is to some extent a pseudoissue at this point, although it is certainly cited often enough to warrant consideration here.

The perceptual–functional debate is really an argument about the nature of concept formation, viewed through early use of lexical categories. In natural language, a relatively small proportion of words serve as proper names (i.e., identifications of single individuals). Rather, most words serve to identify categories of objects, events, or relationships in which individual members are similar but not identical. The infant's problem in learning these words is to determine the nature and limits of the categories to which words differ. He must learn to identify the members of a given class, and distinguish those members from other classes. The child's rules for using a given lexical item often differ markedly from adult uses of the same word. This is evident from a variety of phenomena, including "overextension" (e.g., a child who calls all animals "kitty"), "underextensions" (e.g., the word *kitty* used only to refer to a particular cat, or to a subset of cats), and "overlaps" (e.g., use of the word *open* to refer to the action of opening a door, as well as actions like unbuttoning a coat, turning on a light, unscrewing a knob). Presumably all of these phenomena could be located in comprehension as well as production (see Dichotomy 3). Until recently, most reports have concentrated on lexical "mistakes" in production alone.

In reviewing the literature on production errors in lexical development, Clark (1973) concluded that early categorization is based primarily on perceptual similarities. Above all, early semantic features are based on shape, followed by size, sound, movement, and material, with a few examples based on taste. At least initially, color seems to be taken into account very rarely. Furthermore, Clark maintains that overextensions based on function (e.g., "rollability" of balls extended to anything else that rolls in using the word "ball") are very rare indeed.

By contrast, Morehead and Morehead (1974), and above all Nelson (1973) maintain instead that the infant first categorizes his environment on the basis of functional rather than perceptual similarities. Objects are considered equivalent (i.e., they can be named by the same word) if they can be used to complete the same actions or if they fulfill the same functions. Nelson arrived at this conclusion based on the results of a study of the first 50 words in 18 subjects:

> It is apparent that children learn the names of things they can act on, whether they are toys, shoes, scissors, money, keys, blankets, or bottles as well as things that act themselves such as dogs and cars. The common attribute of all of the most frequent early referents is that they have salient properties of change—that is they do things (roll, run, bark, meow, go and drive away) [pp. 31–32].

Note however that **Nelson is describing the objects and events that the child chooses to name** (e.g., socks and shoes rather than larger pieces of clothing). She is, then, arguing that functional features direct the child's attention to things in the world to be categorized, and motivate the first selection of lexical items for acquisition. This is not a claim about the features that are ultimately derived and used for recognition of new category members. As Bowerman (1976) documents amply in her review, production errors are indeed based almost exclusively on the more static, invariant attributes of objects—basically the list provided by Clark in her earlier review. This "debate" has led Nelson (1977a, in press) to a clarification on several counts. First, she has expanded the definition of "function" to refer essentially to "changing" as opposed to "static" features. Hence, "wetness" would be a "perceptual" feature of water, but a "functional" feature of diapers. In other words, perceptual–functional should be revised to read "trait–state," or inherent properties versus changing attributes.

Nelson reports several experiments on teaching a new lexical item to very young children, indicating that such changing features do indeed direct acquisition in the initial stages. This has led to her second clarification: Functional features determine the "acquisition" of the concept because of their strong attentional pull; after increased familiarity with the concept–word pairings available to him, the child "extends" the concept on the basis of the more reliable, repetitive, stable perceptual features. This revision has, in our view, rendered the Clark–Nelson positions much more compatible. It is also worth noting here Nelson's prediction that functional features will eventually be used to define superordinate categories (i.e., categories of use such as "vehicle"), perceptual features will be retained in categorizing lower-level lexical items (i.e., "cars"). In addition, Nelson feels that functional features will go into the formation of syntactic relations to a much greater extent than perceptual features. This is the beginning of a rapprochement between the substantive–function debate and the perceptual–functional distinction. Function words in Bloom's sense, and functional features in Nelson's sense, both merge into the relational terms that permit grammar to develop.

To summarize, the perceptual–functional debate concerning the content of word meanings has undergone a series of changes in the last few years. This "debate" may be resolved if we assume that functional and perceptual features are involved in very different aspects of lexical acquisition. Functional features (e.g., rollability) direct the child's attention to interesting objects and events whose names should definitely be learned. Perceptual features (e.g., roundness) are the stable, dependable features that form the semantic core of word meanings once the words are acquired. This resolution of a debate over the content of lexical categories leads us into a third issue, concerning the structure of lexical categories.

Prototypes and Features in Category Structure

The third distinction to be considered here also pertains to the internal structure of the categories underlying first words, in this case the distinction between prototypes versus features in the organization of word meanings. Even more than the functional–perceptual feature debate, this particular dichotomy has proven to be a false issue. Bowerman (1976) reviews an emerging debate centering around Eleanor Rosch's work on the internal structure of natural categories (e.g., Rosch and Lloyd, 1978). Rosch had proposed that natural categories are defined in terms of a prototypic or "best" member, the member that shares the greatest number of features in common with other members, and the fewest number of features in common with other categories. In adult categories, the prototype is a central tendency member that may be derived across a series of exemplars. In the categories of young children, Rosch and Mervis (1975) suggest that prototypes are usually the first exemplars that children encounter (e.g., the family dog as opposed to the publically approved "typical" dog). New instances are assigned category membership on the basis of "family resemblance" to the prototype, along a continuum from central to peripheral membership. As noted in Chapter 2, adults typically rate a "robin" as the best member of the category "bird"; parrots are acceptable birds; ostriches are downright lousy birds; bats are "a sort of bird" only under the most extenuating circumstances. At the center of the category, agreement is high. At the outer edges of the category, judgments are fuzzy and imprecise, varying from one person to another. Another characteristic of such category structure is that members can overlap with the prototype and yet share no overlap with one another. This is the essence of the "family resemblance" notion: Jane has the family eyes; Robert, the family nose; Helen (the prototype) has both the eyes and the nose. This last point marks a radical break with traditional models of classification, in which "true classes" are defined by an intersecting set of properties shared by **all** members. For example, triangles may vary in shape or size, but **all** triangles must have three and only three angles connected by a closed set of lines. This model is usually called the "criterial attribute model." There are several reasons why the prototype model (as opposed to traditional criterial definitions) has appealed to child language specialists.

First of all, the notion of organization around a prime exemplar fits nicely with examples of early child speech and subsequent overextensions: *Daddy* is the term applied to all men, *kitty* begins as a name for the family cat and becomes the word used to identify any four-legged beast or furry object.

Second, children extend their limited lexical resources to a wide and heterogeneous set of new instances in a fashion that could be paraphrased as, "I don't know what this is, but it's a sort of kitty." These instances often share little or no overlap with one another, although they may overlap with the prototypic *Daddy, kitty,* etc., via family resemblance (Bowerman, 1976).

Third, some experiments comparing overextension in comprehension versus production suggests that children have more precise definitions available for the "best" member of a class than is apparent in their overextended productions. For example, Thomson and Chapman (1975) report that children who cheerfully call all men *Daddy,* when presented with a picture of their own father and another man, are quite clear in the choice of the prime exemplar when asked, *Which one is the Daddy?* The same applies to kitty, doggie, and other overextended items. If the class of daddies were defined merely in terms of a stock set of features shared by both stimuli, there would presumably be no such bias.

Fourth, research on nonlinguistic categorization (e.g., Bruner, Olver, and Greenfield, 1966; Flavell, 1971; Vygotsky, 1962) suggests that until at least 3–4 years of age, children will sort and classify objects according to what are called "complexive groupings." In these sortings, objects are placed in the same class or group via a heterogeneous and unsystematic feature match. For example, the child may place the doll, the banana, and the car together stating *the dollie wants to eat the banana, and ride in the car.* Here car and banana share no overlap with one another; they are related only by union with "nonoverlapping features of the doll (e.g., eating, riding). This is precisely the sort of organization that Rosch demonstrates in adults, under Wittgenstein's rubric "family resemblance." The prototype is the best approximation to the "union" of the set of features that various members of the "family" or class may have. Again, this contrasts with "scientific" categories, or classes that are defined in terms of a minimum set of criterial attributes, or features that **every** member of the class must have to be a member of that class. As Piaget and a number of other researchers have demonstrated, categorization by criterial attributes is extremely difficult for children before 5–7 years of age. If children's linguistic categories were organized in terms of complexive groupings or prototypes instead of "true classes" or categories with criterial attribute definitions, the same model of category structure could be used to describe performance in both linguistic and nonlinguistic domains.

As Palmer (1978) and Rosch (1978) have noted, the opposite of a prototype organization for categories is the criterial attribute structure. **This structural issue is independent of the mode in which that organization is represented,** for example, as a list of discrete features, or as a continuous, analogue mental image. For example, the prototypic member "robin" could be stored in terms of a long list of features that share maximal overlap with other birds. Or it could be stored as an actual image of a bird that is compared with other potential birds in analogue or continuous fashion (e.g., similar to laying two slides over one another to determine the degree and areas of overlap). In either case, the category is "defined" in terms of a central-to-peripheral organization with imprecise boundaries, in which two candidates can be members of the same class by "family resemblance" to the best member, without any overlap with each other. By some historical accident many psychologists (including child language researchers) have confused prototype as a **category structure** with the issue of discrete–featural versus analogue–imagistic **representation of that structure.** It is fairly clear, for the four reasons outlined above, that the prototypic structure fits the data on early categorization better than criterial attribute structure. It is also the case that many facts in overextension, underextension, and overlap in early speech seem to reflect extension of a lexical class on the basis of one or two clear features rather than some global image. For example, Bowerman reports her daughter's use of the word *moon* to describe any object with a crescent shape—hangnails, half-cookies, a plate viewed from an oblique angle. Because researchers initially confused prototypes with mental images, they have had difficulty reconciling these different facts. However, within Rosch's model both types of data are perfectly compatible. Indeed, she has carried out several experiments demonstrating how prototypes are derived and used in artificial situations that can be defined **only** in terms of discrete features.

We are beginning to emerge from this initial confusion, and in the process many researchers have come to appreciate the power and flexibility of prototype theory in explaining a variety of findings about early word use. For example, Bates and MacWhinney (1978) have argued that grammatical categories like "subject" may be defined in terms of a coalition of family features based on a prototypic sentence subject that is both an agent and a topic. They argue that many psycholinguistic facts about the use of grammatical categories, including "fuzzy" judgments about the grammaticality of certain kinds of sentences, can be explained if this heterogeneous and "fuzzy" type of category structure is the one that people actually use in sentence processing. Similar proposals have been offered by other researchers as well (e.g., de Villiers, 1978; Lakoff, 1977). Regardless of whether this approach works for early grammar, prototype theory does seem to be a fruitful model for describing early word classes and the novel uses that children make of lexical items. The initial dichotomy between prototypes and feature models has proven to be a simple misunderstanding of Rosch's theory. This "debate" should be unpacked into two orthogonal dimensions: prototypic structure versus criterial attribute structure, and featural representation versus analogue representation.

Nonreferential versus Referential Words

A fourth distinction involves different levels of word use rather than the content or internal structure of early words. This is the distinction we introduced early (see Chapter 2, page 40) between nonreferential and referential speech. As described in Chapter 2, this dichotomy is actually a continuum in the way that words are used, from a highly restricted set of contexts for the "word game" (e.g., *Where's Daddy* is responded to by looking toward the garage door regardless of Daddy's actual location), to a relatively decontextualized set of rules for naming a class of objects in a variety of situations, (e.g., *Daddy* used to define father—or for that matter any adult male—in various contexts). Nonreferential word use does not "stand for." "substitute for," or "represent" particular referents. Instead, these sounds are merely used to accompany or participate in a narrow set of events involving those referents.

In the preceding chapter, we reported that:

1. Nonreferential speech tends to precede referential speech.
2. Levels of nonreferential speech are correlated with the later onset of true naming.
3. Nonreferential and referential speech show the same patterns of correlation with various communicative and cognitive measures.

However, the quantitative measures used in Chapter 3 necessitated a crude but arbitrary division of this decontextualization continuum into two artificial classes. A more careful qualitative look at the same data will demonstrate that the transition from one level of word use to another is gradual and continuous. The same gradual transition has been reported—albeit under different names—by a large number of authors including Carter (1975), Gruendel (1977), Bowerman (1976), Holzmann (1977), and Greenfield and Smith (1976). Some of the confusions between functional versus substantive word **classes,** and perceptual versus functional **features** may in fact be due to a failure to distinguish between referential versus nonreferential **uses** of lexical items. This issue should be clearer when we have presented all of the qualitative data from our own study.

Referential versus Combinatorial Meanings

A fifth distinction dates back to the early diary studies, described by deLaguna (1927), Leopold (1939), and others as "global" versus "differentiated" meanings for one-word speech. DeLaguna and Werner and Kaplan (1963) have argued that first words are in fact "holophrases" or diffuse and unanalyzed sentences fused together in a single unit. Greenfield and Smith (1976) refute this notion, arguing instead that the apparent diffuseness and plasticity of one-word speech results from a failure to distinguish between "referential" and "combinatorial" meanings:

> Earlier approaches to one-word speech seemed to have erred in not distinguishing the referential from the combinatorial aspects of meaning. The term holophrase expresses this error, for it implies that a word somehow "contains" a whole sentence. To earlier observers a word appeared global or holophrastic because they failed to see that this "sentential" meaning did not inhere in the word itself, but resulted from the word being systematically combined with non-linguistic elements. Of course, the "meaning" of this combination of word and situation elements differs from the referential meaning of the single word, but the nature of this difference parallels the contrast between the "meaning of a whole sentence and the referent of a single component word [p. 29].

Thus, for Greenfield and Smith, when a child says *Daddy* in one instance pointing to Daddy's shoe, and *Daddy* in another instance commanding Daddy to pick her up, the "referential" meaning of *Daddy* is the same: adult male human, perhaps this particular human with characteristics that distinguish him from other adult males. However, the "combinatorial" meaning of those expressions is located in the juxtaposition of the *Daddy* utterance with situational features (e.g., the shoe and the pointing gesture to indicate a possessive relation between Daddy and shoe, or the arms lifted upward and plaintive expression combined to request that Daddy act as agent to lift the child in the air).

Basing their analysis on combinatorial as opposed to referential meanings, Greenfield and Smith have traced the semantic functions that first words come to serve through the one-word stage. They describe a developmental sequence that proceeds from performative functions (e.g., *hi* in greeting, *mmm* in demands for any object), to functions implying a relationship between an entity and an action (agent, object, dative, state or action of agent, state or action of object), to functions implying a relationship between two entities (e.g., locatives, possessives), and finally to functions that imply a modification of an event (e.g., adverbs of manner and time). This developmental sequence is related to the other issues we have reviewed so far. The passage from performative functions to naming and relational functions seems quite similar to our distinction between nonreferential and referential speech. Also, some of the later changes in semantic function overlap considerably with the substantive–functional and perceptual–functional analyses described earlier. We are also reminded of the suggestion by Bloom, Nelson,

Sinclair, and others that functional items develop into "syntactic" relations, substantive and/or perceptually defined items develop into differentiated "lexical" structures. How do we distinguish (*a*) combinatorial versus referential **uses** of words and (*b*) **definitions** of words as inherently "functional," "relational," "perceptual," "substantive," or "denominative"? At this point, the various dichotomies have begun to collapse. For now we will leave them that way, returning at the end of the chapter when our own data are available for comparison.

Referential versus Expressive Styles

A sixth and final distinction regards a rather different dimension: the individual "style" of the infant in the acquisition and use of first words. Nelson (1973), reporting on the first 50 words of 18 subjects, reports two different styles of acqusition. "Referential" children acquire a high proportion of object names (e.g., *ball, shoes, dog*), and also seem more concerned with solitary play with objects (Starr, 1974). Expressive children tend to acquire words and idiomatic phrases that carry out particular social interactions (e.g., *mommy* and *daddy*, as well as *no, yes, want, please, stop it, go away*). Starr reports that expressive children seem to spend more time in social interaction than solitary play with objects.

The referential–expressive distinction has been criticized on a variety of grounds (see Bowerman, 1976), particularly the weakness of the criteria for dividing social versus referential uses of words. However, Rosenblatt (1975), Starr (1974), and Ramer (1976) have replicated the distinction with other samples of children. Furthermore, there is a study by Dore (1974) which, from a rather different perspective, comes up with quite similar findings. Dore noted in two subjects a very different use of intonation during early language development. One of his subjects—termed "message oriented"—had a rich intonational repertoire, patterns that were used to carry out a variety of social functions. The other infant—termed "code oriented"—used words primarily to identify and describe objects and events in the environment. The code-oriented child (corresponding to Nelson's referential children) acquired a vocabulary much more rapidly than the message-oriented child and tended to use more nouns than pronouns in his first sentences.

In Chapter 7 we will return to these different styles of acquisition for a much more detailed discussion. At this point, we want to stress the overlap between this stylistic analysis and divisions by other authors into functional versus substantive speech, referential versus nonreferential meanings, perceptual versus functional features of objects, and referential versus combinatorial aspects of meaning. Analyses of style, content, and use all revolve around some very similar phenomena.

There are several reasons why we believe we can contribute a frame piece to pull these different analyses together:

1. We have captured the antecedents of language, and the very first uses of words from 9 to 12 months.
2. While our study lacks the detail and precision of diary studies, we do have data on a larger sample of subjects than any of the preceding studies.
3. We have data not only on language production, but also on imitation and comprehension.
4. The findings on language can be compared with developments in nonlinguistic domains as well, in particular "motor naming" in symbolic play.

Progress within Domains

In Appendix 4.1, we have grouped together all the language and gestural examples for each child, proceeding from left to right presenting (*a*) language imitation, (*b*) language comprehension, (*c*) language production, (*d*) number of words, (*e*) gestural imitation and routines, and (*f*) symbolic play. Numbers from 1 through 4 to the left of each example represent the session at which that example first occurred. This appendix combines both the maternal interview examples and the instances that we actually observed in the home sessions. Because the correlations between interview and observation variables were significant (see Chapter 3), we felt justified in combining the data for this more qualitative analysis.

The results are arranged from examples for the child with the smallest number of words by Session 4 to the child with the largest number of words by Session 4. Remember that in Chapter 3 we have divided words into two groups: referential and nonreferential. In this chapter, because we want to highlight the continuity in development from nonreferential to referential use, that division has been dropped. As a result, Appendix 4.1 reflects a language production range from 0 to 36. If a word or sound underwent a change in use from one session to another (e.g., *mama* used initially as a general request, and later used only in reference to the mother), this change is noted in the contextual material provided in the Appendix. Similarly, if a word or sound underwent a clear phonological shift (e.g., *ma* becomes *mama* or *mommy)*, the change is also noted. However, despite changes in use and/or phonological expression, each word received only one count. With the data arranged in this format, it is fairly easy to observe (*a*) the progress in word use within particular domains and (*b*) the reciprocal influences among these five domains of symbol development.

The left-to-right order that we used in Appendix 4.1 makes it easier to pass from the first uses of a particular word or scheme (typically in imitation and/or comprehension) to subsequent use in spontaneous production. However, it will be more convenient to discuss the results in a slightly different order: (*a*) vocal imitation, (*b*) gestural imitation and routines, (*c*) language production, (*d*) language comprehension, and (*e*) gestural production.

Vocal Imitation

There is little of qualitative interest to report here. Basically, the development of vocal imitation (or more precisely, level of complexity of imitation) is the same sequence observed by Piaget: (*a*) imitation of familiar sounds, to (*b*) imitation of sounds not previously in the child's repertoire, through (*c*) imitation of new words. This is nothing more than a replication of the Hunt and Uzgiris findings for development of vocal imitation, based on Piaget's model. What is more interesting is that children differed markedly in the frequency and types of vocal imitations that they engaged in. We will have more to say about individual differences in the use of imitation in Chapter 7.

Gestural Imitation and Routines

Here too the developments observed from 9 to 13 months are basically a replication of Piaget's predictions, and findings by Uzgiris and Hunt. Level of complexity of gestural imitation proceeds from (*a*) imitation of familiar gestures, already in the child's repertoire, to (*b*) imitations of new gestures, but only when the child can observe his own execution of the gesture as well as the model's, (*c*) imitation of new gestural schemes even when the child cannot see his execution of the model (e.g., putting his fingers in "rabbit ear" formation behind the head), and (*d*) deferred imitation of action schemes in the absence of the model. Examples of deferred imitation are essentially the symbolic play schemes, grouped separately here under gestural production. As was the case with vocal imitation, the relative frequency and number of imitated gestural schemes and routines varies considerably from one child to another. Here too, we will postpone a discussion of individual differences in imitation to Chapter 7.

Language Production

First, we should stress again that the 9–13-month age range is a critical phase for the appearance of language. Although the children studied here ended up at very different levels of language use at the end of the research period, even the most advanced children by Session 4 were extremely limited in anything like language production in Session 1 (e.g., Subject 25: 2 words; Subject 24: 4 words; Subject 23: 2 words).

Second, a very striking aspect of this study is the enormous homogeneity or similarity in the first words used by these children. All of the first words consist of (*a*) accompaniments to action schemes that the child is applying to persons or objects (similar to action judgments or function words described earlier), and (*b*) names for persons or objects to which those schemes apply (similar to denominations or substantives on page 144). Table 4.1 summarizes all the words used by our subjects, divided into word schemes accompanying actions and word schemes referring to persons or things. Next to each entry, the number of children using that particular word or word class is noted. Many of the single examples are onomatopoeiac animal names, which occurred in the same kinds of routines with parents: labelling animals in books.

From Table 4.1 it is clear that all the children tend at the beginning of language to "talk about the same things." It is also striking, as Nelson has already noted, that the first words generally refer to small and manipulable objects. For example, among articles of clothing we find words designating items that the child is first able to take off or put on alone: socks and shoes. This provides support for Nelson's view that lexical categories tend to be formed around exemplars that undergo interesting changes of stage—although the category may not be "defined" in terms of those changes in state.

There is, as noted above, superficial resemblance between the divisions made in Table 4.1 (words accompanying action schemes versus words naming persons or objects) and Bloom's function–substantive distinction. However, the relationship is only indirect. Initially, our children used **all** these words—both words like *papa* and words like *bye*—as procedures, or portions of a complex action scheme. In almost all instances, words used in the first sessions occurred in extremely restricted contexts, when the child applied a certain routine action. In the last session, the same terms (or new terms) were applied instead on a much wider variety of contexts, linked primarily by the presence of a particular class of referent objects or events. Words like *mama* and *papa* are particularly significant examples. *Mama* was frequently used at the beginning as a lament or a general request (see S 4, Session 3; S 18, Session 1). Papa was used exclusively in specific situations or games that were associated only with the father (see *papa* in S 21, Session 2, pronounced only when he hears the sound of the door; or *dada* in S 20, Session 1 to request being picked up, and/or in a game of taking father's pen from his pocket). In the last sessions we find the same words used to name or call the mother or father only (S 4, Session 4, and S 18, Session 2, for *mama;* S 21 in Session 4, and S 20, Session 3, for *papa*).

This is, then, a replication of the phenomenon discussed in Chapter 2, the passage from nonreferential to referential use. This passage is not restricted to names of persons and objects. For example, the expression *che e* ("What's that") was used initially by S 14, Session 2 only while playing on the telephone. By Session 3, the same sound was used in response to sounds coming from the front door. By Session 4, the child used *che e* whenever she responded to something new. Similarly, S 10, Session 2 produced *bye* only while putting down the telephone receiver; by Session 4 he used it whenever anyone left the room or the house. In other words, the division in Table 4.1 between words designating schemes versus words designating people contains within **both** categories a passage from language games in narrowly defined action schemes, to language games in a broader contextual range.

Thus, the developmental sequence that we propose for all the words on the basis of our production data is the following:

1. The child uses words to accompany action schemes, as procedures at a narrowly defined point in a given context (e.g., *papa* in going toward father as he enters the door; *bye* while putting down the telephone receiver).
2. The child uses words to "anticipate" or "remember" these same schemes (*papa* in anticipation of father's appearance; *bye* prior to playing with the telephone; *bam* before playing the piano, in example from Chapter 2).
3. The child uses words to designate or name action schemes (which can be carried out either by himself or by others), and to designate the agents and objects of action schemes (*papa* to call or name or request something from father; *bye* when either he or others are talking on the telephone).

TABLE 4.1
Types of Words Produced[a]

	Action words
Greetings (14):	**Affirmation (2):**
Bye	Yes
Byebye baby	Si (= yes)
Chi e (= who's there)	
Hi	**Requests (20):**
Ta-ta (ciao = bye)	numerous consonant-vowel sounds
Tao (ciao = bye)	
	Refusals (12):
Telephone greetings (9):	Ah
Ah	Hmm
Apo (pronto = Hello)	Mm
Bye	Na, nanana
Byebye baby	Nene
Che e (= what's there)	No
Chi e (= who's there)	Pfff
Da	Uh-uh
Hello	
Hi	**Object Manipulation (6):**
Ponto (pronto = Hello)	Ba-ba
Ya	Chetta (questo = this)
	Oh
	Ta-ta
	Whatha (what's that)
Exchange (12):	**Kiss/Cuddle (4):**
Bah/dah	Caa (cara = dear)
da (= give)	Kiss
Dadu (thank you)	Ma
Ga (got)	Nanna, ninna (= rockabye)
Grazie (= thanks)	
Hey woo (hey you)	**Hide (6):**
Please	Cuccutete (cucusettete = peekaboo)
Ta, te, tie (tieni = take)	Dee (there)
Tazie (grazie = thanks)	Peek
	Pu (non c'e piu = allgone)
	Tetete (cucusettete = peekaboo)

Action words

Indication (5):
Da (there)
Look
Pe, Pee (pretty)
See
That

Warning (3):
Bada (= careful)
Bua (Italian baby word = hurt)
Hot

Read/Write (3):
Ba (book)
Write
Lalala (while reading book)

Other (4)
Haha (surprise)
More
Up
Whee (excitement)

Throw down (2):
Boom
Uh-oh (singsong intonation)

Persons, animals, and things

Persons

Mother (17):
Ma, mamma
Mommy, Mom
1 personal name

Siblings (5):
Ba (brother)
4 personal names

Father (20):
Babbo
Da, dada, daddy
Eda
Pa, papa
2 personal names

Other Children (7):
Bebe (*bambini* = children)
8 personal names

Grandmother (6):
Gnagna (= grandmother,
Grandma, grandmama
Nonna (= grandmother)

Self (3):
Bebe
Butch
Good girl

(continued)

TABLE 4.1 (continued)

Persons, animals, and things

Grandfather (2):
Nonno (= grandfather)
1 personal name

Aunt (2): Zia (= aunt)

Uncle (1): Zio (= uncle)

Babysitter (3):
Tata (= nurse)
1 personal name

Animals

Family Dog (6):
Ba
Bow-wow
4 personal names

Dogs (5):
Ba, baba
Bow-bow, Bow-wow
Boo, Bubu
Gog
Dog

Cats (8):
Ca
Gaga
Kitty
Mao

Ducks (4):
Duck
Quaqua
Pepe (specific duck)

Cows (4):
Mm
Moo, Muh
Mucca

Horses (3):
Opop
Tch-tch

Other Animals (8):
Beh (sheep)
Birdie
Chuchu (= pig)
Coco (chioccia = hen)
Cra (= frog)
Hiho (= donkey)
Kiki (chicchirichi = Cockadoodle doo)

Persons, animals, and things

Things

Food (14):		Clothing (3):	
	Ahm		*Bee* (beads)
	Caee (candy)		*Pappe* (*scarpe* = shoes)
	Cookie		*Socks*
	Mm		
	Mpa	Doll (5):	
	Pappa (Italian baby word for food)		*Baby*
	Toto (toast)		*Bamba, bimba* (*bambola* = doll)
	Yum		*Ndee-ndee* (baby)
			Tata
Drinks (6):			
	Acca (*acqua* = water)	Bell (8):	
	Acqua (= water)		*Ba, Ba-ba*
	Appa (*acqua* = water)		*Ball*
	Ba (cup)		*Boom*
	Bumba (Italian baby word for drink)		*Palla* (= ball)
	Juice		
	Mm (milk)	Flower (1):	
			Haha (derived from sniffing)
Vehicles (6):			
	Aeo (*aereo* = airplane)	Cigarette (1):	
	Brrr, brrrm, Brr-brrr		*Fiu*
	Ga (car)		
	Hoo (airplane)	Hairdryer (1):	
	Voom, vroom, vrmmm		*Ffff*
Pictures (2):		Pacifier (1):	
	Tweetie (poster)		*Cucco* (*ciuccio* = pacifier)
	Picture		

[a]Numbers in parentheses indicate number of children producing words in this class. Note that occasionally the number of words produced exceeds the number of children producing the class of words, since one child may produce several words in one class.

4. The child uses words to "categorize" new persons, objects, and events within a much broader range of contexts (e.g., *papa* to designate men he sees for the first time; *bye* used when someone enters or leaves the room, leaves by the front door, or carries some object away).

This progression can be characterized as a general tendency toward "decontextualization," essentially a broadening of the **range** of contexts in which a word can be used, and the **temporal point** in a given context at which the word can occur. This decontextualization characterizes the earliest stages in word use. It should be distinguished from later stages in word use that involve overextension and overlap "errors." Such errors in categorization would, in our framework, be typical only of the fourth level in the development of reference. In fact, the most important development in later phases probably involves learning to **limit** the contextual range of a word back into norms corresponding to adult use.

Language Comprehension

The same phenomenon of progressive decontextualization that characterized language production can also be seen in comprehension. The child passes from a type of comprehension that is highly ritualized, or tied to a specific situation, to a type of comprehension that covers a variety of situations. We discussed this sequence in Chapter 2 in the light of our earlier work and that of other investigators (e.g., Huttenlocher, 1974). The decontextualization phenomenon clearly replicates in the comprehension examples in this study. For example, S 24, Session 1, shows examples of comprehension only in stereotyped routines (e.g., in response to *Where are your little thoughts?*, she touches her head). By the fourth session, the same child correctly brings a variety of objects to several receivers upon request. A particularly clear example is in S 20, who understands the word *dolly* in Session 2 apparently in reference only to a particular doll. By Session 4, she would bring any doll to the experimenter upon request.

The comprehension findings in our study are fairly imprecise. A better understanding of how and when decontextualization occurs will require much more detailed case histories of words in individual children, both in production and comprehension (e.g., Gruendel, 1977). We will say more about methods in the study of language/context relations later on in the book, under general considerations for future research (Chapter 6).

Symbolic Play

Of all the manifestations of symbol use described here, gestural production in symbolic play is the hardest to define. We struggled with the problem of defining and operationalizing symbolic play in Chapter 2. Under the definitions we provided, the child may be subjectively engaged in gestural "naming" either by selecting a conventional gesture associated with a particular object–event (e.g., putting a phone receiver to his ear), or by selecting and reproducing an action that looks much more like his usual sensorimotor manipulations of the same object (e.g., shaking the receiver and cord). If we had direct access to the child's mind, we might be able to distinguish symbolic versus nonsymbolic uses of these later, sensorimotor schemes. But we do not. **We can be comfortable in inferring symbolic use of a gesture only when the gesture looks like it could not have been discovered accidentally in the course of object manipulation.** For that reason, we have classified actions as symbolic play in this study only when the physical form of the action must have been derived through imitation of a "conventional" pattern. If the child puts a receiver to his ear, we can be reasonably certain that this gesture is not just a by-product of exploring the object's physical properties. However, if the child sticks his finger in the inviting holes of the telephone dial, the act could be simple exploration rather than reproduction of the social convention of dialing. In Chapter 3, correlations of symbolic play with other variables are based on a conservative estimate of symbol use, classifying as "symbolic" only those gestures which were quite unlikely to arise out of sensorimotor exploration. In the examples reported in Appendix 4.1 we were somewhat less conservative. Questionable instances of conventional gestures were included when they seemed to lead to or accompany clearer instances of symbolic play with the same objects.

We based our qualitative analysis of gestural production on recent work by Nicolich (1975), which extends Piaget's (1962) observations into more precise classifications of play from 9 to 24 months. The use of Nicolich's scheme seemed warranted on several counts. Her method of data collection was very similar to ours: a longitudinal study, with children observed in the home in the presence of their mothers. The children were videorecorded in play with a variety of objects similar to the toys used in our study. Finally, although Nicolich continued her observations through 24 months, the ages and levels of linguistic production of her five subjects were, at the beginning of her study, similar to ours.

Table 4.2 summarizes the Nicolich taxonomy. The first level includes

TABLE 4.2
Sequence of Symbolic Levels According to Piaget[a]

Nicolich levels and criteria	Examples
Sensorimotor Period	
1. Presymbolic Scheme: The child shows understanding of object use or meaning by brief recognitory gestures. No pretending. Properties of present object are the stimulus. Child appears serious rather than playful.	The child picks up a comb, touches it to his hair, drops it. The child picks up the telephone receiver, puts it into ritual conversation position, sets it aside. The child gives the mop a swish on the floor.
2. Autosymbolic Scheme: The child pretends at self-related activities. Pretending. Symbolism is directly involved with the child's body. Child appears playful, seems aware of pretending.	The child simulates drinking from a toy baby bottle. The child eats from an empty spoon. The child closes his eyes, pretending to sleep.
Symbolic Stage I	
3. Single Scheme Symbolic Games Child extends symbolism beyond his own actions by:	
A. Including other actors or receivers of action, such as doll or mother.	Child feeds mother or doll (A) Child grooms mother or doll. (A) Child pretends to read a book. (B) Child pretends to mop floor. (B) Child moves a block or toy car with appropriate sounds of vehicle. (B)
B. Pretending at activities of other people or objects such as dogs, trucks, trains, etc.	

4. Combinatorial Symbolic Games
4.1 Single Scheme Combinations: One pretend scheme is related to several actors or receivers of action.

    Child combs own, then mother's hair.
    Child drinks from the bottle, feeds doll from bottle.(4.1)
    Child puts an empty cup to mother's mouth, then experimenter, and self (4.1)

4.2 Multischeme combinations: Several schemes are related to one another in sequence.

    Child holds phone to ear, dials.
    Child kisses doll, puts it to bed, puts spoon to its mouth. (4.2)
    Child stirs in the pot, feeds doll, pours food into dish (4.2)

5. Planned Symbolic Games: Child indicates verbally or nonverbally that pretend acts are planned before being executed.

5.1 Planned Single Scheme Symbolic Acts
Transitional Type: Activities from levels 2-3 that are planned.

    Child finds the iron, sets it down, searches for the cloth, tossing aside several objects. When cloth is found, she irons it. (5.1)
    Child picks up play screw-driver, says "tooth-brush" and makes the motions of toothbrushing. (5.1)

Type A. Symbolic identification of one object with another.

Type B. Symbolic identification of the child's body with some other person or object.

5.2 Combinations with Planned Elements: These are constructed of activities from Levels 2-5.1, but always include some planned element. They tend toward realistic scenes.

    Child picks up the bottle, says "bab," then feeds the doll and covers it with a cloth (5.2)

    Child puts play foods in a pot, stirs them. Then says "soup" or "Mommy" before feeding the mother. She waits, then says "more?" offering the spoon to the mother. (5.2)

---

a From Nicolich, 1975.

brief recognitory gestures, "enactive naming" such as putting a phone receiver to the ear. These are distinguished from later acts primarily by their brevity and lack of playfulness. Level 2 consists of re-enactment of the child's own behaviors (e.g., pretend sleeping). Level 3 schemes are role reversals, in which the child takes on another's role (pretend cooking) or applies his own role to another receiver (putting the dolly to bed). Levels 4.1 and 4.2 involve sequential applications of the same scheme to different objects, or different schemes to the same object. At Level 5, the child engages in planned and appropriate sequences of schemes within conventional cultural "scripts" (e.g., feeding sequences that are roughly accurate from start to finish). Finally, the last levels involve substitutions of abstract objects for realistic ones.

For the most part the categories were relatively easy to apply although we had some difficulty with the brevity criterion for Level 1. Table 4.3 presents our data grouped by types of actions (e.g., feeding sequences) within the Nicolich categories. Just as the linguistic vocabularies of our 24 children were very similar, note that the symbolic play "vocabularies" also show a great deal of overlap from one child to another. Although the frequency and absolute number of gestural schemes varies across children, all of our subjects were drawing from the same stock of conventional actions.

Though Nicolich's **categories** fit our data, we did not find the same **sequence** among those categories. Table 4.4 contains the symbolic play levels reached by each of our children according to the Nicholich system. All of our subjects produced examples classifiable at least at Level 2 (such as pretend sweeping). Most of the children reached Levels 3A or 3B (pretending at the activities of others), almost a third attained Level 4.1 (single schemes with a series of objects or actors), and only three produced very marginal instances of Level 4.2 (related schemes with the same object). We have too few examples of Level 4.2 to draw any firm conclusions about the equivalence of Levels 4.1 and 4.2. Note, however, that almost half the sample performed planned symbolic acts of the transitional type, that is planned schemes of Type 3A and 3B but with inappropriate objects (Level 5.1). Nicolich regards play with inappropriate objects (such as playing telephone with a spoon) as a much higher form of symbolic play than Levels 4.1 and 4.2 (multischeme combinations performed with realistic objects). Given that some of the children in our sample first applied simple pretend schemes to inappropriate objects (Level 5.1) during the same session or even before they produced multiple-scheme combinations of Type 4.1 we propose the following, tentative revision of the Nicolich scale:

1.   The child recognizes appropriate use of an object by carrying

TABLE 4.3
Gestural Conventions Grouped According to Nicolich Levels (See Table 4.2)

1. Presymbolic schemes: The child recognizes the appropriate use of objects with a brief gesture

   Putting on necklace (9)[a]
   Placing telephone receiver against ear (7)
   Rocking to music (6)
   Pushing cars or objects with wheels (3)
   Putting empty cups, silverware, or artificial food to lips (3)
   Rubbing silverware against empty plate (2)

2. Autosymbolic schemes: The child pretends to carry out a self-related activity

   Pretending to drink (19)
   Pretending to eat (11)
   Pretending to sleep (9)
   Pretending to comb hair (6)
   Pretending to dress (2)
   Pretending to wash (2)

3. Single-scheme games with other-related activities

   A. Other agents or patients take on the child's role
      Kissing, cuddling, hugging dolls etc. (19)
      Giving food and drink to dolls, etc. (17)
      Dressing or undressing dolls, etc. (10)
      Putting dolls to sleep (4)
      Combing or washing dolls, etc. (3)
      Making others telephone (1)

   B. Carrying out the activities of others
      Pretending to telephone (15)
      Pretending to read or write (5)
      Pretending to clean (household chores) (4)
      Drives car (2)
      Cooks (2)
      Puts on lipstick (1)
      Other adult actions (gardening, carpentry) (6)

4. Multiple schemes (without planning)

   4.1 Combinations of single schemes: One scheme applied to a series of agents or patients
       Giving food or drink to serveral recipients (6)
       Combing several dolls or persons (2)
       Making dolls or persons kiss each other (1)

   4.2 Multischeme combinations
       Scrapes fork on plate, then eats (1)
       Pretends to paper wall, imitating brush movements and then feeling for lumps (1)
       Brushes doll's hair while feeding doll (1)

5. Planned symbolic games

   5.1 Planned single-scheme symbolic acts transitional type:
       Pretending to dress with inappropriate objects (4)
       Telephoning with inappropriate objects (3)
       Pretending to drink with inappropriate objects (3)
       Pretending to eat with inappropriate objects (2)
       Pretending to sleep using inappropriate pillows, etc. (2)
       Pushing an object without wheels in vehicle fashion (2)
       Hugging or cuddling nonsocial objects (1)
       Feeding others with inappropriate objects (1)

[a]Numbers in parentheses indicate number of children showing the behavior.

TABLE 4.4
Comparison between Number of Words Produced and Level of Symbolic Play[a]

Subject	Nationality	Sex	Number of words	Symbolic Play Levels demonstrated				
1	American	M	0	2				
2	Italian	M	2	2	3A			
3	I	F	2	2	3A			
4	I	M	2	2	3A			
5	A	F	4	2	3A-B			
6	I	F	5	2	3A-B			
7	A	M	5	2	3A-B			5.1
8	I	F	7	2	3A			
9	A	F	8	2	3A		4.2	
10	A	M	8	2	3A			
11	A	M	10		3A-B			
12	A	F	10	2	3B			5.1
13	I	M	11	2	3A-B			
14	I	F	11	2	3A-B			5.1
15	A	M	12	2	3A-B		4.2	
16	A	F	14	2	3A-B	4.1		5.1
17	A	F	14	2	3A-B			5.1
18	I	F	15	2	3A-B			5.1
19	A	F	15	2	3A-B	4.1		5.1
20	A	F	15	2	3A-B	4.1	4.2	5.1
21	I	M	18	2	3B			
22	I	M	20	2	3A-B	4.1		5.1
23	A	M	20	2	3A-B	4.1		5.1
24	I	F	22	2	3A-B	4.1		5.1
25	I	F	36	2	3A-B	4.1		5.1

[a] According to Nicolich, 1975.

out a brief "motor naming" of the object (e.g., putting the receiver briefly to the ear).

2. The child plays at carrying out actions that are an actual part of his repertoire (e.g., pretend sleeping).
3. A: The child pretends to carry out actions with other people in which the child's own role is reversed (e.g., the child feeds the doll).

B: The child pretends to carry out actions that are typically associated with the activities of others. In other words, he takes on the adult role (dusting or vacuuming).

4. The child plays at carrying out actions with "inappropriate" objects for those actions (e.g., playing telephone with a spoon or eating with a stick).

5.1. The child applies a play scheme sequentially to a series of different agents or objects (e.g., feeding Mommy, then the experimenter, then the dolly)

5.2. The child applies a sequence of different, related schemes to the same realistic object (e.g., washing, feeding, and putting the dolly to bed).

This revised sequence corresponds roughly to observations by Inhelder, Lezine, Sinclair, and Stamback (1971). The Piagetians prefer to reserve the term "symbol" for performances in which schemes are carried out with a substitute object. It does not seem useful or necessary for us to draw such an arbitrary line across what appears to be a smooth progression in the way that schemes are used. **In fact, we believe that this progression represents the same process of decontextualization that we discussed earlier with regard to language production and comprehension.** The application of the play scheme to increasingly abstract objects (e.g., literal phone receiver, to spoon) suggests that the child needs progressively less contextual support to play the same game. Furthermore, the role reversals suggested in Levels 3A and 3B show a similar flexibility, a break from the narrow rules of the original game in which the gesture was derived. Finally, the combinations of schemes in Levels 5.1–2 show still more flexibility, in which the rules for using schemes are defined in terms of each other rather than the strongly constrained contexts in which each individual scheme was acquired. Nicolich notes that, by 24 months of age, "planned" sequences begin to predominate. For example, bathing the doll always precedes putting the doll to bed. In other words, "decontextualized" play schemes begin to be "recontextualized" with respect to one another, placed into a plan structure very similar to the "scripts" discussed by Schank and Abelson (1975). (See Nelson, 1977, for an extension of script theory to early child language and play.) One of the most interesting aspects of Nicolich's study is the finding that such planned play sequences begin at the point where syntactically structured multiword utterances predominate in the child's speech. Hence "syntax" seems to appear simultaneously in language and in play. That brings us to our next point, a comparison among the five domains of symbol development.

Relationships among the Five Domains

Comprehension versus Production

In this study, we had no means of assessing the comprehension of conventional gestures. Hence our discussion of the role of comprehension must be restricted to language. Not surprisingly, our findings support the common observation that comprehension precedes production. An examination of the Appendix uncovers numerous examples in which a word appears in language comprehension, and one or two sessions later enters into the child's productive vocabulary. For example, S 11 seems to understand *kitty* and *byebye* in Session one, and produces both spontaneously in Session 4. S 17 in Session 1 responds to her dog's name by looking around the room; in Session 4 she calls him by the same name. The same thing happens with S 16 for the word *cat,* understood in Session 3 and produced in Session 4. S 20 responds to *bye* in Session 2 by waving, and actually says *bye* while waving in Session 4. S 18 plays an Italian form of peekaboo in response to *facciamo cucusettete* in Session 2; in Session 3 she says *cucutete* during the same game. S 19 from Session 1 seems to understand both *hot* and *bye;* she produces them in the 2nd and 3rd sessions, respectively. S 22 understands *where's Anna, where's Mamma,* and *where's Grandma* in Session 2, demonstrated by pointing to the correct person. In Session 3 he calls his mother, in Session 4 he calls both *Anna* and *Grandma* by name.

The relationship between comprehension and production seems to be related not so much to the phonetic form of the word, but to the particular referents and situations of use. For example, in Session 2, S 5 responds to *where's (dog's name)?* by turning and looking for the dog. In Session 3 she names the dog, but uses the word *bowbow.* Even when the same word is involved in both comprehension and production, in many cases the child's reproduction differs markedly in phonological structure from the adult version. If comprehension does play a facilitative role in language production, we suggest that comprehension directs the child to particular games and essentially teaches him how to play. When production finally begins within those games, the child may already know enough about the "script" to lexicalize portions that are quite different from the ones that got him interested in the first place.

In sum, comprehension tends to precede production, and there is considerable overlap between the word meanings that are expressed and understood from 9 to 13 months. These qualitative findings are consistent with our correlational results in Chapter 3, indicating strong correlations between comprehension and production.

Imitation in Both Comprehension and Production

The correlational results in Chapter 3 suggested that imitation is related to the production of symbols, in play and in language. Our qualitative results on language and gestural imitation are limited, but generally consistent with the qualitative findings. We again find considerable overlap in content, with the same meanings appearing in imitation, comprehension, and production. The evidence on developmental sequencing is much less clear.

Let us begin with a comparison of vocal imitation and language comprehension. In the first session, S 1 apparently understood *where's daddy;* in Session 3 he imitated *dada* (i.e., uttered that sound immediately after an adult model, with no clear intention to use the word appropriately as a name or a portion of an understood routine). In Session 2, S 6 seemed to understand *mamma,* and she also reproduced it in imitation. By Session 4, *mamma* was part of her productive vocabulary. S 6 also understood *ciao* in Session 3, and imitated it in Session 4. S 19 both understood and imitated *daddy* from the first session, with spontaneous use appearing in Session 2. From examples like these (many more can be found in Appendix 4.1), it appears that children often imitate words that they already seem to comprehend in earlier sessions, or in the same session. It does not appear to be the case that imitation marks the very first notice of a word, preceding any sign of comprehension. In short, children tend to imitate familiar words, at least in this age range.

The same conclusion is upheld by the data comparing imitation and production. In the above examples, *mamma* (S 6) and *daddy* (S 19) were understood and imitated in the same session, but were not produced spontaneously until much later. This is a very common pattern. *Hi* and (*dog's name*) were imitated by S 14 in Sessions 2 and 3, and produced in Sessions 3 and 4. S 25 imitated *papa* and *zia* (aunt) in the first session, producing both in the third. The same child imitated *pappa* (shoes) in Session 2 and produced it in Session 4. If we found nothing but examples like these, we would reach the familiar conclusion that imitation precedes and perhaps facilitates production.

However, we also have a few cases in which the child imitates words that have already appeared in his spontaneous repertoire. For example, S 17 produces *dada* in Session 2, but imitates the same word immediately after an adult model (with no obvious communicative intent) in Session 3. In Sessions 3 and 4, S 1 imitates a series of words that she clearly comprehends and uses spontaneously, including *papa* (=quaqua, food) and *pappa* (food). Finally, there are a number of cases in which the same word is both imitated and produced for the first time in the same session, including *opop* (S 2, Session 2), *bye* (S 10, Session 2), *bamba* (doll—S 13, Session 4), and *goodgirl* (S 20, Session 4). In short, all possible combinations occur: Imitation precedes, follows, and coincides with production.

What do we conclude from this? In contrast with the relatively clear sequencing from comprehension to production, imitation seems to occur at any point in the process of lexical acquisition, at least in this age range. But notice that imitation almost always involves the **same** meanings that occur in all other forms of language use. There is no evidence to support the view that children imitate completely unfamiliar or discrepant sounds. Instead, they seem to imitate words that have already become familiar, in comprehension if not in production. Piaget has proposed that, toward the end of the first year, children pass from a stage of imitating only familiar schemes to a stage of imitating novel schemes. Our data suggest that this stage model must be modified. From 9 to 13 months, children do **not** seem to imitate novel speech—even though they show all other signs of being in Stages 5 or 6, when novel imitations should be relatively easy. The problem lies, of course, with our definitions of "novel" and "familiar." Imitation seems to be reserved for words that are **relatively** new, in the process of being acquired—a rehearsal of things that are already "under study." Since Piaget examined imitation only as compared with spontaneous production, he may have missed the fact that children's language imitations tend to involve material that is at least relatively familiar in comprehension.

Similar patterns occur for the relationship between gestural imitation and gestural production. Again, we find all possible sequences. In some cases the children imitate actions which they already produce spontaneously. For example, S 9 pushes a little car across the rug in Session 2; in Session 4 she carries out the same gesture immediately after seeing the adult push the car. In other cases, children imitate a gesture in one session but do not produce it spontaneously until much later. For example, S 17 imitates bringing a toy plate to her mouth in Session 3; in Session 4 she carries out a similar gesture without an adult model. Note, however, that while the sequence from imitation to production may vary, there is considerable overlap in content between these two aspects of gestural development. As was the case for vocal imitation, gestural imitation is certainly not reserved for completely unfamiliar acts.

Language and Symbolic Play

In Chapter 3, we reported significant positive correlations between various quantitative measures of language and symbolic play. Furthermore, these two types of symbolic activity enter into very similar patterns of correlations with other cognitive capacities. Both are correlated with tool use and manipulative play, and with imitation. Neither are correlated with spatial relations and object permanence. Finally, both types of symbol use seem to relate to preverbal communication with gestural and vocal conventions. In this section, we want to examine this relationship further, comparing both the content and the qualitative structure of language and symbolic play.

Table 4.4 lists our subjects in order from those with the smallest total number of productive words (both referential and nonreferential) to those with the largest number of words. In addition, Table 4.4 presents the highest level of symbolic play reached by each child, according to the revised version of the Nicolich scale we reported on page 164. A glance at this table indicates that the children who are advanced in language are indeed generally more advanced in play. (Note: These are not the same measures reported in Chapter 3, although the quantitative patterns are the same. The two new measures correlate with each other both within and across sessions, and enter into similar patterns of relations with the cognitive and communicative measures. See Chapter 5 for more details.)

Once again we find a remarkable overlap in "content," in this case between vocal versus gestural naming. Table 4.5 summarizes the "vocabularies" for these two types of naming. In the left hand column, we report the kinds of conventional actions used by the children in their primitive symbolic play and communication. These include greetings, telephone play, food games, doll care games, dressing and undressing, and imitations of adult activities like cleaning and vacuuming. Next to each class of gestures we list the number of children who demonstrated some token of that class. In the right-hand column, we have listed words used by children in our sample which correspond directly to the same action schemes—greeting and goodbye words, words associated with telephones, food, doll care, adult activities. Here too we list the number of children demonstrating at least one word within that class. **What is particularly striking about this table is that the two "vocabularies" are virtually the same.** There are a few actions that have no corresponding words. Also, the large class of proper names in the children's vocabularies are not clearly associated with a class of gestures. It is certainly the case that all of these children did associate particular activities with particular people (e.g., some children prefer to be fed by the mother). Hence the word–action relationship applies there as well. But since the idiosyncratic actions associated with various individuals were not the clear, conventional sort that characterize the gestural naming classes in Table 4.5, they are excluded from this analysis.

TABLE 4.5
A Comparison of Gestural and Vocal Vocabularies (Number of Subjects with Such Schemes in Parentheses)

Gestural		Vocal	
Waving hello/goodbye	(5)	*Hi*	(5)
		Bye	
		Byebye Baby	(9)
		Tao (ciao)	
		Ta-Ta	
Placing phone to ear only	(5)	*Hello, Hi, Ah*	
		Che e (who's there)	
Other phone schemes	(15)	*Chi e* (who's there	(9)
Making others phone	(1)	*Apo, pronto* (speaking)	
		Bye, byebye baby	
Cuddling, hugging, kissing	(19)	*Kiss*	
Pretending to sleep	(9)	*Cara* (dear)	
Making others sleep	(4)	*Nanna, Ninna* (Rockabye)	(2)
Empty containers,		*Appa, Acqua, Acca*	
utensils, to lips	(3)	*Juice*	*(5)*
		Bumba, Ba	
		Ahm, Yum, Mm, Mpa	
		Pappa	(13)
Pretend drinking	(19)		
Pretend eating	(11)	*Cookie*	
Making others eat, drink,		*ToTo* (toast)	
take child's pacifier	(17)	*Cucco* (pacifier)	(1)
		Caee (candy)	(1)
		Mm (milk)	(1)
Put on necklace	(9)		
Pretending to dress	(2)	*Bee* (beads)	(1)
Dressing or undressing doll	(10)	*Socks*	
		Pappe (shoes)	(1)
Pushing cars or other objects			
in vehicle motion	(5)	*Vrmmm*	(3)
		Brrr	(3)
		Ga (truck)	(1)
		Aereo (plane)	(1)
Sniffing flowers or other			
objects	(1)	*HaHa* (sniff noise)	(1)
Pretending to read or			
write	(5)	*Ba* (book)	(1)
		Write	(1)
		Lalala (reading)	(1)
Hiding games, peekaboo	(10)		
		Cucutete	
		Tetete	
		Dee (there)	(4)
		Peek	
		Pu (allgone)	(2)

(continued)

TABLE 4.5 (continued)

Gestural			Vocal	
Giving, Taking	(25)	*Da*		
		Ta, te, tie (take)		
		Bah/Dah		
		Grazie (thanks)		(21)
		Please		
		Dadu (thank you)		
		Ga		
		Hey woo (hey you)		
Communicative pointing	(22)	*Da* (there?)		
		See		
		Pe (pretty)		(5)
		Pee (pretty)		
		That		
		Look		

We should stress that these parallels emerge only when we construct vocabularies **across** children. It was **not** the case that each child who had an entry in gestural naming had an equivalent entry in vocal naming. As a matter of fact, such double entries were fairly rare, suggesting the hypothesis that in the early stages one name per activity (either a gestural or a vocal name) is enough for the child's purposes in identifying, recognizing, or classifying situations by a referential act. However, on the basis of the parallels in content that we do find across children, we feel justified in concluding that these children are talking about the same things whether in the gestural or the vocal mode.

In addition to these remarkable parallels in content, we also find similarities in levels and sequences of development between these two domains. At the end of the respective sections on language production and on symbolic play, we summarized the findings with some proposed "stages" (using that term in its loosest sense). If we set these two proposed sequences alongside each other, the parallels become obvious:

1. The child recognizes the appropriate use of an object by briefly carrying out an associated activity.

1. The child uses a word as a procedure or part of a routine or game.

2. The child "pretends" to carry out his own familiar activities (e.g., sleeping) outside of its usual context (i.e., temporal decontextualization).

2. The child uses a word to anticipate or remember the scheme with which it is typically associated (i.e., temporal decontextualization).

3. The child "pretends" to carry out his own familiar activities outside of their usual context (i.e., decontextualization through role reversal).

4. The child carries out actions with objects that are inappropriate, or related quite abstractly to the original object (i.e., reference with decreased contextual support).

3. The child uses words to designate actions carried out by himself or others, or to designate the agents or objects of such actions (i.e., decontextualization through role reversal).

4. The child uses words to categorize new persons, objects or events (i.e., reference with decreased contextual support).

These are parallels that can be described in terms of the gradual decontextualization of the gestural or vocal scheme from the "game" in which it originally occurred. The rules of the reference game change across time until the gestural or vocal symbol is used flexibly, in a variety of contexts, and to categorize or recognize new instances.

This sequence of developments carries us only to the beginning of the productive one word speech. We have no further information in our data on parallels in formal structure between language and symbolic play after this point. However, Nicolich (1975), in the study of five children discussed earlier, reports that structural parallels in these two domains continue at least through 2 years of age. She finds that, at the point at which children begin high frequency application of the same scheme to a succession of objects (e.g., feed dolly, feed mommy), they also begin to use the most primitive sorts of two-word pivot–open constructions (e.g., *allgone shoe, allgone daddy*). This is presumably the point where we have just left our children, since only a few of the subjects in our study had begun using successive applications of single schemes and none of them had begun to use two-word utterances. Later still, Nicolich reports that the onset of planned multischeme play sequences corresponds to the onset of syntactically planned multiword speech. These parallels suggest some very strong claims about the formal organization of symbolic structures in two very different domains. Clearly, the findings need to be replicated with a larger sample (work of this sort is already underway in some ongoing research by Nicolich, personal communication). However, given the structural parallels that occur up through 13 months, we would certainly not be surprised to see yoked developments in language and play continue in the second year of life.

How do we explain these overlaps in content and structure? To some extent, the overlap in content may be an effect of infant culture. That is, these children are acquiring gestural conventions and language conventions within the same game situations. Often, the first gestural routines are in fact responses to set linguistic cues—for example, *where's your belly button?* or *wave byebye.* Hence the relationship between language comprehension and gestural development is situational as well as cognitive. However, the fact that language and gestural development often involve the same games does not explain why children tend to be at the same developmental "levels" within those games for both gesture and speech.

In Chapter 2 we presented a model for the internal structure of symbols at these early stages, arguing that vocal and gestural symbols are cognitively equivalent in terms of the subjective vehicle–referent relationship. Our findings support that analysis. At this point in development, the only difference between the two domains is in the modality of expression. **Indeed, we see no evidence to suggest that a 13-month-old is in any way biased toward the development of vocal language as opposed to gestural language.** Evidence concerning the acquisition of American Sign Language as a native language (e.g., Newport and Ashbrook, 1977) suggests that deaf children acquire their manual–visual code just as rapidly as hearing children acquire speech. Furthermore, the semantic relations expressed in ASL develop in the same sequence that has been reported for hearing children. Our findings support the view that the human symbol-using system is extraordinarily plastic, and relatively modality free. This does not mean that we have no special preparations, not available in other species, for processing information in the acoustic-articulatory modality. However, at the early stages the "cognitive" organization underlying symbol use in gesture and in speech appears to be the same. Our children are biased toward the acquisition of "culture." The capacity for language is only one part of that preparation.

Conclusion

We have found strong correspondences between symbol development in play and language in three aspects: correlations in frequency and rate, overlap in referential content, and parallels in qualitative levels and sequences of development. Within language, we found a developmental progression from what we have termed "nonreferential" to "referential" uses of words. The nonreferential words are not names for actions or entities; rather, they are procedures that are used in restricted contexts that may **include** particular actions or entities. As such, they are what

Piaget (1962) has called "first verbal schemes" or "preconcepts" (pp. 215–244), a transitional form between sensorimotor activities and true concepts. However, the distinction between these preconcepts and true naming does not, in our view, imply a discontinuous development. In true reference or naming, the vocal gesture is used to anticipate, recognize, and identify, or remember a class of objects or events. This is **not** a shift from procedure to "mental object" (Bates, 1976, Chap. III). Rather, naming is a **type** of procedure, a different sort of language game than the more narrow and context-bound uses that typify nonreferential speech. **What happens between 9 and 13 months is that the rules of the language game change, from a rigidly structured and context-bound use to a more flexible use in which the major invariant across contexts is the involvement of a referent object or event.**

What brings about the change in the rules? We do not have an explanation in the material causal or hardware sense. Nor are there any major environmental, efficient causal events that can account for this shift in word use. It does appear, however, that this change in the rules reflects a general pattern of decontextualization, one which occurs in both linguistic and nonlinguistic functioning. One of our goals for future research will be to locate and perhaps quantify this shift in several domains during the first two years of life (more on this in Chapter 6 when we discuss implications for future research in more detail).

The model of symbol use that emerges from these findings is consonant with Wittgenstein's (1958) theory of meaning in language, as a set of language games with rules for using words **and** sentences in contexts. As Werner and Kaplan (1963) have demonstrated in experiments on word acquisition, this game–theoretic approach characterizes adult lexical acquisition as well. We often know how to use a word without being able to define that word when asked. Even when we do have a clear and explicit definition available for a word, that knowledge could still be characterized as a game with clear and precise rules. We have argued elsewhere (e.g., Bates, 1976; Bates and Rankin, 1978; Volterra, Camaioni, and Bates, 1975) that semantics can be viewed as a subset of pragmatics, or rules for using language in context. Furthermore, the same game–theoretic approach that Wittgenstein applied to language can be applied to other forms of cultural knowledge, including the primitive conventional gestures observed in our children.

If we take this approach back to the six controversies outlined earlier, we can obtain a more unified picture of the development of first words.

First, the distinction between substantives and function words can be shown to contain two issues. Bloom's report that Allison began with high-frequency function terms and then moved on to high-frequency use of substantives may, in part, be an artifact of the nonreferential to referential progression that we have described. Hence what Bloom and Sinclair both treat as separate semantic "classes" may in at least some instances be based on different "levels of use." However, even when the level of use is the same across the substantives and function words, we have stressed that both names for objects and words designating relations are based on procedures. In fact, they **are** procedures, both at the nonreferential level and at the level of true naming. Hence, in our view the internal, cognitive status of functions–action judgments versus substantives–denominations is essentially the same. The developmental course of both types of procedures involves a shift in the rules of use such that the procedure begins to be defined in terms of the perception or awareness of a particular kind of entity, event, or relationship, across a variety of situations. At each developmental level, the difference between substantives and function words has to do with the kinds of referents (entities, events, relationships) involved in that language game or procedure. However, both kinds of words are in themselves functions.

We can also reanalyze the distinction between functional and perceptual features in terms of this Wittgensteinian approach. In our model, all language games are procedures, uses, and hence functions. This would include language games whose rules take into account static perceptual features, as well as rules involving changing or dynamic features. Hence the function–perception distinction is **not** between a use-based definition of a word versus a perceptually based definition. Instead, **words are all uses, but they may be governed by different kinds of perceptions.** As we noted earlier, the Clark–Nelson "debate" seems to have been resolved for those investigators as well, with Nelson's proposal that concepts are **formed** on the basis of the dynamic (and hence attractive) aspects of a referent class, while they are **extended** on the basis of the more reliable, stable, static features of that same referent class. Hence these different kinds of features relate to different moments in learning the rules of a language game.

The third issue regards the internal structure of lexical categories, in particular the distinction between prototypes and featural models. As we explained earlier, this has proven to be a pseudoissue. The difference between prototype category structures versus criterial attribute structures is independent of the mode of representation of that structure (i.e., as a set of discrete features or as a continuous, analogue image). As Rosch (1978) has noted, the prototype model of categories is based on Wittgenstein's approach to meaning, including the notion that category members may be related to one another by family resemblance along nonoverlapping sets of "family traits." Hence the internal structure of a lexical category is fairly loose and flexible, and the category is defined more in terms of its center than its imprecise, "fuzzy" boundaries. These principles, in turn, are consonant with the view that the "stuff" of which categories are made is use, or rules for use. What changes from 9 to 13 months is that the "center" or prototypic definition of words changes from a single, tightly defined use, to several interrelated rules specifying a variety of situations in which that word best applies.

The fourth debate listed earlier was the distinction between nonreferential and referential speech. Since this is the key that we are using to organize the other issues, we can proceed directly to the fifth distinction, between referential versus combinatorial meaning. Here too we would argue that the "mental stuff" of which both kinds of meanings are made is use, language games. Referential meaning concerns the rules that regulate the naming game, for identifying and classifying objects, events, relations. Combinatorial meanings are precisely that: combinations of uses, undoubtedly including some new rules that transcend the situations covered by naming alone. Greenfield and Smith (1976) suggest that referential and combinatorial meaning are dichotomous. We propose instead that there is psychological continuity between these two aspects of meaning. In some cases a single lexical item may be used to map a "referential" meaning (in Greenfield and Smith's sense), that is also paraphraseable by whole clauses (i.e., "combinatorial" meanings). The single item and the whole clause can be viewed as two ways of getting the same communicative work done.

The final issue concerns individual differences in language use, along the referential–expressive dimension described by Nelson (1973). As Nelson points out, the referential and expressive children are using language to accomplish different things. The referential children seem more involved in the naming game, and the categorizing function of language. The expressive children are more involved in social functions of language, to regulate interactions. There are probably other differences as well, concerning the kinds of analysis children use in cracking the linguistic code. We will go into this issue in much more detail in Chapter 7, and can postpone the question of analytic styles until then. For present purposes, we suggest that these style differences can also be incorporated within a Wittgensteinian, language-game theory of meaning. The emphasis here is on what is being done with words, how they are being used.

To summarize, the field of child language research has been divided regarding:

1. The developmental levels of word use (i.e., in terms of contextual freedom)
2. The kinds of features that predominate in the rules for using words
3. The structure of the categories that underlie word use
4. Individual differences in the things children want to accomplish with words

Each of these questions is equally relevant to the study of culture acquisition in general, as it is reflected in the exercise of cultural conventions in symbolic play. Our understanding of the emergence of symbols will be greatly enhanced if future research on these issues includes a study of both language and action.

Appendix 4.1

The Corpus of All Instances of Language Imitation, Language Comprehension, Language Production (with Cumulative Word Count), Gestural Imitation, and Symbolic Play as Derived from the Maternal Interviews and from Direct Observations during Four Home Visits

The following 41 pages present the materials described in the above heading in a tabular format. The column headed "Number of words" represents a cumulative word count, including both referential and nonreferential words. If a word occurred in two slightly different versions (e.g., *dada* and *daddy*), it was only counted once. If a similar sound occurred consistently with two very different meanings (e.g., *ba* as a dog's name and for a ball), it was counted twice. When an item is followed by "(u.c.)" it means that the context in which the item was produced was unclear (e.g., the mother reported that the baby said *kitty*, but did not specify the precise context in which the word was produced). Subject numbers begin with the child who had the smallest number of words produced by Session 4, and continue through the subject with the largest productive vocabulary.

Language imitation	Language comprehension	Language production	Number of words[a]	Gestural imitation	Symbolic play
		Subject 1			
1. ah *dada*	1. *sister* (looks to side) *no* (obeys, gets upset) *light* (looks to ceiling) *Where's daddy?* (also looks to ceiling)	1-4. no entries		1. _____ (imitates sister banging hand against dinner table)	1. no entry
2. no entry				2. *hide* (imitates E lifting pant leg during object permanence game) *stacking blocks* (tries unsuccessfully to build tower after demonstration)	2. *drink* (holds cup to mouth and makes swallowing movements)
3. ah (in singsong rhythm) *dadad* *goya-goya* *tch* (tongue click)	2. *Where's kitty?* (turns & stares at cat) *night-night* (when in bed puts his head down) *don't touch that* (stops)			3. _____ (imitates knocking blocks together) *blinks eyes* _____ (M reports numerous efforts to imitate her face and hand movements)	3. *eat* (bats fork briefly against toy plate)
4. *rrrr* car noise)	3. *Where's the light?* (looks to ceiling) *Daddy* (looks to any man in room, or looks around for F if he is absent) *sister* (seeks around room if absent)			4. *car* (imitates E moving car around, but only by tapping car against floor)	4. no entry
	4. *byebye* (waves) *ta* (gives object when M or F say this) *Where's kitty?* (points at a distance to cat) *juice* (after nap, becomes excited when M says this)				

(continued)

			Number of words	Gestural imitation	Symbolic play
Language imitation	Language comprehension	Language production		Gestural imitation	Symbolic play

Subject 2

Language imitation	Language comprehension	Language production	Number of words	Gestural imitation	Symbolic play
1. no entry	1. *ciao – bye* (waves ciao) clap your hands (claps) *no* (stops briefly)	1. no entry		1. *waves ciao* *claps hands*	1. no entry
2. *mamma*		2. *mm* (request and refusal sound)	1		2. no entry
3. no entry	2. *Give a kiss* (gives kiss)	3. no entry		2. *peekaboo* (with cloth)	3. *drink* (sucking movements from empty bottle)
4. *opop* (horse sound)	3. *Make a face* (grimaces) *Where's the tram?* (looks to outside window)	4. *opop* (horse sound, uses only after requested *How does the horsey go?*)	2	3. ___ (imitates M's grimaces) (imitates E shaking coughing gesture)	4. *drink* (now more elaborate drinking movements from various empty containers)
	4. *How does the horsey go?* (gives horsey sound *opop*) *no* (now also shakes head) *Give Luisa your hand* (offers hand to E) *Let's feed the fish* (drops cup already in hand, picks up fish, but does not feed fish)				

1. ha-ha (will only imitate older sister)
2. no entry
3. no entry
4. ahm (food sound)

---

1. no (stops)
   Where's ___? (sister's name, looks around for sister)
2. There's papa (looks around for F)
   where's the music? (asked after music-box has stopped, B. bats at the wind-up handle)
3. Where's papa? (asked when F is absent, B. responds by waving goodbye)
4. Where's mama? or Grandma? or papa? or ___? (sister's name) (in all instances B. responds by looking around room until correct person is located)
   Give the block to Mommy (gives block to M)

---

1. ahah (request sound)
2. no entry
3. baba (while manipulating any object)
4. no entry

1

1. waves ciao
2. ___ (imitates putting object on top of own head)
   claps hands
3. no entry

2

4. hide (imitates covering eyes with hands)
   ___ (imitates making toy dog walk)
   ___ (imitates placing toy fish against toy bear)
   car (imitates rolling fish along ground)
   comb (imitates combing own hair)

---

1. no entry
2. no entry
3. drink (drinking movements from various empty containers)
4. feed (feeds doll with baby bottle)
   comb (combs doll's hair with comb; combs own hair with comb)
   hug (hugs toy dog)
   dance (rocks back and forth to music)

(continued)

185

Language imitation	Language comprehension	Language production	Number of words	Gestural imitation	Symbolic play
		Subject 4			
1. caca ("raspberries") ___ (coughing sound)	1. *no* (stops)	1. no entry		1. no entry	1. no entry
2. *woo* = boo *ba-ba*	2. *Let's go see the horses* (leans toward horse poster in his bedroom)	2. no entry except. shaking head in "no" gesture in refusals		2. *clap hands* ___ (imitates putting small doll on boat)	2. *dress* (places doll's shoe against doll's foot)
3. *ta-ta bamba* = bambola = doll	3. *Be nice* (becomes more gentle in scratching face) *Clap your hands* (claps) *Wave ciao* (waves) *Wash your hands* (rubs hands together) *Go spank* (hits hand against surface)	3. *mamma* (anger cry) *papa* (u.c.)b	1 2	3. *waves ciao* *hide* (imitates hiding by putting cloth over own head) *spank* *wash* (imitates handwashing gesture) ___ (imitates F working with flowers in garden)	3. *hug* (hugs doll) *feed* (places toy bottle against doll's mouth) *sleep* (makes lullaby sounds and rocking movements against various types of cloths)
4. no entry	4. *shoes* (overhears in adult conversation, goes to own room and takes shoes out of closet) *Get up* (pulls up to kneeling position) *Kiss the kitty* (kisses cat)	4. *mamma* (while following M, but also still as anger cry)		4. no entry	4. *drink* (drinking movements from empty cups)

(continued)

Subject 5

#				gesture	symbolic play
1	*ah* *dada*	*bath* (crawls to bathroom but only if she is undressed at the time)	*ah* (orienting or comment sound to novel things)	no entry	no entry
2	___ ("raspberries") ___ (coughing sound) *bzzz* *mmmm* = mama	*Where's* ___ (=dog's name; looks to window) *byebye* (waves when F asks)	no entry	no entry	no entry
3	*hi* *mama* *oooo* = book *tch* (tongue click)	*Where's bow-wow?* (looks to door, but only when she has heard garage door open also) *Soooo big* (lifts arms and hands in wide gesture)	*bow-wow* (says to family dog only)	___ (wide-armed gesture in response to M saying *So-o-o big*)	*telephone* (puts receiver near her ear) *hide* (deferred imitation of peekaboo game)
4	*no* *la-la-la* (rough imitation of M's singsong *telephone*) *wrah-wrah* (breathy growling sound) *th* = there it is	no entry	___ (gurgling noise in food requests) *hey-woo* (ritual request sound, also said while receiving an object)	no entry	*hug* (cuddles dolls) *telephone* (places receiver on shoulder) *feed* and *eat* (feeds doll with plate, fork and cup on separate instances several times and brings to own mouth) *dress* (puts on necklace) ___ (deferred imitation of game of alternating between clapping hands and putting hands between knees)

Language imitation	Language comprehension	Language production	Number of words	Gestural imitation	Symbolic play
		Subject 6			
1. *dada*	1. *no* (gets upset)	1. no entry		1. *claps hands*	1. no entry
mama	*Clap your hands* (claps)			*waves ciao*	
tata				*claps fists together*	
2. *mamma*	2. *Where's mamma?* (smiles and looks to door for absent M)	2. *ah* (acute refusal sound)	1	2. *peekaboo* (puts cloth back over E's face)	2. *dress*(takes off doll's shoe)
brrr					*telephone* (babbles into receiver)
tata = imitation of "papa"		3. *da* = give (while giving and in requests)	2		
	3. *Ciao* = Bye (waves)	4. *da* (same as above)	3	3. no entry	3. *drink* (drinking movements from empty cup)
	Give me the necklace (gives)	*te* = *tienie* = take (identical to *da*, for giving and in requesting)			
	4. *Where's Grandma?* (turns and seeks in room)	*mamma* (in approaching M to put head on lap)	4	4. *telephone* (imitates dialing)	4. *hug* (rocks, hugs, and pats doll)
	Where's brother? (turns and seeks in room)	*chetta* = *questa* = this (said while manipulating objects)	5	(imitates E pressing bulb to make toy frog leap)	
	Give me the ball (throws ball)			(imitates movements of toy frog leaping)	
	Give me the telephone (gives telephone)				
	Where's Papa? (when F is absent, takes adult's hand and pulls over to door)				

1. no entry	1. *no* (stops, then smiles and "teases" M)	1. *eh* (request sound) *ma* (while cuddling M)	1	1. ___ (wide-armed gesture to adult saying *So-o-o big*) ___ (hand-to-mouth gesture in indian whoop)	1. *telephone* (chews at receiver and babbles into telephone) *feed* (feeds doll, u.c.)b *vacuum* (runs vacuum cleaner)	
2. *tch* (tongue click)			2			
3. *brrr* *bzzz* ___ (jack-in-the-box sound)	2. *let's go* or *come over* (comes to speaker) *no* (now shakes head)	2. *ha* (request sound)	3	2. no entry	2. *drink* (puts cup to mouth and tilts head back) *telephone* (lifts receiver to mouth but not to ear, and vocalizes *ah*) *hug* (hugs bunny) *eat* or *cook* (stirs wooden spoon in pot) *converse* (elaborate "pretend talking" with much arm waving)	
4. *brrr* (now in deferred imitation) *bzzz* (now in deferred imitation)	3. *Where's your Peter Rabbit book* (goes and gets correct book) *sit down* (sits)	3. *mama* (u.c.) *dada* (u.c.) *ah* (into phone receiver)	4	3. ___ (imitates E putting ring to own eye) ___ (imitates E bouncing small dolls up and down on clipboard) *write* (imitates E writing on clipboard) ___ (imitates E's "glasses" gesture, putting fingers over eyes.)		
	4. *cookie* (u.c.) *cracker* (u.c.) *flap-flap* (in bedtime routine only, flap arms) *patty-cake* (claps) *hi* (waves) *byebye* (waves)	4. *mama* (in lament or request, said also to F) *dada* (said only to F) ___ (dog's name; says to dog)	5	4. ___ (imitates M watering flowers with spray)	3. *drink* (from empty cup and from baby bottle toy) *eat* and *feed* (eating movements with fork	

(continued)

189

Language imitation	Language comprehension	Language production	Number of words	Gestural imitation	Symbolic play
		Subject 7 (continued)			and plate, with bucket and shovel; also feeds E) *sleep* (puts head on pillow outside bed context) *car* (moves toy car around saying *brrr* in deferred imitation of E) *brush* (brushes teeth) 4. *dress* (puts dog's bowl on head as hat) *sleep* (now sleeping movements on E's lap) *telephone* (now puts receiver to ear and mouth at once) *eat* (varied pretend eating with many different utensils and offers beads on shovel to E in feed gesture) *clean* (bites plate, then picks up cotton-ball and swabs plate with it)

Subject 8

1. *papa* *mama* *baba*	1. *Where's L* (dog's name, turns to outside window where dog is kept)	1. *aah* (aspirated request sound)	1	1. *sleep* (imitates putting doll in carriage)	1. no entry
2. *eh* = Chi e = Who's there? *te-te* *ze-ze* *ta-ta* ___(Indian whoop)	2. no entry	2. no entry		2. *claps hands* ___(hand-over-mouth gesture) ___(imitates putting baby duck on top of larger one)	2. *dance* (bounces up and down to music)
3. no entry	3. *Where's Chip-Chop?* (points to correct character in wall poster) *Where's Scaramaka?* (same as above)	3. *papa* (on seeing F)	2	3. ___(imitates batting stone against pen)	3. *wave* (waves ciao to children outside window) ___(game with M of putting small things in mouth and pretending to choke; M regularly responds with mock horror)
4. *oo-oo* (horse sound) *ah-oh* = Buon giorno = good morning (imitates with singsong intonation) *ahah* = cara = dear	4. *Where's papa?* (looks around room) *Mama's coming* (looks toward outside door) *Give the dolly* (rocks doll) *feed the dolly* (puts toy bottle against doll's mouth)	4. *mamma* (whenever she needs help) *da* = give (while offering or receiving) *hee* (request sound) *babbo* (while approaching F) *mao* = cat (u.c.)[b] *ahm* (food sound, says during game of eating pretend crumbs)	3 4 5 6 7	4. no entry	4. *eat* and *feed* (pretends to eat small crumbs, also extends to E to eat. Does same with nonexistent crumbs, saying *ahm*)

(continued)

Language imitation	Language comprehension	Language production	Number of words	Gestural imitation	Symbolic play

Subject 8 (continued)

Language imitation	Language comprehension	Language production	Gestural imitation	Symbolic play
	Put the dolly's socks on (looks at doll's feet and moves socks toward feet, but does not put on) *Feed the kitty* (places bottle against kitty's body, but not to mouth) *Where's the kitty?* (takes cat out of mouth, looks at it, places it on ground)			*spank* (hits fist against a table where she has hurt her head) *hug* (pets doll, kitten) ___ (game with M of pretending to bite each other)

Subject 9

Language imitation	Language comprehension	Language production	Number of words	Gestural imitation	Symbolic play
1. *hi* *daddy*	1. *no* (stops, gets upset) *wave* (waves) *pattycake* (claps) *bath* (shows excitement) *daddy* (looks to F if present, to door if F is absent)	1. *oh* (while manipulating toys, "comment" sound) *dada* (u.c.) *hi* (u.c.)	1	1. *pattycake* (imitates by shaking flower in hand)	1. *drink* (from empty cup)
	2. *roll-'em-up* (new hand gesture in pattycake)	2. no entry	2 3	2. *stacking blocks* (imitates of M)	2. *car* (moves toy car back and forth on wheels)
	3. *bottle* (u.c.) *mama* (u.c.) *cracker* (u.c.)	3. *mama* (when angry or distressed or in request) *dada* (when happy) *see* (while pointing and turning to listener for eye contact)	4	3. ___ (imitates gesture by E of tilting head from side to side)	3. *kiss* (kisses picture of babies) *hug* (hugs stuffed bunny and doll in separate instances) *drink* (sucks from empty bottle)
2-4. no entries	4. *no* (now shakes her head)		5	4. ___ (imitates E putting ring to own eye by also putting ring to own eye)	

1. ah
2. grrr (lion sound)
   ___ (whistles)
   ___ (sings to music)
   ___ (imitates accordian)
   bye (immediate and deferred imitation)
   why (said in imitation of sister's frequent why questions)
3. ___ (own name, stops and turns to speaker)
   no (stops)
4. no entry

dee (said twice at appropriate point in peeka-boo game)
4. uh (request sound)
   hmmm (acute refusal sound)

6. dress (imitates E putting doll shoe to doll's foot, then puts shoe to doll's face)
7. car (imitates E moving toy car around floor making noises)
8.

dress (puts on necklace)
4. telephone (receiver to ear)
   hide (deferred imitation of object permanence game)
   eat (scrapes toy fork on plate and puts to mouth, later puts fork in shoe with similar tapping movement)

Subject 10

1. no entry
2. bye (says to telephone)
3. bye (now frequent and appropriate use)
   dada (to F and to doll)
   cookie (requesting any food or milk)
4. no entry

1. claps hands (against cotton ball in imitation of E)
2. stacks blocks (in imitation of M)
3. no entry
4. no entry

1. no entry
2. drink (drinking movements with empty vessels complete with swallowing sounds)
   telephone (holds receiver and dials)
   hug (hugs doll)
   sleep (sleeping movements outside bed context)

(continued)

193

Language imitation	Language comprehension	Language production	Number of words	Gestural imitation	Symbolic play
		Subject 10 (continued)			
3. _tch_ (tongue click) _dada_ (said out of context several minutes after M had reported it to E)		_grrr_ (formerly called lion noise, has now become general request sound)	4		4. _hug_ (now extended to foam rubber ball)
(throughout session B frequently imitates various of his reported sounds when M says them to E)		4. _bye_ or _byebye_ _baby_ (to telephone and to any one leaving) _hi_ (to anyone passing outside) _birdie_ (u.c.) _grandma_ (u.c.)	5 6 7 8		
4. _brrr_ (vacuum cleaner)					
		Subject 11			
1. _tch_ (tongue click)	1. _no_ (stops) _Where's Dada_ (looks always to same door)	1. _mommy_ (while crawling after M) _dada_ (u.c.)[b]	1	1. no entry	1. no entry
2. _dadada_	(own name, turns to speaker)	2. _hi_ (u.c.)	2	2. _pattycake_	2. _drink_ (drinking movements from bells on highchair)
3. _doodle-do-do_ = cockadoodledo	_blanket_ (looks at blanket)	3. _juice_ (names, also when others are drinking)	3 4	3. _peekaboo_ _claps hands_ _dance_ (in bouncing game)	3. _hug_ (pets kitten)
4. _yay_ = hurray	_kittycat_ (u.c.) _bottle_ (u.c.) _byebye_ (u.c.)	_to-to_ = toast (u.c.) _kiss_ (u.c.) _eh_ (request sound)	5 6 7	4. _stacks blocks_ _kiss_	4. _eat_ (stirs fork around in cup) _telephone_ (receiver to own and M's ear)

2. pattycake (claps, even when overhearing word in adult conversation)
block (goes and gets)
duck (goes and gets)
blanket (goes and gets)
baby's book (chooses correct book from several others)
ball (u.c.)
cookie (u.c.)
juice (u.c.)
bunny (u.c.)

3. *bouncy-bouncy* (bounces)
peekaboo (puts hands to eyes)
brush your hair (brushes own hair)
Where's mama's nose? (touches M's nose)
Go play piano (goes to piano and plays)
Go get mama the ball (retrieves ball and gives to M)

4. *kitty* (when cat comes in room)
socks (u.c.)
byebye (u.c.)

8
9
10

telephone (receiver to own and M's ear)

(continued)

Language imitation	Language comprehension	Language production	Number of words	Gestural imitation	Symbolic play

Subject 11 (continued)

Language imitation	Language comprehension	Language production	Number of words	Gestural imitation	Symbolic play
	4. Where's _____? (at this point will point correctly to most familiar figures in books, to correct body parts, and will pick up correct toys. M has stopped keeping track of vocabulary)				

Subject 12

Language imitation	Language comprehension	Language production	Number of words	Gestural imitation	Symbolic play
1. no entry	1. no (stops) S_____ (dog's name, looks around floor for dog)	1. no entry	1	1. *dance* (bounces in imitation of sister)	1. *Car*(?) (pushes mirror around the floor making motor-like sounds)
2. *yum* *hi* *no* tch (tongue click)	2. *Daddy* (looks around room) _____ and _____ (two sister's names, also looks around room)	2. *dada* (u.h.) *yum* (to comment on foods she likes) *uhuh* (request sound)	2 / 3	2. *pattycake* *waves byebye* (imitates banging blocks together) (unsuccessfully tries to imitate E building tower)	2. *car* (rolls wheeled fish around on various surfaces)
3. *mama* *dada* *Sit*_____ (dog's name)		3. *na* (refusal sound, with headshake) *hi* (request for attention) *eheh* (request sound)	4	3. *car* (imitates E moving truck around floor)	3. *telephone* (receiver to ear) *dress* (puts on necklace) *car* (deferred imitation of M moving truck around with motor sounds)
4. *fish* *yes*			5		

nnnn (deferred
imitation of
motor sound after
car game)
(at this point M
reports that B
often imitates
key words in
sentences; M has
stopped keeping
record)

pattycake (claps)
peekaboo (hides be-
hind blanket)
4. Where's Daddy? (will
crawl to another room
until she finds F)

6 pe = pretty (said
   to a variety of
   objects)
   ___(imitates E. shak-
   ing rattle)

7 Whastha? = What's
   that? (whispered
   sound said
   frequently while
   manipulating ob-
   jects)
   Mom (from bed in
   morning when she
   wants to get up)
   dada (names F)
   S___ (names dog)
   da (while giving
   objects)
   4. car (imitates E.
   sliding toy car
   around floor)

8

9
10

4. eat (eating
   movements with
   empty spoon)
   sleep (sleeping
   movements with
   blanket outside
   bed context)
   read (pretend
   reading with
   babbling from
   books)
   dance (bounces
   to music)

Subject 13

1. prrr (imitates
   brother only)
   mama
   gna-gna
2. ca-aa = cacca
   bamba = bambola =
   doll

1 mamma (when M is
   present (u.c.))
   papa (when F is
   present (u.c.))
2 gna-gna = nonna =
   Grandma (u.c.)

1. pattycake (claps
   when grandmother asks)
   no (stops, gets upset)
2. pattycake (now claps
   when anyone asks)

1. claps hands (imita-
   tion of grandmother)
2. waves ciao
   claps fist together
   (imitates E)
   peekaboo
3. telephone (places
   receiver behind
   ear)
4. telephone (babbles
   into receiver)

1. no entry
2. no entry

(continued)

197

Language imitation	Language comprehension	Language production	Number of words	Gestural imitation	Symbolic play
		Subject 13 (continued)			
3. *tu-tu* (train sound, imitates while playing with train) —(at this point M reports that B imitates many words from his brother, but she has stopped keeping record)	3. *Where's Papa?* (looks to F in room if F is present) *How is the food?* (nods head and makes happy face)	2. *mamma* (names and requests M) *nonna* (names and requests grandmother) *papa* (says when F returns home) *da* = give (while requesting or giving) *bamba* = bambola = doll (u.c.)	4	3. *train* (imitates moving train across floor saying *tu-tu*) 4. *feed* (imitates brother giving bottle to doll) *dress* (imitates E putting on handkerchief, first around neck, then on head)	*drink* (drinking movements from tiny toy cups) *hug* (cuddles cat)
	4. *Call papa to the telephone* (calls to F on phone) *Where is the telephone?* (looks toward room or place in room where telephone is kept) *Where is papa* (looks to door) *Blow a kiss* (blows kiss) *Make like a lion* (roars) *Make kittykitty* (makes cat sound and gesture)	*tata* = doll (u.c.) *appa* = acqua = water (says to request water, and when he sees water glass)	5 6 7		
4. *tete* = bubusettete (sound made in peekaboo game)		3. *mamma* (calls M from another room) *pappa* (names F when he is home) *dada* (names brother) *da* (to request objects) *bamba* = bambola = doll (to request or name any toy)	8		

(continued)

1. tatta
   mama
   Che e? = What's this?
2. nana
   mamma
3. papa

*S*___ = own name

1. no entry
2. *wave ciao* (waves)
   no (stops)
   Who's there (during telephone game, M says this and B responds *pa* = papa)

tata (to family maid)
pappa = pablum (when he is hungry or looking for food, or to comment on cooking)   9

4. *papa* (looking for F when F is absent)
   tetete = cucusette (peekaboo sound said at correct points in peekaboo game)   10
   ga-ga (to cat)   11

Subject 14

1. *mm* (request sound)
2. *mamma* (as request sound when she sees M)
   Che e = Who's there (while playing with telephone)
3.

1. no entry
2. *wave ciao* (waves)

1. *waves ciao*
   claps hands
2. *dance* (imitation of M)
   car (imitates running car along floor)
   ___ (imitates pulling truck along by cord)   3

1. no entry
2. *dance* (dancing movements to sound of music box)
   telephone (receiver to ear, says *Who's there?* into phone)

Language imitation	Language comprehension	Language production	Number of words	Gestural imitation	Symbolic play

Subject 14 (continued)

Language imitation	Language comprehension	Language production	Number of words	Gestural imitation	Symbolic play
	3. *Clap your hands* (claps) *dance* (bounces up & down) *S* ____ (brother's name, turns and seeks brother in room)	*Pa* = papa (in response to M saying *Who's there* in telephone game) *da* = give (in both giving and taking) *te* = tieni = take (in both giving and taking)	4 5 6	*dress* (imitates E putting doll's shoe against doll's foot) *peekaboo* (with E using E's hand over own eyes instead of own hands)	*eat* (eating movements, with empty chewing, of plastic fruit) *feed* (puts plastic banana to E's mouth)
	4. *Show me the phone* (shows phone) *Where's S* ____ *?* (brother's name, goes to brother if present, looks to door if absent) *Show me the cat* (goes and gets toy cat but does not show) *Where's mamma?* (while in F's arms, reaches out toward M)	3. *pappa* = pablum (for both water and food, both as request and in comment on seeing it) *da* = give (in giving and in demanding objects) *tie* = take (only while giving) *Che e* = Who's there? (while playing telephone, and whenever she hears telephone, door, or related sounds)	7	3. ____ (imitates E putting container on head, but puts back on E's head instead of own head) ____ (imitates E scratching own ear) *feed* (imitates E giving doll bottle to doll) 4. no entry	3. *drink* (drinking movements from any empty container, including bottles) *dress* (puts on necklace puts doll's shoe to doll's leg) *hug* (hugs doll, with singing sound) 4. *sleep* (sleeping movements against book as pillow)

4. *mamma* (when look-
ing for M and to
call any other
person)

papa (u.c. often
says after saying
mamma)

che e? = both
"Who's there?" and
"What's there?"
(said in noting
anything new)

8

grazie = thanks
(said while re-
ceiving objects)

ta = tiene = take
(said in showing,
in giving and in
receiving)

9

cucco = *ciuccio* =
pacifier (both
to name and re-
quest pacifier)

10

caa = *cara* = dear
(said while car-
ressing anything
or anyone)

11

vrrm (while mov-
ing toy car)

(continued)

Language imitation	Language comprehension	Language production	Number of words	Gestural imitation	Symbolic play
1. mama 2. no entry 3. eye 4. no entry	subject 15 1. no (stops, bites hand, gets upset) (dog's name; looks to dog if present, out window if dog is absent) hot (u.c.) daddy (u.c.) 2. put it back (gets upset) you're not going (gets upset) love the baby (hugs doll) here's the bus (looks in direction of bus) spit it out (spits out object) teddybear (u.c.) hat (u.c.) (several adult names, u.c.) 3. no entry 4. give it to mama (gives)	1. mmm (refusal sound, or complaint while looking for M) 2. ma (request sound) ma up (one instance only, in request to be picked up) (car sound in car game) 3. da (while pointing to F and while pointing to dog) (dog's name, u.c.) ga (while giving of showing, may be derived from What have you got? mom (in requests to M only) ball (naming any ball)	1 2 3 4 5 6 7 8	1. pattycake (imitates game of kicking can) (imitates knocking blocks together) 2. hide (imitates E in object permanence game, by hiding diaper pins under cloth) (imitates F playing music conductor with waving movement) 3. no entry 4. ___ (imitation of M gardening) dress (puts pail on head as hat in imitation of E)	1. no entry 2. feed (feeds apple to doll) car (scoots blocks along floor making motorlike sounds) clean (washing movements with hands and dry rag) hug (hugs doll) kiss (kisses doll) drink (drinking movement from empty cup) hide (deferred imitation of object permanence game) 3. write (writing movements on paper)

1. ba-ba-ba dada ("raspberries") (F's laugh) leh-lo = hello 2. pa = poppy (grand- father)	1. no (stops, becomes dejected) don't (stops, be- comes dejected) 2. Look at the kitty (looks at cat)	1. telephone (dialing and picking up receiver) pattycake 2. brush (imitates holding toothbrush to bunny's face)

Session 16

	1. dada (one instance while showing toy to F) duck (says once very clearly while holding duck)	1
		2

1. no entry

2. telephone (u.c.)[b]
   drink (from
   various empty cups
   accompanied by
   empty slurping)

4. ah (request sound)   9
   umm (request sound)
   boom (u.c.)   10
   nanana (refusal   11
   sound)
   write (u.c.)   12

vacuum (vacuum
movements with
vacuum attachments)
dance (dances to
music)
(elaborate
deferred imita-
tion of parent's
wallpapering,
with brush move-
ments and feeling
for lumps in wall)

4. eat (eating move-
   ments with fork
   and plate, trans-
   fers "food" from
   plate to bucket
   with fork)

(continued)

Language imitation	Language comprehension	Language production	Number of words	Gestural imitation	Symbolic play
		Subject 16 (continued)			
bzzz rrrr (tongue roll) sh-sh-sh-sh	3. monkey (looks to stuffed monkey)	ba-ba (says once looking at ball) ca (looking at cat once)	3	3. hug (imitates cuddling doll and bunny)	3. hug (hugs doll) drink (also from toy bottle) telephone (with vacuum cleaner attachment) feeds (M with spoon)
3. ook = book or look	4. bed (becomes angry, protests) bye (waves) pattycake banana (u.c.) hug the dolly (hugs doll)		4	(M holds ring to B's eyes and B puts back to	
4. (at this point M reports frequent imitation of names and intonation contours while reading books together, but provides no further examples)		2. Butch (own nickname, u.c.)	5	own eyes; then M puts ring to own mouth, and B puts	feeds (M with spoon)
		kitty (u.c.) dada (u.c.)	6	ring to her own mouth)	4. sleep (with blanket, outside bed context) telephone (with control box on heating pad) read (extensive babbling and turning pages in imitative style) cards (deferred imitation of playing at cards) dress (puts embroidery hoop on head as hat) eat and feed (stirring with fork, fork to mouth also feeds E with fork)
		muh (cow, u.c.)	7		
		see (u.c.)	8		
		eh (request sound)	9		
		3. see? (looking at objects and pictures) mama (request for drink)	10	3. hide (imitates E in object permanence game hiding object under screen)	
		mmm (food request) duckie (names ducks and other objects, not clear which)	11	(imitates running toy animals along ground making noises)	
		Tweetie (names figure in wall poster)	12	(imitates M folding clothes) eat (imitates eating movements with toy fork to mouth)	
		4. bye (initially said only to self, now only to others)	13		
		pretty (u.c.)	14	kiss (imitates kissing dolls)	

1. *blah* (with tongue out)
   eeee (high-pitched squeal)
   ba-ba (rough imitation of dog's name B___)

2. *ah* = bah (sheep sound)
   hoo-hoo = woof-woof (dog sound)
   tch (tongue click)

3. *dada* = Where's daddy?
   brrm (truck sound)
   mooo (cow sound)
   a-ooo = peekaboo

4. *ba-ba* = ball

---

1. *no* (hesitates, cries)
   Daddy (looks to front of house)
   B___ (dog's name, looks to back of house toward yard)

2. *Bye* (waves)
   Are you Puff the Magic Dragon?
   Where's the duck book? (answers qua-qua)

3. *Where's Daddy?* (responds dada and looks around)
   cat (looks around for cat)
   butterchurn (new object in GM's house, goes over to it when asked)

   (at this point M reports very frequent and varied comprehension, but cannot provide further examples)

---

1. *mama* (while crying in anger)

2. *ah* (request sound)
   qua-qua (response to *Where's the duck book?*)
   Ba (calling dog B___)
   dada (u.c.)
   mama (u.c.)

3. *quack* (names duck)
   uh-uh (clear adult-like "no" sound, in refusals)
   mmm (names cows)
   gog = dog (u.c.)
   bye (u.c.)
   hi (u.c.)
   ___ (reported sound for cat (u.c.)

4. *uh* (request sound)
   baba (in throwing ball)
   ba (from dog's name B___, to all dogs including in books)
   cat (to all cats)
   bird (u.c.)

1
2
3
4
5
6
7
8
9
10
11
12
13
14

---

1. *pattycake* (against M's hand)
   ___ (movement of rocking head back and forth)
   ___ (imitates M going back and forth to cupboard for pots)

2. ___ (pats own head after M bounces ball off own head)

3. *eat* (imitates E's plate-to-mouth gesture)
   claps hands (imitates aunt clapping hands even if she hears aunt clapping from another room)
   ___ (imitates M pointing to dog in book)

4. ___ (imitates M gardening)
   dress (imitates E putting pail on head as hat)

---

1. no entries

2. *drink* (drinking movement, to mouth, for empty cups and bucket)

3. *smell* (sniffs flower)
   sleep (briefly places head on pillow during testing)

4. *smell* (sniffing gesture now to foam ball, cotton ball, and flowers).
   hug (hugs doll)
   eat (eating movements with empty fork and plate)
   hide (deferred imitation of child hiding his eyes the day before)
   dance (bouncing movements to music, hums)

(continued)

Language imitation	Language comprehension	Language production	Number of words	Gestural imitation	Symbolic play
		Subject 18			
1. no entry	1. no (stops briefly) Here's papa (turns to F) Let's do "cappocetta" (bangs forehead against M's in game)	1. mama (when she needs help) ca (brother's name, u.c.) papa (u.c.)	1 2 3	1. claps hands eat (imitates brother's empty eating movements) (game with M of banging foreheads together) (rhythmic back and forth rocking in imitation of mechanical dog)	1. eat and feed (puts plastic fruit to mouth, offers to E; M reports frequent empty eating movements while brother is eating)
2. ___ (M's cough) ca tata tao = ciao = bye (in imitation of waving at the same time)	2. Where's L? (brother's name, will turn to door but only when there has also been a knock on door) Where's papa? (also looks to door) Pat the dolly (pats doll's head) Let's do peekaboo (hides head behind arm)	2. na (in refusals) mm-mm (in reaching for bottle) ma (pulling on M's skirt during requests) mama (names when present, calls when absent) papa (names when present, calls when absent)	4 5 6	2. shakes head no nods head yes waves ciao	2. drink (drinking movements with own cup when empty) hug (hugs doll, but only on command) dress (puts on necklace and shows off) hide (initiates peek-aboo)
3. ca (rough imitation of brother's name) cucu = cucusettetete = peekaboo	3. Rock the dolly (rocks doll back and forth and hums. Will also do same to isolated word rock)	ca (brothers name, names when present, calls when absent) nonna (to call grandmother, only when grandmother is present)	7 8	3. ___ (imitates hand-to-mouth gesture with Indian whoop) (imitates E dropping block along inclined plane) feed (imitates E putting doll bottle against doll's mouth)	3. dress (now puts on string as necklace; takes doll's shoe the color of hat doll usually wears and puts on doll's head) feed (imitates E putting doll bottle against doll's mouth)
4. meow (imitates while pointing to cat in book) papa = qua-qua (while looking at duck in book) ndaa = da = give azie = grazie = thanks pappa = pablum opla = oops bu b-b-b	4. How does the kitty go? (answers Mm-mm)	tata (name for nurse, u.c.) pappa = pablum (names whenever she sees it)	9	4. dance (imitates dancing with shaking arms)	4. telephone (babbles into receiver)

3. *cuccutete = cuccuset-
   tete* (at appropriate
   points in peekaboo
   game)
   nanna = rockabye   10
   (during game of rock-
   back and forth)
   tata (M describes   11
   this as a "pretend
   talking sound")
   dada (in manipulating 12
   or requesting objects)

4. *no* (while shaking
   head no)
   mao = meow (names   13
   cats and pictures of
   cats)
   tao = ciao = either   14
   "hi" or "bye"
   Chi e? = Who's there? 15
   (while playing tele-
   phone, or when some-
   one knocks at the
   door)

(continued)

Language imitation	Language comprehension	Language production	Number of words	Gestural imitation	Symbolic play
		Subject 19			
1. _no_	1. _no_ (shakes head, hesitates)	1. no entries		1. no entry	1. _drink_ (puts empty cup to lip)
nice	_hot_ (u.c.)				
Daddy (deferred imitation of hisses and growls heard the day before)	_byebye_ (u.c.)	2. _hmm_ (request sound)	1	2. _feed_ (imitates E putting doll bottle against doll's mouth)	2. _drink_ (more complete drink from empty cup)
	baby (u.c.)	_no_ (refusals, while shaking head)	2		
	Where's daddy? (looks around)	_Daddy_ (says at bottom of stairs when F disappears)		_pattycake_	_feed_ (feeds jumping jack doll; scrapes fork against plate and offers fork to M, but does not carry to M's mouth)
2. _okay_	_Be nice_ (becomes more gentle in patting dog)	_hot_ (says to stove or radiator)	3	_waves byebye_	
hot			4	_write_ (imitation of adult writing movements)	_dust_ (dusting movement with rag)
3. ___ (Indian whoop)	2. _Get the slinky_ (picks up slinky)	3. _bye_ (u.c.)	5	_car_ (imitates M playing with slinky toy)	_write_ (writing movements with pens or crayons)
sssss		_Shh_ (to name dog)	6		
thankyou		_Sh___ (u.c.)		3. _clean_ (imitates M wiping with cloth)	_hide_ (deferred imitation of object permanence game during entire week after experimental session)
stay (to dog, in imitation of M calling dog)	3. _Where's ___?_ (=dog's name; looks around room)	_hi_ (to someone at door)	7	___ (imitates F working with screwdriver in shop)	
	Where's the dog? (as above; looks around room for dog)	4. _picture_ (observed in free play, u.c.)	8	_type_ (while M works on own typewriter, B imitates on another old typewriter)	3. _telephone_ (receiver to ear, touches dial)
4. ___ (own name)	4. _Love the doggie_ (hugs dog)	_pee_ = _pretty_ (to pictures, to comment on interesting objects, and while giving)	9		_hug_ (cuddles toy dog)
	Love the duckie (hugs duck)	_see?_ (while pointing)	10	_cook_ (stirs in bowls and pots while M is cooking)	_dress_ (puts doll's shoe on doll's head)
	Where's your bottle? (goes to kitchen to get bottle)	___ (babysitter's name, used to summon him)			_sleep_ (sleeping movement on pillow outside bed context)
	cookie (u.c.)	_beee_ = _beads_ (while walking toward beads)	11		_dress_ (tries to put on necklace)

cracker (u.c.)
pop (u.c.)
eye (u.c.)
nose (u.c.)
Comb your hair (combs hair)

13 baby (while hugging doll)

14 ga (said twice to toy truck, may be saying car)

15 caee (to candy bowl)
hi (in telephone play)

4. hug (imitates E cuddling doll; also extensive patting and cuddling imitation of babysitter)
(imitates parents gardening)

eat and feed (eating movements with fork, offers fork to E)
drink (drinks from empty cup and offers to E)
hug (wide variety of human and animal toys)
telephone (tries to put rubber ball to ear like receiver, while looking at telephone)
brush (brushes own hair and babysitter's hair)
domestic tasks (types, gardens, dishwashes, tool work in garage after M and F)

Subject 20

1. tch (tongue click) da-da-da

2. ha-ha-ha ("raspberries")

3. rrrrr (car sound)

1. no (stops, gets upset)
mama (u.c.)
___ (own name, u.c.)
M (brother's name, u.c.)
dada (looks around room)
peekaboo (plays peekaboo)

1. ah (in reaching toward things she wants)
dadada (said during game of taking pen from F's pocket; also said when she wants to be picked up, into telephone and in imitations)
mama (when upset)

1. hug (imitates both parents hugging doll)
rock (imitates F rocking back and forth)
(imitates F's lipsmacking gesture to M)

2. peekaboo
claps hands
stacks blocks

1. peekaboo (plays alone, putting towel over head)
telephone (puts receiver behind her neck)
dress (puts on necklace)

2. drink (drinking movements out of any cupshaped object)

(continued)

Language imitation	Language comprehension	Language production	Number of words	Gestural imitation	Symbolic play
4. good girl pretty allgone (only imitates M)	2. Go get Daddy (seeks F who has just hidden) byebye (waves) dolly (own doll only, u.c.) book (u.c.) ball (u.c.) shoe (u.c.) 3. allgone (u.c.) banana (u.c.) Uncle C (looks around room for uncle) 4. Where's the ball? (seeks and finds despite difficulties) Bring Daddy the flower (gets flower and brings to F) Take the baby to Inge (takes doll and gives to E) Where's the book? (goes and gets book) Close the door (closes door) night-night (lies down) nap (lies down)	whee (noise of excitement) 2. bah (while looking at book) wah-wah-wah (request sound) beh-beh-beh (request sound) la-la-la (while "reading" books, turning pages) 3. dadee-dadoo (while crawling after F) bah (request sound) dah (request sound) (lipsmacking sound in food requests) 4. ba (while searching for and giving ball; also said in "naming") boo (also said during ball search) ndee-ndee = baby (?) (while giving doll) bye (while waving)	4 5 6 7 8 9 10 11 12 13	3. dress (imitates putting ring on self) 4. feed (imitates M burping doll) (at this point M reports that B will try to imitate almost anything M does. M has stopped keeping record)	eat (eating movements with empty spoon) dress (puts any piece of cloth on her head) read (babbling and pretend reading with books) feed (sticks pacifier in other people's mouths and laughs) 3. wave (waves byebye when F kisses M, including outside context of leaving) hug (hugs doll to face) sleep (sleeping movement on pillow outside bed context) feed (feeds E with empty fork; also feeds doll) brush (brushes own hair; also brushes doll's hair while feeding doll) wash (washes doll's face with cloth) dress (dresses doll) (elaborate instance in which B recreates stuffed ring from Piagetian test by placing cotton ball in empty ring)

ding-a-ling (makes
telephone gesture
with empty hand)
telephone (u.c.)
cookie (u.c.)
milk (u.c.)
tree (u.c.)
pretty (u.c.)

dadoo (=rough version 14
of playmate's name,
to playmate and to
photo of playmate)
good girl (says to 15
self, u.c.)
whuh (request sound,
acute)
ahaha (acute request
sound)

4. *telephone* (with empty
hand against ear as
well as phone)
dress (puts on lipstick)
eat (with empty spoon and
bowl)

Subject 21

1. *mamma*
   papa
2. ("raspberries")
   ___ *ga-ga*
3. no entry
4. *voom-voom* (car
   sound)

1. *mamma* (u.c.) 1
   papa 2
   pfff (aspirated sound 3
   made in refusals and
   in disgust)
   ahm-ahm (food request) 4

2. *mamma* (names M)
   mm (request sound) 5
   ta-ta (while waving 6
   ciao)
   papa (when he hears
   doorbell)
   brrr (for objects 7
   that make noise)
   fffff (to name hair- 8
   dryer)

1. *clap your hands*
   (claps, but only
   with grandmother)
   pablum (responds
   with ahm-ahm food
   sound)
   wave ciao (waves)
2. *Where's the dolly?*
   (goes to own room
   and points to doll)
   ___ (own name, re-
   sponds from another
   room by saying eh)
3. *stick out your tongue*
   (sticks out tongue)

1. no entry
2. ___ (imitates E putting
   cup on head – first
   puts back on E's head,
   then puts on own)
   hide (imitates E in
   object permanence
   game putting objects
   under screen)

1. ___ (initiates game of
   knocking off F's hat)
   ___ (as soon as he sees
   grandmother, begins
   clapping hands in recognition of pattycake game)
   ___ (waves ciao when he sees
   M put on coat)
2. no entry
3. *converse* (game of pretending to talk into speaker
   at downstairs door)
   feed (puts toy bottle
   against doll's face)

(continued)

Language imitation	Language comprehension	Language production	Number of words	Gestural imitation	Symbolic play
	3. Make a puppet (turns hand in handpuppet gesture)	3. papa (context again unclear)		3. ___ (imitates rolling rings on stick) At this point M reports many complex and persistent imitations of adult actions; M has stopped keeping record)	4. drink (drinking movements from closed bottle)
		nonna (to name grandmother)	9		
	4. Let's go to the car (goes to outside door)	4. bumba (baby word for water)	10		
	Turn on the light (turns on light)	boom (when something falls)	11		
	Let's go see the fish (goes to fish tank)	pu = non c'e piu = allgone (when something falls)	12		
	How does the doggie go? (says bow)	brr-brr (while climbing into car)			
	Where's mamma? (looks around for M)	vroom (while moving mechanical toy)		4. feed (imitates E feeding doll) claps hands	
	Let's play ball (throws ball)	L___ (to name cousin)	13		
	Throw it to mamma (throws ball to M)	4. bow-bow (when he sees dog or cat; also in answer to How does the dog go?)	14		
		vroom (to name cars or motorcycles)			
		A___ (F's name, to name F)	15		
		papa (also to name F, and when he hears motorcycle sound)			
		da = give (while giving or receiving)	16		
		tie = take (while giving only)	17		

(open-close mouth
gesture to name fish)
tch-tch (to name
horses)   18

Subject 22

1. pappa = pablum
   Chi e? = Who's
   there?
   ta-ta
   (siren sound)

2. ba-ba
   bua = hurt
   no

3. mamma
   ba

4. ah-ah (singsong
   sound)
   sheh = pesce = fish

---

1. Who's there? (crawls
   to door, imitating
   sound Who's there?)
   no (stops briefly)

2. Get me the doggie
   (picks up toy dog)
   Give me the doggie
   (drops toy dog)
   Where's the bow-wow?
   (points to toy dog)
   Where's Anna? or
   Mamma? or Grandma?
   (in each instance
   points to correct
   person)

3. mamma (names in
   variety of contexts)
   papa (names in variety
   of contexts)

4. Eda (another name
   for F, u.c.)
   Ba (to name sister
   M___, and to request
   or accompany supported
   walking. Probably
   derived from game of
   walking with sister)
   da (while talking
   into toy telephone)

---

1. no entry

2. pappa = pablum (names
   both food and water)
   no (spontaneous pro-
   duction, u.c.)
   ta-ta (while manipu-
   lating various ob-
   jects)

---

1. waves ciao
   hide (imitates gesture
   of hiding behind door)

2. clap (claps hand
   against piano)
   ___ (imitates gesture
   of pushing against
   wall)

3. sticks out tongue
   clap hands
   hug (imitates cuddling
   doll)

4. no entry

---

1. no entry

2. telephone (receiver to
   ear, babbling into
   receiver)
   eat (eating movements
   with plastic fruit)

3. dress (puts on necklace;
   puts doll's shoe against
   doll's foot)
   telephone (telephone
   movements now with variety
   of objects)
   hug (hugs and rocks doll)
   drink (drinking movements
   from empty cardboard box)
   sleep (sleeping movements
   using variety of objects
   as pillows)
   flute (makes motion of
   playing flute)

1
2
3
4
5
6
7
8

(continued)

Language imitation	Language comprehension	Language production	Number of words	Gestural imitation	Symbolic play
		Subject 22 (continued)			
	3. *Clap your hands* (claps)	4. *A* ___ (names one of sisters)	9		4. *hug* (also rocks toy kitten)
	Wave ciao (waves)	*nonna* (names grand-mother)	10		*comb* (combs own hair with empty hand)
	Rock the dolly (rocks doll)	*palla* = ball (to all balls)	11		*telephone* (plays telephone with empty hand in receiver position)
	Get your pacifier (picks up pacifier)	*bua* (=Italian word for "hurt", used correctly)	12		*feed* (feeding movements to self, to M, to doll, but not in clear succession)
	Bring the ___ *to Daddy* (correctly brings variety of toys, cup, other objects to F; at this point record was no longer kept)	*bada* = watch out (u.c.)	13		(deferred imitation of odd leg gesture by F; continues this for several days)
		si = yes (while nodding)	14		
		nene = no (in refusals)	15		
	4. *Do a somersault* (puts self into somersault position)	*haha* (surprise sound)			
	Clean your nose (rubs nose)	*da* = give (while giving)	16		
	Spin around (puts self in position for spinning game)	*ta* = *tieni* = take (while giving)	17		
	Where's Papa? (seeks F outside room)	*opop* = horse sound (while pointing to horse in book)	18		
	Bring me the tele-phone (brings telephone to speaker)	*apo* = *pronto* = hello (while receiver to ear)	19		
	Make mamma talk (brings telephone to M)	*acca* = *acqua* = water (while pointing to fountain)	20		
	Sit down (sits)				

Subject 23

Vocalizations / words said	Comprehension (responds to)	Words produced	No.	Imitation	Symbolic play
1. *dada*	1. *come here* (comes)	1. *dada* (says to begin horsey games again with F; also as general happy sound) *mama* (whenever he needs help)	1 2	1. no entry	1. *drink* (mouth to drink position on empty cup)
2. no entry	2. *no* (stops and smiles) *hello* (with telephone, u.c.) *milk* (u.c.) *turn around* (u.c.) *byebye* (waves, but only with F)	2. *dadu* = thank you (while giving or receiving) *ya* (u.c.) *byebye* (u.c.)	3 4 5	2. no entry	2. *drink* (now licks cup, drinking movements, then vocalizes into cup) *dress* (puts bear's hat on and off in game with M) *hug* (pets and hugs toy bunny) *cook* (deferred imitation of stirring in bowl with egg whisk)
3. *hello* ___ (Indian whoop) ___ (friend's name)	3. *Where's the ball?* (crawls across room and gets ball) *Give mama a kiss* (smacks lips from a distance, only for M) *Whoop like an Indian* (makes whooping sound) *stop* (overhears on tape recorder and stops, turns and offers keys to tape recorder)	3. *hello* (says into telephone) *mmm* (for milk) *dog* (names toy and real dog) *that* (while pointing or showing) *Jeh* (while playing with friend *J*) *ba* (names balls) *look* (u.c.) *mama* (u.c.) *hot* (u.c.) *yes* (u.c.)	6 7 8 9 10 11 12 13 14	3. ___ (M's hand-to-mouth Indian whoop gesture) (characteristic hand-to-nose gesture in game with M) *car* (regularly imitates older boys in moving trucks and cars around floor)	3. *hide* (deferred imitation of object permanence game) *drink* (plays tea with neighbor child, drinks from cup and extends for refill) *sleep* (sleeping movements on pillow outside bed context) *hug* (hugs teddybear) *telephone* (receiver to ear) *eat* (extensive eating movements with various objects, including chair bottom as plate)
4. *brrrr* (car sound) *uhoh* (singsong adult sound) *eekoo* = peekaboo	4. *no* (now shakes head) *peekaboo* (obeys by shutting box with object in it)	4. *eh* (request sound)		4. ___ (puts ring back on E's head after E demonstrates) *ball* (imitates older boys in overhand throw of ball) *sleep* (sleeping movement)	

(continued)

Language imitation	Language comprehension	Language production	Number of words	Gestural imitation	Symbolic play

Subject 23 (continued)

Language comprehension	Language production	Number of words	Symbolic play
nose (points correctly in book)	mommy (u.c.)	15	4. dress (tries to put doll's shoe on own foot)
ear (points correctly in book)	uh-oh (with adult singsong intonation, says while throwing objects, and while examining and playing with objects)		eat and feed (eats from empty utensils, and also feeds E)
mouth (points correctly in book)			drink (now with swallowing)
hair (points correctly in book)	D___ (friend's name)	16	car (rolls toy car on floor)
byebye (waves)	peek (in peekaboo game and while putting object in box)	17	comb (combs own hair)
kiss (kisses)			feed (puts pacifier in doll's mouth)
Comb your hair (combs hair, but only if he is already holding comb)	please (u.c.)	18	wave (waves to TV when M pulls him away from it)
cereal (runs and gets highchair)	baby (u.c.)	19	___ (deferred imitation of various Piagetian tests)
juice (goes to sit down and wait)	more (u.c.)	20	
touch the flowers (touches)			
grandpa (shows excitement)			
Get the shoe (goes and gets)			
water (u.c.)			
milk (u.c.)			

Subject 24

	1. no (shakes head)	1. qua-qua = duck (u.c.)	1	1. shakes head no	1. no entry

Column 1

1. mama
   papa
   qua-qua (duck sound)
   ahm (food sound)
   bow-bow (dog sound)
   ("raspberries")
   ___ (whistling sound)

2. beh (sheep sound)
   moo (cow sound)
   P___ (aunt's name)
   M___ (cousin's name)
   bello = pretty
   cacca = acqua = water
   brrr (tongue roll)
   tick-tock
   nonno = grandpa

3. ___ (Indian whoop)
   uh-oh (adultlike surprise sound)

4. opop (horse sound)
   coco (hen sound)
   T___ (aunt's name)

Column 2

1. no (shakes head)
   Give a kiss (kisses)
   Clap your hands (claps)
   Wave Ciao (waves)
   Let's hit heads

2. (places forehead a-gainst adult's)
   Where are your little thoughts? (places hand against head)

2. Where are your ears? (touches own ears)
   Where's your nose? (touches own nose)
   Get your toys or Where are your toys? (goes over to toy-chest)
   Where's Daddy? or Mamma? or Luisa (E) (turns to correct person. M reports that B does this correctly in almost any group of adults)
   Where's the kitty? (points to cat in book)

Column 3

1. qua-qua = duck (u.c.)   1
   bow-bow = dog (u.c.)   2
   papa (names)   3
   mama (names)   4

2. ahm (name for any food 5
   or drink)
   P___ (names aunt)   6
   M___ (names cousin)   7
   bebe = baby (points   8
   and names own reflec-
   tion in mirror)

3. bow-bow or boo = ĉog   9
   (in answer to How does
   the dog go?
   mao = cat (ditto)   10
   moo = moocow (ditto)   11
   beh = sheep (ditto)
   flu (on seeing ciga-   12
   rette)
   brrrm (on seeing any   13
   wheel)
   boom (first while   14
   throwing a plastic
   peach, later on show-
   ing off the same peach)

Column 4

1. shakes head no
   waves ciao
   claps hands (handpuppet ges-ture in game)
   rock (characteristic lullabye rocking gesture)

2. ___ (imitates hand-to-lip gesture)

3. ___ (imitates pulling her own ear)

4. rock (now carries out lullabye gesture with nothing in her arms)
   ___ (imitates E making the toy kitten walk)

Column 5

1. no entry

2. dress (places doll's shoe against own foot)
   rock (rocks doll, and occasionally does the same with plastic fruit)
   telephone (receiver to ear, babbling)

3. eat (eating movements with plastic fruit)
   ___ (says mao = cat, while petting aunt's fur coat; deferred imitation of aunt's performance the day before)

4. dress (places doll's shoe against doll's foot)
   feed (puts baby bottle against doll's mouth saying ahm = food sound; puts baby bottle against mouth of toy kitten)
   hug (hugs and/or rocks doll, toy kitten, frog, and mechanical doll)

(continued)

Language imitation	Language comprehension	Language production	Number of words	Gestural imitation	Symbolic play
		Subject 24 (continued)			
	Where's the bunny? (points to bunny in book)	_M___ (cousin's name, now extended to name all male children) *bebe* = baby (now to name all female children)	15		*kiss* (kisses toy kitten; makes kitten and doll kiss each other; kisses picture of kitten and frog in book)
	3. ___ (at this point M reports that B now points correctly to most of the known figures in her books; M has stopped records) *Give me your hand* (shakes hands)	*haha* (aspirated sound used to name flowers, derived from sniffing gesture)	16		
	Where are your eyes? (squeezes eyes shut) *What's this?* (answers by naming thing or person indicated by adult) *How does the ___ go?* (on request, gives appropriate sounds for cat, dog, cow)	4. *no* (in refusals) *ta* (while giving objects) *voom* (names any moving mechanical object) *boom* (names balls or any falling object - see peach example above)	17 18		
	4. *Where's your car?* (says *voom* and turns to car) *Bring the ___ to ___* (brings named object to named recipient in wide variety of combinations. M has stopped keeping record)	*pu = non c'e piu =* allgone (said when an object disappears or when she has finished an activity such as turning book pages)	19		

How does the frog go?
(says craaa)
Do you want to give me the frog? (shakes head "no")
Where's papa? (seeks in various rooms)

20 *mac* = cat (names cats in books while pointing, and without adult prompting. But does occasionally make errors)
boo or *bow-bow* = dog (ditto)
21 *craa* = frog (ditto)
moo = moocow (ditto)
22 *nonno* = grandpa (names grandfather, also names grandparents house on arrival)

Subject 25

1. ___ (pig sound)
opop (horse sound)
papa
zia = aunt
2. *ecco* = here it is
B (M's name)
peppe = *scarpe* = shoes
talco = talcum powder
issa = upsedaisy

1. *Clap your hands* (claps)
wave ciao (waves)
2. *Where's F___?* (looks around room for cousin)

1. *eh-ah* (request sound)
B (rough approximation to M's proper name, u.c.)
2. *mimimi* (request sound)
da = give (says while giving)
tazie = *grazie* = thanks (says while receiving only; both *da* and *tazie* are said in exchange sequences on-

1. *waves ciao*
claps hands
2. *dress* (imitates E placing doll shoe against doll's foot)
___ (ritual gesture in imitation of M in song game)
3. *sticks out tongue*

1. no entry
2. no entry
3. *dress* (takes off doll's shoe)
comb (combs own hair with brush or with empty hand)
4. *dress* (puts on necklace)

(continued)

219

Language imitation	Language comprehension	Language production	Number of words	Gestural imitation	Symbolic play

Language imitation	Language comprehension	Language production	Number of words	Gestural imitation	Symbolic play
bubu (dog sound)	___ (on request will	ly after M has said		*hush* (places index	*feed* (puts baby bottle
papa (*Dov'e andato*	make the appropriate	*How do you say?*)		finger against side	against doll's mouth,
papa = Where did	noises for *hen, roo-*	*no* (u.c.)	6	of nose in imitation	places both kitten and
Daddy go?)	*ster, duck, donkey,*	*hihihi* (donkey sound	7	of *hush* gesture)	doll, separately, against
	and either *puppy* or	said on request)			mouth of cup to drink)
3. *zitta* = hush	*dog*)	*kiki* (rooster sound,	8	4. *shrug* (characteristic	*drink* (drinking movements
	How do you say? (When	on request)		Italian gesture mean-	from various empty paper
4. (at this point M	M says this during	*bubu* (dog sound, on	9	ing "alligone")	containers)
reports that B tries	an exchange of ob-	request)			*kiss* (kisses own image in
to imitate with per-	jects between M and	*coco* (hen sound, on	10		mirror on command)
sistence virtually	B, or between B and	request)			*telephone* (dials and says
any new word which	someone else, B says	*qua-qua* (duck sound;	11		*ya* into receiver)
interests her. M	*da* while giving and	like all the above			*rock* (rocks toy kitten)
has stopped keeping	*tazie* [= thanks] while	animal noises, said			___ (gives large shrug
record)	taking)	only in response to			gesture as comment when
		request *How does the*			something disappears)
	3. ___ (on request now	*go?*)			*wave* (waves "ciao" spon-
	also makes the appro-	*nonna* = grandma (names	12		taneously when someone
	priate sounds for *pig*	or calls)			leaves)
	and *baby chick*)	*B* (M's name, to			___ (deferred imitation of
	Where's papa? (looks	name or call)			a game of putting a block
	for F all over house)				on her own head, something
	Hush (responds with	3. *da* = give (while giv-			M showed her several days
	gesture of putting	ing or requesting,			before)
	index finger to side	spontaneous now)			
	of nose)	*te* = *tieni* = take			
	puppy (when M is talk-	(while giving only,			
	ing to E about a pup-	also spontaneous now)			
	py, B overhears and	*mamma* (in requests)			
	says *baba*, her own	*pappa* = pablum (u.c.)	13		
	word for puppy)	*zia* = aunt (u.c.)	14		

4. _____ (on request, now also makes the appropriate sounds for birdie, cat, mosquito, car, moocow, and airplane)

Sing (sings)

What do we do now? (makes Italian shrugging gesture with palms joined)

Clean your mouth (cleans mouth)

Where's papa? (goes to F's studio)

Where's the moon? (looks to sky)

Rock the kittycat (rocks cat)

Kiss the kittycat (kisses cat)

Give the kitty a drink (puts cup to cat's mouth)

Make Mommy telephone (hands telephone to M by cord)

Kiss _____ (own name, kisses own reflection in mirror)

hiho = donkey (names pictures)	
baba = dog (names in pictures)	15
chuchu = pig (names in pictures)	
pio-pio = baby chick (names in pictures)	16
papa (to name or call F)	17
ro (in refusals)	
tazie = grazie = thanks (says only in receiving)	
agghi (very strong request sound)	18
aeo = aereo = airplane	19
zia = aunt (names)	
zio = uncle (names)	20
M_____ (grandfather's name, names)	21
D_____ (Nonna D_____ = one of grandmother's names, names)	22
C_____ (names cousin F_____)	23
Pe_____ (names cousin	24
F_____)	
Pi_____ (names teddy-bear)	25

(continued)

Language imitation	Language comprehension	Language production	Number of words	Gestural imitation	Symbolic play
		Subject 25 (continued)			
	Where are ____'s shoes? (own name, touches one of her shoes and says shoes)	*Pepe* (names specific duck character in book)	26		
	pappa = scarpe =	*mucca* = moocow (names)	27		
		mao = kitty (names)	28		
	Where's your leg? (touches own thigh)	*brr* (answer to *How does the car go?*)	29		
	Where's the baby? (says *bimba* = "baby" and looks around; may be calling to doll)	*hooo* (answer to *How does the airplane go?*)	30		
		pappe = scarpe = shoes (names)	31		
		ninna = rockabye (while rocking doll, in singsong)	32		
		acqua = water (names)	33		
		palla = ball (names)	34		
		bimba = bambola = doll = doll (names mechanical baby doll)	35		
		ya (says into toy telephone)	36		

a This represents a cumulative word count, including both referential and nonreferential words. If a word occurred in two slightly different versions (e.g., *dada* and *daddy*), it was only counted once. If a similar sound occurred consistently with two very different meanings, e.g.,*ba* as a dog's name and for a ball, it was counted twice.

b "(u.c.)" after an item means that the context in which the item was produced was unclear (e.g., the mother reported that the baby said kitty, but did not specify the precise context in which the word was produced).

Chapter 5

RELATIONSHIPS BETWEEN COGNITION, COMMUNICATION, AND QUALITY OF ATTACHMENT

Inge Bretherton
Elizabeth Bates
Laura Benigni
Luigia Camaioni
Virginia Volterra

Social and cognitive development are inextricably intertwined: Without being able to interpret the behavior of social companions, one cannot respond to them appropriately; and interpreting the meaning of behavior in turn requires cognitive processes at some level. In this chapter we are not asking **whether** one should expect levels of cognitive functioning to be reflected in the expression and comprehension of social behavior. We assume that this must be the case. Rather, we are asking a more specific question regarding how cognitive and communicative competence might be influenced by the quality of the relationship between and infant and his or her mother (or major caregiver).

The idea that social interaction is in some way involved in symbol formation is not a new one. In his theory of symbolic interaction, G. H. Mead (1934) proposed that individual cognition is a reflection of social exchange, the internalization of interaction in the form of "significant symbols" which can have the same effect on both the speaker and the listener. In *Symbol Formation* (1963), Werner and Kaplan emphasize the role of the relationship between addressor and addressee in the emergence of symbols in infancy. For traditional psychoanalytic theory and for the neo-Freudian "object relations" theorists (e.g., Kernberg,

1976) the symbolic function—in the Piagetian sense—is believed to arise during the oral stage as a product of emotionally charged interactions between infant and caregiver. A similar theme is apparent in much of the recent research on mother–infant interaction (see Lewis and Rosenblum, 1977, and Schaffer, 1977, for reviews). For example, Bruner (1977) has suggested that preverbal interaction provides the scaffolding that is essential for the emergence of language, as well as the major categories of early semantics and syntax. Attachment theory, as formulated by Bowlby (1969, 1973) and Ainsworth (1973) has added a second idea here: That the harmoniousness of the relationship between mother and child contributes to the emergence of symbolic thought **directly** via mother–child interaction, but that it also contributes **indirectly** by enhancing the child's capacity to explore the environment on his or her own.

Attachment theory emphasizes the role of the mother as a source of security. The infant's propensity to seek proximity to the mother or other major caregiver—at first excercised by signalling behavior and later by locomotor following and approach—is seen as fulfilling a protective function. A curious infant who has a tendency to remain in fairly close proximity to the mother is less likely to come to harm than an infant who pays no heed to the whereabouts of his or her caregiver. Like Piaget (1952), Bowlby and Ainsworth think of the infant as an active explorer, set on discovering the world; but unlike Piaget, Bowlby and Ainsworth see the infant's exploratory tendencies as being held in check by an opposing propensity to remain within some degree of proximity to the mother and to withdraw to her should anything unusual or frightening occur. Bowlby, rooted in psychoanalysis but also inspired by both modern and classical ethology (e.g., Lorenz, 1935; Hinde, 1966) worked out the normative aspect of attachment theory. Ainsworth (see Ainsworth, 1973, for a short overview), on the other hand, set herself the task of developing a methodology which would make it possible to assess individual differences in mother–infant interaction. She hypothesized that if indeed infants use their mother as a secure base from which to explore the world and as a secure haven to which to flee if danger threatens, then mothers who do not respond reasonably promptly and appropriately to their infants' signals, especially in stressful situations, may produce infants who are less prone to explore the environment because of anxiety about their mothers' accessibility and responsiveness. Ainsworth's methodology will be described shortly. Suffice it here to say that her ideas inspired many studies in which investigators sought to establish relationships between the quality of mother–child attachment and cognitive and communicative functioning. Two hypotheses have generally been advanced by these investigators as to why such relationships might be expected:

Hypothesis 1: Infants who can feel assured of their mother's availability and responsiveness, especially in situations of stress, can devote themselves more fully and enthusiastically to interacting with the physical environment. In other words, because these infants can use the mother as a secure base from which to launch out into the world, they can learn more about the environment and about properties of objects by teaching themselves (the attachment–exploration hypothesis)

Hypothesis 2: If infant and mother can achieve an interactive style in which harmony and affective synchrony predominate, the infant has increased opportunity to acquire cognitive and communicative skills through interaction with the mother (the attachment–teaching hypothesis).

Hypothesis 1 ascribes the influence of quality of attachment on cognitive development to motivational factors: The baby is freed for exploratory activities if he does not anxiously have to keep track of the caregiver's whereabouts. Exploration and attachment are seen as functioning in a dynamic balance which may be disturbed if the mother is too unresponsive or too inconsistently responsive to her infant's security-seeking behavior.

Hypothesis 2 explains the predicted effect of the mother–infant relationship on cognitive and communicative functioning through motivational **and** learning factors. The feelings of satisfaction which derive from pleasurable interactions are believed to lead to further interactions (positive feedback) and it is within such mutually satisfying interactions that the infant first discovers that his or her behaviors (signals) have an effect on others—that is, that they have communicative value. Also, within the context of interactions a baby can acquire cognitive skills through playing games such as peekaboo (learning about object permanence) and through direct teaching (being shown how to stack blocks, or to play "telephone").

In order to monitor the process whereby a mother–infant couple develops more or less harmonious styles of interaction one can (like Ainsworth, Blehar, Waters, and Wall, 1978) make detailed and frequent observations, recording the transactions between baby and mother in a variety of naturally occurring situations. Such observations make it possible to witness the emergence of fairly stable interactional patterns for each mother–infant dyad in the course of the first year. Alternatively, one can take the same shortcut that we have elected here, observing infants for 20 minutes in what has become known as "the strange situation" (Ainsworth and Wittig, 1969). Infants' behavior in this situation, which we will describe forthwith, has been shown to relate to many aspects of the quality of caregiver–infant interactions throughout the first year of life. These relationships will be discussed in some detail later.

The strange situation is a miniature drama staged in a laboratory playroom. Three actors, baby, mother, and a stranger participate in a standard sequence of eight episodes (described in more detail in Table 5.1). The procedure permits assessment of the degree to which infants can use their mother as a secure base from which to explore the unfamiliar playroom and toys and the degree to which the introduction of potentially stressful events (encounter with a stranger, departure of the mother from the playroom) disrupt an infant's exploratory activities and heighten attachment behavior directed towards the mother. Although the purpose which lay behind the design of the strange situation was to demonstrate individual differences in the interplay of a baby's attachment and exploratory behavior, the serendipitous but ultimately more important finding was that individual differences in this situation— especially behavior to the mother during reunion with her—were systematically related to many measures of dyadic functioning in the home environment. The patterns observed by Ainsworth in the strange situation were as follows:

Group B infants: These infants explored the toys provided in the playroom with alacrity as long as they were alone with their mothers during Episode 2. When a stranger entered in Episode 3, they showed some decrease in play activity although they were usually not undone by the stranger's presence. B babies tended to cry after their mother's departure from the room at the end of Episodes 3 and 5, but their crying often did not start immediately. When the mother returned in Episodes 5 and 8, B infants were usually active in seeking proximity, contact and/or interaction with her. If they had been distressed during separation they were relatively easily soothed.

Group A infants: This group of babies behaved much like Group B before separation, although they were on the whole less wary of the unfamiliar person in Episode 3. They did not cry when left with the stranger in Episodes 4 and 7, although some became distressed when left alone in Episode 6. Group A babies engaged in search for the mother while she was absent in Episodes 4, 6, and 7, but on her return tended not to greet her, to turn away from her after a partial approach, to ignore her and snub her in other ways.

Group C infants: This group was generally less able to use the mother as a secure base from which to explore the playroom in Episode

TABLE 5.1
The Strange Situation Procedure

Episode	Duration	Participants	Events
1.	30 seconds	Mother, Baby	The observer shows mother and baby into the room and leaves after instructing the mother where to sit and where to put the baby down.
2.	3 minutes	Mother, Baby	Mother puts the baby down close to her chair and at a distance of 5 feet from the toys. She may respond to the baby but has been asked not to initiate social interaction. The baby is free to explore, but if the baby does not move, the mother may take him to the toys after 2 minutes.
3.	3 minutes	Mother, Baby, Stranger	This episode has three parts. The stranger enters, greets Mother and Baby, and sits opposite the Mother quietly for 1 minute (responding to the baby's social bids if any occur). During the second minute, the stranger engages the mother in conversation. The stranger then gets down on the floor and attempts to engage the baby in play for the third minute. At the end of Episode 3, the mother leaves "unobtrusively" (the baby usually notices).
4.	3 minutes or less	Baby, Stranger	The stranger sits back on her chair, responding to any social or play bids the baby might address to her. If the baby becomes distressed, the stranger attempts to comfort him. If this is not effective, the mother is asked to return before the 3 minutes are up. (And the stranger leaves).
5.	3 minutes	Mother, Baby	The mother calls the baby's name outside the door and then enters, comforting the baby if necessary and then reengaging him in play. If the baby is not distressed, the mother goes to sit on her chair taking a responsive, but noninitiatory role. At the end of the Episode, the mother leaves, saying *Byebye. I'll be back soon.*
6.	3 minutes	Baby alone	The baby remains alone for 3 minutes unless he becomes distressed, in which case the stranger enters.
7.	3 minutes or less	Baby, Stranger	The stranger attempts to comfort the baby if needed. Otherwise, she sits on her chair, responding to but not initiating any social bids. If the baby cannot be comforted, the mother returns early.
8.	3 minutes	Baby, Mother	The mother enters as the stranger leaves. She behaves as in Episode 5.

2. During that episode and even more during Episode 3, C babies were often found to be passive, sticking close to the mother. They were usually wary of the stranger and tended to cry the moment their mothers left the room, strongly resisting the stranger's attempt to comfort them. Upon the mother's return they showed strong proximity and contact seeking (often but not invariably by signaling rather than active approach). However their proximity promoting behaviors were accompanied by angry, tantrumy resisting behaviors (squirming in the mother's arms, pushing away toys she offered).

The behavior by which these three groups were most clearly distinguished was their behavior on reunion with the mother, rather than the behavior during her absence, although this also contributed to the classification.

A number of highly interesting relationships emerged when the patterns observed in the strange situation were compared with the behavior of the mother–infant pair in the home. The mothers of Group B infants were distinguished from those of Groups A and C by responding more appropriately and promptly to their infants' crying during the first quarter of the first year of life. They tended to pace face-to-face interactions (Blehar, Liebermann, and Ainsworth, 1977) and feedings (Ainsworth and Bell, 1969) more contingently upon the baby's behavior and were observed to initiate more interactions as well as to engage in more tender careful holding of their babies during the first 3 months. This maternal behavior during the first quarter was related to infant behavior in the last quarter of the first year. During the 9–12-months period, B infants enjoyed physical contact more, although they sought it less often. Instead of communicating with the mother by whining, crying and fussing, B infants had by the last quarter developed a clearer and more extensive repertoire of communicative signals (Bell and Ainsworth, 1974). In addition, B infants also scored higher on the Griffith's Scale of Infant Intelligence. In sum the interactions between B dyads were smoother and more harmonious, and B infants seemed more **competent.** Both A and C mothers were less responsive to their babies' signals, but A mothers (more than B and C mothers) frequently rejected their infants' initiatives, especially bids for physical contact (Main, 1976). C mothers, on the other hand, tended to be inconsistent rather than rejecting in response to their infants' signals (Ainsworth *et al.*, 1978).

These findings by Ainsworth and her colleagues have led to a number of further studies in which investigators looked for relationships between strange situation behavior, and both infant and maternal behavior in the first, second, and third year of life. Only one group of these studies concerns us here: those which were inspired by the finding that B infants had developed a larger and more readable repertoire of communicative behaviors in the last quarter of the first year (Hypothesis 2) and those which predicted cognitive differences between B and non-B infants on the basis of Hypotheses 1 and 2.

The major findings of these studies are listed in Table 5.2. It is apparent at first glance that a large number of studies **did** find the predicted relationship between quality of attachment (as measured indirectly by the strange situation) and cognitive or communicative functioning. Although a substantial number of studies did **not** show correlations between attachment and cognition or communication (in some of these studies the means were in the predicted direction but fell short of significance) it is important to note that, so far at least, no study seems to have discovered a negative relationship. In all cases where significant relationships did emerge, they always favored B infants over non-B infants.

The strange situation was validated for 12 months by Ainsworth *et al.* (1978), but some investigators have used it with infants aged 18 months. Both Connell (1975) and Waters (1978) independently found that if the strange situation is administered to groups of infants at 12 and 18 months, there is a very high probability that the infants will be reclassified into the same groups (81% and 95%, respectively). It may be inferred that it is a meaningful procedure at 18 months also. One study cited in Table 5.2 used the strange situation with 28-month-olds. Until validations against behavior in other situations are made, we cannot be sure that being placed into the A, B, or C group at 28 months is equivalent to being classified into these groups at 12 or 18 months, but the possibility cannot be ruled out a priori.

Hypothesis 1, the idea that securely attached infants teach themselves by exploring the inanimate environment more eagerly and/or intensely and effectively, was tested by a small number of studies. One of these (Harmon *et al.*, in press) discovered that total amount of toy manipulation did not distinguish 12-month-old B infants from A infants. A significant difference emerged, however, when combinatorial (nesting, stacking) and symbolic play (using a toy telephone appropriately) were separated out from the more primitive schemes of banging and shaking. Main (1973), like Harmon *et al.*, observed infants' exploratory play in a laboratory situation where the mother was available but encouraged not to interact with her infant unless the baby invited it. Main's group of 20-month-old Group B toddlers engaged in substantially longer bouts of exploration with one object or a set of objects (such as a toy stove and a set of pots) than non-B children. Moreover, the B

TABLE 5.2

Findings of Studies Relating Strange Situation Classifications and Ratings with Cognition and Communication

Age at Strange Situation	Relationships of Strange Situation classification or ratings with	At age (months)		Sample size
		Significant Relationships with Cognitive/Play Variables[a]		
12	DQ (Griffiths Scale)	12	Bell and Ainsworth, 1972	23
12	DQ (Griffiths Scale)	8.5,11,15	Bell, 1978	33
	IQ (Stanford-Binet)	30		
12	DQ (Bailey)	20.5	Main, 1973	40
11.5	Person Permanence	10,11	Bell, 1970	33
11	Person Permanence	8.5,11,14.5	Bell, 1978	33
11.5	Object Permanence	14.5	Bell, 1970	33
11	Object Permanence	14.5	Bell, 1978	33
12	Means-End Relations (Uzgiris-Hunt)	11,12	Bretherton, Bates, Benigni, Camaioni, and Volterra, this volume	25
18	Tool Use (with Mother's Help)	24	Matas, Arend, and Sroufe, 1978	48
12	Quality of Exploration	20.5	Main, 1973	40
12	Quality of Cognitively Mature Play (Combinatorial and Symbolic Play)	12	Harmon, Suwalski, and Klein, in press	36
18	Duration of Symbolic Play Bouts	24	Matas et al., 1978	48
12	Level, Breadth, and Frequency of Symbolic Play	11,12	Bretherton et al., this volume	25
	Frequency of Combinatorial Play	11		

Significant Relationships with Communicative Variables[a]

12	Clarity and Variety of Communicative Signals	9-12	Bell and Ainsworth, 1972	23
12	Communicative Gestures	11,12	Bretherton et al., this volume	25
12	Observed Vocabulary Size and Imitation of Words Uttered by Mother	18	Connell, 1975	55
12	Number of Morphemes/Utterance	20.5	Main, 1973	40
28	Percentage of Utterances that are Questions	36	Pentz, 1975	31

No Significant Relationships with Cognitive/Play Variables

12	DQ (Bailey)	11.5,18	Clarke-Stewart, 1973	38
12	DQ (Cattell)	14	Connell, 1975	26
	IQ (Stanford-Binet)	30		
11	DQ (Bailey)	24	Bell, 1978	33
	IQ (Stanford-Binet)	36		
18	DQ (Bailey)	24	Matas et al., 1978	48
12	DQ (Bailey)	3,8,11	Hock, 1976	164
12	Object Permanence, Space, Imitation (Uzgiris-Hunt)	10,11,12	Bretherton et al., this volume	25
12	Object Permanence, Combined Means-End + Space Scale	13	Clarke-Stewart, 1973	38
12	Level and Duration of Symbolic Play	20.5	Main, 1973	40
12	Combinatorial Play	10,12	Bretherton et al., this volume	25

(continued)

TABLE 5.2 (continued)

Age at Strange Situation	Relationships of Strange Situation classification or ratings with	At age (months)		Sample size
	No Siginificant Relationships with Communicative Variables			
12	Language Competence	18	Clarke-Stewart, 1973	38
28	MLU, Imitation of Maternal Utterances	28,36	Pentz, 1975	31
	Comprehension	36		
	Percentage of Utterances that are Questions	28		
	Number of Utterances	28,36		
12	Referential versus Expressive Style, Comprehension of Commands	18	Connell, 1975	44
12	Number of Different Words Uttered, Number of Words per Utterance	20.5	Main, 1973	40
12	Comprehension, Referential and Nonreferential Words (Maternal Interview and Observation Variables)	10,11,12	Bretherton et al., this volume	25

[a] In all cases where significant relationships were found, Group B infants always perform at a level superior to Group A infants, or Group A and C infants combined. In those studies where interactive ratings were used, proximity and contact seeking correlate positively with cognitive performance and avoidance resistance correlate negatively with cognitive performance.

toddlers exhibited considerably more positive affect in the course of play (smiling at or about the toys, which is not to be confused with smiling at mother). B toddlers were also judged to be more intensely engaged in their play. A shape box was treated as a problem solving toy by a substantial number of B children, but only by one A child.

Studies in which attempts were made to link strange situation behavior to performance on Piagetian tasks or on standardized developmental tests have cited both Hypotheses 1 and 2 when predicting positive correlations between quality of attachment and competence. Bell (1972), who undertook the first such study, suggested that infants whose mothers responded to them consistently and contingently would develop person permanence before object permanence (i.e., she predicted a positive decalage for person permanence in B babies from stages 4 to 6). Bell did indeed find this to be the case, first in a sample of white middle-class infants (1972) and later in a sample of black, underprivileged infants (1978). In both studies Group B infants showed a positive decalage for person permanence; infants of Groups A and C, however, showed either a positive decalage for object permanence or no decalage at all. B infants also reached a higher level on person permanence than did A and C infants on object permanence. At 14.5 months, B infants in both of Bell's samples were more advanced on object permanence as well. Clarke-Stewart (1973) tested infants on object permanence, schema level, means–end relations, and spatial relations using the Uzgiris–Hunt Scale (1975). No differences between strange situation groups emerged in her study, but since she did not test for person permanence separately her results cannot be compared with Bell's. A tool-use task which could be regarded as an extension of the Uzgiris–Hunt means–end scale was presented to a group of 24-month olds by Matas, Arend, and Sroufe (1978). The children had to weight down a lever to raise candy through a hole in a plexiglass container and to put two sticks end to end to obtain a lure from a tube. The difficulty of these tasks was such that the children needed to enlist the help of their mothers in order to succeed with this task, so no data are available on the children's absolute performance level. However, these investigators report that B children spent significantly more time on the task than did A and C children combined, that B children showed fewer frustration behaviors while attempting to solve the task, that they complied with maternal suggestions more often and showed more positive affect. Matas *et al.* propose that the greater affective support these children have come to expect from their mothers leads to greater competence in problem-solving situations.

Turning now from performance on Piagetian tasks to level of achievement on DQ and IQ tests, we find an almost equal number of studies which demonstrate significant effects and no effects. Indeed, in some longitudinal studies significant effects favoring B children were found at some ages, but not at others. In Main's (1973) study, B infants not only obtained higher test scores on the Bayley Scale, but entered into the test situation with much more cooperativeness and "gamelike spirit" than the A and C toddlers. Bell (1978), for her underprivileged sample, reported significant differences favoring B infants at 8, 11, 15, and 30 months, but not at 24 and 30 months. In the Matas *et al.* investigation, B toddlers performed better than did A and C children at 23 months, but the difference between the means was not statistically significant. Clarke-Stewart (1973) also found no differences in performance on the Bayley test at 12 and 18 months. Hock (1975) did not use the Ainsworth classifications for her enormous sample. Instead, she employed the rating scale for interactive behavior during the reunion episodes which were also developed by Ainsworth *et al.* (1978). At neither 3, 8, nor 11 months did she find correlations of DQ with proximity and contact seeking, or with proximity avoiding and contact resisting, although her own independent measure "quality of mothering" was positively correlated with DQ at these ages. Connell (1975) administered the Cattell Scale to a group of children at 18 months and the Stanford–Binet Test to a second group of children at 30 months without finding significant differences between B and non-B children.

Let us now finally discuss the studies which predicted relationships between communicative competence and quality of attachment, for example, studies which sought to verify Hypothesis 2 according to which the development of communicative behavior should be facilitated in dyads where the mother gives contingent feedback to the infant's signals. Hypothesis 2 would lead one to expect that B infants would discover sooner than A and C infants that their gestural and vocal signals could influence the mother's behavior. Moreover, the mother's contingent responsiveness could be related to an earlier discovery of the efficacy of gestural and vocal signals but could, conceivably, also contribute to their ritualization (if your mother usually pays attention to your requesting gestures, you can afford to ask for an object by opening and closing your hand while reaching toward the object rather than by attempting to grab it or by making fussy sound until you obtain it). Other than our own study, which we will shortly describe, no other investigations beyond the original one by Bell and Ainsworth (1972) have looked at preverbal communication in B versus non-B infants. There are a number of studies, however, in which language communication was found to be correlated with strange situation behavior. Main (1973) assessed language competence in her 20-month-old toddlers during a laboratory playsession using three different measures: number of morphemes per utterance, number of words per utterance, and number of different words spoken. Only the first of these variables was significantly related to strange situation group. For the other two measures the means favored Group B without being significantly different. Connell (1975) who, as we have already mentioned, did not observe DQ scores to be different at 18 months, did report significant differences in vocabulary size (as observed independently in the home) between strange situation groups. At 18 months, B children, especially girls, had substantially and significantly larger vocabularies than did A children, but they did not, as Connell had predicted, use an expressive as opposed to a referential style of speech (Nelson, 1973). Connell had expected such differences because he found that B dyads interacted more at home than A dyads, but it is not clear to us why he expected that more social interaction would ipso facto lead to more talking about people and why less interaction should lead to more talking about things. In fact, one might postulate the opposite: Children whose mothers are less responsive may have more occasion to say *I want, gimme, come over here,* and *no* (I should note here that Connell thinks of the differences between A and B children in terms of sociability, rather than in terms of the quality of the mother–infant relationship). Clarke-Stewart (1973) measured language competence in terms of a composite variable which includes both language comprehension and production. No correlations between language competence and strange situation group were found in her sample. The most thoroughgoing study of child language as related to the strange situation was undertaken by Pentz (1975). Pentz found evidence for two speech styles in the mothers of his 28-month-olds (an informational–referential style and a directive style), which split into three styles when the dyads were seen again at 36 months (a social–expressive style appeared in addition to the two above-mentioned styles). However, only tenuous relationships between maternal speech style and child language competence emerged from his data. Furthermore, child language turned out not to be significantly related to strange situation variables. Only one child language measure out of nine (number of utterances which were questions at 36 months) was correlated with strange situation group. The other eight measures (number of utterances at 28 and 36 months, proportion of maternal utterances imitated at both ages, MLU at 28 and 26 months, proportion of utterances which are questions at 28 months, and scores on a comprehension test at 36 months) did not significantly differentiate between B and non-B children. Of course, Pentz's findings have to be treated with some reservation since he did use the strange situation for an age for which it has not been validated.

Considering the studies reviewed so far as a whole, we can make the following statements:

1. A substantial number of investigators have discovered positive relationships between quality of attachment as measured by the strange situation and cognitive functioning as assessed in a variety of ways. There is also a substantial number of studies in which the expected correlations were not found, but no investigation has as yet shown A or C children to perform at levels superior to B children.
2. Relationships between quality of attachment and language competence so far reported have been weaker, with a higher proportion of studies finding no differences in language competence between A, B, and C children.

Possible interpretations of the findings cited so far will be discussed as we add the results of our own study to the joint data bank. Our study was undertaken with two purposes in mind: First, to confirm the findings reported by Bell and Ainsworth (1972), who reported that group B children had a more extensive and more easily comprehensible repertoire of communicative gestures during the period between 9 and 12 months (verification of Hypothesis 2). Second, we wished to test for possible relationships between cognitive functioning and quality of attachment (verification of Hypotheses 1 and 2) in a group of babies who were observed repeatedly in a short-term longitudinal study.

Method

The procedures used for collecting data related to the cognitive and communicative behavior of our sample of 13 American and 12 Italian infants have already been described in some detail in Chapter 3. We will therefore limit ourselves here to explaining the Strange Situation procedure and the measures associated with it. Second, we will explain the prorating procedures which had to be applied to the cognitive and communicative measures. Last, we will define all cognitive and communicative variables used in this chapter, including some which do not appear in Chapter 3.

The Strange Situation

The Strange Situation consists of a standard sequence of 8 episodes as already described in Table 1.1. It was conducted in a laboratory playroom (the Italian playroom was about 3.5 x 5 m, the American playroom was about 3.5 x 3.5 m). The rooms contained three chairs which were arranged along three walls to form a triangle. The mother and stranger (when present) sat on two chairs facing one another; the third, a child's chair, stood against the wall opposite the observation window and had age-appropriate toys heaped on and about it (see Figure 5.1).

One member of the American research team (I.B.) who was familiar with the Strange Situation procedure visited the Italian team in Rome in order to run a number of training sessions. In both countries the sessions were videotaped. In addition a narrative report, divided into 15-second intervals, was dictated by I.B. for the American sample, and by L.B. for the Italian sample. At the time of making these dictations none of the cognitive–communicative data had been analyzed, let alone prorated, making the operation of a halo effect unlikely.

The ratings and classifications for the American subsample were made by Mary Main (University of California, Berkeley), who graciously volunteered her services for this task. She used the narrative records supplemented by videotapes for hard-to-classify cases. Ratings and classifications for the Italian subsample were made by I.B. with the aid of E.B., who translated the narrative records. In order to establish her reliability with Main, I.B. separately classified and rated the American subsample. Reliability coefficients for the interactive ratings ranged from 0.87 to 0.96. There was one disagreement (within Subgroup B) out of 13 classifications (92% agreement). The following measures were used to assess strange situation behavior.

Figure 5.1. *The physical setup of the strange situation.*

Classifications: The three major behavior patterns observed by Ainsworth and Wittig (1969) in their first strange situation study have already been described in the introduction. Further subdivisions within the three major patterns were made by Ainsworth, Bell, and Stayton (1971). Groups A1 and A2 showed a considerable amount of avoidant behavior to the mother upon reunion, but Group A2 also showed some proximity-seeking behavior (approaching the mother, then turning away before the approach was completed). Group B2 also exhibited some avoidant behavior, but in this group avoidant behavior was overshadowed by proximity seeking. Group B1 tended not to approach the mother on her return. Instead, B1 infants interacted with the mother over a distance by showing toys, looking at her and vocalizing. Groups B3 showed high levels of proximity seeking and contact maintaining but tended to go back to exploration of the toys after having touched base with the mother, unlike B4 infants who stuck close to the mother throughout and who became highly distressed upon separation. The major difference between B4 and C infants was that the latter exhibited angry behavior as well as contact-seeking and contact-maintaining behavior during reunions with the mother. Within Group C, the C1 subgroup was more passive during the mother-and-baby-alone Episode and tended to use more signaling in order to achieve contact than did Subgroup C2, who displayed more overt anger and tantrumy behavior during reunions (and separations). For the purposes of this study infants were assigned subclassification scores which indicate their distance from the normative B3 group as follows: B3 = 4; B1, B2, and B4 = 3; A2, C2 = 2; A1, C1 = 1. These classification scores were highly correlated with ratings of proximity and contact seeking, contact maintaining, and proximity and interaction avoidance in the reunion episodes (.71, .66 and −.76, respectively). There was only one C2 and one B4 infant in this study. Hence we did not use contact-resisting (one of the interactive measures devised by Ainsworth) in our data analysis.

In addition to the classification scores, we used the interactive ratings for behavior to the mother during reunions which are described in much more detail in Ainsworth *et al.* (1978). As previously mentioned, it was this group of reunion behaviors which turned out to be most strongly related to infant, maternal and dyadic behaviors in the home throughout the first year.

Proximity and contact seeking (Proximity): This includes active behaviors such as approaching the mother or clambering up on her, gestures such as reaching or leaning towards her, intention movements such as partial approaches, and vocal signals such as directed crying.

Contact maintaining (Contact): This rating applies to situations where the baby has either been picked up or made contact with the mother on his own initiative. Clinging to the mother, sinking into her, holding the mother's knee while standing next to her, and resisting release if the mother attempts to break contact, or trying to clamber up again if the mother sets the baby down are the kinds of behaviors included in this scale.

Proximity and interaction avoiding (Avoidance): This measure includes behaviors such as failing to greet the mother on her return, ignoring her, pointedly looking or turning away in a situation which usually elicits greeting or proximity, and interaction seeking, as for instance after the mother's absence.

The scales give a combined rating for intensity, duration, and/or latency of an interactive behavior. Several examples of behavior are given for the seven points of the scale, the raters task being to match the observed behavior to the complete examples provided in the scale.

Interactive ratings were made for Episodes 5 and 8, and for both Episodes summed (e.g., Proximity 5, Proximity 8, and Proximity T). The age of the American subsample on the day they visited the laboratory for the strange situation was within + 12 days and −3 days of their first birthday. The Italian subsample was on average two weeks older than the American sample at the time they were seen in the strange situation, being within + 15 days and −9 days of 12.5 months. Since the strange situation is not a measure of achievement, but a procedure for assessing the quality of the interaction which has been validated for the period from 11 to 12.5 months, we do not believe that this age difference influenced our results. Further support for this view comes from Connell (1975) and Waters (1978) who found that even with an age difference of 6 months (e.g., from 12 to 18 months), the vast majority of infants were reclassified into the same strange situation categories. Although we partialed out the effects of nationality from all our measures (as was also done in Chapter 3), there were no differences between the two subsamples on any of the strange situation measures prior to applying the partialing out procedure.

Prorating of the Cognitive and Communicative Measures

The 13 American and 12 Italian infants who participated in our study were seen four times, at monthly intervals, in their homes. Although the mean age for each visit was 9.5, 10.5, 11.5, and 12.5 months, the range for the first visit (and the monthly subsequent visits) was ± 2 weeks from the mean, that is an infant could be anywhere from 9 to 10 months during the first session. In Chapter 3 we were mainly interested in comparing the performance of each infant with himself, but in this study we had to be able to compare the infants to each other. The scores for all cognitive and communicative measures were therefore prorated to derive scores for 10, 11, and 12 months by using the following formula for 10 months and analogues thereof for the succeeding sessions:

10-month score = 1st session score + (2nd session score − 1st session
score) × number of days from 1st session to 10
months/number of days between 1st and 2nd sessions

In order to compensate for small differences in method and for cultural differences, nationality was partialed out of all correlations reported in this study, as was done in Chapter 3.

In any session, if a behavior was shown by less than one-third of the total sample, it was not included in the correlational analysis in order to avoid the possibility of spuriously high or low correlations which we might have obtained with highly skewed data base. Because of this we did not have scores for all four sessions in Chapter 3. Similarly, in this analysis we do not have scores at all three prorated ages. In the section which follows the numbers in parentheses after the behavioral definitions indicate the age levels for which scores met our criteria for inclusion in the correlation matrix.

Communicative Measures

COMMUNICATIVE GESTURES

The same four gestures which we already identified in Chapter 3 as forming a Gestural Complex were included in this analysis: communicative pointing, showing, giving, and ritual requests.

We not only asked the mother whether and how her baby used these four gestures, but independently observed whether a baby produced a particular gesture during any one of our home visits. Whereas the interview provided us with information on **whether** an infant was capable of a specific gesture, the observations also noted the relative frequency with which the gesture occurred (1 = behavior seen only once, 2 = behavior seen two to four times, 3 = behavior seen five to nine times, and so forth in increments of 5).

Chapter 3 gives the results for each of the measures taken individually. In the analysis to be reported here, three summary measures of gestural communication were constructed from the interview and from the observation data by combining the four gestural variables. We believed that such a composite measure would give a more stable indication of the "general" level of gestural communication which the infant had attained than each of the separate gestural measures. The summary variables were generated as follows.

For each of the four gestures there were two levels whose definition is given below:

1. **Communicative Pointing**
   a. Pointing in a social context, but without looking back to check if the adult is attending = 1
   b. Pointing to an object, then checking back with adult = 2
2. **Showing**
   a. Showing an object already in hand = 1
   b. Picking up an object in order to show it to the adult = 2
3. **Giving**
   a. Giving an object to the adult which the baby is already holding = 1
   b. Picking up an object in order to give it to the adult = 1.5
   c. Picking up an object and crossing the room in order to give it to an adult = 2
4. **Ritual Requests**
   a. Requesting an object by stretching out the hand with a ritual grunt = 1
   b. Requesting an object with a ritual gesture (opening and shutting the hand) or a wordlike sound = 2 (Babies could also request by pointing to the object, but for the purposes of creating the summary measure this was included under communicative pointing.)

For the interview-derived gestural measures scores for Communicative Pointing, Showing, and Giving were available for 11 and 12 months only, but Ritual Requesting scores were obtained at 10, 11, and 12 months. For the observation based (relative frequency) measures scores for Communicative Pointing and Giving were available at 11 and 12 months, and scores for Showing and Ritual Requesting at all three age levels.

Interview Communicative Gestures (10, 11 and 12) and Observation Communicative Gestures (10, 11, and 12) were the two summary measures which were created by adding the highest level attained on each communicative gesture for each child (the maximum score being 8 in each case). A third summary variable, Frequency of Observation Communicative Gestures (10, 11, 12), was obtained by adding the relative frequencies of the four gestures, without regard to their level.

LANGUAGE MEASURES

As you will recall from Chapter 3, measures of language comprehension and production were also obtained from both the maternal interview (conducted during each home visit) and from our independent observations. The individual interview and observation measures were the following:

Interview Comprehension (10, 11, 12): The number of different words, other than *no*, which the child was reported to understand.

Interview Comprehension Level (10, 11, 12): Understanding of words in context. Level 1 implies understanding only within a specific routine (e.g., *peekaboo* is understood only while playing peekaboo); Level 2 implies understanding while the object referred to is present; and Level 3 applies to comprehension when the object is not present (e.g., going to find Daddy in the next room when his name is mentioned).

Interview Nonreferential Words (11, 12): Ritual vocalizations used by the child during specific activities (e.g., saying *pattycake* while clapping the hands).

Interview Referential Words (11, 12): The number of different referential words used by the child as reported in the maternal interview.

Observation Comprehension (10, 11, 12): The relative frequency of instances of comprehension noted during the home visit.

Observation Nonreferential Words (11, 12): The relative frequency of nonreferential words used during routines (e.g., *heeyouah* when giving and taking objects) as observed during the home visit.

Observation Referential Words: The relative frequency of applying a referential word to label an object or activity (saying *ba* while showing the ball to Mommy).

As we did for gestures, three summary language variables (not used in Chapter 3) were constructed in the interest of obtaining a stable overall measure of language comprehension and production.

Interview Language (10, 11, 12): This refers to the total number of different words comprehended added to the total number of different nonreferential and referential words produced by the child, as reported by the mother. It is thus a qualitative measure.

Observation Language (10, 11, 12): This is a qualitative measure, constructed by adding together the relative frequencies of comprehension, referential and nonreferential word production.

Number of Words (10, 11, 12): This variable was obtained from interview and observation combined (see Volterra *et al.*, Chapter V). It represents the cumulative number of nonoverlapping nonreferential and referential words produced at each age level.

Cognitive Measures

Two kinds of cognitive measures were used in this analysis: scores for four domains of sensorimotor development and scores derived from the interview and observation for two categories of play.

SENSORIMOTOR DEVELOPMENT

The infants were tested with the Uzgiris–Hunt (1975) subscales for object permanence, spatial relations, imitation, and means–end relations during each home visit, so that we have data on all these domains prorated for 10, 11, and 12 months. For object permanence, means–end relations, and spatial relations we used the scale scores presented in the Uzgiris–Hunt Scale. Because of difficulties in persuading the infants to imitate the items of the imitation subscale, we had to simplify that scale so that we had two levels of gestural and vocal imitation which were added for each child. This adaptation of the scale is described in Chapter 3.

PLAY MEASURES

We investigated combinatorial and symbolic play separately. **Symbolic Play** is defined as appropriate use of objects (phoning with a toy telephone, eating with a toy fork after scraping the empty plate, hugging the doll or teddybear), as well as using an inappropriate object for pretending (which did not occur very frequently at the ages we studied; see Chapter 4). Combinatorial Play consisted of activities such as stacking rings on a pole, emptying and filling containers, nesting cups, and building towers with wooden blocks.

As before, we obtained independent measures from the maternal interview and from the observations we made during the home visits. Apart from Symbolic Play Level (see Chapter 5), all of these measures were also used in the analysis described in Chapter 3.

Interview Combinatorial Play (10, 11, 12): The number of different combinatorial schemes (stacking and unstacking rings, building towers, nesting objects) which the mother reported to us during the interview.

Observation Combinatorial Play (10, 11, 12): The relative frequency with which we observed combinatorial schemes to occur during the home visit.

Interview Symbolic Schemes (11, 12): The number of different symbolic schemes which was derived from the maternal interview.

Observation Symbolic Schemes (11, 12): The number of different symbolic schemes the child performed during our observations at home.

Observation Symbolic Play Frequency (11, 12): The relative frequency with which any symbolic scheme was observed to occur during the home visit.

Symbolic Play Level (11, 12): The level of all schemes reported by the mother and observed during the home visits was assessed using the revised Nicolich scheme reported in Chapter 4 (Volterra *et al.*). The lowest level was assigned to merely using a toy to carry out a familiar activity oneself, a higher level was assigned to making a doll or other person perform the activity, and the highest level to performing a sequence of appropriate actions, such as lifting the toy phone receiver, dialing, and then vocalizing into it.

Results

Sensorimotor Development and Strange Situation Behavior

As already reported in Chapter 3, the four domains of sensorimotor functioning were not significantly correlated with each other. It appears that, at the ages we were studying, these abilities were not developing at similar rates within each child. In other words, we seemed to be assessing separate aspects of intelligence with each of our measures.

Of the four sensorimotor abilities which we investigated, only the means–end scale was significantly related to the 10 strange situation measures. For object permanence, only 2 out of a possible 30 correlations were significant at $p < .05$, for imitation none whatsoever, and for spatial relations only one.

Table 5.3 shows how strong and consistent were the relationships between the attachment variables and means–end relations, especially at 11 and 12 months. Overall, 20 out of 30 possible correlations between means–ends and the strange situation are significant at the .05 level. Moreover, all are significant in the predicted direction, that is, we find positive correlations with measures of proximity and contact seeking as well as with contact maintaining during the two reunion episodes, but negative correlations with avoidance of the mother upon her return in Episodes 5 and 8. At 11 and 12 months, 90% of the 20 possible correlations are significant at the .05 level, and 75% at the .01 level. (This pattern of stronger relationships at 11 and 12 months is, incidentally, repeated throughout this analysis.)

TABLE 5.3
Correlations between Means-End Relations and Strange Situation Classification
and Ratings[a]

	Means-End Relations		
	10 months	11 months	12 months
Strange Situation Class		0.33	0.48**
Proximity 5		0.50**	0.51***
Proximity 8	0.38*	0.48**	0.36*
Proximity T	0.34*	0.58***	0.51***
Contact 5		0.49*	0.51***
Contact 8		0.44*	0.42*
Contact T		0.58***	0.57***
Avoid 5		-0.47**	-0.31
Avoid 8		-0.52***	-0.54***
Avoid T		-0.58***	-0.49**

[a]Nationality was partialed out of all correlations.
*$p < 0.05$ (one tailed).
**$p < 0.01$ (one tailed).
***$p < 0.005$ (one tailed).

Of the studies listed in Table 5.2, only Clarke-Stewart (1973) investigated possible relationships between means–end relations and strange situation behavior. Unfortunately she combined the spatial and the means–end scores into one measure, thus possibly obscuring relationships which may have been present. Bell (1972, 1978) found relationships between strange situation group and the infants' scores on person permanence. When the object permanence (as opposed to person permanence) scores were compared to the strange situation group in both of Bell's samples, no significant differences between the B and non-B groups emerged. Her results are thus comparable to ours.

A number of investigators (e.g., Schaffer and Emerson, 1964) have suggested that attachment of the infant to the mother in Bowlby's use of the term requires that the child have attained at least Stage 4 in the development of the concept of the object. In other words, a child who cannot hold an absent object in mind would not be expected to show search behavior for the absent mother, to start crying well after the mother has left the room and to show angry behavior upon her return. Since all the children in our sample were, at 12 months, already well into Stage 5 of object concept development, such a pattern could not appear in our data. However, other cognitive abilities are involved in the organization of a control system which regulates a child's proximity to the mother in stressful situations. **It may be that the capacity for goal-directed behavior which is necessary both for means–end behavior (tool use) and for regulating proximity-seeking behaviors to the mother underlies the correlations shown in Table 5.3.**

Play Measures and Strange Situation Behavior

Of the two play categories, combinatorial and symbolic play, the latter turned out to be much more strongly related to strange situation variables than the former.

SYMBOLIC PLAY

The two observational measures of symbolic play showed the strongest association with the 10 strange situation variables. As Table 5.4 indicates, the observed relative frequency of symbolic play was most consistently related to strange situation variables. At 11 and 12 months (we have no 10-month scores for any of the symbolic play measures since this behavior was only sporadic during the first session) 85% of the 20 possible correlations reached the .05 level of significance and 70% are significant at the .01 level. Almost equally strong were the relationships between number of different schemes observed during the home visits: Of the 20 possible correlations with strange situation measures 75% were found to be significant at the .05 level, though only 25% at the .01 level. Whereas the first measure tells us how often an infant was observed to engage in a symbolic play scheme, the second is a measure of the variety or richness of his or her schemes.

The weakest relationships were found for number of symbolic play schemes reported by the mother, only 20% of these being significant at the .05 level. On the other hand level of symbolic play (as measured according to the revised Nicholich scales presented in Chapter 4) was more strongly related to the strange situation variables: Forty-five percent of all possible correlations were significant at the .05 level and 15% at the .01 level. Interestingly, for both of the latter measures significant correlations occurred only with proximity seeking and contact maintaining, not with the avoidance scores.

COMBINATORIAL PLAY

Combinatorial play schemes reported by the mother were not related to the strange situation variables at all, but frequency of combinatorial play as we observed it during the home visits was significantly related to the strange situation variables at 11 months when 50% of the 10 possible correlations were significant at the .05 level. In all, the relationships to combinatorial play are not very impressive.

Our findings are supported by those of Harmon *et al.* (in press) who reported that cognitively mature play (as opposed to toy manipulation in general) was more frequently seen in securely attached as opposed to avoidant 1-year-olds. Harmon *et al.* did not present separate scores for the two measures of play, but lumped both symbolic and combinatorial play together under the same rubric so we cannot be sure either one play measure contributed more to the differences between B and non-B infants than the other. Matas *et al.* (1978) report that in their 24-month-old B children symbolic play bouts were longer than those of A children. Thus, there may be relationships of strange situation behavior with symbolic play into the third year of life. Main (1973), it should be noted, did not find that her B toddlers performed at a more advanced level in symbolic play or that they engaged in it more often. She did, however, use a much more stringent definition of symbolic play (pretending with an inappropriate object, such as "shaving" with a plastic toy wrench).

Though expected correlations of strange situation behavior with play have often been linked to Hypothesis 1 (the attachment–exploration hypothesis which postulates that securely attached infants are better at teaching themselves), our own observation of maternal behavior in the home suggests that infants may first acquire symbolic schemes through interaction with the mother (Hypothesis 2, the teaching hypothesis). Many of the mothers in our sample spontaneously hugged the babydoll and cooed to it, or pretended to have a conversation on the toy telephone. Although we did not count it as symbolic play if the child immediately imitated such actions, many infants may first acquire symbolic schemes through imitation of the mother's playful behavior rather than through reenacting the mother's hugging of a real baby or talking on the phone to another adult. In other words, infants may first become aware of the possibilities of "pretend" through play rather than through observation of the real-world activities of others. Interestingly we observed much less spontaneous maternal demonstration of combinatorial play (emptying and filling containers, building towers) in our sample.

Relationships between Communication and Strange Situation Measures

COMMUNICATIVE GESTURES

We investigated the hypothesized relationships between communicative gestures and strange situation variables in two ways: first, by cor-

TABLE 5.4

Correlations among Strange Situation Variables, Means-End Relations, and Symbolic and Combinatorial Play[a]

| | Symbolic Schemes | | | | Symbolic Play Frequency | | Symbolic Level | | Combinatorial Schemes | | | Combinatorial Play Frequency | | |
| | Interview | | Observation | | Observation | | Obs. + Int. | | Interview | | | Observation | | |
	11	12	11	12	11	12	11	12	10	11	12	10	11	12
Strange Situation Class			0.47**	0.37*	0.51***	0.46*	0.38*	0.29					0.37*	0.30
Proximity 5	0.31	0.28	0.77***	0.45*	0.55***	0.31	0.50**	0.37*						
Proximity 8	0.45*	0.43*	0.41*	0.32	0.50**	0.51***	0.33	0.34*				0.29	0.34*	
Proximity T	0.45*	0.43*	0.70***	0.45*	0.62***	0.50**	0.49**	0.42*						0.25
Contact 5			0.77***	0.35*	0.49**	0.26	0.47**	0.28						0.34*
Contact 8			0.31	0.33	0.40*	0.51***		0.26				0.27	0.25	
Contact T			0.64***	0.43*	0.55***	0.51***	0.35*	0.34*						0.26
Avoid 5			-0.38*	-0.38*	-0.25	-0.56***						-0.33	-0.51***	
Avoid 8			-0.34*		-0.49**	-0.48**						-0.25	-0.34*	
Avoid T			-0.42*	-0.37*	-0.42*	-0.61***	-0.26					-0.35*	-0.51***	
Means 10	0.71***	0.71***		0.30	0.29	0.26	0.31	0.50**	0.47**	0.48**	0.43*	0.25		
Means 11	0.53***	0.54***	0.50***	0.36*	0.37*	0.48**	0.44**	0.55***	0.25	0.30		0.26		
Means 12	0.30	0.27	0.41*	0.33	0.29	0.38*	0.50**	0.56***						0.34*

	(1)	(2)	(3)	(4)	(5)	(6)	(7)	(8)	(9)	(10)	(11)	(12)	(13)	(14)
Int.Symb.Sch.11 (1)	1.00													
Symb.Sch.12 (2)	0.97***	1.00												
Obs.Symb.Sch.11 (3)	0.36*	0.41*	1.00											
Symb.Sch.12 (4)	0.54***	0.55***	0.55***	1.00										
Obs.Symb.Freq.11 (5)	0.37*	0.38*	0.69***	0.53***	1.00									
Symb.Freq.12 (6)	0.38*	0.43*	0.47**	0.72***	0.52***	1.00								
I+O Symb.Lev.11 (7)	0.48**	0.46*	0.64***	0.53***	0.47**	0.41*	1.00							
Symb.Lev.12 (8)	0.56***	0.61***	0.53***	0.67***	0.35*	0.52***	0.76***	1.00						
Int.Comb.Sch.10 (9)	0.61***	0.65***	0.40*	0.40*	0.27	0.30			1.00					
Comb.Sch.11 (10)	0.55***	0.57***	0.46*	0.46*	0.46*	0.31			0.88***	1.00				
Comb.Sch.12 (11)	0.30	0.35*	0.37*	0.37*					0.54***	0.82***	1.00			
Obs.Comb.Freq.10 (12)	0.30	0.38*	0.30	0.40*					0.49**	0.59***	0.49**	1.00		
Comb.Freq.11 (13)	0.26	0.26	-0.26	0.35*					0.34			0.74**	1.00	
Comb.Freq.12 (14)	0.29	0.37*	0.25	0.40*					0.36*	0.52***	0.55***	0.36	0.51***	1.00

a Nationality has been partialed out of all correlations.

* $p \leq 0.05$ (one tailed)

** $p \leq 0.01$ (one tailed)

*** $p \leq 0.005$ (one tailed)

relating the three summary measures of gestural communication with the attachment measures, and, second, by looking at the relationships between strange situation behavior and the individual gestures which entered into the summary measures (communicative pointing, showing, giving, and ritual requesting).

Of the three summary measures only those two which measured "level" of gestures were related to the strange situation measures. No relationships at all (either positive or negative) were found with the observed relative frequency of gestural communication and the attachment variables. **Hence, sheer quantity of communication regardless of level did not distinguish the strange situation groups from each other.** Moreover, and somewhat contrary to our expectations, the relationships between gestural communication and strange situation behavior were not as strong as the relationships with either means–ends or the play measures (see Table 5.5). Thirty-seven percent of all 30 possible correlations between level of communicative gestures as reported during the maternal interview were significant, and if only the 11 and 12 months data are taken into consideration, we find 55% significant correlations out of a possible 20. For the observed level of gestural communication, all significant correlations occurred at 11 and 12 months. At these two ages, 35% of the 20 possible correlations were significant at the .05 level. (As may be seen from Table 5.5, the two summary measures of gestural communication level were significantly intercorrelated although they were based on quite independent data sources.)

The relationships are weaker when we look at the pattern of correlations between strange situation variables and individual gestures. Table 5.6 shows all significant correlations obtained. Out of a possible 100 correlations with frequency of communicative pointing, showing, giving, and ritual requesting, 20 were significant at the .05 level, all but one in the predicted direction. Twelve out of a possible 90 correlations with the interview measures (level of each gesture) were significant. This indicates that we were justified in using a summary measure as a more stable assessment of the infant's gestural level. Of the individual measures, by far the most successful predictor of strange situation behavior was communicative pointing. Taking the observation and interview measures jointly, 35% out of a possible 40 correlations were significant at the .05 level and 20% at the .01 level. The relationship of the attachment measures to communicative pointint is especially interesting in view of the findings to be reported in the next section, and in view of the fact that pointing was one of the best gestural predictors of language (see Chapter 3).

LANGUAGE

Three summary language variables were entered into the correlation matrix together with the 10 strange situation measures: observed language (a frequency measure of comprehension and production), interview language (a qualitative measure of comprehension and production derived from the interview), and a production measure (Number of Words), which was jointly derived from interview and observations. For none of these three summary measures did we find a single significant correlation with the strange situation. Table 5.5 shows the relationships of the strange situation variables to all three summary language variables, a well as the relationships of these language variables to means–end rela tions and to each other. Note that the summary production measure, number of words, is more highly correlated with means–ends than are the other two language variables.

When the individual language measures (which were used to form the summary variables) were correlated with strange situation variables, a similar picture emerged. Only 4 out of a possible 100 correlations with the individual interview language variables were significant and, what is more, 3 out of these 4 were not in the predicted direction. For the observed language measures, none of the 70 possible correlations reached a conventional level of significance.

Our findings are somewhat surprising in view of the fact that gestural communication is highly related to the summary language variables. As may be seen in Table 5.5, 92% of all possible intercorrelations of the summary language and gestural variables are significant. Moreover, the summary measures of gestural communication were also strongly related to the individual language measures of production and comprehension.

Table 5.7 shows that of all possible correlations between gestural communication (interview and observation) and language production and comprehension measures 73% were significant at the .05 level or less. Similarly, 69% of the correlations with the observation language and production measures reached at least the .05 level of significance.

We had expected, using Hypothesis 2 (the attachment–teaching hypothesis) as the basis of our argument, that B infants might be more advanced in both gestural and language communication than A and C children. Our expectations were borne out only for gestural communication, but not for language development. Although Connell (1975) found that B children had larger vocabularies at 18 months, and although Main (1973) showed that B toddlers had more morphemes (though not more words) per utterance than did A and C children

TABLE 5.5

Correlations of Gestural and Verbal Communication with Strange Situation Classification and Ratings[a]

	Interview Communicative gestures			Observation Communicative gestures			Int. + Obs. Number of words			Interview Language			Observation Language		
Strange Situation	10 Mos.	11 Mos.	12 Mos.	10 Mos.	11 Mos.	12 Mos.	10 Mos.	11 Mos.	12 Mos.	10 Mos.	11 Mos.	12 Mos.	10 Mos.	11 Mos.	12 Mos.
Class	0.29	0.44*	0.34*		0.25										
Proximity 5		0.27	0.33		0.37*										
Proximity 8		0.45*	0.45*		0.44*	0.44*	0.26								
Proximity T	0.26	0.43*	0.46*		0.48*	0.36*									
Contact 5			0.30		0.31										
Contact 8				0.27	0.38*	0.32	0.26								
Contact T		0.26	0.26	0.28	0.45*	0.30									
Avoid 5		-0.38*	-0.34*					0.25							
Avoid 8		-0.35*	-0.31		-0.28										
Avoid T		-0.43*	-0.38*		-0.26										

252

	C1	C2	C3	C4	C5	C6	C7	C8	C9	C10	C11	C12	C13
Means 10	0.33	0.43*	0.52***	0.26	0.50**	0.50**	0.37*	0.45*	0.44*	0.31	0.41*	0.44*	0.28
Means 11	0.31	0.48**	0.47**	0.29	0.57***	0.46*	0.26	0.34*	0.42*		0.25	0.33	
Means 12		0.39*	0.35*	0.29	0.50***	0.30	0.32	0.45*	0.54***		0.33	0.39*	0.27
Int.Comm.													
Gest.10	1.00												
Comm. Gest.11	0.87***	1.00											
Comm. Gest.12	0.70***	0.86***	1.00										
Obs.Comm.													
Gest.10	0.42*	0.41*	0.42*	1.00									
Comm. Gest.11	0.58***	0.69***	0.66***	0.73***	1.00								
Comm. Gest.12	0.57***	0.68***	0.76***	0.55***	0.84***	1.00							
Int. + Obs.													
Number of words 10	0.28	0.33	0.31	0.37*	0.61***	0.49**	1.00						
Number of words 11	0.34*	0.40*	0.39*	0.47**	0.71***	0.57***	0.92***	1.00					
Number of words 12	0.44*	0.49**	0.50***	0.51*	0.77***	0.65***	0.81***	0.95***	1.00				

(continued)

TABLE 5.5 (continued)

	Interview Communicative Gestures			Observation Communicative Gestures			Int. + Obs. Number of Words			Interview Language			Observation Language		
	10 Mos.	11 Mos.	12. Mos.	10 Mos.	11 Mos.	12 Mos.	10 Mos.	11 Mos.	12 Mos.	10 Mos.	11 Mos.	12 Mos.	10 Mos.	11 Mos.	12 Mos.
Int.Language 10	0.67***	0.60***	0.46*	0.34*	0.55***	0.51***	0.64***	0.66***	0.66***	1.00					
Language 11	0.63***	0.64***	0.55***	0.56***	0.71***	0.61***	0.68***	0.80***	0.81***	0.90***	1.00				
Language 12	0.67***	0.67***	0.63***	0.60***	0.66***	0.76***	0.69***	0.82***	0.87***	0.86***	0.97***	1.00			
Obs.Language 10	0.41*	0.41*	0.49*	0.53***	0.51**	0.51**	0.38*	0.43*	0.46*	0.58***	0.66***	0.69***	1.00		
Language 11.		0.30	0.32	0.36*	0.56***	0.51**	0.55***	0.58***	0.55***	0.66***	0.69***	0.68***	0.79***	1.00	
Language 12	0.38*	0.54***	0.65***	0.38*	0.62***	0.64***	0.41*	0.52***	0.60***	0.52***	0.67***	0.71***	0.70***	0.78***	1.00

[a] Nationality was partialed out of all correlations.

* $p < 0.05$ (one tailed)

** $p < 0.01$ (one tailed)

*** $p < 0.005$ (one tailed)

TABLE 5.6

Correlations between Strange Situation Variables and Individual Communicative Gestures[a]

	Communicative pointing		Giving		Showing		Ritual requests	
	Interview	Observation	Interview	Observation	Interview	Observation	Interview	Observation
Strange Situation Class	0.36[c]					0.49[c], 0.45[d]	0.36[c]	0.39[c]
Proximity 5								
Proximity 8	0.35[c], 0.36[d]	0.49[c], 0.50[d]						
Proximity T		0.46[c], 0.39[d]				0.41[c], 0.38[d]	0.34[c], 0.37[d]	0.36[c]
Contact 5						0.35[c]		0.34[c]
Contact 8	0.36[c], 0.41[d]	0.59[c], 0.43[d]						
Contact T		0.52[c]						
Avoid 5			-0.38[d]			0.34[b]		-0.57[b]
Avoid 8		-0.35[c]						
Avoid T		-0.34[c]	-0.34[c], -0.38[d]					-0.49[b]

[a] Nationality has been partialed out of all correlations. r = 0.34, p < 0.05 (one tailed); r = 0.47, p < 0.01; r = 0.51, p < 0.005 (one tailed).
[b] 10 months.
[c] 11 months.
[d] 12 months.

TABLE 5.7
Correlations between Interview and Observation Communicative Gestures and Interview and Observation Language Measures[a]

	Number of words comprehended			Comprehension level			Number of non-referential words			Referential words
	10	11	12	10	11	12	10	11	12	12
Interview										
Int.Comm.Gest.10	0.81***	0.80***	0.78***	0.70***	0.55***				0.34*	0.29
11	0.65***	0.71***	0.68***	0.58***	0.44*			0.39*	0.51***	0.30
12	0.54***	0.63***	0.62***	0.46*	0.45*			0.32	0.42*	0.37*
Obs.Comm.Gest.10	0.35	0.53***	0.58***		0.38*	0.29	0.25	0.41*	0.39*	0.40*
11	0.41*	0.57***	0.63***	0.33	0.38*		0.55***	0.65***	0.68***	0.57***
12	0.44*	0.52***	0.59***	0.36*	0.49**	0.32	0.44*	0.57***	0.61***	0.49**

	Comprehension frequency			Frequency of non-referential words		Frequency of referential words	
	10	11	12	11	12	11	12
Observation							
Int.Comm.Gest.10	0.52***	0.41*	0.54***				0.34*
11	0.46*	0.39*	0.61***		0.36*		0.39*
12	0.46*	0.36*	0.66***		0.43*	0.40*	0.55***
Obs.Comm.Gest.10	0.38*		0.39*				0.27
11	0.39*	0.44*	0.49**	0.33	0.50**	0.44*	0.54***
12	0.42*	0.46*	0.53***	0.32	0.51***	0.49**	0.60***

[a] Nationality was partialed out of all correlations.

* $p < 0.05$ (one tailed)   ** $p < 0.01$ (one tailed)   *** $p < 0.005$ (one tailed)

combined, a glance at Table 5.1 indicates that not many relationships between strange situation behavior and language competence have been found at this and later ages. Although Alison Clarke-Stewart (1973) reported that total verbal stimulation between 12 and 18 months (whether it was rated to be appropriate or not) was correlated with the infants' language competence, she found no language related differences among strange situation groups. Pentz (1975) suggested that his negative findings could be explained if one assumed that language development is buffered against variations in mother–child interaction within a fairly wide range. This does not imply that severe affective deprivation would not be expected to leave its mark on a child's developing language competence. It may be that the threshhold at which such deficits could be shown lies outside the range of variation encompassed by mother–infant dyads used in strange situation studies. It is, however, also possible that relationships of strange situation behavior (or inferred harmoniousness of interaction) with language could be shown if we used different measures. For instance, in dyads where there is much interaction one might expect a child to develop a more elaborated vocabulary describing internal states (especially emotional states). Logically, it is not necessary to think of a social–expressive capacity and a referential style as being mutually exclusive. It would also not be unreasonable to suppose that B children, earlier than A and C children, might acquire a less egocentric style of communication, a style which demonstrates greater understanding of the partner's knowledge and point of view. We plan to test these hypotheses in the near future.

The Overall Pattern of Relationships between Attachment, Cognition, and Communication

We have so far presented data which demonstrate:

1. Strong correlations of strange situation variables (and by inference with quality of attachment) with means–end relations, but not with any of the three other sensorimotor domains which we investigated (object permanence, spatial relations, and imitation).
2. Fairly strong correlations between strange situation variables and symbolic play, as opposed to weak correlations with combinatorial play.
3. Fairly strong correlations of strange situation variables with gestural communication level (not frequency), but none whatsoever with language competence (production as well as comprehension).

4. Correlations of strange situation variables with qualitative measures of cognition and communication (means–end relations, symbolic play level, number of symbolic schemes, level of communicative gestures) and—less often—with quantitative measures (frequency of observed symbolic schemes, frequency of combinatorial play). This suggests that our findings cannot just be ascribed to a general effect of sociability. B infants, for many measures, showed higher absolute levels of performance, but did not necessarily engage in any of these more frequently than A and C infants.

5. For two measures—gestural communication level and number of symbolic schemes—both the interview-derived and the observation-derived scores were correlated with the strange situation variables. Since these two measures were based on independent sources of information, the significance of our findings is thereby strengthened.

One way of clarifying the intercorrelations between the domains of attachment, language, gestural communication, and cognition is to present them in the form of a diagram.

Figure 5.2 shows the interrelations between these domains at 11 and 12 months, the period during which most of the significant correlations occurred. Although an attempt was made to do so, it proved impossible—within the limitations of a two-dimensional figure—to represent strength of association between two domains in terms of proximity. Information about the degree to which domains are related is therefore carried by the thickness of the interconnecting lines. Since each domain was assessed at two ages (11 and 12 months) and frequently by a set of variables rather than by a single variable (e.g., 10 strange situation measures, 4 symbolic play measures) the thickness of the inter-

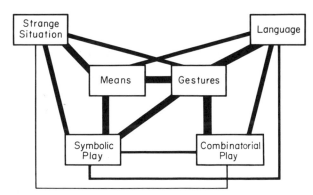

Figure 5.2. *Proportions of significant correlations between domains (at 11 and 12 months).*

connecting lines stands for the number of significant correlations divided by the number of possible correlations between each pair of domains. Thus, the statement that 100% of all possible correlations between level of gestural communication and combinatorial play are significant means that out of all possible correlations between the two measures of gestural communication level (4 scores per child) and the two measures of combinatorial play (5 scores per child) all of the 16 correlations are significant at the .05 level or less. Table 5.8 shows the percentage of significant correlations between all pairs of domains in addition to the number of correlations on which this calculation was based. As may be seen, the means for those correlations which were significant ranged from .34 to .53.

We have already drawn attention to the fact that no significant correlations occurred between language and attachment (as measured by the strange situation), despite the fact that both of these domains were related to many of the same variables.

Indeed, Figure 5.2 can be taken apart to yield two independent networks which are depicted in Figure 5.3. Figure 5.3 makes it apparent that the group of the three most strongly intercorrelated measures, namely, means–end relations, symbolic play, and communicative ges-

TABLE 5.8
Percentage of Significant Correlations-Possible Correlations between Cognition, Communication, and Language.

Correlated domains	Number of possible correlations	Percentage of significant correlations	Mean of significant correlations
Strange Situation			
X Means-End	20	90%	0.50
X Gestures	40	50%	0.41
X Symbolic Play	80	58%	0.47
X Combinatorial Play	40	12%	0.43
X Language	60	0%	
Means-End			
X Gestures	8	87%	0.40
X Symbolic Play	16	75%	0.47
X Combinatorial Play	8	12%	0.34
X Language	12	42%	0.43
Gestures			
X Symbolic Play	32	79%	0.48
X Combinatorial Play	16	100%	0.53
X Language	24	92%	0.46
Symbolic Play			
X Combinatorial Play	32	31%	0.38
X Language	48	27%	0.46

NETWORK I

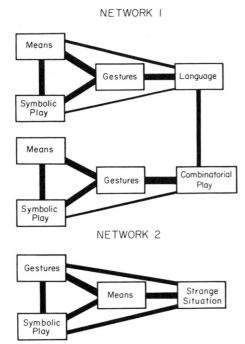

Figure 5.3. *Correlational networks at 11 and 12 months.*

tures are related both to the language domain and to the attachment (strange situation) domain. Network 1 shows that out of a triangle formed by means–end, gestures and symbolic play, means–end relations correlated most strongly with attachment. Network 2 is made up of two correlated "factors," namely, language and combinatorial play, both of which are most strongly related to gestural communication and more weakly to means–end relations and to symbolic play. We can infer from this that the portion of the variance which accounts for the intercorrelation of attachment with the three triangle measures is quite independent from that portion of the variance which accounts for the correlations with language and combinatorial play.

It is only fair to emphasize here that Figures 5.2 and 5.3 represent a web of relationships which may hold true only at a particular period (11–12 months). The pattern might well be very different 6 months later. As we have already pointed out in Chapter 3, the level of development attained in a particular domain may affect further progress in another domain only during particular stages of development. Once a criterion level is attained in both domains, they may, if only for a time, diverge and develop at differential rates. For example, our study would seem to show that once Stage 4 object permanence is attained, the organization of a control system which regulates attachment behavior—as suggested by Bowlby (1969)—may be influenced by the capacity for goal-directed behavior which also underlies tool-use or means–end behavior but not be much affected by further development in the object-permanence domain. Language competence, on the other hand, which seems to be quite unaffected by quality of attachment during the 11–12-month age-range, may turn out to be so affected at a later stage in development.

Discussion and Conclusions

Let us now evaluate our findings in conjunction with the results of those other, similarly conceived studies which we listed in Table 5.2. It has been suggested that the superior functioning so frequently observed in B children is really a pseudofinding which is to be more parsimoniously explained by B children's more enthusiastic approach to problem-solving situations and by their greater cooperativeness with testers. In other words, although there **appears** to be substantial, though not unequivocal, support for Hypotheses 1 and 2 (the attachment–exploration and the attachment–teaching hypotheses), children have not really developed superior levels of ability but are merely using the abilities they have more efficiently.

This possibility has been entertained by Main (1973) and by Matas *et al.* (1978). Main raised the question as to whether the higher DQ scores attained by the B toddlers in her study could be attributed to the cooperative and gamelike spirit with which B children entered into the testing situation. Matas *et al.* suggested that B children differed from non-B children not in terms of their "smartness" but in terms of the style with which they approached a new and difficult task (longer attention span, less frustration, and more positive affect, less help seeking from the mother but using mother's help more effectively when provided). Matas *et al.* predict a relationship not between "level" of competence and strange situation group, but between "sense" of competence and strange situation group.

Are our results and those obtained by others only measuring "sense" of competence? We would like to suggest an alternative interpretation which encompasses but extends the position taken by Matas *et al.* As we see it, the "sense of security" which an infant derives from a harmonious relationship with the mother is related primarily to achieving a "sense of competence" or effectance (White, 1959). "Level of competence" in specific domains is, we propose, more strongly related to maternal stimulation (both amount and quality of stimulation) in these domains. Although Hypothesis 1 (the attachment–exploration hypothesis) predicts both a sense of competence and higher levels of competence in B children, this may, in fact, hold true only when maternal (caregiver) stimulation is held constant.

For infants whose mothers vary greatly in how effectively and how intensively they stimulate their infants verbally and/or through play with toys and other interesting objects, the maternal input may overshadow gains which the infants may also be making through their own discoveries. We still believe that more self-teaching leads to more actual mastery, not only to a sense of mastery (Hypothesis 1). However, the effect of maternal stimulation may, at least in infancy, be stronger than the effect of self-teaching, especially within a harmonious relationship (Hypothesis 2). Let us illustrate this point with the aid of unpublished data kindly furnished to us by Alison Clarke-Stewart (personal communication, 1978).

Clarke-Stewart's (1973) study of mother–infant interaction during the period from 11 to 18 months assessed maternal social behavior (social stimulation and social responsiveness) as well as investigating the mother's role as a mediator of the inanimate environment through play and instruction. Clarke-Stewart undertook two factor-analyses of her data, of which one focused on infant behavior and the other was concerned with maternal behavior. In each analysis one factor explained the major portion of the variance. Because of the variables which loaded highly on these factors, the infant factor was labeled "infant competence" and the maternal factor "maternal optimal care," although I will refer to this factor as "maternal competence" from here on. Table 5.9 shows highest factor loadings for both these competence factors.

Looking at the maternal side of Table 5.9, we encounter many old acquaintences: social responsiveness and stimulation, responsiveness to distress, positive affect shown toward the baby, and rejection which is negatively related with competence. In addition, measures, which we did not discuss in relation to the strange situation and its correlates, put in an appearance here. These variables have to do with cognitive and language stimulation, with the mother's effectiveness in stimulating the baby with objects and with adjusting her stimulating behavior to the age (and presumably abilities) of the baby. On the baby's side, we encounter variables which are concerned with social interaction (and which we would expect to relate to strange situation behavior): positive affect to the mother, using the mother as a reassuring presence as well as a playful companion (the attachment measure in the home lumped both

TABLE 5.9
Variable Loadings on Maternal and Infant Competence Factors[a]

Maternal variable loadings on maternal competence factor		Infant variable loadings on infant competence factor	
Verbal Stimulation	0.89	Language	0.81
Social Responsiveness	0.88	Bailey DQ (18 months)	0.77
Social Stimulation	0.87	Schema (Uzgiris-Hunt)	0.69
Responsiveness to Distress	0.88	Attachment at Home	0.65
Referential Speech Ratio	0.78	Positive Emotion to Mother	0.63
Stimulation with Objects	0.77	Looking at Mother	0.63
Appropriateness of Behavior for Baby's Age	0.76	Play Level	0.60
		Vocalizes to Mother	0.57
Positive Emotion to Baby	0.71		
Effectiveness of Stimulation with Objects	0.58		
Rejection of Baby	-0.56		

[a]From Clarke-Stewart, 1973.

of these components of attachment together), even the mere frequency of looking at and vocalizing to the mother. In addition, the infant competence factor also has high loadings on language and cognitive performance.

Are these factors related to behavior in the strange situation? The answer turns out to be that they are, but the correlations—although highly significant—do not explain the total variance represented by these factors. The correlation of the infant competence factors scores with the dichotomous B versus non-B variable was .42 (df 35, $p < .01$), the correlation with the maternal competence factor was .39 (df 35, $p < .01$). More revealing than the correlation coefficients are the scatterplots for both factors which are shown in Figure 5.4.

The scatterplots do show that a highly competent infant is much more likely to belong to Group B rather than to Groups A or C, and that a highly competent mother is much more likely to have a Group B infant. However, there is a lot of overlap between the two distributions. **Since the correlation between the maternal and infant competence factor scores was .67 (Clarke-Stewart, 1973) we may infer that other aspects**

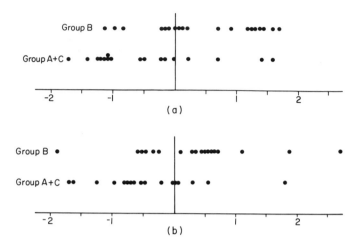

Figure 5.4. *(a) Correlations between strange situation group and infant competence factor scores. (b) Correlations between strange situation group and maternal competence factor scores. (From Clarke-Stewart, personal communication.)*

of the mother–child interaction contribute to competence (as measured here) over and above those aspects which are associated with the child's strange situation classification.

We suggest that the additional variance may be explained by the extent to which a mother acts as a mediator of the environment for her child: by the amount of object stimulation in which she engages, and her effectiveness in this task, the age appropriateness of her stimulation with objects, as well as her level of verbal stimulation. We assume that the mother's social responsiveness and stimulation, as well as her responsiveness to distress, are related to quality of attachment as measured by the strange situation. However, it has **not** been shown that the mothers who are most responsive and stimulating socially are **consistently** also those who engage in more toy play and instruction and who talk most to their infants (although Bell [1978] reports that the B mothers in her black, disadvantaged sample were more likely to be the "superteachers").

If it is the case that quality of social interaction and quality of maternal stimulation are somewhat orthogonal inputs into the child's developing competence, then we may expect that a mother's stimulation of the infant in specific domains should be related to her child's competence in these very domains. In addition, we would expect such stimulation to be more effective within a harmonious relationship and less effective within a disharmonious one. Variations of maternal stimulation **within** A and C dyads may, we suggest, also facilitate cognitive and language development, but the magnitude of the effect may be somewhat dampened by the quality of the interaction within which this stimulation occurs. **In other words, we need in the future to study relationships between maternal stimulation of cognitive and language development within A, B, and C dyads, as well as investigating differences between A, B, and C dyads, which has most frequently been the case hitherto.**

The possibility remains that maternal sensitivity as demonstrated during early social interactions tends not to be a good predictor of maternal sensitivity and effectiveness in teaching specific skills. Harmoniousness of mother–infant interactions may not be as cross-situational as we have tended to assume, especially during the later stages of infancy and toddlerhood. Ainsworth and her colleagues (Ainsworth *et al.*, 1978) have found that mothers who modulated their behavior contingently upon their infants' behavior tended to do so consistently, whether it was in face-to-face interactions, feeding interactions, or interactions involving close physical contact, but they have not looked at whether these same mothers were effective teachers for their infants, in terms of amount as well as in terms of skill. The findings reported by Matas, Arend, and Sroufe (1978) certainly support the idea that harmoniousness of interaction is cross-situational and has long-term stability, but further substantiation of this point is vital. We suggest that cross-situational stability of maternal sensitivity—or better still, its dyadic correlate, harmony of mother–infant interaction—be studied by devising a series of standardized situations analogous to the strange situation, each of which would tap some aspect of the reciprocal roles in which mothers and infants engage (including the teacher–pupil role). The behavior of the dyads should then be categorized independently in order to assess the degree to which harmony is or is not situation specific. If, on further study, it turns out that harmony is a **general** characteristic of dyads, the usefulness of the concept is thereby strengthened. Even if interactive harmony is **not** situation bound, however, harmony of a relationship may still not affect infant development in all domains equally (in contrast to what is suggested by Hypotheses 1 and 2). In some domains, and language may be one of those domains, development may be buffered against variations in interactive harmony. It has been found (Goldfarb, 1945; Spitz, 1965) that **severe** social deprivation has a devastating effect on language development, but the lesser variations in interactive harmony found in the mother–infant dyads which have been included in strange situation studies may have little or no effect on language development (thus making "amount" and "type" of stimulation a much more influential input).

Our data show that B infants were more advanced than A and C infants in symbolic play, means–end relations, and communicative gestures. We take this to mean that the mothers of B infants stimulated these activities more skillfully and more frequently. The lack of association between strange situation group and language could, within our framework, be due to any or all of the following:

1. The B mothers may not have been different from non-B mothers in terms of amount of language stimulation.
2. Harmoniousness of interaction is not a general property of dyads, but is limited to specific interaction categories, so that one would not expect strange situation classifications to be related to language interactions.
3. Language is buffered against variations in mother–infant interaction represented by the range of middle-class dyads who were studied in the strange situation.

Can we gain further insight from the area of developmental psycholinguistics? There are presently two major lines of research which are aimed at uncovering associations between specific aspects of the mother–child relationship and language. One of these is the literature on interaction patterns in early infancy (see volumes edited by Lewis and Rosenblum, 1977, and by Schaffer, 1977, for review). The other is a growing body of research on motherese or the speech of caregivers to children.

The work on early interaction between mothers and infants, while not exclusively undertaken by language specialists, was generally based on the idea that interaction can be viewed as communication or protoconversation (e.g., Bruner, 1977; Freedle and Lewis, 1977; Kaye, 1977; Sander, 1977; Stern, Beebe, Jaffe, and Bennett, 1977). Because of the time-consuming nature of microanalysis, these studies were generally limited to small samples and focused on describing the temporal and behavioral patterning of interactions, not on uncovering the influences of interaction quality on later language development. It makes sense to postulate that the interaction rules acquired during the infant's preverbal period should facilitate the acquisition of language, but data testing this hypothesis have yet to be collected.

The second line of research, the study of motherese, **has** focused on individual differences: that is, on whether a mother's ability to tailor her speech to the perceived needs of her child has some impact on language acquisition (see Snow and Ferguson, 1977, for a review of this work). Some correlations have indeed been found (Cross, 1977) but these turn out, upon removal of confounding factors, to be limited to very specific linguistic structures such as questions with fronted auxiliaries (Newport, Gleitman, and Gleitman, 1977).

On the whole, then, the relationship between maternal input and child language is not impressive, and neither is the association between dyadic harmony (as measured by the strange situation) and language. On the other hand there are a number of tantalizing positive findings which we reviewed earlier (Clarke-Stewart, 1973; Connell, 1975; Main, 1973). One way out of this confusing situation may be to peel apart the various hypothesized influences (dyadic harmony, amount, quality, and style of maternal language stimulation) and assess their relative contribution to language development within the same sample over a period of time. There remains the possibility that consistent effects of maternal or dyadic behaviors on language development will not show up until language is well established and that correlations of language variables with strange situation behavior would appear if we studied social aspects of language development such as level of egocentric speech, discourse ability, verbal expression of affective and other internal states, and differentiation of "I" and "you."

Taking the body of findings listed in Table 5.2 as a whole, we can say that the quality of the relationship which has developed between infant and mother within the first year or 18 months appears to be related to many aspects of intelligence, although—for reasons as yet unclear—the effects are much stronger for cognitive measures than for language competence. When we first introduced the topic of infant–mother attachment we used the term in a restricted sense, linking it to social interaction between the partners and to the mother's function as a secure base. It has become evident (Bretherton, in press) that there are additional components which play an integral part in the functioning of the mother–infant relationship. One of these components is the interaction of mother and child as teacher and pupil.

The Piagetian school of research has justifiably emphasized the child's active role in teaching himself about interesting and novel aspects of the inanimate and animate environment. While it is undoubtedly true that infants explore, such behavior may at this young age be more strongly related to acquiring a "sense" of competence and autonomy than to the actual "level" of competence (for example, Clarke-Stewart, 1973 found that DQ was predicted not by how many toys were available to the child, nor by how much time mother and child spent in the same room, but by how much toy play and positive social interaction occurred between the partners. Similarly, Carew (1975) reported that up to the age of $2\frac{1}{2}$ years later IQ was related not to the complexity of the child's own solitary play, but to the complexity of the play in which the mother involved her child).

Attachment theory as well as Piagetian theories have tended to minimize the role of the mother as a mediator through whom the child comes to discover the environment. We feel it is time that the role of the mother as a teacher be reintegrated into both cognitive and attachment theories. In other words, we are suggesting further testing of the two components of Hypothesis 2 (see page 225) separately. Hypothesis 2, in its revised form, reads as follows:

(*a*) If the mother and infant can achieve an interactive style in which harmony and affective synchrony predominate and

(*b*) if the mother stimulates and challenges her child

the infant's communicative–cognitive competence will be enhanced because:

(*a*) Within a harmonious relationship the infant is likely not only to achieve **more** interactions but also **more contingent** interactions;

(*b*) within a relationship where the mother actively teaches and encourages her baby, the environment comes to meet the baby halfway, as it were. Aspects of the environment with which the baby is ready to cope are selectively made available by the caregiver: That is, their discovery is not left entirely up to the baby's own initiative.

Hypothesis 2, in its new form, would predict superior performance levels for infants high on *a* and *b*. It would also predict some facilitation of cognitive–communicative development by either *a* or *b* alone (although the cognitive–communicative style of babies high on *a* might differ from that of babies high on *b)*. Lowest performance levels would be expected for babies low on both *a* and *b,* that is babies whose interaction with their caregiver is relatively inharmonious **and** whose caregiver does not provide high levels of stimulation.

Furthermore, we must make an effort to verify the extent to which harmony of interaction and maternal teaching style are cross-situational, issues which should be explored by observing the same infants in a variety of different interactive situations (such as the strange situation, unstructured play situations, and structured teaching situations). We suggest that a **separate** classification system be developed for each category of interaction, allowing examination of the degree of overlap **and** the degree of nonoverlap between the different classifications. Once this is done we will be in a much better position to determine what kinds of relationships between dyadic harmony and infant cognitive–communicative development we should expect to find (e.g., very specific relationships, or cross-situational relationships). We may also gain further insight into the reasons why some areas of infant competence (such as language) appear to be less sensitive to environmental variations than other areas (such as symbolic play, means–end relations, and gestural communication).

Chapter 6

NEXT STEPS:
A FOLLOW-UP STUDY AND
SOME PILOT RESEARCH

Elizabeth Bates
Inge Bretherton
Vicki Carlson
Karlana Carpen
Marcia Rosser

Correlational studies are difficult to interpret because we do not control the world that creates our results. Unless measures are chosen carefully, we may find interesting patterns that are produced by such uninteresting factors as age, IQ, or trivial but pervasive task effects. There are ways around some of these problems. In the results presented so far we factored out the effects of nationality and (where relevant) age. Low correlations with locomotor development suggest that our results are not picking up gross differences in maturation (Chapter 3). Low correlations among the cognitive measures permit us to rule out general IQ as an explanation (Chapter 3). Though certain aspects of the mother–child relationship have probably affected our findings, there is no single factor of "good mothering" that can account for the relationships to language (Chapter 5). Finally, we used a variety of methods to assess the same developments: interview versus observation, frequency versus level of development, single measures versus summary variables. Insofar as the results are consistent across these measures, they are probably not created by the side effects of a particular method. In short, we feel confident that the patterns reported in the last few chapters reflect interesting and nontrivial relationships among communicative and cognitive developments. We still cannot elevate our correlations to the level of cause. Correlations do not prove cause, but they do tell us where to look for causes: We have narrowed the range of inquiry, specifying new places to look and things to do. Having surrounded the phenomena of interest with a correlational net, the next step is to send a search party into the interior.

This chapter is primarily "notes from the field," a report on pilot work and research in progress by the American team. The results are certainly not conclusive. We present them here to illustrate new directions, and to provide an early warning on some possible dead ends.

The work is based on three themes that emerged in the Italian–American study:

1. Local homology
2. Sensitive periods
3. Decontextualization

In extending the research beyond the 9–13-month age range, we have added another key concept:

4. Predictive power across time

Before turning the results, let us examine these issues one at a time.

Local Homology. The correlational findings of Chapters 3 and 5 support the neo-Piagetian view of local or specific structural relationships among sensorimotor developments (e.g., Fischer, in press). Like Uzgiris and Hunt (1975), we found no evidence for general operative principles unifying performance within a given stage. The emergence of symbols in language and in play is predicted by a subset of preverbal communicative measures (e.g., giving, showing, pointing, ritualized requests). Play, imitation, and tool use predict language development; object permanence and spatial relations do not. Some of these measures correlate with mother–child attachment, others do not (notably language). In short, if there are homologies between language and nonlinguistic systems in this age range, they seem to involve some fairly specific and heterogeneous set of structures. These patterns suggested two lines of new research, one devoted to cognitive factors, the other to social development. First, we decided to go "inside" imitation, play, and tool use to find out more precisely how these developments relate to language. Second, we proposed a more detailed exploration of mother–child interaction during early play and language games, to see if different styles of interaction relate to performance on our cognitive and communicative measures.

Sensitive Periods. The concept of local homology seems to apply both across and within sessions. Some of our measures were correlated only at particular sessions, suggesting that certain items are more sensitive predictors of future development than others. For example, the means–end scale at $9\frac{1}{2}$ months accounted for most of the correlations between means–ends and the various communicative measures. This is the period when the children first began to use cloth supports and strings to pull in objects. The combined vocal–gestural imitation scale was a more sensitive predictor at $11\frac{1}{2}$ months, when imitation of novel models began to predominate. Correlations with combinatorial play were distributed fairly evenly across sessions; correlations with symbolic play were relevant only in the last sessions. Note that all of these measures were varying across children at every session, or they would have been excluded from the matrix. So this "sensitive period" effect is not a statistical artifact. We decided to follow up on these patterns, focusing new research on the sensitive periods for each measure, to discover which aspects of tool use, play, and so on, were having an effect.

Decontextualization. The results of Chapters 3 and 5 pointed us toward a more detailed investigation of specific quantitative relationships. However, as noted in Chapter 4, there is also a general qualitative change that holds up across measures in the passage from presentational to representational knowing. In tool use, language, and symbolic play the children begin with highly restricted, context-bound behaviors that seem to depend heavily on perceptual support. Across this 4-month period the same schemes are gradually "decontextualized," occurring in a broader range of situations with decreasing perceptual support. This pattern suggests that there is a developmental variable of decontextualization that applies across aspects of symbolization, something "in the child" that is changing across domains. To observe this passage in more detail, we set out to design more continuous or graded measures of tool use, symbolic play, and language, to see whether these three domains are changing separately or in unison along a continuum of contextual dependence.

Predictive Value across Time. All of the results presented so far pertain to a relatively brief and intense period of development. How strong is the predictive value of the same variables beyond the 9–13-months range? For example, tool use at 9 months was related to language at 13 months. We doubt if it would predict the children's verbal scores on the Graduate Record Exam 21 years later. Indeed, most infant intelligence measures predict very little beyond the first 2 years of life (Bayley, 1958). Sensitive periods provide a particularly clear window on development, where we can detect the interdependence of structures as they are being built. This does not mean that two domains will continue to covary after the construction is complete. For example, there may be something about the discovery of tools at 9 months which is integrally involved in the discovery that things have names. Hence the first child on his block to discover tools may be at an advantage in applying this "something" 4 months later. But depending on what that "something" is, it may be irrelevant once everyone has made the same discovery. If the homology taps into some robust and pervasive capacity (e.g., anticipatory imagery, social sensitivity) then its predictive value may hold up for months or years. If, on the other hand, the homology between a linguistic and non-linguistic measure involves a skill that varies only in particular periods in infancy, then correlations should disappear across time. In sum, by extending the age range in a correlational study and determining the predictive strength of measures across time, we can learn more about the nature of the underlying structures that created our results.

We will begin by describing a small follow-up study at 19 months, carried out with 11 of the American infants in our international study. Then we will describe some ongoing research on causal understanding around the 10-month "sensitive period." Finally, we will present a few illustrations from research on adult–child interaction and contextual dependence during language comprehension and play.

Six-Month Follow-Up

Approximately 6 months after data were collected for the international study, we were able to locate 11 of the 13 American families involved in that research. They all graciously agreed to participate in a brief follow-up session in their homes. The purpose of this follow-up was twofold:

1. to determine the time course and predictive strength of some of our old measures
2. to pilot test some new measures relevant to later development, and maximize continuity with the first study

We were particularly interested in developing some more standardized measures of language comprehension and imitation, together with some techniques for eliciting symbolic play with realistic versus abstract objects. The focus here was on the concept of decontextualization in language and in play. We hypothesized that there would be correlations among measures with a common degree of abstractness versus contextual dependence.

Method

SUBJECTS

The 11 American infants included 5 girls and 6 boys, averaging $18\frac{1}{2}$ months of age within a range of 17–19 months. To reduce the variance due to age differences, all scores from the earlier study were corrected according to prorating procedures similar to those described in Chapter 5. These procedures produced three between-session scores for the earlier study: A', B' and C', averaging 10, 11, and 12 months, respectively. For each child the prorated scores represent performance 6 months, 7 months, and 8 months prior to the follow-up testing date.

PROCEDURE

The F-session measures were designed by M.R., who was present at all the home visits, accompanied by either E.B. or I.B. Measures included the following: informal observations of communication and play, maternal interviews based on a vocabulary checklist, standardized tests for language comprehension and imitation, videotaped free play with the mother, and elicited symbolic play with abstract versus realistic objects. The highest items from the various Uzgiris and Hunt scales were administered to all the children, but since they had almost all reached ceiling on these scales, the measures were dropped from the analyses. An audiorecorder was left running throughout the home visit, to record the interview with the mother as well as any spontaneous speech by the child.

Informal observations of communication and play were made on standard coding sheets with space for notes. The variables of interest included the familiar communicative gestures from Chapter 3 (giving, showing, and pointing), instances of combinatorial or symbolic play, and contextual notes for spontaneous language.

The maternal interview was based on a checklist of vocabulary items that had been sent to the mother several days prior to the visit. This checklist included lexical items based on our earlier research, as well as suggestions from the current literature on language at 18 months of age. Mothers were asked about both comprehension and production of these items. In addition, we also asked about multiword combinations that had occurred since the 13-month session. (The checklist is included in Appendix 6.1.) As described in Chapter 3, the interview was carried out informally, probing for anecdotes and additional information that would help us to determine the contextual range of the child's word use.

The language imitation test was administered by the mother. It consisted simply of a picture book with short sentences written under each picture (e.g., *The kitty is soft, The girl eats cake*—see Appendix 6.1 for the full list of sentences). The mother was asked to show the book to the child, reading each sentence and doing whatever she could to elicit imitation. In addition to audiorecordings, the experimenter took notes on both linguistic and nonlinguistic responses by the child, using a standardized coding sheet.

The language comprehension test was administered by the experimenter (M.R.). Based on reports by Huttenlocher (1974) and Sachs and Truswell (1978), the test consisted of a randomized set of 30 commands. Twenty-four of these commands were predictable plausible acts like *Give the dolly to Mommy*. Six of the commands contained the same kinds of lexical items, but the child was asked to carry out implausible acts such as *Smell the ball*. Sachs and Truswell had demonstrated that children at the one word stage are capable of responding to implausible commands (albeit reluctantly), and they argue that this is particularly strong evidence that children are responding to the linguistic structure of the utterance rather than to cues involving high-probability actions. We were particularly interested in this portion of the test because of its relationship to our notion of contextual dependence. Responses to the commands were recorded by the observer (E.B. or I.B.) on coding sheets with space for notes; linguistic responses by the child were audiorecorded. (The full set of commands is presented in Appendix 6.1.)

There were two parts to the elicited symbolic play task. In the first portion, the experimenter used a set of realistic toys (vehicles, dolls, furniture, utensils, etc.) and tried informally to engage the child in pretend play. The schemes that we tried were based primarily on our earlier observations of spontaneous play (see Chapter 4, Appendix 4.1). In the second portion, we again tried to elicit familiar schemes. This time, however, the objects were all fairly abstract: tinker toys, nesting cups, blocks, etc. The elicitation was informal here as well, paced according to the child's interest. Typical sequences included telephoning with a Tinkertoy stick and a block, driving a block while making motor noises, eating from a nesting cup with a stick. Both of the symbolic play tasks were videorecorded for later analysis. Notice that this measure is quite different from our recordings of spontaneous play. Elicited symbolic play is a hybrid including aspects of imitation and comprehension. The focus here was on the ease with which such behavior can be elicited from the child, the complexity and creativity of the child's play in response to the adult, and the difference between play with suggestive toys and play with abstract objects.

Five minutes of free play between the mother and the child were videorecorded. A battery of toys suitable for pretend play and for combinatorial play were provided for this purpose. In addition there was a shape box, the only toy which the mother was specifically asked to use, although she was not told for how long she was to play with it. One of our interests was, in fact, the kinds of play in which the mother would choose to engage her child, in order to determine whether this was correlated to some of our other measures of symbol development.

The order of presentation of the tasks was varied depending on the child's level of interest, as described in Chapter 3.

ANALYSES

Due to equipment failure, 3 of the 11 videotapes were lost. Hence we were forced to analyze some measures separately for 11 versus 8 children. A total of 15 measures were derived for the full sample of 11 at the F-session. Nine measures based on the videotapes were derived for the subsample of 8. (Details of scoring procedures are provided in Appendix 6.2.)

Table 6.1 lists the 15 F-session measures for all 11 children, the 9 augmented or additional measures derived for the video sample of 8, and the means and standard deviations for all 24 scores. Notice that once again there are interview and observational records for some of the same behaviors. Also, the scores for language and play include frequencies, number of different schemes produced, and a few scores representing qualitative levels. This plethora of scores complicates the correlational analyses, but it also permits us to generalize some of the findings beyond particular task effects.

The 15 measures for the full sample include 4 measures of language comprehension (number of words reported by the mother, comprehension of plausible commands, comprehension of implausible commands, and a total score for comprehension testing), 3 measures of language production (number of words reported by the mother, number of different words observed, frequency of meaningful speech), and 1 language imitation score (the standardized test described above). There are 3 measures of play (number of different symbolic schemes observed, number of different combinatorial play schemes observed, frequency of observed symbolic play) and 4 measures of nonverbal communication (frequency of observed giving, showing, and pointing, plus a nonverbal summary score).

For the subset of 8 children, a second set of scores were derived to include information from the videotapes. First, the observation scores

TABLE 6.1
Means and Standard Deviations for Measures Used in the Follow-Up Study

Measures	Abbreviation[a]	Mean	Standard Deviations
Interview			
1. Language Comprehension	FMI Comp	115.86	39.98
2. Language Production	FMIProd	58.86	42.59
Observation Notes			
1. Gestural Communication			
Communicative Pointing	FPoint	10.09	8.34
Show	FShow	4.64	6.33
Give	FGive	9.32	6.42
Total	FCommGest	24.05	11.74
2. Language Comprehension (Percent of Commands Administered)			
Plausible Commands	FComp 1	0.59	0.20
Implausible Commands	FComp 2	0.48	0.26
Total	FComp	0.57	0.20
Production			
Number of Words	F#Words	8.64	6.87
Frequency of Language	FLFreq	16.73	17.27
Language Imitation	FLImit	11.09	7.45
3. Play			
Number of Symbolic Schemes	F#SymbPl	6.18	3.31
Frequency of Symbolic Play	FSFreq	8.91	4.68
Combinatorial Play	FCombPl	3.05	2.96
Videotapes			
1. Language			
Augmented Number of Words	FOV#Words	11.13	8.87
Augmented Frequency of Language	FOVLFreq	23	25.12
2. Play			
Augmented Number of Symbolic Schemes	FOV#SymbPl	6.75	3.62

(continued)

TABLE 6.1 (continued)

Measures	Abbreviation[a]	Mean	Standard Deviations
Augmented Frequency of Symbolic Play	FOVSFreq	9.38	4.37
Elicited Symbolic Play, Realistic Toys	FESymbRe	21.19	7.92
Elicited Symbolic Play, Abstract Toys	FESymbAb	18.81	8.89
Elicited Symbolic Play, Highest Level	FESymbLev	4.94	1.12
Combinatorial Play	FVTCombPl	14.75	6.46

[a]The abbreviations listed in this table will be used in all following tables using the above measures.

for language and play were all augmented to include a combination of instances on and off camera. Exceptions were the play schemes in the elicitation task. This two-part task was analyzed separately with a coding scheme designed to reflect the child's highest level of sophistication, and the breadth and complexity of his performance. For example, low scores were given for simply cooperating with the experimenter's games (e.g., allowing E to put the telephone receiver to his ear). Higher scores were given for active participation, ranging from simple imitation with the modeled objects, to imitations carried out on different objects, to creative play adding components that were not modeled by the experimentor. Scores were adjusted for variety of play within each of these levels. This procedure yielded four scores for each child: breadth of performance on realistic toys, breadth of performance on abstract toys, a summary score for breadth, and a single score reflecting the highest level reached overall regardless of variety. Appendix 6.2 describes these scoring procedures in more detail.

All of the analyses described so far were carried out by K.C. The coding scheme for elicited symbolic play was developed and applied jointly by K.C. and I.B. We have made no systematic efforts to establish reliabilities for these measures, a factor which must be kept in mind in interpreting the results.

Finally, the complete set of F-session scores was compared with a subset of the more interesting measures from the 9–12-month sessions listed in Table 6.2. These include the Uzgiris–Hunt scales (object permanence, means–ends, space, and imitation), several measures of sym-

TABLE 6.2

Measures from Sessions A', B', and C' Which Were Entered into the Follow-Up Correlation Matrix

Measures	Abbreviations	Defined in
Interview		
1. Gestural Communication		
Communicative Point	Cpoint	Appendices 3.2, 3.3
Show	Show	Appendices 3.2, 3.3
Give	Give	Appendices 3.2, 3.3
Ritualized Request	RitReq	Appendices 3.2, 3.3
Level of Communicative Gestures	CommGest	Method section, Chapter 5
2. Language		
Comprehension Level	CompL	Appendices 3.2, 3.3
Number of Words Comprehended	#Comp	Appendices 3.2, 3.3
Nonreferential Words	NRefWd	Appendices 3.2, 3.3
Referential Words	RefWd	Appendices 3.2, 3.3
Language Summary Measure, Comprehension, and Production	Lang	Method section, Chapter 5
3. Play		
Symbolic Play Schemes	SymbPl	Appendices 3.2, 3.3
Combinatorial Play	CombPl	Appendices 3.2, 3.3
Observations		
1. Gestural Communication		
Communicative Point	CPoint	Appendices 3.2, 3.3
Show	Show	Appendices 3.2, 3.3
Give	Give	Appendices 3.2, 3.3
Nonritualized Request	NRitReq	Appendices 3.2, 3.3
Ritualized Request	RitReq	Appendices 3.2, 3.3
Level of Communicative Gestures	CommGest	Method section, Chapter 5
Frequency of Communicative Gestures	CommGestFreq	Method section, Chapter 5
2. Language		
Frequency of Comprehension	Comp	Appendices 3.2, 3.3
Nonreferential Words	NRefWd	Appendices 3.2, 3.3

(continued)

TABLE 6.2 (continued)

Measures	Abbreviations	Defined in
Number of Referential Words	RefWd	Appendices 3.2, 3.3
Number of Words, Referential and Nonreferential, Produced[a]	# Words	Method section, Chapter 5
Language Summary Measure, Comprehension, and Production	Lang	Method section, Chapter 5
3. Play		
Number of Symbolic Play Schemes	#SymbPl	Appendices 3.2, 3.3
Frequency of Symbolic Play Schemes	FSymbPl	Appendices 3.2, 3.3
Highest Level of Symbolic Play[a]	SymbLev	Method section, Chapter 5
Combinatorial Play	CombPl	Appendices 3.2, 3.3
4. Uzgiris-Hunt Scales		
Object Permanence	ObjP	Chapter 3; Uzgiris and Hunt, 1975
Spatial Relations	Space	Chapter 3; Uzgiris and Hunt, 1975
Means-End	Means	Chapter 3; Uzgiris and Hunt, 1975
Imitation	Imit	Chapter 3, Method section
5. Locomotion	Loco	Appendix 3.4

[a]These measures were based on a combination of observational and interview data.

bolic and combinatorial play, individual and summary variables of early language and of nonverbal communication.

Results

One of the most surprising findings in our follow-up study is the fact that very little had changed in the intervening 6 months. Compared with the burst of events that occurs from 9 to 13 months, this period is something of a plateau—a fact also noted by Nelson (1973). Only one of our children was reported to use multiword speech. Their vocabularies had expanded (from a mean of 8.2 on the 12½-month maternal reports to a mean of 58). The symbolic play repertoire was richer and more stable. But all of this seems to be just more of the same. We suspect that the major developments of the 13–18-month range take place "underground," a consolidation and gradual decontextualization of the schemes acquired in the first year. There are some indications in our data supporting this view, particularly in performance on abstract symbolic play and comprehension of implausible commands. Overall, however, the 18-month level seems to be a calm moment before a linguistic storm that occurs with the subsequent onset of multiword speech.

Turning to the correlational findings, we have followed the format of Chapter 3, listing significant relationships in tabular form. Table 6.3 lists all of the significant correlations of the 15 F-session measures for 11 children, both within the F session and with the earlier measures. Table 6.4 lists significant correlations of the 9 videomeasures for 8 children, again within the F session and with sessions A′, B′, and C′. For 11 children, a correlation of .49 is significant at $p < .05$, with a one-tailed test. For 8 children, the $p < .05$ level requires a correlation of .58. There were considerably more significant relations than would be expected by chance, even in correlations spanning 6–8 months. But the patterns were somewhat different from the ones reported in Chapter 3.

Readers interested in the correlational details are referred to Tables 6.3 and 6.4. Given the pilot nature of many of the F-session measures, we do not want to milk these findings for more meaning than they deserve. Instead, we will restrict ourselves to a brief characterization of the patterns that emerged, first for the follow-up session itself and then for the cross-lag correlations between the earlier measures and the follow-up study.

SESSION F—ELEVEN CHILDREN

First, the comprehension test worked better than we expected, given the difficulties inherent in telling 18-month olds what to do. The plausible versus implausible commands were correlated at .88. Furthermore, the three scores for the comprehension test (implausible, plausible, total) were all related to language comprehension and production in the interview (ranging from .55 to .72). The other language correlations were less impressive, suggesting that the single "Language Complex" of Chapter 3 has diverged by 18 months into separate and more variable language skills. The interview measures correlated with one another (77), but with very few of the other F variables. The two measures of observed spontaneous speech (number of Words, Language Frequency)

TABLE 6.3

Significant[a] Positive Product-Moment Correlations between Follow-Up Measures for Eleven Children and Measures of Gestural Communication, Language, and Cognition for Sessions A' - C'

Follow-up Measure	Follow-up	Session A' Interview	Session A' Observation	Session B' Interview	Session B' Observation	Session C' Interview	Session C' Observation
Interview Comprehension	FMIComp 0.78 FCommGest 0.51 FComp 1 0.67 FComp 2 0.56 FComp 0.67	RitReq 0.49 CommGest 0.62	Show 0.76 CommGest 0.70	#Comp 0.64 Lang 0.62	ReFwd 0.58 #Words 0.49	#Comp 0.58 Lang 0.51	Comp 0.57 #Words 0.51
Interview Production	FComp 1 0.73 FComp 2 0.60 FComp 0.72 FLImit 0.65	RitReq 0.57 CommGest 0.61	Show 0.62 CommGest 0.62	RitReq 0.52 #Comp 0.55 #SymbPl 0.52 Lang 0.57	Show 0.64 RitReq 0.64 CommGest 0.69 CommGest Freq 0.56 ReFwd 0.69 #Words 0.59 SymbLev 0.61 Mean 0.55		CommGest 0.55 ReFwd 0.74 #Words 0.66 Symblev 0.55
Observation Communicative Point	FCommGest 0.63 FSFreq 0.76 FCombPl 0.53	RitReq 0.64 CommGest 0.70	Show 0.77 RitReq 0.63 CommGest 0.64 Mean 0.60	CPoint 0.49 RitReq 0.51 CommGest 0.54 Lang 0.50	NRefwd 0.51	CPoint 0.53	
Observation: Show	FCommGest FLFreq 0.71						
Observation: Give	FCommGest 0.49		CommGest Freq 0.61		Show 0.80 Give 0.69 CommGest Freq 0.49 Lang 0.78		Give 0.54 NReFwd 0.78 Lang 0.68

(continued)

283

TABLE 6.3 (continued)

Follow-Up Measure	Follow-Up	Session A' Interview	Session A' Observation	Session B' Interview	Session B' Observation	Session C' Interview	Session C' Observation
Observation: Communicative Gestures	FLFreq 0.65 FSFreq 0.74		Show 0.75 CommGest 0.62 CommGest Freq 0.59	Show 0.56	Show 0.49 #Words 0.54		#Words 0.52
Observation: Language Comprehension 1	FComp 2 0.88 FComp 0.99 F#Words 0.62 FLFreq 0.49 FLImit 0.49	CommGest 0.55	Show 0.67 CommGest 0.57 CommGest Freq 0.55		Show 0.71 CommGest Freq 0.54 RefWd 0.54		RefWd 0.54
Observation: Language Comprehension 2	FComp 0.93 FLImit 0.57	CommGest 0.57			Show 0.52 RitReq 0.57 RefWd 0.54		
Observation: Language Comprehension Total	F#Words 0.58 FLImit 0.52	CommGest 0.57	Show 0.64 CommGest 0.54 CommGest Freq 0.55		Show 0.68 RitReq 0.49 CommGest Freq 0.52 RefWd 0.56		RefWd 0.51
Observation: Number of Words	FPoint 0.50 Show 0.51 FCommGest 0.65 FLFreq 0.88 F#SymbPl 0.54	NRefWd 0.54	Show 0.54 RitReq 0.81		RefWd 0.64		
Observation: Frequency of Language	F#SymbPl 0.52	NRefWd 0.68	RitReq 0.70				

Observation:					
Language Imitation		#Comp 0.57, Lang 0.55		CPoint 0.57, CPoint 0.50	RefWd 0.78
Number of Symbolic Play Schemes	FPoint 0.81, FCommGest 0.76, FSFreq 0.97, FCombPl 0.68	RitReq 0.59, CommGest 0.56, NRefwd 0.51, Lang 0.49	Show 0.78, RitReq 0.57, CommGest 0.69, CommGest 0.73, Freq 0.59, #Words 0.61, CombPl 0.57, Imit 0.57	NRefwd 0.63, #Words 0.62	RefWd 0.54, #Words 0.54
Frequency of Symbolic Play		RitReq 0.51	Show 0.81, RitReq 0.51, CommGest 0.78, CommGest 0.74, Freq 0.74, #Words 0.71, CombPl 0.51, Imit 0.57	Lang 0.51, NRefwd 0.75, #Words 0.69	RefWd 0.51, #Words 0.61
Combinatorial Play	FSFreq 0.60	NRefwd 0.68	CommGest 0.74, Imit 0.64		

[a] $r = 0.497$ (df 10), $p < 0.05$ (one tailed).

$r = 0.658$ (df 10), $p < 0.01$ (one tailed).

TABLE 6.4

Significant[a] Positive Product-Moment Correlations between Follow-Up Videotape Measures for Eight Children and Measures of Gestural Communication, Language, and Cognition for Sessions A'-C'

Follow-up Measure	Follow-up	Session A' Interview		Session A' Observation		Session B' Interview		Session B' Observation		Session C' Interview		Session C' Observation	
Observation and Videotape Number of Words	FCommGest 0.68	NRefWd	0.81	RitReq	0.89								
	FComp 1 0.61			Imit	0.77								
	F#Words 0.99												
	FLFreq 0.97												
	F#SymbPl 0.69												
	FSFreq 0.63												
	FOVLFreq 0.93												
	FOV#SymbPl 0.82												
	FOVSFreq 0.59												
Observation and Videotape Frequency of Language	FShow 0.73	NRefWd	0.80	RitReq	0.73								
	F#Words 0.87			Imit	0.70								
	FLFreq 0.98												
	FOV#Words 0.93												
	FOV#SymbPl 0.61												
Observation and Videotape Number of Symbolic Play Schemes	FMIComp 0.69	RitReq	0.68	Show	0.87	Show	0.65	Show	0.59	RefWd	0.64	#Words	0.68
	FPoint 0.75	CommGest	0.81	RitReq	0.75	CommGest	0.65	RefWd	0.63				
	FCommGest 0.86	NRefWd	0.80	CommGest	0.83	Lang	0.60	#Words	0.72				
	FComp 1 0.72	Lang	0.72	CommGestFreq	0.78								
				#Words	0.64								

								Show	0.59	#Words	0.80
								RefWd	0.61		
								Lang	0.60		

Category			Imit	0.70					
	FComp	0.69							
	F#Words	0.84							
	FLFreq	0.71							
	F#SymbPl	0.93							
	FSFreq	0.93							
	FOV#Words	0.82							
	FOVLFreq	0.61							
	FOVSFreq	0.94							
	FESymbAb	0.64							
	FESymb	0.74							

Observation and Videotape Frequency of Symbolic Play	FMIComp	0.84	RitReq	0.79	Show	0.95	Show	0.74	Show	0.74	Show	0.59
	FMIProd	0.71	CommGest	0.90	CommGest	0.92	Give	0.66	Give	0.68	RefWd	0.61
	FPoint	0.75	Comp	0.66	CommGest Freq	0.81	RitReq	0.72	RitReq	0.67	Lang	0.60
	FCommGest	0.79	CompC	0.65			CommGest	0.80	CommGest Freq	0.74		
	FComp 1	0.76	NRefWd	0.70	#Words	0.75	Comp	0.61				
	FComp 2	0.59	Lang	0.87	Mean	0.62	NRefWd	0.59	NRefWd	0.69		
	FComp	0.74					Lang	0.81	#Words	0.81		
	F#Words	0.62										
	F#SymbPl	0.87										
	FSFreq	0.92										

(continued)

TABLE 6.4 (continued)

Follow-up Measure	Follow-up	Session A' Interview	Session A' Observation	Session B' Interview	Session B' Observation	Session C' Interview	Session C' Observation
	FOV#Words 0.59 FOV#SymbPl 0.94 FESymbRe 0.59 FESymbAb 0.62 FESymb 0.76						
Videotape Combinatorial Play							
Videotape: Elicited Symbolic Play Realistic Toys	FMIComp 0.69 FGive 0.85 FCommGest 0.61 FSFreq 0.58 FOVSFreq 0.59 FESymb 0.77	NRefWd 0.62 CombPl 0.65	Show 0.70 CommGest 0.68 CommGest Freq 0.71	CombPl 0.68 NRefWd 0.76 Lang 0.76	Show 0.62 Give 0.77 CommGest Freq 0.74 #Words 0.76 Lang 0.63	RefWd 0.82 Lang 0.61	#Words 0.71
Videotape: Elicited Symbolic Play Abstract Toys	FPoint 0.65 FComp 2 0.73 FComp 0.63 F#SymbPl 0.64 FCombPl 0.78 FOV#SymbPl 0.64	RitReq 0.67 CommGest 0.78	Show 0.63 RitReq 0.75 CommGest Freq 0.78		RitReq 0.78 RefWd 0.80 CombPl 0.88		

Videotape: Elicited Symbolic Play Total

	FOVSFreq 0.62				
	FESymb 0.80				
FMIComp 0.68	RitReq 0.75	Show 0.84	RitReq 0.68	Give 0.80	RefFwd 0.72
FMIprod 0.59	CommGest 0.76	CommGest 0.77	Lang 0.65	RitReq 0.62	RitReq 0.59
FPoint 0.66	NRefwd 0.59	CommGest Freq 0.96	CombPl 0.60	CommGest Freq 0.71	
F#SymbPl 0.77	Lang 0.63				
FSFreq 0.76		CombPl 0.73		#Words 0.58	
FCombPl 0.61		Mean 0.61		Lang 0.65	
FOV#SymbPl 0.74				CombPl 0.57	
FOVSFreq 0.76					
FOVSymbRe 0.77					
FESymbAb 0.80					

Videotape: Elicited Symbolic Play Level

		Space 0.74	Give 0.70	Give 0.58
			Space 0.80	Space 0.80

[a] $r = 0.582$ (df 7), $p < 0.05$ (one tailed).

$r = 0.750$ (df 7), $p < 0.01$ (one tailed).

were correlated more often with nonverbal measures than with the rest of language, suggesting that by 18 months variability in the use of single words indexes motivational factors in social interaction more than underlying linguistic skill. The language imitation test did correlate with elicited comprehension and with the mother's report of productive vocabulary, so there is some consistency across language measures. But they are not as tightly related as they were at the dawning of symbol use.

The measures of nonverbal communication (giving, showing, pointing, and one summary variable of gestural communication) are still correlating positively with other measures at 18 months of age. Not surprisingly, the strongest relationships are with the summary variable, which predicts several aspects of language including frequency of spontaneous speech. In other words children who are communicating frequently are using both language and gesture. In addition, gestural communication was also related to aspects of play. Hence the predictive strength of gesture at 9–13 months continues 6 months later.

For symbolic and combinatorial play, the pattern of relationships has changed considerably from 12 to 18 months. The number of different play schemes is still related to spontaneous speech (number of words + .53, word frequency + .51), but not with the interview language measures for the imitation and comprehension tests. Combinatorial play is even more isolated from language at 18 months, correlating only with symbolic play and pointing. Note however, that when instances of play from the videotapes are added, more relationships emerge with communicative variables. So the earlier relations among symbols in language and in action have not disappeared 6 months later, but they do seem to have weakened and diverged somewhat.

SESSION F—EIGHT CHILDREN

For the subsample of 8 children, we ran the entire matrix of variables from Sessions F, A′, B′, and C′. The patterns were very much the same for this subsample and for the full sample of 11 children. Hence, in this section we will discuss only the nine separate video-measures.

Five of these scores were versions of the measures reported above, augmented to include instances from the videorecords: number of words used, number of different symbolic play schemes, number of combinatorial play schemes, and frequency of both symbolic play and speech. Most of the additions to play come from the filmed segment with the mother, since elicited play was treated separately.

For the language measures, the augmented scores are more strongly related to other variables than those reported above, but in very similar patterns. The number of words used went from a mean of 9.8 to 11.1, and frequency increased from 17.8 to 23. The scores are correlated with one another, and with aspects of gestural communication. Correlations with symbolic play are even stronger, reaching .82 for number of play schemes versus number of words. However, these spontaneous speech measures are still isolated from the other language variables, correlating only with comprehension of plausible commands. This underscores the view that number of words used and frequency of meaningful speech relate more to social–motivational factors than to linguistic skill at 18 months of age.

For the play measures, the augmented scores change the picture radically. When the videorecords are added, scores for combinatorial play are negatively related to the rest of the matrix! Relationships are negative in 21 out of 23 possible instances, 10 of them significant beyond −.59. By contrast, the addition of videotaped instances greatly enhances the positive predictive value of symbolic play, particularly with the various language measures. Frequency of symbolic play now correlates with all of the language measures except imitation. What happened? An examination of the means and standard deviations suggests that something unusual has occurred. With additions from the play segment with mother, the means for the number of combinatorial play instances go from 2.6 to 14.7. By contrast, the symbolic play means go from 5.75 to 6.75 for number and from 8.37 to 9.3 for frequency. In other words, a small change in symbolic play has led to increased significance of the correlation coefficients, while a large change in combinatorial play has led to negative relationships. Why? Notice that most of these increases come from the play segment with mother, where there was an opportunity to play with the shape box as well as other combinatorial toys or to engage in fantasy play. In fact, the increase in the mean for combinatorial play was mainly due to play with the shape box (which involved repeated dropping of objects into a container). There is thus a suggestion that children who spent more of the 5-minute play segment with the mother engaged in fantasy play tended to be more adept at symbol use in general, whereas children who spent more of the interaction with the mother involved in shape-box play tended to be less adept at symbol use. This conclusion is, of course, highly tentative and will require much more systematic study. But, returning to the theme outlined in Chapter 5, there is some reason to believe that the dyad's preferred mode of interacting—which is partly governed by the mother's preferred mode of teaching—may have an important influence on early symbol development.

Turning now to the measures of elicited symbolic play, our pilot technique yielded a few surprises. First of all, play with abstract toys (such as Tinkertoy phones, stick spoons) was not significantly related to play with realistic toys (.23), even though all children were given the opportunity to do both. We have not, then, found the graded continuum of decontextualization which we had in mind. Furthermore, the measure of highest level of symbolic play reached was useless, relating only randomly to the rest of the matrix, whereas the complexity scores taking breadth and variety of play into account, were reasonably good predictors of other behaviors. Both abstract and realistic pretend play related to aspects of language, but in somewhat different patterns. The same was true for gestural communication and spontaneous symbolic play. The most interesting finding for our purposes was the fact that abstract play correlated with comprehension of implausible commands while realistic play did not. In other words, children who have decontextualized their symbolic play schemes are likely to be the ones who attend to implausible linguistic cues. This suggests that our idea of decontextualization across domains deserves further investigation.

CORRELATIONS OF THE NINE TO TWELVE MONTHS DATA WITH THE F SESSION

We will look at the cross-session correlations from two directions: from the earlier study looking forward, and from the F session looking back.

The forward correlations from A', B', and C' can be summarized very simply. The noncommunicative measures have no predictive value up to 18 months. Object permanence, space, means–ends, imitation, symbolic play, and combinatorial play all related randomly to the F-session measures. By contrast, the communicative measures were surprisingly robust from 9 to 18 months of age. Many of the early language variables, both interview and observation, predicted later levels of language, play, and gesture across a variety of measures. The same was true for the early gestural measures, particularly the summary variables. The most striking finding was the fact that the gestural measures for Session A' were by far the best predictors of later developments. The interview summary variable at A' was related positively to the F session in 86% of the 24 possible relations (including the video measures). The observational summary variable at A predicted the 24 F-session measures 58% of the time. **In other words, the earliest manifestations of intentional communication were the most sensitive indicators of later developments in symbol use.** A similar pattern can be observed within language. The performative words measure in the interview was a fairly weak measure within the ABCD matrix itself (Chapter 3)—but it was correlated reasonably well with behavior at 18 months.

To summarize so far, communicative variables from 9 to 12 months have considerable predictive strength, particularly at the earliest stages; cognitive variables from the A', B', and C' sessions do not. That this does not mean, however, that language and cognition are "unhooked" at 18 months becomes clear when we look backward from F to A', B', and C', to see which 18-month measures are most related to early developments.

Starting with F-session language, none of the 18-month spontaneous speech measures were particularly sensitive to earlier developments, although the relationships that did occur were primarily from A'B'C' language to later word use. The same was generally true for the language imitation test. The comprehension test related back to earlier measures at better than chance levels, but only for observed language and gesture. The 18-month interview measures for comprehension and production were, by contrast, quite strongly related to earlier measures. Furthermore, these two variables correlated better with the A'B'C' observational measures than the A'B'C' interviews, so these relationships are probably not simply an effect of good interviews getting better over time. In sum, language at 18 months can be predicted by earlier developments, but the relationships are not overwhelming. Predictions are strongest for the vocabulary reports by the mother.

Later gesturing was also related to earlier communicative abilities, both nonverbal and verbal. There is no evidence then, for the replacement hypothesis proposed in Chapter 3 (i.e., that increased language skill comes to replace gestural communication). Instead, the children seem to be expanding their repertoires and using all of the communicative means at hand at least up to 18 months of age.

In contrast with language, symbolic play at 18 months seems to be quite sensitive to earlier developments. This was true for the frequency and number variables in the full sample of 11, and for the augmented scores from the videotapes for the sample of 8. For elicited symbolic play, scores for realistic toys correlated back to A'B'C'; scores for play with abstract toys did not. Interestingly, these correlations are **not** with symbolic play in the earlier sessions. Instead, later developments in gestural "language" are best predicted by early developments in vocal language. In other words, the links we observed earlier between first words in language and action have not broken down in the intervening 6 months. But they may have changed somewhat. One possibility is that the two domains began as "equal partners"; as the vocal mode comes into its own as a communicative device, it may come to dominate over other symbolic activities, influencing the content and frequency of symbolic play. Obviously, we need to know a great deal more before we can interpret these findings. All we can conclude for now is that the various forms of symbolic activity are linked somehow from 9 to 18 months.

Causal Understanding at Nine to Ten Months

Building on the notion of sensitive periods, we have focused some of our recent research efforts on the development of causal understanding around 9–10 months of age. Recall from Chapter 3 that tool use (i.e., means–end relations) at 9 months was a reasonably good predictor of communication and symbol use up to 13 months of age. This finding is supported by several other studies as well. Sugarman (1973) also found parallels between tool use and intentional communication at Piaget's sensorimotor stage 5 (i.e., around 10 months). Harding and Golinkoff (1977) found that the onset of intentional vocalizations in the same period correlates with understanding of other human beings as agents. In studies with various types of language disorders, Snyder (1975), Snyder and Woods (1977), and Curcio (1977) report correlations between the Uzgiris–Hunt means–end scale and degree of language deficiency. Finally, our own results in Chapter 5 suggest that tool use is related to other aspects of social development as well, notably the quality of mother–child attachment at 12 months of age.

In short, there is something about causal development from 9 to 13 months that is a particularly sensitive indicator of social and communicative developments in the first year of life. What is this "something"? Causality is a cover term for a number of dimensions. As Piaget (1954) has noted: "Causality must definitely be conceived as intelligence itself to the extent that the latter is applied to temporal relations and organizes a lasting universe [p. 315]." Causal development includes both static and dynamic relations. For example, the means–end scale requires some kind of insight into support relations, spatial contact, and the fact that intervening links can be used as substitutes for direct reaching (see Chapter 7, p. 324). There is no obvious way in which this static causal task involves knowledge of agency or dynamic events. By contrast other aspects of causal development require knowledge of action and the flow of energy from one source to another, objects setting one another in motion (Michotte, 1963). Is this a completely separate development from static tool use, or is the same kind of analysis involved in both? Furthermore, dynamic causality differs depending on whether the object set in motion is animate or inanimate. The ability to operate on inanimate objects, through inanimate means, will draw primarily on knowledge of efficient causality (see Chapter 1, page 15). By contrast, the ability to operate on animate beings and in particular human agents will require knowledge of final causality, that is, awareness of goals and their influence on voluntary activity (see Chapter 1, page 16). Animate beings tend to go off by themselves; inanimate objects typically do not. A means that works with an inanimate entity may not work with a human agent—and vice versa. We now know that social and nonsocial instrumentalities are correlated in some gross way in the first year of life. How specific is this relationship? When does the difference between the two types of causality make a difference for the child? How do social and nonsocial developments interact with static versus dynamic problem-solving in infancy?

One of our research goals has been to watch 9–10-month-olds solving a variety of problems figuring out how to make things work. For the moment, we are simply trying to map out the behavioral landscape associated with causal understanding at this sensitive point in development. The eventual goal is to relate a set of causal measures, varying along different dimensions, to the development of communication and symbol use—putting together Wittgenstein, Peirce, and Michotte in the arena of infant research. All that we have to report here is a few first steps in the development of causal measures.

Means–End Relations with Static Tools

One problem with the Uzgiris–Hunt means–end scale is the heterogeneity of the items. At around 9 months the relevant items form a rough continuum from pulling an object on a cloth, to using a string, to using a stick set next to the goal. However, the next items are radically different: putting a filled ring on a ringstack, and placing a long strand of beads in the opening of a narrow cup—both of these supposedly tapping foresight and representation in problem solving. One of our interests in tool use (described in more detail in the next chapter) is to determine whether there is a continuum of decontextualization in this domain that parallels the changes in language and symbolic play. This kind of hypothesis requires a more graded set of items, in which the relationship between the tool and the goal is suggested by degrees. Using the Uzgiris–Hunt scale as a starting point, we designed a graded set of tool use items reflecting differences in shape, texture, and color. The shape gradations were the following: a cloth support, a thick string, a thin string, a hoop which made a breakable contact with the goal and was relatively easy to pull in, a crook set around and behind the goal, a crook set beside the goal so that the child would have to furnish the spatial contact, and a stick set beside the goal. The goal toy for all these items was a fuzzy red or blue wind-up toy with eyespots. The six types of tools were constructed in all combinations of red and blue, covered with fuzzy or flat cloth.

In our first study with these instruments, 40 9-month-old infants each received the full set of eight tool-use items (cloth through stick), in one randomized order. The tool and goal were matched or mismatched in a between-subjects design, with 10 infants in each cell: same color–same texture; same color–different texture; different color–same texture; different color–different texture. There were two equally plausible hypotheses concerning the effect of the color–texture variations:

1. A similarity between tool and goal would help the child to see the relationship.
2. A difference between tool and goal would clarify the situation, helping the child to attend to both and hence arrive at the solution.

The results for the items were very much as expected. The items fell into three equivalent sets, in the following order of difficulty: contact (cloth support, thick string, thin string), breakable contact (hoop, crook behind, and touching the goal), and no contact provided (crook beside the goal, stick beside the goal). The color–texture manipulations supported Hypothesis 2. There was a significant color by texture interaction across items: the same–same combination was the most difficult, though any of the three contrasting combinations were equally good. This effect was consistent across items, not interacting with item difficulty. In other words, difference clarifies more than similarity helps.

In ongoing research, we are developing more gradations within the tool-shape continuum. The new scale has been incorporated within a second short-term longitudinal study from $10\frac{1}{2}$ to $13\frac{1}{2}$ months, to determine what aspect of the tool use measure (if any) is most associated with subsequent developments in communication and symbol use. One hypothesis is that the noncontact items involve what has been termed "anticipatory imagery"—a type of representation that involves active transformations rather than recall. Johnston and Ramstad (1977) have analyzed the behavior of older language-impaired children on a variety of cognitive tasks. They report that the discriminating tasks seem to involve some form of anticipatory imagery. It is possible that the tool use measure at 9 months of age taps into this same capacity, and bears the same sort of relationship to language disorder and to normal language development.

Means–End Relations with Dynamic Events

Social tool use involves procedures to make human beings do things. Human beings are (usually) active, somewhat unpredictable in their movements, and responsive to signals from a distance. As such, they perform rather differently from toys that can be raked in with a stick, knocked off tables with one swipe, and so forth. The correlations we obtained in previous research related static means–end relations to procedures for making people work. Isn't there some point in between? Our second line of research on causal development has been an exploration of dynamic cause–effect relations at 9–10 months of age.

Carlson (1977) investigated causal understanding with an apparatus just one step removed from static means–end toys. The goal event was a bouncing plywood bunny in red pajamas, mounted against a plywood board and covered with a transparent plexiglass screen. After demonstrations (created from behind the board) the only way to make the bunny event recur was to manipulate a wooden button 6 inches to the right of the bunny (see Figure 6.1). Bunny and button were held together by a pivot behind the board, so that they moved together in a

Figure 6.1 *Carlson's (1977) apparatus for investigating causal understanding.*

similar vertical arc. The toy was designed so that a false connecting rod at the front could be used, suggesting a direct spatial contact. Or, alternatively, the rod could be removed so that the bunny and button moved together in the same arc, at the same time, but without spatial contact. In many ways, then, this toy obeyed the same laws of physics that govern the tool-use situation described earlier: Goal and means look different, but they move together in similar ways and (in one condition) are in spatial contact.

Carlson administered the bunny task to 72 infants, with 24 infants at 6, 9, and 13 months of age, respectively. Half the infants saw the bunny with the connecting rod, half without. The results were fairly straightforward. Very few 6-month-olds solved the problem; they either pounded away at the plexiglass screen covering the bunny, or fidgeted with the button alone without even looking at the bunny event. Nine-month-olds took a while to solve the problem, but eventually learned to move the button while looking directly at the bunny effect. Thirteen-month-olds solved the problem immediately, and complained of boredom very soon. Interestingly, the false connecting rod had little effect. It did not affect the probability of problem solving at any age. However, when the rod was absent children did spend significantly more time attending to the button itself. This may have meant that the link between cause and effect was mysterious and interesting. However, it may also mean that the button stood out as a separate entity, a figure against ground interesting in its own right. If we compare this finding with the tool-use results described above, there is further support for the view that a noticeable difference between cause and effect increases the infant's interest in both.

Once again, 9–10 months of age proved to be a pivotal moment for this kind of problem solving. In ongoing research, Carlson has designed a series of new causality toys in which the cause and event are even more dissimilar. One toy involves a button that must be moved toward or away from a window; when the child moves the button in the appropriate direction, a new picture appears in the window. A second toy is a barking mechanical puppy that goes off when the child moves a button toward or away from the goal. A third toy is the experimenter herself, who waves and calls the child's name when a button is moved toward or away from the experimenter's hand. The point of these experiments is to vary the logic of the cause–event relation, using the same kind of cause in situations in which it bears less and less relation to its effect. Variations include temporal relations between cause and effect, movement toward or away from the goal (according to Kohler, 1927, an important variable in the phylogeny of intelligence), and contact or no contact. After we sort out these various aspects of causal knowledge in older infants, our eventual plan is to relate the different aspects of causality to developments in the communicative and social domains.

Language, Context, and Social Interaction

Turning again to the decontextualization theme, another of our interests is the relationship between language comprehension and the support provided by the social and physical context. At first we planned to experiment with contextual support as an independent variable, administering a series of commands to infants (similar to those used in the follow-up study and reported earlier in this chapter) while varying such factors as degree of gestural support, and physical proximity of the items in question. Rosser set out to design such a series of experiments, and soon decided that the whole effort was premature. It was totally unclear which aspect of the situation should be varied first, or for that matter what threads in the whole fabric of mother–child conversation are properly defined as "context." There are a few experiments in the literature relevant to such experimental manipulations (e.g., MacNamara, 1977). As far as we could tell, their major findings were that children become confused when a natural situation is rendered massively unnatural by separating language, gesture, eye contact, etc. Since our focus was not on ways to confuse infants, Rosser (research in progress) made the wise decision to return to naturalistic analyses, to define in much greater detail those aspects of context that mothers use as a function of the child's sophistication and the difficulty of the message.

After 2 years of data collection and poring over tapes, a coding scheme has been developed which seems to divide the stream of infant–mother interactions into some natural categories, at least for the 15–24-months age range that has been analyzed so far. Rosser is analyzing behavioral and linguistic categories, for mother and child, in a free play situation with a standard set of toys, and in a command sequence similar to the one pilot tested in our follow-up study. The mothers are told to get messages across any way they can; we are looking at how they do that, in excruciating detail.

In a second study, we are applying the Rosser coding scheme to videotapes of 48 infants (at 12, 18, and 24 months of age) engaged in 5 minutes of free play with one of four unfamiliar female adults. Beeghly-Smith and Bretherton (1979) had already analyzed the same tapes in order to assess how adult strangers initiate and maintain playful interactions with older infants. They found that each stranger had her own distinctive style of play (a discriminant analysis was significant at $p <$ .0001). First, the strangers differed in how actively they guided the infants' play as opposed to how much they let themselves be guided by the infant. Second, strangers differed in the extent to which they gave specific verbal directions *(Would you like to put this block in the bucket?)* as opposed to commenting on the infants' actions and giving verbal encouragement *(Good girl!)*. Other variables which served to distinguish the strangers' interactive styles were the frequency with which they repeated their utterances, and how often they laughed. A fifth variable, which just missed significance ($p <$ .06), was the number and type of games that the strangers tried out with the infants. Interestingly, the four strangers did **not** differ along a sixth dimension, ratings of "interactive harmony" obtained by independent raters. In other words, although these four women each had different styles, these styles do not fall along a dimension of good–bad or sensitive–insensitive. Rather, all four had their successes or failures depending on how well their styles fit the infants' preferences. Finally, these style differences cannot be attributed to the effects of particular infants assigned to the four strangers. First, the 48 infants had been assigned randomly to the strangers in groups of 12. Second, the four groups of infants were all observed prior to the 5-minute play session. At this point none of the adults actively engaged the infants in play, but did respond warmly to the infants' social overtures (Bretherton, 1977). The infants who subsequently played with the four different strangers did not differ significantly before they were invited to play by the stranger. Having thus delineated interactive styles which seem to be independent of harmony and which are not primarily influenced by individual differences between infants, we are now about to examine whether the four strangers also differed in the way in which they used nonverbal contextual cues to get verbal messages across to their infant playmates. Since one would expect harmony of interaction to be related to the stranger's effectiveness in communicating with the infants we are also predicting that communicative styles, if any are found, will not lie along a value dimension.

As already mentioned in Chapter 5, many investigators have suggested that early mother–infant interaction can be viewed as protoconversation, a prelude to later verbal dialogue (see Lewis and Rosenblum, 1977, and Schaffer, 1977, for reviews). So far research in this area has concentrated on identifying the parameters which allow us to describe the synchrony (or asynchrony) of a mother–infant interaction: the temporal patterns of eye-to-eye contact and reciprocal vocalizations as well as the duration of kinesic phrases (Stern and Gibbon, 1977). The work which will ascertain whether the quality of early mother–infant interactions is related to later discourse ability remains as yet to be done. Even when infants first begin to understand spoken words the adults who interact with them still continue to use nonverbal behavior to clarify their verbal messages. We know of only one study (Shatz, in press) in which an attempt was made to relate a mother's gesturing during speech to the child to facilitation of the child's comprehension (measured in terms of the child's response), with very limited results. It is of course possible that, as we stated in Chapter 5, language development is buffered against environmental variation within the range usually found in middle-class homes. On the other hand our new, very detailed coding scheme may capture differences in maternal communicative style which are related to the infant's later language competence.

The findings reported in this chapter, like those outlined in Chapters 3, 4, and 5, have all raised very specific questions, much more detailed than the general issues that guided our first research efforts. These new questions have, in turn, forced us to refine our measures considerably. We are now about to launch a second short-term longitudinal study in which we will ask the new, specific questions with new, refined measures. What we have in mind is more than replication of earlier results. Although we are looking at the same phenomena, we have added lenses to our instruments in the hopes that we will see much more. Of course, we have not been alone in our quest for more finely graded measures or for better understanding, especially in the areas of symbolic play and imitation (Killen & Uzgiris, 1978; Nicolich, 1977; Wolf, personal communication). In fact, our new longitudinal study has incorporated instruments, advice, and insight from our colleagues in this field. Some of the main issues in the new research include the following:

1. There is a developmental discontinuity between the manipulation of tools that are in contact with the goal, and the ability to provide contact between tool and goal when none is provided. Is this developmental passage related to similar qualitative changes in communication, play, and understanding of causality?
2. Is the ability to decontextualize verbal commands (e.g., to obey implausible commands like *Kiss the ball*) related to decontextualization of symbolic play (e.g., drinking from a block) and imitation (e.g., imitating a familiar scheme in an unfamiliar context)?
3. How does a mother support her verbal messages with gestural, postural, and facial cues? How much does the child depend on this kind of contextual support at different stages in symbol development?

We are also encouraged that this work may have implications for research and intervention with language-disabled children. Snyder (1975, 1978) has applied several of our measures to language-impaired children, and is providing the kind of converging evidence recommended in Chapter 1 (i.e., "mirror image" correlations). In studying normal and deficient development, we are gradually moving from an exploratory phase based primarily on naturalistic observation, to an experimental phase where we can ask (and occasionally answer) much more specific questions. Let us stress one more time, however, that our current hypotheses are working hypotheses. For the moment, the most that we can offer with any conviction are some interesting new directions, and new places to look.

Appendix 6.1

(This was sent to M in advance of session to fill out, then gone over with
E during the interview)

How many words do you estimate your child understands when he hears some-

one use them? _____

How many words do you estimate your child says? _____

Please check which of the following words your child *understands* in

Column A and which he *uses* him- or her-self in Column B. In the blank

after each work please fill in any variant of the listed word that you or

your child uses (e.g., "baba" instead of bottle).

	Write Word	A *Understands*	B *Uses*

Names of Family Members

   Mommy

   Daddy

   Maternal Grandmother

   Paternal Grandmother

   Maternal Grandfather

   Paternal Grandfather

   Brothers

   Sisters

Other (Please list)

Pet's Names (please list)

(Note: The following words were originally presented in the format
illustrated above.)

Toys and Common Objects

    Doll

    Ball

    Teddy bear

    Blanket

    Truck

    Car

    Block

    Others (Please list)

Household Objects

    Plate

    Cup

    Knife

    Spoon

    Fork

    TV

    Radio

    Stereo/Record player/hi fi

    Others (please list)

Furniture

    Sofa/Couch

    Chair

    Table

    Bed

    Potty

    Crib

    Playpen

    Others (Please list)

Rooms

    Kitchen

    Living Room

    Bathroom

    Others (please list)

Activities

    Baths

    Dinner

    Lunch

    Breakfast

    Shopping

    Play

    Changing diapers

    Others (please list)

Places

    Store

    Movie

    Gas Station

    Mountains

    School

    Playground/park

    Others (please list

Outside

    Plant

    Tree

    Bush

    Flower

    Swing

    Sandbox

    Others (please list)

Animals
>   Dog
>   Cat
>   Cow
>   Horse
>   Others (please list)

Clothes
>   Hat
>   Coat
>   Dress
>   Socks
>   Shoes
>   Pants
>   Pajamas
>   Others (please list)

Food (Please check whether your
    child knows the general term listed,
    e.g., "fruit," and list whatever
    specific words in that category
    he/she uses or understands, e.g.,
    "orange.")
>   Cereal

>   Fruit

>   Vegetables

>   Meat

>   Desserts

>   Drinks
>>   Milk
>>   Juice

>   Candy

>   Snacks

>   Others (please list)

Greetings
>   Hi
>   Hello
>   Goodbye/byebye
>   Others (please list)

Modifiers
>   Red
>   Blue
>   Green
>   Big
>   Little
>   Fast
>   Others (please list)

Prepositions
>   In
>   On
>   AT
>   To
>   Under
>   Others (Please list)

Articles
>   A
>   An
>   The

Request Words
>   Get
>   Give
>   Bring
>   Take
>   Show
>   Go
>   Come
>   Help
>   Please

Request Words (continued)

    Help

    Please

    Up

    Down

    Others (please list)

Verbs

    Run

    Jump

    Swing

    Push

    Fall/fall down

    eat

    walk

    play

    Others (please list)

Pronouns

    I

    My

    His

    Her

    He

    Him

    Hers

    She

    You

    Your

    That

    This

    Me

    Here

    There

    Others (please list

Miscellaneous (Please list anything not covered above)

"Comprehension Task"

The blanks in the following commands were filled in with words that C understood. These were selected by E during the maternal interview concerning the vocabulary checklist, and were subjected to a brief comprehension check prior to beginning the command section of the comprehension task.

"Plausible" Commands

1. Where's _____?

     1   2

2. Where is the _____?

     1   2

4. Where is the _____?

     1   2

5. Show the _____to Mommy.

     1   2   3

6. Bring the _____over here.

     1   2   3

7. Give that to Mommy.

     1   2   3

8. Where is Mommy's _____.

     1   2   3

9. Throw the _____.

     1   2

11. Where is your _____?

     1 2   3

12. Put the _____under the _____.

     1   2   3   4

13. Show Mommy the _____.

     1 2   3

14. Where is your _____?

     1   2   3

15. Kiss the _____.

      1   2

16. Where is the _____?

      1   2

18. Give the _____ to Mommy.

       1   2   3

19. Where is my _____?

    1   2   3

21. Where is (C's name)'s _____?

     1   2   3

22. Put the _____on the _____.

    1   2 3   4

23. Sit down.

    1   2

25. Where is Mommy's _____?

    1   2   3

26. Put the _____on the _____.

    1   2   3   4

28. Show the _____to me.

    1   2   3

29. Put the _____under the _____.

    1   2   3   4

30. Make Mommy see the _____.

      1 2   3

                        "Implausible" Commands

3. See the _____to Mommy.

    1   2   3

10. Give the _____to the _____.

    1   2   3

17. Come the _____over here.

        1   2   3

20. Put the _____in the _____.

    1   2   3   4

24. Give the _____to the _____.

    1   2   3

27. Give me to Mommy.

    1 2   3

"Imitation Task"

The mother was given a notebook of pictures, each depicting a sentence to be imitated. We had M put C on her lap and try to interest C in the book. M read the model sentences and tried to get C to repeat them by asking such things as *Can you say that?* An effort was made to preserve the order of items, although this was not always possible as some C's turned the pages by themselves.

1. Bird. (with a picture of a cardinal)

2. Sleep. (with a picture of a baby in bed)

3. The kitty is soft. (with a picture of a white angora cat)

4. The kitty bakes pie. (with a picture of a white cat wearing a long dress placing a pie on top of an old-fashioned stove)

5. Mouse. (with a picture of a mouse)

6. Eat the little bunny. (with a girl holding an ice cream cone in one hand and feeding a bunny a spoonful of ice cream with her other hand)

7. Dogs. (with a picture of a large and a small poodle)

8. The girl brings dinner. (with a picture of a girl carrying a turkey)

9. The little girl sits. (with a picture of a girl sitting on a park bench)

10. Show the cake to daddy. (with a picture of a tiger with a bow on her head holding a cake out to another tiger holding a newspaper)

11. The mommy is pretty. (with a picture of a woman with earrings and flowers in her hair. The woman is winking)

12. Hug. (with a picture of a little girl hugging a puppy)

13. Sit on the ball. (with a ridiculous picture of a baby wearing a football helmet and sitting on a football)

14. Boy. (with a picture of a boy wearing a straw hat)

15. Mommy reads the book. (with a picture of a bear wearing glasses and holding a book in front of a baby bear who sits on her lap)

16. Birds. (with a picture of two chickadees sitting on a branch)

17. Make the dog eat. (with a picture of a baby holding a cupcake
    above the head of a puppy which looks very attentively at the
    boy)

18. The white lamb jumps. (with a picture of a lamb jumping over a
    fence)

19. Give mommy a present. (with a picture of a kitten handing a
    "mommy" cat a wrapped box tied with a ribbon)

20. Kiss. (with a picture of a boy and girl standing under mistletoe —
    their lips pucked and about to touch)

21. The girl eats cake. (with a picture of a girl eating a piece of
    pink birthday cake)

22. Ride in the basket. (with a picture of a girl riding a bicycle
    with a puppy in a basket on the handlebars)

23. The girl's doll. (with a picture of a girl sitting at a table with
    a doll in her lap. The girl is drawing a picture)

24. Lamb. (with a picture of a white lamb staring at his tail which
    is made out of a bit of fluff)

25. Feed the dog. (with a picture of a boy holding an ice cream cone.
    A puppy is jumping up and licking the boy's cheek)

26. The dog swings high. (with a picture of a dog swinging on a trapeze)

27. Mice. (with a picture of two mice kissing atop a chandelier)

28. The dog's balloon. (with a picture of a dog sitting with five
    balloons tied to his tail.

29. The boy rides fast. (with a picture of a boy and a dog riding a
    motorcycle)

"Elicited Symbolic Play"

"Abstract" toys included tinker toys, a mirror, two unpainted wooden "people,"
nesting cupts, wooden blocks. C was allowed to interact with the toys for
2 minutes. E then approached and demonstrated several symbolic games, involving C in the demonstrations when possible. Games initiated by E included
telephoning with a stick, running a block around on the floor like a car,
pretending to eat with a stick from one of the nesting cups, pretending
to drink from another of the nesting cups. "Realistic" toys included a
doll house with assorted furniture, a family of small wooden dolls, and a
car. Again, C was allowed to interact with the toys for 2 minutes, after
which E approached and demonstrated several symbolic games. E encouraged
C to engage in the modeled activities. These included putting the dolls
to bed, taking them for a ride in the car, setting them in chairs at the
table and making them "eat," making them go up the dollhouse stairs.

Appendix 6.2

Maternal Interview

Comprehension score (FMIComp): 1 point for each item comprehended, as reported by M in interview and on vocabularly checklist.

Production Score (FMIProd): 1 point for each item produced, as reported by M in interview and on vocabulary checklist.

Observation Notes

"Gestural Communication" (FCommGest): Criteria for communicative pointing (FPoint), showing (FShow), and giving (FGive) were the same as those specified in Appendix 3.2. One point was scored for each instance of a behavior and the total points summed to derive a summary measure of gestural communication.

Language

"Comprehension Task": For scoring purposes, all commands were divided into semantic subunits, each of which could be the basis of a behavioral response. E.g., *Where is the ball?* was considered to have two subunits, a request for indication and a specification of the particular object to be located; *show the ball to Mommy* was counted as having three subunits, a request for a particular action and showing, with both an object and a recipient specified. (For a complete list of commands and subunits, see Appendix 6.1.) One point was scored for each subunit which the child acknowledged behaviorally, and the sum was divided by the total number of subunits that had been administered, since the number of commands given was somewhat dependent on the child's willingness and ability to cooperate. There were 24 "Plausible" commands, with 69 subunits, and 6 "Implausible" commands, with 19 subunits. "Implausible" commands included both grammatically anomalous but semantically intelligible sentences such as *See the ball to Mommy* and grammatically correct but semantically improbable sentences such as *Give me to Mommy*. (Again, see Appendix 6.1 for a complete list.) Separate scores were calculated for "Plausible" commands (FComp1), "Implausible" commands (FComp2), and the total (FComp).

"Number of Different Words (F#Words): Verbalizations were counted as words if they resembled their adult counterpart phonetically, or if they were used in a consistent referential fashion. No attempt was made to distinguish between referential and performative words, and imitations were not included.

"Frequency of Language" (FLFreq): 1 point for each instance of word production.

Language Imitation" (FLImit): 1 point for each instance of a phonetically similar verbalization following a model. Imitations of intonation contour only were not counted. This score was based primarily on performance during the Language Imitation Task (see Appendix 6.1), but any spontaneous imitations were also included.

Play

"Number of Different Symbolic Play Schemes (F#SymbPl): Criteria for symbolic schemes were similar to those mentioned in, Appendices 3.2 and 3.3, 1 point for each different symbolic action.

"Frequency of Symbolic Play" (FSFreq): 1 point for each instance of symbolic action.

"Combinatorial Play" (FCombPl): 1 point for each instance of combining two objects systematically (criteria similar to those contained in Appendix 3.2), for example, putting an object inside another object. Only constructive combinations were scored, for example, removing an object from inside another one did not count. Combinations involving more than two objects received 2 points.

Videotapes

"Augmented measures": Criteria for number of different words (FOV#Words), frequency of language (FOVLFreq), number of different symbolic play schemes (FOV#SymbPl), and frequency of symbolic play (FOVSFreq) were the same as above, except that instances from both observation notes and videotaped interactions were counted.

Play

"Elicited Symbolic Play", with a set of abstract toys (FESymbAb), and with a set of realistic toys (FRWymbRe), was scored according to the following coding system. (See Appendix 6.1 for a brief description of the task.) A total score (FESymb) was obtained by summing FESymbAb and FESymbRE. The qualitative score (FESymbLev) was equal to the highest score obtained for any single symbolic scheme.

Symbolic Behavior	Score
Cooperation: C is a cooperative but passive recipient of E's symbolic play activity, e.g., allows E to put stick to his or her mouth in offering C a bite of pretend food.	1
Participation: E offers or presents C with the toys she has been using and C imitates the modeled behavior using these instruments.	2
deferred participatory imitation, i.e., of a previously demonstrated scheme	+0.5
C supplies some, but not all, of the toys used in the symbolic activity.	+0.5
Following a command: C executes an undemonstrated symbolic behavior at E's suggestion.	2
Imitation: C executes a modeled symbolic behavior with objects of his or her own selection.	3
Deferred imitation with objects of own selection	+0.5
C applies scheme to agents other than self (in abstract toy situation) or dolls (in realistic toy situation), e.g., C offers M a bit of pretend food.	+0.5

C uses objects of a type not used by E, e.g., C uses an overturned table as a car.   +1

Spontaneous Symbolic Play: C engages in umprompted novel symbolic behavior, e.g., spontaneously converses, intelligibly, while pretending to telephone E.   4.5

Additional Parts: When C's symbolic scheme includes more than one modeled behavior, either simultaneously, e.g., sound effects or verbalizations, or sequentially, the first gestural component is coded according to the previous criteria, and each elaboration is scored as an additional part.   +1.5

Errors or Attempts: When C;s execution of the modeled symbolic behavior is flawed, e.g., E models putting the doll in a chair at the table, and C then puts the doll on the table, or only approximate, e.g., E models making the doll go up the stairs, and C then waves the doll over the stairs while moving it to the second story, the behavior is coded according to the above criteria, but an error or attempt deduction is made.   -0.5

"Combinatorial Play" (FVTCombPl): Criteria were the same as those for FCombPl, the observation measure, except that combinations requiring skilled manipulation, e.g., putting a shapebox form through the correct opening, received an additional 0.5 points. Score was based on the first 3 minutes of videotaped M-C interaction.

Chapter 7
THE BIOLOGY OF SYMBOLS:
SOME CONCLUDING THOUGHTS

Elizabeth Bates

Chapter 1 reopened an old question: Are there parallels in the ontogeny and phylogeny of the capacity for symbols? What are the "old parts" that went into the evolution of this relatively new machinery? Can we find evidence for the same construction process in the development of human children today? I proposed a search for prerequisites to language, based on a model of "homology through shared structure." Within this kind of model, we would expect correlations between linguistic and nonlinguistic aspects of symbol development, based on the view that these different aspects of symbol use share underlying cognitive structures or "software."

Chapter 2 presented a description of the period from 9 to 13 months, a critical period in the emergence of communicative intentions, conventional signaling, and the idea that things have names. Some working definitions were presented for "convention," "intention," and "symbol," together with criteria for inferring these structures in the behavior of human infants. This led us to a model of the internal structure of symbols, reworking the traditional views of Peirce, Piaget, Werner, and Kaplan. The purpose of this section was to locate the seams and joints of symbol structure, the places where various "old parts" could have come together in the evolution of this new capacity. In Chapter 3, we presented our correlational findings for communicative and cognitive development from 9 to 13 months, in a sample of 25 American and Italian children. These results suggested several specific or "local" homologies with language development: symbolic play, imitation, tool use, and combinatorial play. Furthermore, the same cognitive capacities that relate to language also relate to some preverbal communications that precede and correlate with language. In short, we have located a package of related structures, capacities that are implicated in the development of linguistic and nonlinguistic symbols. There is also supporting evidence from abnormal language development, and from comparisons across species, suggesting that the same capacities that are **present** when language emerges are **absent** when language fails to emerge.

In Chapter 4, we took a more qualitative look at the structure and content of early symbol use, both in language and in play. Some striking parallels emerged between gestural and vocal naming, suggesting that these early stages in symbol use are in some sense modality free. In language and in action, children are symbolizing the same small stock of concerns. These findings were discussed in the light of six controversies in the literature on first words. We have offered a Wittgensteinian "language game" approach to early naming, an action-based view of symbol development that seems to pull together some of the debates about the nature of first words.

Chapter 5 was devoted to the role of social factors in cognitive and communicative development. In particular, we focused on individual differences in the mother–child attachment relationship. Quality of attachment was related to the use of conventional signals like pointing, giving, showing, and ritual requesting. It was also related to tool use and symbolic play. However, individual differences in attachment did **not** correlate significantly with language development. Apparently language and social development (at least those aspects of social development tapped by traditional attachment measures) relate to different "aspects" of the same cognitive and communicative skills. We certainly do not conclude from this that language development has nothing to do with human relationships. As Bruner (1977) has pointed out, language is acquired in a dialogue, and must in some way reflect the structure of that dialogue. We need to find measures of interaction and social skill that map into these two-party constraints on language.

Chapter 6 included some illustrations of ongoing research based on four themes derived from earlier work: specific or local homologies; sensitive periods; decontextualization; and predictive strength across time. Eleven of the 25 infants we had studied from 9 to 13 months were seen again at around 18 months. One of the most striking findings from that follow-up was that very little happens between 13 and 18 months of age, at least in those aspects of symbol development studied here. This plateau (which has also been reported by a number of other investigators) may reflect a period of consolidation, where the gains that were made in the first year are exercised. There may be new things happening "underground," including a gradual decontextualization or "freeing up" of language, tool use and symbolic play schemes. In any case, this "time-out" period underscores the dramatic changes that did occur from 9 to 13 months, in the critical moment for the emergence of symbols. Some of our current research is focussed on decontextualization across domains, from nine months through two years of age. However, our first round of findings suggests that developments within the 9–13-month sensitive period vary in their predictive strength beyond that stage. For example, we have no evidence so far that cognitive developments at 9 months correlate with symbol use and communication beyond 13 months. On the other hand, communicative developments at 9 months continue to correlate with symbol use at least as late as 18 months of age. In current work, we are trying to learn more about the inner workings of tool use, imitation, symbolic play, and the mother–child dialogues where language first emerges. The gross correlations reported in Chapters 3, 5, and 6 have told us more about where to look. Our task now is to determine the specific structural relations that created those correlations, and the critical levels or degrees of various component skills that are required for language to emerge.

In this chapter, I want to return to the evolutionary themes of the first chapter, looking more carefully at the "old parts" that we have located here as they lead to symbols in ontogeny and phylogeny. I will concentrate on imitation and tool use, two skills which seem to relate to language development in very different ways. Using the model of symbol structure outlined in Chapter 2, we will examine the processes that underlie imitation and tool use, as they contribute to the child's analysis of his culture.

Tool Use

Tool Use in Phylogeny: Some Parallels with Language

In our efforts to establish ourselves as unique among species, we humans have come up with various definitions of "man" that suggest discontinuous leaps in evolution. The best known candidate is the defini-tion of man as the unique possessor of a soul. Social scientists have, instead, preferred more behavioral definitions (with implications for a difference in neural hardware). The two favorites have been "Man the Tool User" and "Man the Symbol User" (with particular emphasis on linguistic symbols). In the last two decades, however, evidence has ap-peared suggesting that both these abilities have fuzzy evolutionary boundaries.

Regarding tool use, Kohler (1927) had established that chimpanzees in captivity are capable of tool use and tool construction. Among the more remarkable examples, Sultan was observed shaping and fitting a narrow stick into a wider one to create a long compound tool for raking in bananas. But because Kohler's animals were observed in captivity, in prepared environments, there has always been suspicion of a "circus effect." The suggestion has been that this sort of toolmaking involves processes distinct from natural toolmaking, and hence tells little about the natural abilities and behaviors of this species. For these reasons, Jane Goodall's (1964) observations of tool use and toolmaking by chimpan-zees in the wild had a much greater impact on the definition of man as "the" toolmaking animal. Since Goodall's discovery, there have been many other reports of problem solving through complex object and object-to-object manipulations in other species as well. For an excellent review, with a proposal for a classificatory system based on relative complexity of tool use, see Parker and Gibson (1977). For present pur-poses, my point is that we must now recognize a phylogenetic continuum of tool use, varied in degree of complexity and amount of insight, rather than a radical discontinuity from one type of intelligence to another.

Something similar has happened to our definition of man as "the" symbol-using animal. Recent successes in teaching various types of sym-bolic communication to nonhuman primates have eroded the bound-aries separating human symbol use from the capacities of other species (see Chapter I). There is of course still a great deal of controversy regarding whether these chimpanzee experiments are relevant to lan-guage (see Harnad *et al.*, 1977). For example, if one accepts Hockett's (1960) list of criteria for defining language, then nothing short of human acoustic–articulatory speech can be classified as language (a definition which, incidentally, excludes American Sign Language). In the case of tool use, the discovery of toolmaking in the wild lent greater credibility to the claim that chimpanzees possess at least the precursors of a human-like tool-using capacity. There is as yet no such evidence for the use of symbolic communication in the wild by nonhuman species. One might still argue that the acquisition of communicative symbols by chimpanzees in laboratory settings involves some sort of psychological process that is quite different from natural language acquisition. Obviously, from what has been said so far, I am persuaded by the evidence for continuity. At the very least, it is unlikely that anyone will ever again write an anthropology textbook defining man as unique among symbol users—at least not without a great many qualifying footnotes.

And so there is evidence that tool use and language both evolved gradually. There has also been ample speculation that the two abilities evolved in parallel. A review of the literature on this topic shows that there are at least a dozen distinct theories about why these two abilities should have contributed to one another in human evolution. Only a few of these are relevant to possible parallels in human ontogeny. Nevertheless, they are all worth considering here briefly—if only to illustrate what wonderful ideas people can come up with in the absence of data. I will begin with the noncognitive theories (which have less in common with the ontogenetic position outlined in this book), and move on to theories proposing parallels in cognitive structure for tool use and language. My summaries are drawn from a variety of sources, including Washburn (1960), Hewes (1973), Rensch (1972), Laughlin and d'Aquili (1974), deLaguna (1927), Bruner (1975), and Jolly (1972). Some of them are syntheses of several positions.

Noncognitive Theories

1. The development of the speech channel was facilitated by evolutionary adaptations brought about by the substitution of tools for the functions executed by the large canines and incisors of apes. Gradual changes in the jaw musculature, etc., permitted fine-tuned uses of the articulatory system. In short, animals with small teeth can talk better.
2. Tool use facilitated the development of a gestural system by selecting for refined hand–eye coordination. This theory has (at least) two versions:
   (a) It is more likely that apes will discover symbolic communication in the visual–manual modality because they are using the visual–manual modality regularly and are already highly specialized for it.
   (b) Although tool use would facilitate the initial discovery of a visual–manual language, it would also get in the way of

visual–manual language when both are used at high levels (i.e., it is hard to talk while you work). This situation would facilitate a shift toward language in the acoustic–articulatory modality, to free the hands for work.

3. The use of tools led to the selection for larger brains (without specifying particular qualitative neural connections). The larger brain mass would in turn

   (*a*) Result in still more complex forms of tool use and problem solving.

   (*b*) Increase "quantitatively" the probability that new "qualitative" neural connections could evolve (including neural connections for language unrelated to those involved in tool use itself).

4. Tool use gave impetus to a shift toward bipedal locomotion, which in turn led to a structural alteration of the pelvis, which in turn led to a shorter gestation period in humans (required by the decreasing efficiency of the birth canal in bipedal animals). The shorter gestation period results in infants who are less developed at birth. A common argument among neural biologists is that a species less developed at birth is more "plastic" and better tuned to the environment in its subsequent learning and development.

5. The use of tools increases the likelihood of complex social organization (which in turn interacts to increase the likelihood of language) in a number of ways:

   (*a*) In a tool-using species there will be selective pressures for an increased capacity for observational learning (i.e., imitation), so that the individuals can more rapidly and reliably acquire a complex and plastic tool use repertoire.

   (*b*) Tool use increases the efficiency of hunting and other forms of food gathering, permitting expansion of the population of the troop. The greater size of the social unit may in turn bring about more complex social organization, which can in turn provide an evolutionary pressure for the development of more sophisticated forms of communication.

   (*c*) Tool use will have a particularly strong impact on the relative supply of protein in the diet, which will not only improve the food supply of the group, but also the brain size and efficiency of its members (see 3 above).

   (*d*) Tool use permits the hunting of much larger animals. This capacity will in turn require greater social organization in planning and executing the hunt, and in deciding on the distribution of meat after the hunt. While such increases in social complexity do not logically necessitate symbolic communication, they would be greatly facilitated by it. (It is worth noting in this regard that almost all instances of food sharing in omnivorous primates involve meat.)

(e) Preparation and execution of the hunt, as well as consumption of its products, are typically associated with the evolution of ceremony. Ceremonies generally involve ritual or symbolic objects. While the causal direction is not clear, this association suggests an early connection between hunting and symbolic activity.

Cognitive Theories

6. Tool carrying leads to (and conversely, requires) hindsight and foresight (i.e., concerning what the tool has been and will be used for). This tendency results in cognition being taken out of the immediate situation in which the organism finds itself (i.e., in "displacement" or "decontextualization").

7. The more complex "flake tools" (Washburn, 1960) are the result of a manufacturing process so complex that it would have been difficult to achieve without a complex set of communicative signals and intentional "teaching" through gestural demonstration.

8. The more complex flake tools must also be constructed in a set sequence of steps, which have a syntaxlike structure. The ability to invent, learn, and/or impart such complex construction sequences would facilitate (or be facilitated by) the capacity for syntax in symbolic communication.

9. The power grip–precision grip relationship involved in tool making and tool use could provide a phylogenetic predecessor for the topic–comment relationship in communication, thereby setting the stage for predication.

10. The power–precision grip involved in tool use may increase the likelihood of selection for asymmetric brain development, handedness, and lateralization of function, which may in turn have somehow increased the likelihood of hemispheric specialization for language.

11. The process of tool use and tool making in problem solving requires the development of sophisticated part–whole analysis,

in which the organism must analyze the array, isolate the missing part in the problem, and find or manufacture a substitute for that part. This process of part–whole analysis and substitution of parts within wholes is structurally related to the process of symbolization.

It is of course possible that most or all of these relationships were involved in the parallel evolution of language and tool use. The reader could no doubt come up with several more given time to peruse the list. Most of these historical coincidences, however, bear little relationship to what currently happens in the development of symbols in a human child. The human child probably does not recapitulate shifts in pelvic structure, the analysis of flake tools, or the need to organize socially in order to kill mastodons. However, some of the parallels in the cognitive structure of tool use and symbols may involve the same "software" in the human child today, just as they evolved from some common cognitive structures in the child's ancestors.

It may be a rule of pedantry that he who presents a long list of anything has his greatest investment in the last member of the list. That is certainly true of the above list of theories. I am proposing here that tool use and symbolic activity in human children involve some common structural capacities for part–whole analysis and substitution of parts within those wholes. To illustrate this relationship, we will turn now to an analysis of tool use in human ontogeny.

Stages in the Development of Tool Use in One Situation

Rather than describe the sequence of developments in means–end relations from 9 to 13 months in abstract terms, it is more useful to examine the same sequence within a single problem-solving situation, with a task that is eventually solved by many 1-year-olds as well as by Kohler's chimpanzees: discovery of an intervening support (e.g., a stick) to rake in an object that is out of reach.

This kind of problem-solving situation will require three phases of analysis:

1. Noticing the problem
2. Isolating the missing means
3. Locating a substitute means

The first phase can be divided (very roughly indeed) into three subparts:

1. Noticing the problem
   (*a*) Formulation of the goal (e.g., call up subprogram *Want cookie*)
   (*b*) Test run (mental or literal) of familiar means, e.g., reach out and grab $\longrightarrow$ reaching fails—try and locomote to a better reaching position $\longrightarrow$ locomotion fails
   (*c*) Conclusion: familiar means fail

As we noted earlier, at this point children under 9 months of age typically bail out of the situation altogether. They simply give up, or they begin crying. The crying may eventually result in obtaining the goal if some adult intervenes. But there is no evidence that the child himself has selected crying as an alternate means, since he does not at this point modify or direct his crying signal toward the adult as agent (e.g., making adjustments in the cry contingent on the adult signalling approach to the cookie). In Piagetian terms, this child is at best at Sensorimotor Stage 4, "the use of familiar means to novel ends." At this stage the child has not yet fully "externalized" or objectified causal sources outside himself. Hence he does not employ external causes as means. However, as the child begins to play with combinations of his own, subjective, familiar sensorimotor means, his experiments will yield more and more information about the nature of different objects and the relationships among objects. According to Piaget, the Stage 4 child becomes less and less interested in exercising his stock of schemes for their own sake and more and more interested in the results those schemes yield with different external objects. This gradual shift ends in Stage 5 "tertiary circular reactions" or "experiments to see." Within the domain of tool use, Piaget claims that the Stage 5 child engages in "novel means to familiar ends." In short, having learned to experiment in general, he begins to experiment in problem-solving situations when his familiar means fail. He moves toward means that bear a decreasing resemblance to the old sensorimotor schemes that worked for so many months, and as he does so he comes to understand and use increasingly "externalized" causes within his problem solving. In particular, the child begins to use external objects as tools in situations where he previously used his own arm, hand, locomotion, etc. In the particular problem-solving situation being examined here, the Stage 5 child can move into the second phase of analysis:

2. Isolate the missing means, for example,
   (*a*) Note gap from hand to cookie when normal reaching procedure is employed.
   (*b*) Conclusion: missing component involves physical contact from hand to object.

(c) Formulate subgoal: find substitute for physical contact from hand to object.

We have glossed over these three steps as though they were simple—particularly the conclusion 2b that the missing component involves hand-to-object contact. The capacity to come to that conclusion requires a highly evolved type of intelligence. All of the steps described in "isolating the missing means" form the "part–whole analysis" phase of problem solving. Before a substitute can be found, the organism must be able to isolate the misfiring element, that portion of the whole, global, means–end situation that requires substitution. By Stage 5 the human child is apparently capable of sufficient part–whole analysis to enter into the third phase of the cookie-getting problem:

3. Locate a substitute means (e.g., a substitute part to create physical contact from hand to object):
   (a) Look for supports and links already supporting the object that are within hand's reach (e.g., if the cookie is resting on a cloth, pull the cookie closer by pulling the cloth).
   (b) If the search for existing links fails, find a substitute object that can create a link.

This portion of the process—location of substitutes—may be quite lengthy, and the child's skill at this phase will increase markedly across Stage 5 and into Stage 6 (i.e., the stage of representational means–end relations, as we shall see shortly). The search for substitutes may involve repeated "rerouting" back through the second phase, part–whole analysis. For example, what is involved in establishing physical contact in the gap from hand to object? One crucial aspect of the missing part involves the property of extension in space. If the child has failed to locate a surrounding link, he may have to reanalyze the part–whole relations to isolate the particular aspect of extension in space that will be required in the substitute object. Furthermore, the missing part will have to have other properties as well. For one thing, it must be portable enough to be brought from its original location to be placed in the gap from hand to object. Second, it must have **sufficient** extension in space to fill the hand–object gap. Third—as one of Kohler's chimps discovered in flailing at a banana with his blanket—the object must also have sufficient strength or stiffness to serve as a rake for pulling the goal in. In other words, the original means (the arm and hand) and the substitute means (e.g., a stick) will have to share a number of properties, including shape, extension in space, maneuverability, stiffness in raking action. In a trial-and-error process of problem solving the child may have to discover these requisites a few at a time (moving back and forth between Steps 2 and 3). Later on, at the stage of representational means–end analysis, he may be able to envision each of the requisites prior to the first try, hence choosing an appropriate substitute the first time around.

The duration and probability of success of the last two analysis phases will be determined in part by the perceptual layout of the means–end situation. Kohler has discussed in detail the process leading to the moment of insight, when the animal "sees" the solution by extracting the relevant similarities between missing parts and potential substitutes. In particular, Kohler focused on the degree to which the perceptual situation suggests the solution. This includes factors like proximity to the goal, and the relative salience of the missing attribute in the substitute object. For example, in one instance a wooden box with slats fitted closely together lay near the goal. The chimpanzee had already demonstrated awareness that sticks can be used to rake in a banana. But he did not perceive the sticklike properties of the individual wooden slats in the box. On another occasion, however, one of the slats in the same box was pulled out slightly from the others. The gap between the boards in the second situation made the individual board perceivable as an entity with the appropriate sticklike length and width. The animal immediately ran to the box, ripped out the board, and used it as a stick to rake in the banana. In short, success was determined by an interaction between the animal's current knowledge about substitute means, and the degree to which the situation supported or suggested the eventual solution.

For the human infant, the development from Stage 5 to Stage 6 involves a gradual decrease in the amount of perceptual support needed to "see" a solution (i.e., to extract the necessary similarities between the missing part and the substitute). A particularly clear illustration comes from the Uzgiris and Hunt (1975) means–end test. On this task, a 9-month-old can generally recognize and use a clear support relationship already provided by the environment (i.e., Step 3a above). If the object is already resting on a large, salient cloth support, the child may reach the cookie by pulling the support toward him first. Interestingly, early on the child may not entirely understand the necessity of physical contact between object and support. If the cookie is held slightly above the cloth, many children will pull the cloth toward them anyway (just in case?). However, even a child who fully understands the way that a cloth functions in the support situation may still fail to recognize more tenuous support relations (e.g., a thin string tied around the cookie). Still later, the same child may recognize almost any existing support when the physical contact is already established. But he will fail to provide the link himself (e.g., to pick up a stick lying a short distance from the cookie and use it to create physical contact with the goal). In other words, he "recognizes" supports and uses them, but he does not "produce" or create them. Later still, he may produce links when the stick and goal are both in sight. But he will not represent the missing link to himself and go out in search of a stick. What we have here is a gradual "decontextualization" of the support–link problem, a decreasing reliance on the context to suggest the solution. I have suggested elsewhere (Bates, 1976) that this is an analogue in problem solving to the passage from comprehension to production in language. One of our goals in future research is to determine whether this relationship is also a homologue (see Chapter 6 for a description of our first efforts in this direction).

We propose that there may be a parallel progression from recognition to production of part–whole relations in **three** domains: tool use, symbolic play, and language. Recall the distinction introduced in Chapter 2 between "symbolization" and "representation"—terms that have been interchangeable in the Piagetian literature. "Representation" refers to the "calling up" of an organized action package that defines an object or event, in the absence of perceptual motor support from that object or event. "Symbolization" refers to the selection of **one** part of such an action package to stand for, identify, or recall the whole. Symbolization can, then, take place either presentationally (using the action scheme to "name" an object or event that is fully present in the situation) or representationally. As the evidence presented in Chapter 4 suggests, there is a developmental progression from presentational to representational symbolizing both in language and in action. The child takes an increasingly active role while the amount of perceptual support in the environment becomes decreasingly important. For example, in symbolic play the child may stir with a real spoon in a bowl, in the kitchen where Mother is doing similar spoon things. This would be an example of presentational symbolic activity. In representational symbolizing, the subjective vehicle–referent relationship (Veh_s–Ref_s) must be constructed without perceptual support from the objective vehicle and referent (Veh_o–Ref_o). For example, the child may stir with an empty hand, using a block for a bowl, while playing in the bedroom with no adults around. This developmental progression parallels developments in tool use, as the child becomes capable of increasingly creative solutions to the "extension in space" problem. **Just as the child who is playing can see "spoonness" in a stick, the child who is solving problems may come to see "stickness" in a wide array of objects that can be used to rake in a cookie.**

In other words, I am suggesting that tool use is a type of symbolic activity. There are of course clear differences between symbolizing in play versus problem solving. For example, in order to solve the problem the child may be forced to make a number of modifications in the stick substitute to make it actually work. In play, the constraints from the goal situation are minimal. Few modifications are required for the substitute object to "take" the meaning that the child is attributing to it. As long as the use of an object is divorced from its actual real-life function, the child has greater freedom in the selection of objects to support the internal vehicle (e.g., even an empty-handed gesture may suffice).

The role of the goal situation in constraining possible solutions suggests that symbolic play, language, and tool use will begin to diverge **not** in terms of the underlying capacities they require for part–whole analysis and recognition of substitutes, but in the latitude that the child has in selecting substitutes. In play, where the goal constraints are minimal, the selection of objects is potentially very wide (although as we shall see shortly, constraints from the imitation component may nevertheless bring object selection into line with adult models). In tool use, where the object **must** be adequate if the goal is to be met, the set of possible substitutes will usually be maximally constrained. In language, insofar as language is being used as a means to communicative goal, the constraints of the goal situation will depend on the listener's skill in decoding utterances that bear an unconventional relationship to the situation in which they are used.

In summary, the passage from Stage 4 (familiar means to novel ends) to Stage 5 (novel means to familiar ends) to Stage 6 (representational means–end analysis) involves a gradual process of decontextualization, in which the child requires less and less perceptual support from the environment to call up and/or carry out mental acts of selection, comparison, extraction of similarities, etc. This passage from "presentational symbolizing" to "representational symbolizing" will have structurally similar consequences for the analysis and substitution phase of tool selection in problem solving, symbol selection in play, and symbol selection in language. All three domains should reflect a parallel passage from recognition of relationships to production of relationships, with decreasing reliance on contextual support. Differences among these three domains will derive, at least in part, from the relative amount and type of constraint on substitute selection imposed by the goal situation.

There are predecessors to part–whole analysis in symbol use and tool use in the developmental stages that precede both, in the presymbolic months in which the child is mastering knowledge of objects. Consider the behavior of a Stage 3 child (around 6 months of age) in an object permanence hiding task. If a doll is completely covered with a cloth, this child shows no evidence of knowing that the doll still exists. With no perceptual support from the object, the child apparently cannot keep his "doll program" activated in consciousness long enough to come up with a way to get rid of the cloth. However, if the doll is only partially covered (e.g., with an arm sticking out), the same child can remove the screen and recover the doll. It appears that the "part"—the doll's arm—is sufficient perceptual input to enable the child to call the entire referent back into consciousness long enough to come up with a recovery procedure. He clearly expects the rest of the doll to be under that screen. In the 6-month-old, whole objects come to be recognized from partial perceptual input. There is a sense, then, in which the part stands for or evokes the whole in object recognition, long before the child analyzes and uses part–whole relations in tool use and symbolic activity. The former is, however, a much more passive and "data driven" type of part–whole analysis. The child is not yet actively selecting, imitating, or otherwise producing the relationship.

In Chapter 2, I proposed that vehicle–referent relations appear in problem-solving situations as means–end relations—essentially a restatement of Tolman's theory that stimulus–stimulus relations are stored and used as "means–end readiness." There is ample evidence from the problem-solving literature to suggest that exploration and play with objects outside of a goal situation facilitate the use of those objects to solve a problem later on (e.g., Schiller, 1957). The knowledge gained in play is used in the analyses that will be required to attain a goal. The key factor uniting play and problem solving is the experience of part–whole analysis. If means–ends are a subset of vehicle–referent relations as we have claimed, then it should be possible to analyze and describe a tool use situation in the same Peircian framework adopted in Chapter 2 to describe the structure of symbols. In Figure 7.1, I have described a situation in which a child uses a stick to rake in a cookie.

(a) In the stick and cookie situation (see Figure 7.1), the objective vehicle (Veh_0) is the objectively successful means that must be modelled or discovered for the child to solve the problem. In this particular case, the Veh_0 is the use of the child's own arm in reaching successfully for objects. (Note: It is not the arm itself but "arm use" and all that it involves that comprises the successful means.) The Veh_0 serves as successful means insofar as it is made up of a set of properties that permits completion of the goal (e.g., sufficient extension in space, maneuverability, stiffness).

(b) In this same situation, the objective referent (Ref_0) is the goal situation, with all its various components and relationships among those components. The Ref_0 is defined in terms of the properties

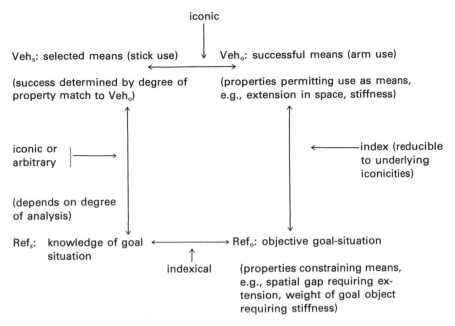

Figure 7.1. *Analysis of tool-use situation in which the child selects and uses a stick to rake in a cookie.*

constraining selection of means, e.g., the spatial gap between the child and the goal–object, the weight of the goal necessitating a fairly stiff raking motion to pull it in. These are the objectively given properties of the situation—although obviously they become relevant only when some human or nonhuman knower has formulated the goal and entered psychologically into the situation. In this sense, the objective means–end relationship is quite similar to the objective sign–referent relationships described by Peirce. The relationships are "real" and "out there." But like the airwaves created by a tree falling in the forest, they are only relevant with regard to their implications for some potential knower.

(*c*) The subjective vehicle (Veh$_s$) in this situation is the means that is selected by the child in trying to solve this problem. In this case the selected means is "stick use" as a substitute for "arm use." **Note that it is not the stick itself that is the Veh$_s$, but the selection of the stick.** The child could, in a representational act of problem solving carried out in the absence of real sticks, have come up with stick selection as his means to the goal. At that point, however, it would do him little good to act out the stick-use gesture with an empty hand (an option that is open to him in symbol selection during play). Interestingly, among Kohler's chimpanzees as well as among children we sometimes observe curious gestures when the problem solver is frustrated, suggesting that the means selection is being partially acted out in the absence of an appropriate object. For example, Kohler's chimps—when deprived of anything sticklike to rake in the banana—were observed to throw rocks at it as though they were trying to achieve extension in space the only way they knew how from their barren cages. However, if it is at all possible to find an object that fits the Veh_s, the child will be constrained to do so to the degree that he still wants to solve the problem and obtain the goal. During means selection, the greater the iconicity (e.g., the relevant property match) between the Veh_s and the objectively determined Veh_o, the greater the odds of success.

(d) Finally, the "subjective referent" (Ref_s) is the child's knowledge of the goal situation. In Piagetian terms, this consists of the entire action-package, or set of potential interactions with the various components and relationships in the objective goal-situation. The Veh_s is selected out as one among the possible actions that could be carried out within that situation.

(a) Regarding the relationships among the various poles in this means–end situation, the Veh_o and the Ref_o—the objective means–end relationship—bear an "indexical" or participatory relationship to one another. Furthermore, insofar as this is a physically real functional relationship, the index should be reducible to some sort of underlying iconicity or similarity of structure that "makes the relationship work." In other words, a scientific explanation of the cookie-getting act would involve pointing out the common direction of movement, the complementary weight relationships, etc., that comprise the physics of cookie getting.

(b) The Veh_s and the Veh_o stand in an iconic relationship to one another, insofar as the selection of means involves an imitation matching the properties of the selected means to the properties of the successful means.

(c) The Ref_s and the Ref_o, in the Piagetian approach taken here, stand in an "indexical" relationship to one another, insofar as all sensorimotor knowledge is comprised of interactions or participations with the external world. However, as is typically the case with participatory relations, the index can be mixed with varying degrees of iconicity as the child's actions are forced into partial isomorphic relations with aspects of the goal situation (e.g., stretching out the arm to cover the gap between actor and goal, hence setting up an iconic relation between child and situation).

(*d*) Finally, the Veh_s and the Ref_s can bear either an "arbitrary," "indexical," or "iconic" relationship to one another, depending on the degree to which the child has analyzed the similarities of structure that make the Veh_s action work as a means to an end. Remember our argument in Chapter 2 that children and adults often use means to ends without understanding how or why they work. It was suggested that "scientific" explanations typically involve reducing a relationship based on contiguity to an underlying iconicity, or similarity–complementarity in structure that unites cooccurring events. Some means to ends are derived through imitation, with little or no analysis of the way the relationship works. Others are worked out privately, through trial and error. In the latter case, it is highly likely that the inventor has been forced to an analysis of iconicities that made the original means and the substitute means work. Imitative means–end relations are likely to be arbitrary, at least at the beginning; "discovered" means–end relations are likely to involve understanding (i.e., relations perceived through similarity rather than contiguity).

I am certainly **not** suggesting that tool use causes symbolization. This is, as we have stated throughout the book, a homology model of language–thought relations, in which various domains of activity share underlying capacities. Tool use involves a capacity for part–whole analysis and location of substitute parts—a capacity that must be shared with symbols in language and in play. However, problems can also be solved through imitation, with analysis of Veh_s–Veh_o relations but no analysis of the Veh_s–Ref_s relationship. **In other words, imitation involves a kind of analysis that is distinct from the kind of understanding that goes on in breaking down part–whole relationships.** Both types of analysis are useful in problem solving; both types of analysis are involved in the emergence of symbols. Later we will discuss how these two processes interact in symbol development. First, we will take a phylogenetic and ontogenetic look at the development of imitation.

Imitation

Perception of contiguity is a process that permits us to identify, recognize and/or recall arbitrarily linked events or events in which the link between sign and referent is poorly understood. Contiguity has been a fairly unpopular topic in cognitive psychology. In an era when our focus has been on the internal elaboration and interpretation of information, mechanisms for uninterpreted learning have been viewed as passive, environmentally driven, and generally pernicious (see Brewer, 1974). The same can certainly be said for imitation. If contiguity is involved in the **incorporation** of arbitrary or uninterpreted relations, imitation is involved in the **reproduction** of arbitrary or poorly understood relations. It is, then, a mechanism that allows us to act without understanding how our actions work. A set piece in social learning theory, imitation has until recently been virtually ignored in cognitive psychology—except to prove that it does not work. For example, in the language acquisition literature a great deal of energy has been expended in demonstrating that imitation contributes little to language development (see Dale, 1976).

More recently, however, interest in the process of imitation has revived (e.g., Kaye, 1970; Moore and Meltzoff, 1977). There are a number of reasons why this happened.

1. Imitation is much less widely distributed phylogenetically than interpreted learning. In lower animals, there are some clear exceptions such as imitated song in certain birds. And there is certainly some evidence for observational learning in nonhuman primates. However, both in degree and range of imitative behaviors humans are vastly superior. If we are to construct a human ethology cataloguing and explaining the specialized behaviors of our species, imitation must be among them.

2. The information-processing mechanisms that permit imitation to take place are a complete mystery. How does the child take visual or auditory input from the behavior of conspecifics (or, in some cases, behavior of animate and inanimate objects) and translate that input into a motor analogue? At present, I am aware of no models that can adequately account for this translation process. (The notion of "analysis by synthesis" cannot explain imitation. It merely labels it.)

3. Imitation has been considered a passive, environmentally driven process simply by "guilt through association" with other traditional learning theory concepts. In fact, imitation is an active process that is very much in the organism's control. So far we have stressed the fact that imitation permits the reproduction of arbitrarily linked or poorly understood relations. **This does not mean, however, that imitation involves no analysis.** There are at least two levels of analysis required for imitation to take place:

(*a*) First, the "selection of models" is an active process, one that is almost always initiated by the organism rather than the human model. Like the selection of symbols (discussed in Chapter 2), the selection of objective vehicles for imitation depends much more on the internal stage of the knower than on the properties of the environment. Uzgiris and Hunt (1975) stress the difficulty of eliciting imitation if the child is not "in the mood"; we certainly confirmed their experience in our own research (see Chapter 3).

(*b*) Second, the "creation of a match" (or partial match) between the objective and the subjective vehicle is certainly a process requiring some very sophisticated perceptual–motor analysis. We have evidence that the child is carrying out such an analysis from the gradual selection of certain properties or features of the model for his first approximations in matching, the correction procedures he employs in perfecting his match, the sequence in which features are selected.

In short, the study of imitation does **not** signal a return to Behaviorism, nor to any other empiricist theory of knowledge. A good theory of imitation will be crucial to any complete, rationalist account of human cognitive development. There is now some evidence available (Gardner and Gardner, 1970; Moore and Meltzoff, 1977) suggesting that even the human neonate may be capable of certain types of imitation, possibly of a reflexive sort (a point which is still controversial—more on this later). The capacities underlying imitation are clearly part of our innate apparatus for the acquisition of culture.

Imitation and Phylogeny

When we are studying human infants, it is not difficult to locate instances of imitative behavior. Because humans engage in so many complex conventional acts—acts which the child is most unlikely to have discovered on his own—all we have to do is find instances in which an infant carries out a version of one of these conventional acts. We can conclude quite comfortably that the **child must have derived that action through imitation** (regardless of the psychological status of that act at the moment it is used—a point that we will return to shortly). A child who sticks his finger in an inviting telephone dial may be engaged in simple sensorimotor exploration, rather than an imitation of adult dialing. But a child who places the telephone receiver in an awkward position on his shoulder is undoubtedly trying to engage in an adultlike telephone behavior.

With nonhumans, it is much more difficult to identify instances of imitation. Just because two organisms are doing the same thing, we cannot conclude that one is imitating the other. What are the criteria for differentiating imitation from other forms of parallel behavior? There seem to be at least four:

1. $Organism_2$ can be said to imitate $Organism_1$ if there is a "temporal delay" between their behavior, with O_2 following O_1. The extent of that delay is a separate issue (see below).
2. O_2 can be said to imitate O_1 if O_2's behavior resembles O_1's, but is at the same time a "partial, rudimentary version" of O_1's display.
3. O_2 can be said to imitate O_1 if O_2 shows awareness of his effort to model O_1 by "repetitions," "corrections," and "other adjustments" bringing his behavior increasingly in line with that of O_1. This may include repeated eye contact or other perceptual checks back to O_1's model.
4. O_2 can be said to imitate O_1 if O_1's behavior is oriented toward and corrected in accordance with a goal, while the same behavior by O_2 is not. Or, alternatively, if both organisms are engaged in trying to solve a problem, O_2 can be said to imitate O_1 if corrections and adjustments in the behavior of O_2 are oriented more toward the behavioral model of O_1 than feedback from the goal situation itself.

These criteria should distinguish imitations from other situations of parallel behavior between organisms, such as the following:

1. Two organisms emit the same behavior
   (*a*) because they are in the same internal state (e.g., contagious crying in neonate nurseries)
   (*b*) because they are solving the same problem and hence coincidentally discovering the same solutions (e.g., two chimps reaching for the same out-of-reach banana)
   (*c*) because they are reacting to the same external stimulus (e.g., kittens playing with the same ball of yarn)
2. O_2 repeats the behavior of O_1 in an expanded and improved version, in order to teach O_1 by presenting a better model.

In applying these criteria, one soon runs into a number of conceptual issues related to the role of imitation in learning.

1. How long a delay can be permitted between the behaviors of O_1 and O_2 if a behavior is to qualify as an imitation?
2. Must imitation always be overt? Clearly the above criteria apply to the recognition of overt imitation. However, **if imitation is defined**

as a match between Veh_s and Veh_o, it is possible to make a
conceptual distinction between overt and covert versions of this
match. These two types of imitation may play somewhat different
roles in learning.

3. The fact that imitation **can** take place without understanding,
prior to any analysis of vehicle–referent relations, does not mean
that it always **does**. It is at least logically possible, according to the
model presented here and in Chapter 2, for **overt** Veh_s–Veh_o
matching to precede, follow, or go on in parallel with vehicle–
referent analysis. **If an overt imitation follows the extraction of
principles that unite vehicle and referent, it may not look like an
imitation in the ordinary English use of the term.** In other words,
many of the above criteria for recognizing imitation (e.g., checks
for feedback to O_1, partial or rudimentary match) may be violated.

4. Criterion 4 for recognizing imitation included a separation of O_2's
imitative behavior from a means–end situation. However, the process and the products of imitation can both be used in problem
solving even when the organism has no idea why or how the means
works in facilitating its end. If O_2 imitates O_1's behavior **in order to
achieve the same goal,** we may not recognize the behavior as an
imitation.

In Chapter 2 we gave definitions for intention, convention, and symbol, plus a list of criteria for recognizing instances of each. The inferred
structures are not "defined" by those behavioral criteria; they are merely
"located" in development by the appearance of behaviors that meet these
criteria. Similarly, we are not defining imitation in terms of the above
four behavioral criteria. **Imitation is defined here as an overt or covert
process of matching subjective actions to objective actions, objects, or
events; in particular, imitation is involved in matching subjective
vehicles to objective vehicles in the incorporation of vehicle–referent
relations, and means–end relations.**

We will examine the above list of problems in the next section, on the
ontogeny of imitation in language, play, and tool use. First, however, we
should briefly examine the small amount of information available on
phylogeny of imitation.

Because the information on imitation in nonhumans is so im-
poverished, there is very little to review in this section. First of all, in
contrast with tool use and certain objects associated with ceremonial
symbolic activity, there are no fossil traces of imitation on which to base
an evolutionary theory. A possible exception regards the geographic
proliferation of particular tools and particular designs, suggesting that
hominids were copying one another's products. This is, however, very

indirect evidence. For the most part we are restricted to the comparative study of existing species. Here too the principal conclusion that derives from the literature is that there simply is not much imitation (as defined above) in nonhumans. The field is restricted almost entirely to our nearest phylogenetic neighbors, except for a restricted class of imitations in birdsong.

As noted earlier, reviews of sensorimotor development in nonhuman primates (Chevalier-Skolnikoff, 1977; Parker and Gibson, 1977) suggest that infrahumans are poorer (relative to human infants) on imitation tasks than on any of the other scales of sensorimotor development (e.g., means–ends, object permanence, spatial relations). An animal like the cebus monkey, capable of Stage 6 representational memory for objects and enormously skilled at problem solving with tools, shows few signs of proceeding beyond sensorimotor Stage 3 or 4 in imitation. As we shall see shortly, Stage 4 is the lowest level at which an animal or child begins to imitate something not already in his repertoire. Kellogg and Kellogg (1933) repeatedly marvel at the gross differences in imitative skill between their human child Donald and the chimpanzee Gua, even though the two infants were raised together in nearly identical circumstances. Indeed, the Kelloggs were tempted to call off their experiment when Donald began imitating Gua's facial expressions and call sounds, using them appropriately to demand food, show excitement, etc. In the end, the Kelloggs suggested that the verb *to ape* may be an inappropriate term for imitation.

Kohler (1927) stressed that the chimps in his study rarely solved problems by imitating the successful solutions of other chimps. When observational learning does occur (i.e., the acquisition of a means to an end through imitation), it is typically restricted to the very young, or to adults low in the dominance hierarchy. For example, in Kawai's (1965) study of Japanese macaques, several important "technological advances" were discovered by one juvenile female of very low status. These included washing sweet potatoes to remove dirt, and washing wheat out in pools of water where sand sinks to the bottom and wheat floats to the top. This female exercised her skills in full view of the troop for years with little impact on group habits. Finally, when a high status member of the troop at last caught on to her trick, the new techniques then spread fairly rapidly. Eventually these procedures became an established part of the group "culture."

So imitation and observational learning are possible among nonhumans, but they are strongly constrained by several factors. First, the direction of who observes and copies whom is based on the dominance hierarchy. Since it is often the low status member who is least conservative and hence most likely to discover improved techniques, this tendency builds a natural conservatism into ape "culture." Second, Jolly (1972) reported that observational learning takes place in nonhumans entirely in the absence of any effort by O_1 to improve his model for learning purposes, to correct O_2, or to engage in anything remotely like teaching. Third, the frequency of imitative behavior is low, suggesting that nonhumans have nowhere near the motivation of the human child to imitate poorly understood events apparently for the sheer pleasure of it.

This brief overview suggests that an increase in the capacity and the motivation to imitate may have been a critical factor in the evolutionary leap into humanlike culture, including language. Such a development dramatically increases the probability that an organism will master new techniques without repeating the trial and error process himself—indeed long before he has any insights into the way the technique works.

Imitation in Ontogeny

The most detailed theory available on the development of imitation in human children is, not surpisingly, Piaget's (1962)—although Piaget borrowed heavily from work by Guillaume (1926, translation 1971). The six sensorimotor substages he outlines for imitation can be briefly summarized as follows.

Stage 1 (stage of reflex behaviors, 0–1 month of age): No evidence for any analysis and incorporation of new behaviors, nor for any repetition of own behaviors after modeling by others. The closest thing to imitation in this period is so-called "contagious crying" in nurseries (cf. Moore and Meltzoff, 1978).

Stage 2 (stage of primary circular reactions, or the ability to maintain voluntary control over basic schemes, 1–4 months): At this point the child will repeat a scheme **already in his repertoire** if the observer repeats that scheme soon after the child initiated it. In effect, it is as though the infant does not distinguish between his own continuation of a basic scheme, versus the continuation by someone else, and hence is "fooled" into going back into the primary circular reaction by the adult feedback.

Stage 3 (secondary circular reactions, or behaviors to make interesting events continue or repeat, 4–8 months): At this point the child will still imitate only behaviors that are already in his own repertoire. Hence there is still no "true imitation" in the sense of analysis of new models. However, now the adult can initiate the exchange without waiting for a spontaneous behavior by the child. Hence the imitation is somewhat closer to an effort to reproduce the environment, rather than a continuation of the child's prior behavior.

Stage 4 (coordinations of secondary circular reactions into new combinations, 8–11 months): This is the first level of true imitation, or an effort to analyze and incorporate new models. At this point, however, the child can imitate only new models that are visible on his own body as he reproduces them (e.g., so that he can compare the adult hand and his own hand in imitating a new finger movement). If a scheme is not visible on his own body, it must be a pattern that is already in his repertoire if the child is to imitate it (e.g., mouth movements, hands behind the head out of eyeline).

Stage 5 (tertiary circular reactions, or creation of novel means and experiments to see what will happen, roughly 10–13 months in our samples): Here the child analyzes new models even when he cannot watch himself reproduce them (e.g., patting the top of the head, making rabbit ears with the fingers behind the head, unusual mouth movements). In this stage the extent and variety of imitation also tends to increase markedly, albeit always in the presence of the model.

Stage 6 (quarternary circular reactions, or representational and fully internalized schemes, 13 months onward): This is the stage of deferred imitations, carried out in the absence of the model, often after considerable lapses of time. It is here that it becomes difficult to distinguish imitation as an acquisition process, from the exercise of schemes that were acquired through imitation.

There are some interesting transition points as the child begins to imitate novel models during State 4. Often the child will correctly reproduce the rhythms and general movement patterns of the adult model, but with the wrong part of the body altogether. For example, eye blinking may be imitated with an open-and-shut movement of the hand. The child has extracted some general movement and temporal properties of the adult model, but has not yet determined the modality in which to instantiate those patterns. Bower (1977) has suggested that amodal information precedes modality-specific information in the development of three-dimensional perception, and that if there is an innate component to depth perception, it may involve precisely that amodal information. It is also possible that amodal information may be more basic in imitation as well.

These observations lead to some recent studies on imitation that may pose serious problems for a Piagetian theory of development through experience and exercise. As noted earlier, Meltzoff and Moore (1978) have provided some evidence for imitation of mouth, eye, tongue, and hand movements in human neonates. The facial imitations, if they prove to be robust and replicable findings, are particularly difficult for Piaget's theory since imitations of behaviors invisible on the child's own body are purportedly not mastered until Stage 5, around 10 months at the earliest. Moore and Meltzoff have even suggested that these imitations provide evidence for some form of mental representation a year before Piagetian age norms. While I think that this particular explanation may be a little farfetched, we have clearly arrived at a point in research where it is necessary to reexamine the traditional Piagetian view of imitation.

This brings us to the four problems mentioned earlier with regard to applying our criteria for recognizing imitation. Briefly restated, these are:

1. the length of the delay permissible between O_1's behavior and O_2's behavior if we are to call O_2's action an imitation
2. the distinction between overt and covert imitation
3. imitation with and without understanding of the vehicle–referent relation
4. imitation inside and outside of problem-solving situations.

All of these issues require a reconsideration of the Piagetian view.

Beginning with the issue of temporal delay, remember that what Piaget calls "deferred imitation" takes place by definition in the absence of the objective vehicle, with a delay of up to several days. Are these really imitations? For Piaget, imitation and play form two ends of a continuum: Imitation is behavior that is almost entirely accomodative (i.e., schemes adjusted to conform to the object being "known"); play is behavior that is almost entirely assimilative, (i.e., schemes applied to objects of knowledge that may be deformed to fit the scheme). In assimilation the world is fitted to what the child already knows. In accommodation the child fits himself to the world and changes his knowledge base. **However, once a highly imitative, accommodative scheme is acquired, the next time it is used it is by definition an assimilation.** So precisely what kind of an act is a deferred imitation? Piaget argues that the child in these situations is creating a match between his overt behavior and some "internal" model of the "objective" model. The internal model is itself an imitation, insofar as all a child actually stores in the Piagetian view of knowledge is actions. Images (like all representations) are nothing other than internal motor commands derived from perceptual-motor interaction with the original object. A mental image of a triangle is created by calling up the perceptual procedures used in interacting with triangles (e.g., eye scan patterns). In other words, during a deferred imitation the child is imitating at the overt level his own internal or covert imitation of an object or event. He is, in short, imitating himself. We could justifiably argue, then, that a deferred imitation involves more assimilation (i.e., calling up a scheme that has already been acquired) than accommodation. In that regard, it really is not imitation at all in the sense of incorporating **new** information by creating a motor analogue. Deferred imitation is actually a form of play, the exercise ("functional assimilation" in Piaget's terms) of an already acquired scheme.

To resolve the issue of temporal delay, we must conclude that deferred imitations do not qualify as imitations. However, it may be useful at this point to introduce a distinction between "imitation as a process" and "imitations as products." The former refers to the incorporation and improvement of subjective vehicles, creating a match to an objective vehicle—the definition provided on page 335. The latter refers to those behaviors that were derived initially from a process of imitation. The deferred imitations that we witness in symbolic play (e.g., putting telephone receivers to the ear, stirring in bowls with a spoon) are the products of imitation, even though they are now being used in the process of play. This view makes it difficult to distinguish deferred imitation from symbolic play. Indeed, the two become essentially the same thing. Take the example of a child alone in his room, stirring with a spoon or saying "spoon." It is very unlikely that the child discovered these behaviors on his own, through experimenting trial-and-error fashion with spoons. Rather, the conventional form of these behaviors suggests that they must have been derived by a matching of the child's motor system to visual input from adult behaviors. Hence these spoon behaviors are necessarily the products of imitation. However, insofar as the adult model is perceptually absent in this situation, the child is not currently engaging in the process of imitating objective vehicles. That does not mean that the child is no longer improving his performance. Indeed, he may show evidence of adjusting or correcting his reproduction (e.g., hesitating and repeating some component of the act more accurately). We can conclude that the child is comparing his overt act with some sort of internal model. However, in this second process nothing new is being incorporated. Rather, the subjective vehicle (which consists of the internalized motor commands initially derived from imitation of the objective vehicle) is in a sense adjusting itself as it is "sketched out" on the plane of action. The products of imitation are now solidly within the child's repertoire. Hence by Piaget's definition they are assimilations, or play.

The notion of "sketching out" knowledge on the plane of action brings us to the second issue, the distinction between overt and covert imitation. There is a sense in which virtually all cultural knowledge involves some degree of imitation. This is merely the trivial observation that French children end up speaking French and using French culture, Chinese children eventually speak Chinese and master Chinese customs, etc. Furthermore, in a procedural or actionbased theory of knowledge like those of Piaget and Werner, **all** learning involves some sort of motor match between the child's actions and the objects he interacts with. The vehicle–vehicle match is particularly direct in the acquisition of culturally specified behaviors that would probably never arise in trial-and-error manipulations of the objects (e.g., the above-mentioned spoon behaviors). However, **the match between the internal motor commands that comprise object knowledge, and the external model, could in principle take place without an explicit, overt enactment of those motor commands.** According to this proposal, all of the child's imitations could potentially take place "underground," where we would have no way of observing them. The four criteria specified earlier for recognizing imitation obviously pertain only to the recognition of "overt imitations." For obvious reasons, the study of imitation has always been restricted to the study of these overt, explicit matching behaviors. Should we ever develop a technology for recording internal motor commands, the question of internal or covert imitations could be addressed at something other than the theoretical level. For the moment, however, we are left with the possibility that overt imitations represent only a subclass of the matching processes involved in cultural learning, a subclass that may have a special function in that learning process. Given the assumption that some sort of imitation process is essential in the acquisition of culture, the question then becomes when and why do imitations take place overtly, on the plane of action?

There are at least two possible advantages of overt versus covert vehicle–vehicle matching:

1. The actual execution of the imitative act provides feedback (auditory, visual, kinesthetic, etc) that may be useful in correcting and improving the match between the external model and the child's subjective reconstruction of the model. This would be an example of the kind of contextual support discussed throughout this book regarding the gradual onset of representation from presentational knowing. This view leads to the prediction that the child will engage in "overt" matching at particularly difficult points in vehicle–vehicle analysis, when the analysis needs to be "sketched out" in action to provide further perceptual-motor support.
2. An overt imitation is perceptually available to other human beings

as well as to the child himself. Hence some children may discover that overt imitation (*a*) attracts adult attention, and/or (*b*) elicits information about the correctness of the match between subjective and objective vehicles.

In other words, we are suggesting that overt imitation will be used when the child is trying to incorporate something that is particularly new, difficult, or discrepant for him. This is perfectly in keeping with findings by Kagan (1976) that imitation is a response to information that is discrepant with the child's current knowledge, but not so far beyond the child's understanding that it is either upsetting, or impossible to perceive. Kagan uses the term "imitation" to refer to what we are calling "overt imitation." As far as I can see, we disagree only on terminology. The distinction between overt and covert imitation will be useful later on, when we turn to a discussion of individual differences in language acquisition.

The third issue involves the relative timing of vehicle–vehicle matching versus vehicle–referent analysis. I have claimed repeatedly that imitation permits the incorporation of relations that are unanalyzed or poorly understood, as well as the "re-presentation" of those relations for analysis long after they have been acquired. However, imitation (in the sense of correcting and improving vehicle–vehicle matches) can continue **after** vehicle–referent analysis. In fact, some children may not engage in "overt" imitation until they have already achieved some understanding of the relationship between the imitated vehicle and its referent. In other words, **imitation can occur prior to, during, or after the process of understanding the vehicle–referent relation.** According to the proposal presented above, we would expect overt imitation to occur more often when the child does **not** understand the situation very well. There may be cases, however, in which overt imitation follows understanding (perhaps for the social reasons mentioned above). This possibility has at least two implications:

1. If the child has already come to understand a sign–referent relationship prior to his first observed overt imitation of the vehicle, then his appropriate use and understanding of the imitated act may obscure its role as an acquisition device. In other words, his reproduction may not **look** like an imitation to the adult, even though it is still serving the function of copying, practicing, and perfecting the adult model. For example, in language the same utterance could be both an imitation **and** a spontaneous production, if the child is using the production as an opportunity to improve his match to adult speech forms.

2. Some confusions in the literature regarding the role imitation in learning may be due to observations of "conservative" children, who wait and watch at length prior to overt exercise of some scheme, versus "risk takers," who are willing to try things out immediately and refine their models at leisure. The conservative children may not seem to imitate at all, since they do not "sketch out" their first reproductions of adult behaviors until some understanding of vehicle–referent relations has been achieved.

This third issue regards whether the child imitates with or without understanding the "nature" of the vehicle–referent relation. The fourth issue regards whether the child imitates with or without understanding what the vehicle–referent relation is **for** (i.e., whether or not it can be used in problem solving). If a child carries out his first overt imitations of an adult act in the process of trying to solve a problem, then once again his action may not look like an imitation. Here too we might expect individual differences among children, in that some infants may imitate only when highly motivated to solve a problem while others may engage in more imitation "for its own sake." The first group of children may not seem to be imitating at all.

To summarize, we have defined imitation as a process of vehicle–vehicle matching. Behaviors derived initially from this imitative "process" are not functioning as imitations when they are executed at great delay. In other words, Piaget's deferred imitations would be classified by our criteria as play with the "products" of imitation. Second, imitation may be either overt or covert, but overt imitation probably occurs in difficult situations, where the child's understanding of the situation is minimal. Third, children may imitate with or without understanding of the vehicle–referent relationship. Fourth, children may imitate with or without understanding of the way the vehicle–referent relationship can be used to solve problems (i.e., as means to ends). In the literature on the development of imitation and its role in acquiring language and other cultural behaviors, most investigators seem to be referring to "overt imitations carried out without understanding of either meaning or use." This restricted use of the term "imitation" has in turn led many investigators to conclude that imitation per se plays little role in acquisition. This should become clearer as we apply our distinctions to the role of various types of imitation in symbolic play, tool use, and language.

IMITATION AND SYMBOLIC PLAY

I have already stated one important difference between our view of imitation and Piaget's: By the definitions adopted here, deferred imitations are actually a form of play. In fact, most of the examples of symbolic play discussed in Chapters 3 and 4 would qualify as examples of deferred imitation of adult conventional behaviors (both indexical behaviors, like vacuuming or cooking, and truly arbitrary "games").

It is also true that in most of our examples of symbolic play, there was no clear sense in which the environment was "deformed" in assimilation to the child's schemes. Most of the gestural naming examples were deferred imitations carried out with appropriate objects—telephoning with a telephone, stirring with a spoon. Some authors—including Genevan researchers like Sinclair (1970) and Inhelder (1966)—have reserved the term "symbolic play" only for those schemes that do deform the environment, through selection of an object and/or context that is inappropriate to that scheme. Hence the enactive or gestural naming of a telephone with a receiver-to-ear action is not seen as a symbolic act, while the same scheme with a stick or with an empty hand is defined as symbolic. Also, these acts are called "deferred imitations" more often when they are associated with appropriate objects; they are called "play" when the object employed in the game bears a more abstract relationship to the appropriate object for that scheme. I have several difficulties with this distinction.

First, this approach creates an artificial distinction between symbolization in play versus language. Sinclair and the other investigators are perfectly content to call the vocal gesture of naming a spoon "spoon" a truly symbolic act. They do not require that the vocal naming be applied to an inappropriate or abstract object before it qualifies as a symbol (e.g., calling a stick "spoon"). It is indeed the case that children go through a period of overgeneralizing words to inappropriate referents. **In fact, they tend to engage in such overgeneralization of words in roughly the same period in which they overgeneralize their gestural schemes to inappropriate objects.** If the act of stirring is truly symbolic only when applied to spoonlike abstractions, then we must also conclude that word use is truly symbolic only when applied to abstract variants on the original referent for that word. On the other hand, if calling a spoon "spoon" is a symbolic act, then so is the recognitory gesture of stirring applied to the same object. Both acts are derived through imitation. Both occur in deferred imitations (and hence, in our view, in play). Both types of acts move from application to a very restricted range, to overgeneralization along a gradient of similarity to the original referent.

Second, if the use of gestural schemes with appropriate objects is defined as nonsymbolic, we must at the very least conclude that it is "presymbolic." In both linguistic and nonlinguistic symbolization, there are correlations between the presymbolic use of conventions and their later symbolic use. Since one type of "naming game" leads directly into the other, the decision to call only the later uses "symbols" seems somewhat arbitrary.

Third, the Genevan definition of symbolic play poses serious problems for the fate of the same play schemes months or years after their first "symbolic" use with inappropriate objects. After a period in toddlerhood of overextending vocal and gestural schemes to inappropriate objects, many preschool children become quite conservative and realistic in their choice of objects for play. Do we really want to claim that dramatic play with realistic toys is no longer symbolic activity? Remember that for Piaget (and for us) the subjective vehicle or symbol (Veh$_s$) is the child's action (overt or covert) as it is used to stand for a larger action-package (Ref$_s$) to which that vehicle belongs. **The symbol is, then, the action rather than the object to which that action is applied.** In the Peircian analyses of symbol structure provided in Chapter 2, the four-way vehicle–referent relations described in Figures 2.1, 2.2, and 2.3 are the same regardless of whether the child is stirring with a spoon, a stick, or an empty hand. Symbolization is not defined in terms of object choice. The question of object choice is related, instead, to the process of "decontextualization," in which symbolic schemes (or tool selection—see page 324) initially require maximum perceptual support from the environment in which they were derived. Gradually, the same schemes require less and less support until they can be carried out with inappropriate objects that provide only a few suggestions of spoons, telephones, etc. Later still, children will learn to restrict the range of application back again to conform with adult rules for using those schemes. There is, then, a "recontextualization" phase that follows the decontextualization of symbols. Nevertheless, the later, more adultlike uses of symbols are still classifiable as symbolic activity, since they involve naming, identifying, or representing some state of affairs.

To summarize, imitation is a process of acquiring sign–referent relations by vehicle–vehicle matching. Deferred imitations, carried out after long delays in the absence of the objective vehicle, are actually a type of symbolic play with the products of imitation. Gestural symbols, like linguistic symbols, can be carried out either with appropriate objects or with more abstract objects. Although the latter is more advanced developmentally, both types of activity should be viewed as symbolic acts. As our correlational findings in Chapter 3 demonstrate, imitation and symbolic play are correlated developments. Indeed, **I suggest that symbolic play is best viewed as imitative play, while combinatorial or manipulative play might be viewed as tool-use play.** This brings us to the next point, regarding the relationship between tool use and imitation.

IMITATION AND TOOL USE

So far we have discussed imitation and tool use as separate skills. The correlations reported in Chapter 3 suggest that the two skills do develop separately, although both relate positively to language and play. The phylogenetic evidence reviewed earlier (e.g., Parker, 1977) also suggests that these two abilities are dissociable across species. Recall, however, the position taken here that vehicle–referent relations can become means–end relations when the child is trying to solve a problem. In trial-and-error problem-solving the child is likely to discover the indexical and iconic relations that make a particular means work in obtaining a goal. However, it is also possible to incorporate new means through imitation, by directly copying someone else's solution to the problem without working the relationship through. In imitation, an organism must analyze vehicle–vehicle relations (in this case the relationship between the "missing means" and the substitute means—see page 324). But he need not analyze the bond between vehicle and referent, i.e., the relationship that makes the means work. Instead, he can simply exploit the observed contiguity between means and ends. With continued experience in using such solutions, the child may **later** come to understand how things work. When this happens, unnecessary components in the imitation (i.e., actions that do not actually function in obtaining the goal) may be dropped, while useful portions are retained.

The relationship between imitation and tool use is relevant to the third and fourth issues described above: Imitation with and without understanding of the vehicle–referent relation, and imitation inside and outside of goal situations. In this case, we are focusing on imitation to obtain goals. The question is how much understanding is required to use imitation in tool use? What is the analytic process by which arbitrarily incorporated means are broken down into a truly productive understanding?

An example of this analytic process that I find useful comes from my own experiences in learning how to cook. At the beginning, I followed recipes slavishly. Since it was a mystery to me how these various actions and ingredients worked, I was afraid to alter or eliminate a single element—going out in the snow to buy forgotten spices an hour before a dinner party. Gradually, as I saw the same recipes permuted in varied forms, I began to eliminate or interchange certain steps in those recipes. Some spices could be substituted for one another, while some produced unpleasant combinations with other ingredients. Steaming was preferable to sauteeing for certain processes; in other recipes either method of cooking would do. And so forth. This process finally led to the abstraction of some principles about ingredients and kitchen procedures, until I was finally able to generate new recipes based only indirectly on the old models. I now have a sort of grammar of cooking, one that I can use both in comprehension of cookbooks and production of meals.

The point is that I had initially acquired a complex skill through something akin to imitation—adopting someone else's means to goals without understanding the part–whole relationships in the recipe. The process of breaking up seemingly arbitrary combinations into combinations based on similarities of structure took place very gradually. The amount of time required for this kind of process will vary with several factors: Amount of experience with the system, lawfulness and regularity of the system, the severity of the constraints within tasks, and perhaps the motivation and curiosity of the knower to understand something he already knows how to do. In many cases of problem solving, imitation may predominate indefinitely over trial-and-error substitution of parts in wholes. This does not mean, however, that imitation and means analysis are opposed. Instead, one supports the other in a complementary fashion. In human evolution, we can speculate that these two approaches to problem solving evolved independently, at least initially (recall how little observational learning was involved in Kohler's study of chimpanzee tool use). The historical coincidence of these two skills may have been one of the great catalysts in the evolution of human culture.

To summarize so far, we are not opposing imitation and tool use in themselves. The continuum introduced in Chapter 2 involves two opposing and interacting modes of analysis: perception of similarity and perception of contiguity. The latter is involved in recognizing and reproducing poorly understood relationships. The former is involved in breaking relationships down into parts, and discovering the class of possible substitutions for each part within the whole. **Problems can be solved through either process, but I suggest that imitative tool-use will occur when simple contiguity predominates. Analyzed, productive tool use (involving perception of similarities) is more likely to occur in trial-and-error problem-solving.** The same approach will apply to the "social tool-use" situation of language acquisition.

IMITATION AND LANGUAGE

The role of imitation in language acquisition is a controversial issue, and the literature is contradictory at best (see Clark, 1978 and Keenan, 1977 for excellent critical reviews). There is evidence to support each of the following conclusions:

1. Imitation is **not** progressive over comprehension or production. In other words, the child will only imitate linguistic forms that are

already a productive part of his repertoire. Hence imitation cannot be viewed as the means for acquiring those forms.

2. Imitation **is** progressive over comprehension and production. The child tends to imitate forms that are either absent in his spontaneous productions, or present at a very low frequency. Hence imitation **is** a means of acquiring new forms.

3. Imitation is progressive for some children, and not for others. Furthermore, some children imitate frequently, others not at all. Hence imitation is an optional strategy in language acquisition.

4. Imitation is a strategy that is useful for acquiring some linguistic forms (e.g., lexical items) but not others (e.g., syntax).

5. Imitation is a strategy that is employed at particular stages in development, and not at others.

In Chapter 4 we reported our own findings regarding the relation between imitation, and both comprehension and production. The reader will recall that these findings were inconclusive, compatible to some extent with any of the above five positions. The one firm conclusion that we do have is that imitation is involved in language acquisition somehow. It is correlated significantly with language development. The content of imitation is the same as the rest of early language. Furthermore, symbolic play (which always involves deferred imitations) predicts language development better than other nonlinguistic variables. Clearly imitation plays some role in language acquisition. Why is the literature on this topic in such a muddle? The distinctions introduced in this chapter may help clarify the seemingly contradictory evidence.

The first conclusion (i.e., imitation is not progressive over comprehension or production) is particularly common in some of the 1960s work on acquisition. For example, Ervin (1964) examined word order in the imitative versus spontaneous speech of three children in a longitudinal study. She concluded that the children only imitated orders that were already present in their spontaneous speech. Hence imitation was not used for acquiring new syntactic rules. Slobin and Welsh (1973) report on elicited imitation of a variety of syntactic devices, with one child, who systematically changed the modelled sentences to conform to rules that characterized her spontaneous productions in the same period. For example, the embedded sentence, *The boy who cried came to my party,* was imitated as a conjoined sentence, *A boy cried and he came to my party.* This phenomenon in elicited imitation has since been reported in numerous studies, including my own (Bates, 1976). There is even a certain amount of evidence (Bloom, Hood, and Lightbown, 1974) that imitations may actually lag behind spontaneous speech in complexity and grammatically, and that a child may incorrectly imitate an utterance that he produced spontaneously himself the day before. Still more recently, Mayer and Valian (1977) have suggested that children's imitations of questions are rarely progressive in syntactic structure over spontaneous production of questions. Instead, children seem to produce partial or complete imitations of adult questions as a means of holding the floor in conversation, stalling and keeping their conversational turn until a better response can be formulated. A similar "placeholding" strategy has been noted in children at the one-word stage by Donahue (1977).

Early evidence for the second conclusion, that imitation does play a progressive role in language development, comes from Brown and Bellugi (1964). In an experiment comparing imitation, comprehension, and production of a variety of syntactic and morphological forms with the same stimulus materials, they conclude that imitation of these forms precedes comprehension, which in turn precedes production (cf. Fernald, 1972, for a methodological critique of this study). Smith (1970) noted that when nonsense words are embedded in sentences, children are more likely to imitate the nonsense words than other lexical items in the sentence. Hence the author concludes that imitation is at least a means of acquiring new lexical items. Similar findings are reported by Bloom *et al.* (1974).

Bloom *et al.* and Kemp and Dale (1973) report that children are most likely to imitate forms that have **just begun** to appear in their spontaneous speech. They are least likely to imitate structures that are well established. However, both these studies also report that imitation is frequent for some children, while others do very little. (In the Bloom *et al.* study the criterion for imitation is an utterance repeating the adult model within five utterances of that model.) Furthermore, children seem to develop unique strategies for using imitation in acquiring new forms. One child in the Bloom *et al.* study tended to imitate lexical items that were rare or absent from his spontaneous vocabulary, but **only** when the new lexical item occurred within the syntactic frames that were the most frequent and stable in his own speech. In other words, an old syntactic vehicle was used to incorporate new lexical items.

These last studies lead to Conclusions (3) and (4): Imitation is a strategy used by some children but not by others, and imitation is useful for acquiring some linguistic forms (e.g., lexical items) but not others (e.g., syntax). However, Nicolich (1975) has suggested that both these conclusions are artifacts of a "developmental" difference in the usefulness of imitation at different stages. In particular, Nicolich reported a sharp increase in vocal imitation at a point at the end of the one word period, when vocabulary is undergoing marked expansion. Shortly after, when multiword utterances begin to predominate, the frequency of imitation drops off. Nicolich argues that apparent individual differences in frequency of imitation may be related to the developmental stage at which a given child is. Furthermore, the conclusion that imitation is used for lexical acquisition but not for syntax may be related to the fact that children are more likely to imitate at the stage in which lexical acquisition is expanding.

How do these contradictory findings relate to the conceptual issues outlined earlier? First, with regard to overt versus covert imitation, they all pertain to the use of overt imitation in language acquisition. In this chapter we have defined imitation as the construction of motor analogues to perceptual input, or Veh_s–Veh_o matching. Any child who will ever learn to produce his native language will have to go through that construction process. Hence by our definition **all** children imitate, and **all** linguistic forms must be imitated. However, it is not logically necessary for all (or any) linguistic forms to be exercised overtly when the motor analogues are first constructed. We suggested that overt imitation—viewed as the "sketching out" of subjective knowledge on the plane of action—is more likely to occur when particularly difficult models are being copied. This prediction fits with the data by Smith, and by Bloom *et al.* that children tend to overtly imitate nonsense words, new lexical items in old syntactic frames, or forms that are just beginning to appear in the child's productive repertoire. Also, individual differences in the frequency of overt imitation may be related to the factors outlined earlier. Some children may experience more difficulty in acquiring linguistic forms than others and hence resort to overt sketching out of those forms. Other children may use overt imitation because of its attention value and/or because they have discovered its usefulness in eliciting feedback about the correctness of the reproduction. In short, overt imitation may be a strategy used by children who are less skilled or precocious in language, or by socially oriented children who are reinforced by adult attention to imitations (see Mayer and Valian on imitation as a device for holding the conversational floor).

A second issue raised earlier regards the relative timing of vehicle–vehicle analysis and vehicle–referent analysis (i.e., the relationship between imitation and understanding). As we noted, if a child sketches out his first overt reproductions of an adult model **after** he has already come to understand the meaning of a linguistic form, then (*a*) imitation may appear to follow comprehension and (*b*) imitations and spontaneous productions may look like (and even be) the very same thing. In either case, an observer might conclude that imitation plays no progressive role in language acquisition. Also, "risk taking" children may be more likely to engage in overt attempts at matching adult models prior to attaining understanding of the way the linguistic device works. More conservative children might construct their motor analogues covertly, until they have gained a better understanding of the meaning of the relationship. The result would be that risk-taking children look like imitators, and conversative children do not.

This issue of timing between reproduction and understanding may also relate to the observation that overt imitation is more common for lexical items than for syntactic forms. First, there are simply a greater number of new lexical items in child language than new syntactic devices. So our probability of observing a child's first overt reproduction of a structure is greater for individual words than for grammatical forms. But there is a second, more subtle reason for the reports in the literature that children do not "imitate" grammar. If we were using the garden variety definition of imitation as reproduction without understanding (i.e., prior to vehicle–referent analysis), then what exactly would it mean to say that a child "imitates" a grammatical rule? He may reproduce word-based order patterns (like those observed by Braine, 1977), idiomatic expressions, or morphological markers that seem inseparable from their lexical root. In my early cooking efforts, I produced dishes that obeyed cooking principles—but those principles were embodied in the recipe, and not in my own productive repertoire. I had imitated the recipe, in the sense of reproduction without understanding. But it would be inappropriate to say that I had imitated the cooking rule. Similarly, if a child reproduces a phrase or inflected item without having analyzed the part–whole relations embodied in the item, it would be inappropriate to say that he "imitated" the grammatical rule. The point I am making is really quite simple: If we have defined rules as productive applications of a principle, and we have defined imitation as reproduction prior to analysis, then by definition a child cannot imitate a grammatical rule! In short, the child's first reproductions based on rules are, in the terms we have used here, imitation after vehicle–referent analysis.

There are, however, two timing issues to be considered here. One is the issue just discussed concerning reproduction with or without analysis of the internal vehicle–referent structure (i.e., part–whole relations and principles of similarity and complementarity that govern substitutions of parts within frames). The second issue regards imitation with or without understanding of the function of an utterance. The first issue pertains to knowing how a communicative means works. The second issue pertains to knowing what it gets you, regardless of how it does it. Just as we are more likely to apply the term "imitation" to reproductions prior to vehicle–referent analysis, we are also more likely to use the word "imitation" to describe reproductions prior to analysis of function. The first time a child uses the word "please," he may well be constructing his first motor analogues or matches to the adult model. Hence, in the terms outlined in this chapter, "please" is an imitation. Suppose, however, that the child's first use takes place quite intentionally in a cookie-getting situation. The child knows what that word will do for him—a sort of magic formula—even if he does not know why (Bates, 1976). In the traditional literature on imitation, if a child reproduces a phrase for the first time in a "payoff" situation, the instance will probably not be recorded as an imitation. Recall the instances described earlier of imitation in nonhuman primates (e.g., a chimpanzee juvenile imitating termite fishing by the mother). Presumably the infant knows what the whole procedure is for. Does that mean that the act is not an imitation? To summarize, we can have imitations with or without analysis of structure, and with or without analysis of function. In the usual literature on language imitation, however, recordings are made only of reproductions prior to analysis of either structure or function.

There has recently been a revival of interest in formulaic speech, the "phrasal lexicon," idiomatic expressions—in short, the use of language in a nongenerative, unanalyzed fashion as an arbitrary means to a goal. These uses were once considered a small and aberrant corner of the language. Upon closer examination, it is becoming clear that much more of language is acquired in this fashion than was originally thought. Ruth Clark (1974) was among the first to document such arbitrary uses of language by children in a paper entitled "Performing without Competence." More recently, Lily Fillmore (1976) traced the role of formulaic speech in the acquisition of English as a second language.

For five Spanish-speaking grade-school children acquiring English from their playmates, there was a period of several months in which **most** of their English was formulaic in nature. Whole phrases like *How do you do dese?* and *Gotcha one cowboy* served as tools used at appropriate points in the social interactions of the children. Gradually, however, they began to break these whole units down into patterns with slots for new material. Table 7.1 (from Fillmore, 1976) illustrates the history of the formula *How do you do dese?* as it moves toward full grammatical analysis. This is one example of movement along the continuum suggested earlier, from arbitrary to iconic Veh_s–Ref_s relations. The formulas were initially acquired by imitation, and used appropriately due to an apparently arbitrary contiguity between the linguistic means and its communicative ends. In a manner similar to the cooking example presented earlier, the children gradually subject such phrases to part–whole analysis, determining which parts are dispensable, what substitutions can and

TABLE 7.1
How do you do dese? From Formula to Productive Speech (Nora)[a]

Structure	Examples
Time II	
Wh (F): How do you do dese?	*How do you do dese?*
Time III–IV	
Wh (Fx)[1]:	*How do you do dese?*
	How do you do dese September
How do you do dese (X)/	*por manana?*
X = NP, PP	*How do you do dese flower power?*
	How do you do dese little tortillas?
	How do you do dese in English?
Wh (Fx)[2]: How do you	*How do you make a little gallenas?*
How did you X/X = VP	*(="ballenas")*
	How do you like to be a cookie cutter?
	(="How would you...")
	How do you like to be a shrarks?
	How do you make the flower?
	How do you gonna make dese?
	How do you gonna do dese in English?
	How did you make it?
	How did you lost it?
Time IV	
Wh (Fx)[3]: How do	*How do cut it?*
How does X/X = Clause	*How do make it?*
How did	*How does this color is?*
	How did dese work? (= "How does this
	work?")
Wh (S): How is freed, preposed	*Because when I call him, how I put*
	the number? (= "How will I
	dial his number?")
	How you make it?
	How will take off paste?

[a]From Fillmore, 1976.

cannot be made. As more of these patterns are broken down, the child may come up with grammatical hypotheses (i.e., higher-order similarities of use and structure that unite this pattern to others). Again, this is a creative, constructive process—hardly the mechanistic, passive sort of induction envisioned in the 1960s. But the process **is** a gradual one. **If the child is to function adequately in his social setting, he must occasionally use imitation prior to understanding as a mode of acquiring some minimal linguistic means.**

To summarize, the apparent contradictions in the literature on imitation in language can be resolved if we make three distinctions about kinds of imitation: overt versus covert, with or without analysis of vehicle–referent relations, and with or without analysis of function or use in a means–end situation.

1. If overt imitation is used to "sketch out" particularly difficult reproductions, we would expect some children to resort to it more often than others. Also, overt imitation may be more likely for particular kinds of linguistic forms. Finally, overt imitations are perceptually available to observers, and hence can provide some ancillary social payoffs. Hence some children may come to rely on overt imitation for social reasons.

2. The acquisition literature has primarily focused on imitation **prior** to understanding of vehicle–referent relations. Conservative children may avoid this strategy, and hence appear not to imitate at all. Also, imitation without vehicle–referent analysis is possible with lexical terms, and with order patterns or morphological markings based on particular words. However, grammatical rules that extend across classes of words will necessarily require some part–whole/substitution analysis before they can be perceived or reproduced at all. Hence the kind of poorly understood, parrotted imitations that psychologists usually study are unlikely to reflect the acquisition of grammatical knowledge.

3. Linguistic forms can be imitated for their own sake, with no particular goal in mind. But they can also be imitated as means to some communicative goal—even when the child has no understanding of the internal structure of a particular form. Imitations used as social tools, like imitations that follow vehicle–referent analysis, probably will not be recorded as imitations in most acquisition studies. If they are included under a researcher's criteria for imitation, then strong individual differences are likely to emerge. Children may vary greatly in their willingness to use a linguistic form as a social means prior to understanding of that form. In other words, children may vary in the degree to which they use "formulaic" (i.e., arbitrary and unanalyzed) versus "propositional" speech (i.e., forms which have been broken down into parts and analyzed for the substitutability of items within frames).

In Chapter 2, Peirce's three types of vehicle–referent relations (icons, indices, arbitrary symbols) were related to two modes of processing: perception of similarity and perception of contiguity. In the next section, we will concentrate on the interaction of these two processing modes in symbolic development, in relation to some of the issues we have raised about individual differences among children.

The Iconicity–Arbitrariness Continuum in Symbol Development

The Iconicity–Arbitrariness Continuum in Language: Individual Differences

To reiterate, we have proposed here that the acquisition and use of vehicle–referent relations involves two processes: perception of similarity and perception of contiguity. Perception of similarity is more likely to be involved in tool use and similar symbolic processes. Whole relationships are broken down into subparts, and the substitutability of subparts is determined by extracting structural similarities (iconicities) that link vehicle to referent, and structural and functional similarities between the vehicle and potential substitutes for that vehicle. Perception of contiguity is involved, on the other hand, in the incorporation of vehicle–referent relations as wholes, purely by association and without necessarily analyzing the nature of the relationship that unites vehicle to referent or permits substitution of one vehicle for another. Imitation provides a means for incorporating and reproducing such arbitrary relationships. Through it, opportunities for analysis can be repeated and prolonged. When sign–referent relations (either arbitrary or analyzed) are exercised in the absence of a goal, the resulting behaviors can be described as exploration and play. When the same sign–referent relations are involved in problem solving, they are described as means–end relations. Insofar as means–end or sign–referent relations can be **partially** analyzed, it is possible for a given relationship to occupy any point along the continuum flanked by iconicity and arbitrariness, perception of similarity and perception of contiguity (see Chapter 2, page 63).

Jerry Morgan (1977) has developed a model for synchronic and diachronic analysis of speech acts, along a continuum very similar to the one proposed here. The model is presented to resolve a controversy over the underlying structure of indirect speech acts like *Can you possibly reach the salt?* The surface form of this speech act is a question, not a command. And yet speakers of English invariably interpret such a question as a request to pass the salt. What sort of linguistic model can describe the native speaker's competence to interpret indirect speech acts?

One model has been offered by Gordon and Lakoff (1971) and by Searle (1975). According to these proposals, the construction and interpretation of indirect speech acts is carried out through reference to a series of conversational postulates (Grice, 1975) or rules about the way lawful conversation is carried out. For example, one conversational rule dictates that speakers will not ask "insincere" questions, i.e., questions requiring answers that are of no interest to either party. Obviously under normal conditions I am not particularly interested in anyone's ability to reach out and pick up a salt shaker. However, such an ability **is** what is called a "felicity condition," a condition that is essential for a request to work. A conversational postulate governing commands is that one does not sincerely request a behavior if the listener is known to be incapable of carrying out that request. Hence being able to reach the salt is a felicity condition for the implicit request, "Pass the salt." By referring to the felicity condition for a request, in a situation in which the normal conditions for a question do not hold, the speaker signals that this utterance is indeed **not** a question but a lead-in to a request. In normal discourse, the lead-in alone is enough. Obviously this model for producing and comprehending indirect forms requires a great deal of analysis of the whole form into a series of explicit and implicit parts. Furthermore, the general rules for producing such indirect forms (i.e., by a combination of felicity conditions and conversational dictums) are highly productive, useful for producing an infinite set of indirect forms.

A different model has been proposed by Sadock (1974). Sadock suggests that many indirect forms are idioms, formulae that are **not** created anew for each item by the application of conversational rules. He marshals evidence to show that idiomatic indirect speech acts are "syntactically defective"; that is, they function as whole, unbreakable phrases that cannot receive the full set of transformations that normal sentences undergo. Given an idiom like *John kicked the bucket,* one cannot grammatically use the passive version of the idiom, "The bucket was kicked by John." Similarly, idiomatic requests like *Can you open the window?* do not function syntactically like normal questions. Sadock does not deny that many indirect speech forms are produced anew through application of conversational rules. However, he demonstrates that the generative speech acts differ syntactically from idiomatic or formulaic speech acts. For example, I can say *Can you please open the window?* but not *Do you please think it's stuffy in here?* Only formulas can take sentence internal "please." Generative indirect requests cannot. According to this model, formulaic indirect requests are acquired or used as whole forms that not only do not, but cannot undergo analysis of the structure into substitutable parts within frames.

Morgan suggests a resolution between these two positions, in which indirect speech acts can be ordered along a continuum from phrases where the relationship between the linguistic means and the communicative goals is analyzable and understandable, to phrases where the relationship between means and goals is no longer transparent. This is essentially the iconicity-to-arbitrariness continuum that we have been discussing here. Morgan suggests that historically many idioms may have originated as transparent, generative phrases in which the means–end relationship was clear. Over time, as the contexts of use increase in variability, the initial context of derivation may be lost. For example, there is an idiomatic "good luck" phrase used by actors before going on stage: *Break a leg!* This particular phrase originated productively from an old superstition that one must wish the opposite of what one desires to "fool" the fates. Apparently a variety of such forms were once possible, produced generatively from this single principle. This custom has become frozen into the single curse just noted. Of course, this form is not entirely opaque. We could probably make a good guess about its origins without being told. There are other examples, however, that have completely lost their origins for most people, like *Goodbye.*

Since this is a continuum rather than a dichotomous classification, we can compare linguistic forms in terms of their relative transparency, e.g., *How do you do?* bears a less obvious relationship to its origins than *How are you?* And so forth. Morgan suggests that historically the direction is typically from analyzed to idiomatic uses of a phrase. In development, on the other hand, the direction of movement across the continuum is often the reverse. At any given point in history and/or for any given individual within a language group, there are linguistic forms that correspond to varying degrees of means–end analysis (or analyzability). Partially analyzed forms may be partially productive in the sense that variations can be made within the formula. However, such partially productive forms may nevertheless bear an obscure relationship to their origins.

There is even evidence (reviewed in Kempler, 1977, and Van Lancker, 1975) suggesting that idiomatic or "automatic" speech involves a different neural basis from propositional speech. For example, there are various forms of aphasia in which idioms remain intact (including partially productive idioms with slots for new lexical items) when propositional or purely productive speech has been lost. Stimulation of the limbic centers in animals may result in elicitation of innate call sounds, threat cries, etc. Stimulation of the corresponding center in humans has been found to result in cursing and/or the elicitations of idioms like *Pardon me.* In recovery from aphasia, there is some evidence that idioms are regained before propositional speech. Finally, there is also a certain amount of evidence pointing to greater involvement of the right hemisphere in the production of formulaic speech by normals.

The suggestions that the two modes have a different neural base does not mean, however, that they are dichotomous. Van Lancker presents a hypothetical continuum from propositional to automatic speech (see Figure 7.2) including a great many forms that lie at the border between these two modes of analysis and use. Examples of forms at the midpoint are "social chatter" and semi-productive conversational expressions like *Is that so? I wouldn't have imagined that X.* Presumably, differences in neural wiring apply not to the expressions themselves, but to the separate modes of acquiring and recalling those expressions. Partially analyzed speech forms would, according to this proposal, involve use of both modes. **I suggest that the perception of contiguity versus the perception of similarity may be, in some direct or indirect fashion, the two modes that create the opposite ends of the continuum from automatic to propositional speech.**

There is evidence, then, for both the linguistic and perhaps the neurolinguistic reality of the iconicity–arbitrariness continuum. So far this continuum has been used to classify different linguistic forms, and the changes that occur in those forms during language development, language loss, and language history. **A further proposal is that many individual differences in style of language acquisition may be based on differential use of the processes that underlie this continuum.**

The literature on individual differences in language acquisition has grown in the last few years. After an initial emphasis on universal sequences and strategies in language development, researchers have come to realize that there is more than one way to acquire a given language. Nelson (1973) was perhaps the first in recent times to draw out attention to different styles in early speech. Since then, a number of related papers have appeared by other authors. While the content varies, these studies point to two predominant styles.

1. First, Nelson (1973) described the period in which children acquire the first 50 words, noting that two distinct vocabulary patterns are clearly discernible in a sample of 18 children. The first group, termed "referential" children, tend to specialize in names of objects. The second group, termed "expressive" children, are more likely to pick up whole phrases (e.g., *Don't do that*) and lexical items that function more to regulate social interaction than to classify and identify things in the world. Interestingly, the referential children tend to be firstborns while expressive children tend to be laterborn. Since the literature on birth order reveals greater linguistic proficiency through life in firstborns (for a review, see Bates, 1975), this finding suggests that the referential children (whether by cause or by coincidence we do not know) have a better "prognosis" for later language development. Starr (1974) has shown that these two styles are consistent from the one-word level studied by Nelson through to two-word speech; to my knowledge there are no studies following the two types of children beyond early word combinations. Nelson attributes

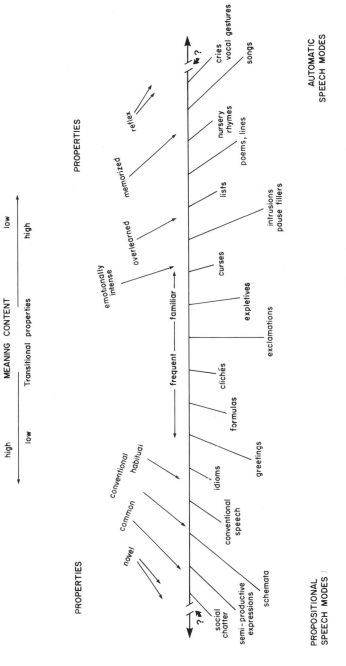

Figure 7.2. A hypothetical continuum of propositional and automatic speech. (Redrawn from Van Lancker, 1975.)

this stylistic difference at the early stages to a greater object orientation in expressive children. And indeed, Rosenblatt (1975) has reported that referential children are more likely to play alone with objects, expressive children are more likely to seek social interaction.

2. Dore (1974), with a sample of two children at the beginning of one-word speech, has noted that one child specialized in the speech act of labelling. The other, at an equivalent stage, tended to babble in adultlike sentence contours without lexical content. He suggests that the former (the "word baby") may be more oriented toward the referential function of language, the latter (the "intonation baby") places greater weight on the "orectic attitude" or communicative function of linguistic expressions. This pattern may well be the predecessor of Nelson's referential versus expressive styles, although there is to my knowledge no data demonstrating this longitudinally.

3. Ramer (1976) has replicated Nelson's referential versus expressive styles, but reports that the expressive style is typical of children who are slower at language learning overall (despite the apparent precocity for a brief time when the use of unanalyzed expressions produces greater MLU's in the expressive children). In addition to their greater use of conversational formulaes, the expressive children are also more likely to use "dummy forms" that give the illusion of adult syntactic rhythms without content. For example, "schwa" sounds are used in the place of articles and other morphemes prior to acquisition of the appropriate inflection for those rhythmic slots. Dummy words with no apparent meaning (e.g., similar to the expression *wida* used by Bloom's subject Allison) occur frequently, giving one-word expressions the "look" of longer sentences. Finally, the expressive children are more likely to use pronouns than nominals. Although pronouns are certainly not devoid of meaning, they are less referentially specific and, like dummy forms, can occur in a wider range of sentence types than particular names (see also Leonard, 1975).

4. Bloom, Lightbown, and Hood (1974), as noted earlier, report that some children are more likely to engage in overt imitation than others. They also report a greater tendency toward pronoun use by the children who are more frequent imitators.

5. In a study of somewhat older children (between MLU 3.0–5.5), Horgan (1977) examined the complexity and patterning of speech in show versus fast language learners. She reports that the more precocious children tend to produce longer and more elaborate noun phrases, and generally talk more about people and things. The slower children have lengthier verb phrases, fewer and less elaborate noun phrases, and tend to engage in less description of people and things. Although Horgan does not make this leap, it seems fair to ask whether the longer verb phrases (e.g., use of auxiliaries, modals) may be the results of a greater

use of stock phrases; the longer noun phrases in the precocious children tend to involve more productive and varied descriptions.

A pattern emerges from these studies in which expressive, idiomatic, imitative, and empty forms seem to be found in one type of child; more productive and descriptive speech typifies the acquisitions of the other type. In addition, the "whole form" style is associated with later and/or slower language acquisition; the productive, analytic form is associated with linguistic precocity. I suggest that the "expressive" child tends to employ acquisition through perception of contiguity, imitating and using unanalyzed phrases as means to ends prior to analysis of vehicle–referent relations. The "referential" child is faster at analysis, so that the use of imitated whole forms is short-lived and infrequent. When he does imitate (i.e., carry out vehicle–vehicle matching in acquiring new speech forms), he may do so in parallel with and/or following a rapid break-down of the new form into its components and the relationships into which that form can enter. Hence his imitations, as noted earlier, do not look like imitations in the ordinary language sense of parrotted ex-pressions.

Both arbitrary and analyzed learning are necessary for rapid and efficient acquisition of language. Nevertheless, individuals may vary in the "relative" use of one process over another, and in the timing of analysis with imitation. This general stylistic difference may yield the varying phenomena reported so far in the individual difference litera-ture in language acquisition. Furthermore, it is possible that this differ-ence in language development may reflect parallel tendencies in other aspects of symbol development, including play and tool use. We will turn now to some possible application of the iconicity–arbitrariness con-tinuum outside of language.

The Iconicity–Arbitrariness Continuum Outside Language: Individual Differences

Gardner and his associates (Shotwell, Wolf, and Gardner, in prepara-tion; Wolf and Gardner, 1979) are currently carrying out a longitu-dinal study of symbolic play, drawing and clay modelling, and several other aspects of symbolic functioning. In a proposal very relevant to the approach taken in this book they report that there are two general styles discernible across symbolic development in all these domains. One style is termed the "patterner." These children seen most interested in break-ing patterns down, permuting their possibilities, setting up symmetries, generally transforming the input model. The other children, termed "dramatists," are particularly concerned with approximations to reality, developing dramatic themes along socially related lines in play, preserv-ing the proper details in drawing, etc. Hence the dramatists are interested in preserving the input model, or developing it along conventional lines. I should note that Gardner does not use these particular terms in interpreting the two different styles. He prefers an interpretation in terms of "preferred modalities," for example, greater visual orientation in patterners. Taking some license with his findings, however, I suggest that these pervasive styles in symbol development may result from differential use of arbitrary versus analyzed learning. The dramatists are more oriented toward preserving whole patterns through perception of contiguity and imitation. The patterners are more interested in rapid part–whole analysis, extraction of similarities, and substitutions within frames.

While the Gardner study is clearly most relevant to the proposals put forth in this paper, there are some other possible relationships to an older literature on "cognitive styles":

1. Kagan (1962) has reported a difference between "reflective" versus "impulsive" children. The impulsive child tends to seize a new means and employ it without careful analysis. The reflective child waits, watches, and considers before adopting a new technique.

2. Another pervasive difference in cognitive style has been termed "field dependence" versus "field independence" (e.g., Witkin *et al.*, 1967). Field-dependent children and adults tend to be controlled more by the objective perceptual properties of the situation; field-independent children are more likely to impose internal interpretations on the same perceptual field.

Other cognitive styles bearing striking similarities to the above two have also been reported in the individual difference literature. All of them seem to overlap to a considerable extent regarding the amount of internal control an individual exercises in a given cognitive task, versus the degree to which performance fluctuates as a function of external factors. Although the authors typically avoid direct suggestions that one style is "better" than another, it is always clear in this literature that "reflectivity" and "field independence" tend to be identified with more precocious and/or more efficient performance in a variety of tasks.

Table 7.2 summarizes these various patterns of individual differences sorted into two columns that reflect the overlap that I perceive among them. With regard to the model suggested here, I propose that the tendency to engage in more arbitrary and unanalyzed use of sign–referent and means–end relations may be related to impulsivity and field dependence. By contrast, the rapid analysis of sign–referent relations and the extraction of iconicities may be related to reflectivity and field independence. This interpretation is supported by the fact that more precocious learning characterizes "referential," "field independent," and "reflective" styles. However, the proposal that all these diverse literatures

TABLE 7.2
Evidence for Individual Styles in Symbol Development

Style 1	Style 2
Referential (Nelson)	Expressive (Nelson)
-- predominance of nouns in first 50 words -- interest in labelling	-- heterogeneity of form class in first 50 words -- focus on social uses of language
-- first borns predominate -- solitary play with objects (Rosenblatt) -- consistency of style to two-word stage (Starr) -- typical of more advanced language learners (Ramer, Horgan)	-- later borns predominate -- social orientation in play (Rosenblatt) -- consistency of style to two-word stage (Starr) -- typical of later language learners (Ramer, Horgan)
Propositional Speech (van Lancker)	Formulaic Speech (van Lancker)
-- associated with left hemisphere	-- associated with right hemisphere
Word-Babies (Dore)	Intonation Babies (Dore)
-- single word utterances -- oriented toward labelling	-- contentless babbling with sentence contours -- oriented toward social functions of language
Elaboration of noun phrases in multiword speech (Bloom *et al.*)	Elaboration of verb phrases in multiword speech (Bloom *et al.*)
High noun/pronoun ratio (Bloom *et al.*)	High pronoun/noun ratio (Bloom *et al.*)
Relatively low use of imitation (Bloom *et al.*; Leonard)	Relatively high use of imitation (Bloom *et al.*; Leonard)
First references to speaker and hearer by name	First references to speaker and hearer by pronoun
No use of empty "Dummy" forms (Leonard)	Use of empty "Dummy" forms (Leonard)
Patterners (Wolf and Gardner, 1979)	Dramatists (Wolf and Gardner, in press)
-- interest in rearranging and playing with component parts	-- interest in reproducing realistic patterns
Elaborated Code, middle class (Bernstein)	Restricted Code, working class (Bernstein)
Field Independence (Witkin)	Field Dependence (Witkin)
Reflective (Kagan)	Impulsive (Kagan)
	Formulaic approach to second language learning in older children (Fillmore)

share some common factor does not mean that the two (if there are only two) styles create the same results in every domain. The consequences of a tendency toward arbitrary versus iconic learning will be very different depending on the particular application.

The reader may have already noted a parallel between all these bipolar styles, and recent (perhaps overpopularized) evidence for hemispheric specialization. It has been proposed (Corballis and Beale, 1976) that the right hemisphere is implicated in "holistic" or synthetic processing, the left hemisphere in sequential, analytic processing. These two different modes do bear at least a superficial relationship to the range of individual differences reviewed here. Most of us, however, have both hemispheres. Insofar as both styles will be essential for the acquisition of culture, we are discussing nothing more than a relative "weighting" of one process over another in development.

A final note on these two styles in development comes from a colleague of ours, regarding parallels between talking and walking in two of her sons. One child learned to walk one step at a time, hesitating after each step until balance was regained. The other began walking by essentially running and falling, correcting himself a little at a time until he had the whole pattern worked out. The more conservative child applied a similar strategy in acquiring single words beginning with one or two well-articulated syllables and making no effort to use the rest of a longer word until he had it right. The other child slurred through whole words with a large number of phonological errors, but preserved the rhythmic patterns of the whole word long before the details were worked out. With a sample of two this coincidence could of course be nothing more than that. But it does at least suggest that processes involved in language acquisition may have consequences in a wide variety of domains.

Heterochrony and the Biology of Symbols

In Chapter 1, a three-part argument was presented concerning the emergence of complex systems:

1. Nature builds new machinery out of old parts.
2. The transmission of new machinery from one generation to the next may involve the same construction route, putting together the same old parts that led to the discovery in the first place.
3. The construction route itself may be selected for through a process called "heterochrony," that is, changes in the relative timing of dissociable components, such that "quantitative differences" in growth lead to "qualitatively different interactions" among the components.

Most of this book has been devoted to the first two arguments. We have used the correlational method to isolate some possible "old parts" that may go into the emergence of symbols in human infancy. It is at least arguable that the same combinations of components that we witness in ontogeny were involved in the evolution of language and human culture. What does timing have to do with any of this?

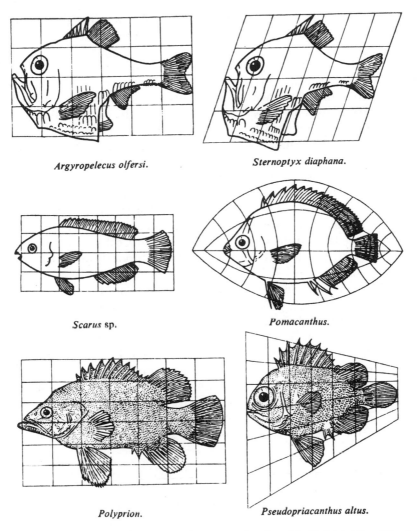

Argyropelecus olfersi.

Sternoptyx diaphana.

Scarus sp.

Pomacanthus.

Polyprion.

Pseudopriacanthus altus.

Figure 7.3. *Comparisons of the topological structure of various fish. (Reprinted from Thompson, 1917.)*

Gould has argued that the evolution of human culture (of the human capacity for acquisition of culture) involved a particular heterochronous process called "neoteny" in which juvenile characteristics are selected for incorporation into the adult phenotype. Juvenile primates are notable for their marked curiosity and interest in learning new things; this capacity for learning presumably has material causal correlates in the form of greater neural plasticity. If this neural plasticity were incorporated in the adult organism, we would have a species with a markedly increased capacity for learning in comparison with other primate adults.

The adult would, in a sense, manifest a sort of "cognitive gigantism" by continuing to grow long beyond the point where his ancestors ceased growing.

A second point that Gould raises is that heterochrony can apply "selectively" to dissociable components (i.e., components with different growth algorithms). His own examples involve fairly simple dimensions like size versus shape in body structure. Perhaps the clearest illustrations of such size–shape interactions (cited in Gould as well) come from Thompson's (1917) comparison of the topological structure of various fish. In Figure 7.3, there are a series of pairs of fish with very different bodily forms. However, a point-to-point Cartesian analysis of these forms reveals that for each pair, the fish on the left is topologically identical to the fish on the right. In other words, these animals come from the same structural blueprint, to which different growth algorithms have been applied: Same deep structure, different transformations, different surface structures—a sort of underwater transformational grammar.

We can make an analogous argument for complex cognitive outcomes. Gould has suggested a "general" change in the growth patterns for cognition, through selection for juvenile neural plasticity in the adult primate. It is possible, however, that some specific cognitive components were advanced ahead of others, until some critical levels were reached permitting the new capacity for symbols to emerge. It is undoubtedly the case that a complex capacity like symbolization requires far more components than the few candidates we have isolated in our correlational studies. However, to explore the role of heterochrony in the evolution of symbols, let us assume for the moment that only three capacities are involved:

1. the capacity for imitation of poorly understood behaviors (Veh_s–Veh_0 analysis)
2. the capacity to analyze whole situations into parts, and locate substitutes for missing parts (Veh_s–Ref_s analysis)
3. a social motivation to communicate, verbally or nonverbally, through sharing reference to external objects, e.g., pointing, giving, etc. (functional intent)

We will abbreviate these capacities to "imitation," "tool use," "communicative intent"—although the reader should keep in mind that we are talking about the capacities that underlie behaviors rather than the behaviors themselves.

Let us also assume that these three capacities are in some way quantifiable. That is, by examining the organism's behavior, we can talk about and perhaps even measure "degrees" or "levels" of these three abilities. This is of course an enormous assumption. The best measures we have are ordinal scales. That is, we have items that sequence reasonably well within imitation, tool use, and communication. However, many of these items are very unevenly spaced across development. For example, in the Uzgiris–Hunt means–end scale, children pass rapidly from pulling a cloth to pulling a string to obtain a goal. The next step—using a stick to rake in the goal—takes much longer. We cannot assume interval data from such ordinal measures. In our current work, we are trying to construct measures that sequence much more evenly across development, so that we can use the child's level of development on the ordinal scale as an estimate of interval or degree in a hypothetical underlying capacity (see Chapter 6). For example, we are trying to locate items **between** string pulling and raking with a stick, forming a more evenly graded continuum of development in tool use. Even if we are successful in this effort, **all the arguments that follow about interacting levels rest on the assumption that ordinal behaviors can be used to estimate interval capacities.**

For purposes of argument, then, we have assumed a minimodel of language development involving three quantifiable capacities: imitation, tool use, communicative intent. In phylogeny, there is reason to believe that these three capacities predated the emergence of language. That is, they were "preadapted" in the service of different functions. **However, once certain critical threshold levels were reached in each of these three domains, it was possible for the same three capacities to join in the service of a new function, the symbolic capacity.** This notion of critical levels is illustrated in Figure 7.4, plotting time against amount for each ability. The dotted lines indicate subthreshold amounts; the unbroken lines indicate that a necessary and sufficient amount of each capacity is now present for use in symbolization. Once threshold is reached in all three domains, a qualitatively new pattern of interaction can emerge, illustrated in Figure 7.4 by the double line for symbolic capacity.

This sort of threshold model is quite common in more precise sciences, for example in models of drug interactions as a function of dosage level. Unfortunately the application of this model to complex behavior is a science fiction enterprise at this point. However, in the model we have described, several interesting questions can be raised. First, what is the threshold level of each of these skills underlying symbols? How much imitative capacity must an animal have to arrive at the "critical moment" of symbol use? How much skill in part–whole analysis? Second, once the threshold level is reached in each domain, will further increases in symbolization require **more** of the component skills? Or is symbol development from that point on dependent only on exercise, on inputs from other domains, etc., with increases in imitation, tool use, or communicative intent having no further impact? This is essentially the issue raised in Chapter 6 regarding predictive strength. For example, it may be that tool use at 9 months involves a capacity that feeds into the 13-month discovery that things have names. Beyond that point, how-

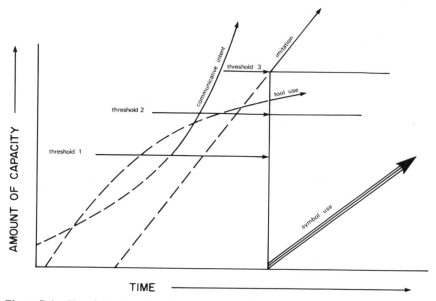

Figure 7.4. *Hypothetical model of the quantitative development of various components of symbol use. (Dotted lines represent subthreshold degrees of capacity; solid lines represent degrees of capacity beyond threshold.)*

ever, "more" tool use capacity may be irrelevant to "more" naming. If we are successful in constructing better ordinal measures for estimating these three capacities, we may be able to determine the levels that are typically reached when symbolization begins, as well as degrees of change in these component skills as symbol use increases. We would predict correlations at least up to the moment of symbol development. However, if criterial levels are sufficient and no further inputs are required for symbol development, then correlations between symbol use and the three component skills may drop to zero in the next few months.

This model may also be useful for comparative work, including comparisons between normal and abnormal development in human children, as well as comparisons across species. We would predict that some language disorders involve limitations in one or more of the components that permit normal language development. For example, children may reach threshold levels in communicative intent and imitation, but remain subthreshold in the analytic capacity involved in tool use. If this were the case, the interaction permitting symbolization could not take place. If we could measure these three capacities "outside" of symbol use, we might be able to pinpoint the "problem area(s)" in this particular child's language delay syndrome. It would be interesting to see whether training in the problem domain could bring the child up to the same levels of competence that characterize normal children when language begins. If that child then showed improvement in language, we would have strong support for the theory of critical thresholds in prerequisite capacities.

What about the symbol-using chimpanzees? If they do not have criterial levels of imitation and/or tool use, how do they learn to use symbols at all? This raises still another question, regarding "prosthetics" or "shortcuts" in language development. For example, suppose that imitation skills permit the acquisition of culture because they facilitate the use of poorly understood behaviors as means to cultural ends. If we can find an alternate route, another way that the animal could master the same poorly understood cultural acts, then the contribution of imitation would no longer be required. In the chimpanzee studies, the "alternate route" to the acquisition of symbols seems to be simple operant conditioning. The animal's hands are literally placed in the shape of the ASL sign (Gardner and Gardner, 1969). Rewards are contingent upon increasingly correct executions of the hand movement. **If a child or chimp does not have criterial levels in one of the component skills leading to symbolization, it may be possible either (*a*) to bring him to criterion through training, or (*b*) find a "prosthetic" or substitute for the component skill.**

A final issue regards individual differences in the "style" of symbol development. It was suggested earlier that the so-called "expressive" style of language development involves greater reliance on imitation of unanalyzed or partially analyzed idioms and formulae, while the "referential" style involves proportionally more vehicle–referent analysis. A similar suggestion was made for the difference between dramatists and patterners in the Gardner *et al.* study of symbol development, with dramatists employing imitation and reproduction of things as they are, while patterners break configurations down into part–whole relations and play with various substitute parts. How do such individual difference come about?

One possibility is that the different styles are acquired through experience. For example, some maternal teaching styles may facilitate an imitative strategy while others foster part–whole analysis. Nelson's (1973) study indicated that firstborns are more likely to become referential children, while laterborns were more likely to develop an expressive style. This would suggest that experiential factors of some sort do indeed influence styles of symbol use. It is also possible, however, that genetic differences between children may increase the likelihood of one or the other of these "routes into language." Returning to the model in Figure 7.4, suppose that Child A develops the criterial level of imitation fairly early relative to other children, or for that matter relative to his own basic growth pattern. By contrast, the criterial level of tool use is available relatively late. When symbolization is finally possible, this child might rely more upon the "stronger" or more mature of his two capacities as he begins the process of symbol development. Child B may show a different pattern, with relative precocity in part–whole analysis compared with the growth of imitative skills. Once criterial levels were available in both domains, Child B would be more likely to rely on his skills at part–whole analysis in acquiring language. **In other words, complex differences in strategy and style might be the result of rather simple differences in the relative timing of component skills.** Again, a simple genetic input results in a complex phenotypic result. This is one area in which behavior genetic research (e.g., twin studies, adoption studies) might contribute to our understanding of language development and the acquisition of culture.

To conclude, we have provided the rough outlines of a biological model for the emergence of symbols. Our results indicate that, at least by 13 months of age, symbol development is modality free. That is, correlations in frequency, level, onset time, and content suggest that gestural and vocal naming are part of the same process. The emergence of symbols is in turn correlated with imitation, tool use, and manipulative play, and the frequency and sophistication of preverbal communication. We know much less about the role of social factors in symbol development. As noted in Chapter 5, individual differences in quality of mother–child attachment are poor predictors of language development, although attachment does relate to symbolic play, tool use, and preverbal communication. We need to know much more about social, "dialogic" constraints on symbolization, in particular those aspects of the parent–child interaction that relate to language acquisition.

For that matter, we need to know much more about everything. Our readers have been very patient, if they have made it to this point, in tolerating a very large ratio of theory to data. Some researchers find the search for nonlinguistic prerequisites to language a frustrating enterprise, since there are so many places to look once we get out of the domain of language proper. They recommend that we restrict ourselves to a detailed description of the object of study (i.e., language). While we agree that "descriptive" studies of language itself are important, we do not believe that they are sufficient to arrive at "explanatory" models of language acquisition.

There is a very, very old joke about a drunk who loses his keys in the bushes late one night. A passerby finds him on his hands and knees, searching a bare piece of pavement directly under a streetlight. "What happened?" asks the stranger. "I lost my keys in the bushes," replied the drunk. "Then why are you looking here?" the stranger asked in bewilderment. The response was one we can all sympathize with: "Because it's so much easier to look out here in the light." We are engaged in a very difficult enterprise thrashing about in the darkness for the causes of the human capacity for symbols. It may be easier to look in the light, but we will have to do what we are doing if we are going to find the key.

REFERENCES

Ainsworth, M. D. S. The development of infant–mother attachment. In B. M. Caldwell and H. M. Ricciuti (Eds.), *Review of child development research 3*. New York: Russell Sage Foundation, 1973, Pp. 1–94.

Ainsworth, M. D. S., and Bell, S. M. Some contemporary patterns of mother–infant interaction in the feeding situation. In J. A. Ambrose (Ed.), *Stimulation in early infancy*. London: Academic Press, 1969. Pp. 133–170.

Ainsworth, M. D. S., and Bell, S. M. Mother–infant interaction and the development of competence. In K. J. Connolly and J. Bruner (Eds.), *The growth of competence*. New York: Academic Press, 1974.

Ainsworth, M. D. S., Blehar, M. C., Waters, E., and Wall, S. *Patterns of attachment: A psychological study of the strange situation*. Hillsdale, N.J.: Lawrence Erlbaum Associates, 1978.

Ainsworth, M. D. S. and Wittig, B. A. Attachment and exploratory behavior of one-year-olds in a strange situation. In B. M. Foss (Ed.), *Determinants of infant behavior*, vol. 4. London: Methuen, 1969. Pp. 111–136.

Ammon, P. R. Cognitive development and early childhood education: Piagetian and neo-Piagetian Theories. In H. L. Hom and P. A. Robinson (Eds.), *Psychological processes in early education*. New York: Academic Press, 1977.

Austin, J. L. *How to do things with words*. Cambridge: Oxford University Press, 1963.

Bayley, N. Value and limitations of infant testing. *Children*, 1958, 5, 129.

Baron, N., Insensee, L., and Davis, A. *Iconicity and learnability: Teaching sign language to autistic children*. Paper presented at the Second Annual Boston University Conference on Child Language Development, Boston, September 1977.

Bates, E. Peer relations and the acquisition of language. In M. Lewis and L. Rosenblum (Eds.) *Friendship and peer relations.* New York: Wiley, 1975.

Bates, E. *Language and context: The acquisition of pragmatics.* New York: Academic Press, 1976.

Bates, E. The emergence of symbols: Ontogeny and phylogeny. In W. Collins (Ed.), *Proceedings from the 12th Minnesota Symposium in Child Development.* Hillsdale, N.J.: Lawrence Erlbaum Associates, in press.

Bates, E., Benigni, L., Bretherton, I., Camaioni, L., and Volterra, V. *Cognition and communication from 9–13 months: A correlational study.* Institute for the Study of Intellectual Behavior Technical Report: Program on Cognitive and Perceptual Factors in Human Development Report #12. University of Colorado, Boulder, 1977.

Bates, E. Benigni, L., Bretherton, I., Camaioni, L., and Volterra, V. From gesture to the first word: On cognitive and social prerequisites. In M. Lewis and L. Rosenblum (Eds.), *Interaction, conversation, and the development of language.* New York: John Wiley and Sons, 1977. Pp. 247–307.

Bates, E., Camaioni, L., and Volterra, V. The acquisition of performatives prior to speech. *Merrill-Palmer Quarterly,* 1975, *21*(3), 205–226.

Bates, E., and MacWhinney, B. A functionalist approach to the acquisition of grammar. In E. Kennan (Ed.), *Developmental pragmatics.* New York: Academic Press, 1978.

Bates, E., and Rankin, J. Morphological development in Italian: Connotation and denotation. *Journal of Child Language,* in press.

Bayley, N. Value and limitations of infant testing. *Children,* 1958, *5,* 129.

Beeghly-Smith, M., and Bretherton, I. *Adult style and infant effects in interactions.* Paper presented at the Biennial Meeting of the Society for Research in Child Development, San Francisco, 1979.

Bell, S. The development of the concept of the object as related to infant–mother attachment. *Child Development,* 1970, *41,* 291–313.

Bell, S. M. *Cognitive development and mother–child interaction in the first three years of life: A study of black disadvantaged children.* Final Report to the Office of Child Development, 1978.

Bell, S. M., and Ainsworth, M. D. S. Infant crying and maternal responsiveness. *Child Development,* 1972, *43,* 1171–1190.

Blehar, M. C., Lieberman, A. F., and Ainsworth, M. D. S. Early face-to-face interaction and its relation to later infant–mother attachment. *Child Development,* 1977, *48,* 182–194.

Bloom, L. *Language development: Form and function in emerging grammar.* Cambridge, Mass.: MIT Press, 1970.

Bloom. L. *One word at a time.* The Hague: Mouton, 1973.

Bloom, L., Hood, L. and Lightbown, P. Imitation in language development: If, when, and why. *Cognitive Psychology,* 1974, *6,* 380–420.

Bolk, L. *Das Problem der Menschwerdung.* Gustav Fischer: Jena, 1926.

Bonvillian, J. D., and Nelson, K. E. Development of sign language in autistic children and other language-handicapped individuals. In P. Siple (Ed.), *Understanding language through sign language research.* New York: Academic Press, 1978.

Bower, T. G. R. Repetitive processes in child development. *Scientific American,* 1976, *235*(5), 38–47.

Bowerman, M. F. Semantic factors in the acquisition of rules for word use and sentence construction. In D. M. Morehead and A. E. Morehead (Eds.), *Normal and deficient child language.* Baltimore: University Park Press, 1976.

Bowlby, J. *Attachment and loss. Vol I: Attachment.* New York: Basic Books, 1969.

Bowlby, J. *Attachment and loss. Volume II: Separation.* New York: Basic Books, 1973.

Braine, M. D. S. Children's first word combinations. *Monographs of the Society for Research in Child Development,* 1976, *41,* serial 164.

Braine, M. D. S. On learning the grammatical order of words. *Psychological Review,* 1963, *39,* 323–348.

Bretherton, I. Young children in stressful situations: The role of attachment figures and unfamiliar caregivers. In G. V. Coelho and P. Ahmed (Eds.), *Uprooting.* New York: Plenum Press, in press.

Bretherton, I. *Beyond wariness: Infants' spontaneous approach to and proximal interaction with unfamiliar adults.* Paper presented at the Biennial Meeting of the Society for Research in Child Development, New Orleans, March 1977.

Brewer W. There is no convincing evidence for operant or classical conditioning in adult humans. In W. Weimar and D. Palerno (Eds.), *Cognition and the symbolic processes.* Hillsdale, N.J.: Lawrence Erlbaum Associates, 1974.

Brown, R. A first language: The early stages. Cambridge, Mass.: Harvard University Press, 1973.

Brown, R. *Why are signed languages easier to learn than spoken languages?* Keynote address to the National Association of the Deaf, 1977.

Brown, R., and Bellugi, U. Three processes in the child's acquisition of syntax. *Harvard Educational Review,* 1964, *34,* 133–151.

Brown, R., Cazden, C., and Bellugi, U. The child's grammar from I to III. In J. P. Hill (Ed.), *Minnesota Symposium on Child Psychology, vol. 2.* Minneapolis: University of Minnesota Press, 1969, 28–73.

Bruner, J. The ontogenesis of speech acts. *Journal of Child Language,* 1975, *2*(1), 1–19. (a).

Bruner, J. From communication to language: a psychological perspective. *Cognition,* 1975, *3,* 255–287.(b)

Bruner, J. S. Early social interaction and language acquisition. In H. R. Schaffer (Ed.), *Studies in mother–infant social interaction.* New York: Academic Press, 1977.

Bruner, J., Olver, R., and Greenfield, P. M. *Studies in cognitive growth.* New York: Wiley, 1966.

Carew, J. V., Cahn, I., and Halfar, C. *Observed intellectual and tested intelligence: Their roots in the young child's transactions with his environment.* Paper presented at the Biennial Meeting of the Society for Research in Child Development, Denver, 1975.

Carlson, V. K. *Causal understanding in the infant.* Unpublished master's thesis, University of Colorado, 1977.

Carter, A. *Communication in the sensorimotor period.* Unpublished doctoral dissertation, University of California at Berkeley, 1974.

Carter, A. The transformation of sensorimotor morphemes into words: A case study of the development of "more" and "mine." *Journal of Child Language,* 1975, *2*(2), 233–250.

Carter, A. *Some evidence for the sensorimotor origins of the expressions "hi" and "bye."* Paper presented to the Society of Research in Child Development, New Orleans, March 1977.

Case, R. Intellectual development from birth to adulthood: A neo-Piagetian interpretation. In R. Siegler (Ed.), *Children's thinking: What develops?* Hillsdale, N.J.: Lawrence Erlbaum Associates, 1978.

Chevalier-Skolnikoff, S. The ontogeny of primate intelligence: Implications for communicative potential. In S. Harnad, H. Steklis, and J. Lancaster (Eds.), *Origins of language and speech.* New York: New York Academy of Sciences, 1977.

Chomsky, N. *Syntactic structures.* The Hague: Mouton, 1957.

Chomsky, N. *Aspects of a theory of syntax.* Cambridge: MIT Press, 1965.

Chomsky, N. *Invited address to the 1977 Convention of the American Speech and Hearing Associations.* Chicago, November 1977.

Clark, E. V. What's in a word? On the child's acquisition of semantics in his first language. In T. E. Moore (Ed.), *Cognitive development and the acquisition of language.* New York: Academic Press, 1973.

Clark, E. V. *Strategies for communicating.* Paper presented at the Biennial Meeting of the Society for Research in Child Development, New Orleans, March 1977.

Clark, P. What's the use of imitation? *Journal of Child Language,* 1977, *1,* 341–358.

Clark, R. Performing without competence. *Journal of Child Language,* 1974, *1,* 1–10.

Clarke-Stewart, K. A. Interactions between mothers and their young children: Characteristics and consequences. *Monographs of the Society for Research in Child Development,* 1973, *38,* serial 153.

Clarke-Stewart, K. A. Personal communication, February 1978.

Connell, D. B. *Individual differences in attachment behavior: Long-term stability and relationships to language development.* Unpublished doctoral dissertation, Syracuse University, 1977.

Corballis, M. C., and Beale, I. L. *The psychology of right and left.* Hillsdale, N.J.: Lawrence Erlbaum Associates, 1976.

Corrigan, R. *The relationship between object permanence and language development: How much and how strong?* Paper presented at the Eighth Annual Stanford Child Language Forum, Stanford, April 1975.

Cross, T. G. Mother's speech adjustments: The contributions of selected child listener variables. In C. E. Snow and C. A. Ferguson (Eds.), *Talking to children: Language input and acquisition.* London: Cambridge University Press, 1977.

Curcio, F. *A study of sensorimotor functioning and communication in mute autistic children.* Unpublished manuscript, Boston University, 1977.

Dale, P. *Language development,* 2nd ed. New York: Holt, Rinehart and Winston, 1976.

Darwin, C. A biographical sketch of an infant. In A. Bar-Adon and W. F. Leopold (Eds.), *Child Language, A book of readings.* Englewood Cliffs, N.J.: Prentice-Hall, 1971.

DeLaguna, G. *Speech: Its function and development.* Bloomington, Indiana: Indiana University Press, 1927.

de Villiers, J. G. *Prototypes in grammatical rule learning.* Paper presented at the Biennial Meeting of the Society for Research in Child Development, San Francisco, 1979.

Donahue, M. L. *Conversational gimmicks: The acquisition of small talk.* Paper presented at the 2nd Annual Boston University Conference of Language Development, September 1977.

Dore, J. *On the development of speech acts.* Unpublished doctoral dissertation. City University of New York, 1973.

Dore, J. A pragmatic description of early language development. *Journal of Psycholinguistic Research,* 1974, *4,* 343–351.

Dore, J. Holophrase, speech acts, and language universals. *Journal of Child Language,* 1975, *2,* 21–40.

Edwards, D. Sensory-motor intelligence and semantic relations in early child grammar. *Cognition,* 1973, *2*(4), 395–434.

Eibl-Eibesfeldt, I. *Ethology: The biology of behavior.* New York: Holt, Rinehart and Winston, 1970.

Ervin, S. Imitation and structural change in children's language. In E. H. Lenneberg (Ed.), *New directions in the study of language.* Cambridge, Mass.: MIT Press, 1964.

Escalona, S. *On precursors of language.* Paper presented at Teachers College, Columbia University, New York, October 1973.

Feldman, C., and M. Shen. Some language-related cognitive advantages of bilingual five-year-olds. *Journal of Genetic Psychology,* 1971, *118,* 235–244.

Ferguson, C. A., and Slobin, D. I. (Eds.), *Studies in child language development.* New York: Holt, Rinehart and Winston, 1973.

Fernald, C. D. Control of grammar in imitation, comprehension, and production: Problems of replication. *Journal of Verbal Learning and Verbal Behavior,* 1972, *11,* 606–613.

Ferreiro, E. *Les relations temporelles dans le language de l'enfant.* Geneva: Droz, 1971.

Fillmore, L. *The second time around: Cognitive and social strategies in second language acquisition.* Unpublished doctoral dissertation, Stanford, 1976.

Fischer, K. W. *A formal theory of cognitive development: Seven levels of understanding.* Manuscript, University of Denver, 1976.

Fischer, K. W. A theory of cognitive development: The control and construction of a hierarchy of skills. *Psychological Review,* in press.

Flavell, J. Stage related properties of cognitive development. *Cognitive Psychology,* 1971, *2,* 421–453.

Fouts, R. S. Acquisition and testing of gestural signs in four young chimpanzees. *Science,* 1973, *180,* 978–980.

Freedle, R., and Lewis, M. Prelinguistic conversations. In M. Lewis and L. A. Rosenblum (Eds.), *Interaction, conversation, and the development of language.* New York: Academic Press, 1977.

Frishberg, N. Arbitrariness and iconicity. In E. Klima and U. Bellugi (Eds.), *The signs of language.* Cambridge, Mass.: Harvard University Press, 1977.

Garcia, J., and Koelling, R. Relation of cue to consequence in avoidance learning. *Psychonomic Science,* 1966, *4,* 123–124.

Gardner, B. T., and Gardner, R. A. Comparing the early utterances of child and chimpanzee. In A. Pick (Ed.), *Minnesota Symposium on Child Psychology,* vol. 8. Minneapolis: University of Minnesota Press, 1974.

Gardner, H. Promising paths toward artistic knowledge: A report from Harvard Project Zero. *Journal of Aesthetic Education,* 1976, *10,* 201–207.

Gardner, J., and Gardner, H. A note on selective imitation by a six-week-old infant. *Child Development,* 1970, *41,* 1209–1213.

Gardner, R. A., and Gardner, B. T. Teaching signs to a chimpanzee. *Science,* 1969, *165,* 664–672.

Gleitman, H., and Rozin, P. The structure and acquisition of reading: Relations between orthographics and the structure of language. In A. Reber and D. Scarborough (Eds.), *Toward a psychology of reading.* Hillsdale, N.J.: Lawrence Erlbaum Associates, 1977.

Goldfarb, W. Psychological privation in infancy and subsequent adjustment. *American Journal of Orthopsychiatry,* 1945, *15,* 247–255.

Goodall, J. Tool using and aimed throwing in a community of free-living chimpanzees. *Nature,* 1964, *201,* 1264–1266.

Goodman, N. *Languages of art.* Indianapolis: Bobbs-Merrill, 1968.

Gordon, D., and Lakoff, G. Conversational postulates. In *Proceedings of the 7th Annual Meeting of the Chicago Linguistic Society.* University of Chicago, April 1971.

Gottlieb, G. Ontogenesis of sensory function in birds and mammals. In E. Toback, L. R. Aronson, and E. Shaw (Eds.), *The biopsychology of development.* New York: Academic Press, 1971.

Gould, S. *Ever since Darwin.* New York: Norton, 1977. (a)

Gould, S. *Ontogeny and phylogeny.* Cambridge, Mass.: Harvard University Press, 1977. (b)

Greenfield, P., and Smith, J. *The structure of communication in early development.* New York: Academic Press, 1976.

Grice, P. Logic and conversation. In P. Cole and J. Morgan (Eds.), *Syntax and semantics. Volume 3: Speech acts.* New York: Academic Press, 1975.

Gruendel, J. *Locative production in the single word utterance period.* Paper presented to the Society for Research in Child Development, New Orleans, April 1977.

Guillaume, P. *Imitation in children.* Chicago: The University of Chicago Press, 1971.

Haeckel, E. *The history of creation,* 2 vols. (trans. E. R. Lankester from 8th ed. of *Natürliche Schöpfungegeschichte*). London: Kegan, Paul, Trench, Trubner & Co., 1892.

Halpern, E., and Aviezer, L. *Psycholinguistic skills and sensory motor development within Piaget's theoretical framework.* Paper presented to the 21st International Congress of Psychology, Paris, July 1976.

Harding, C., and Golinkoff, R. *The origins of intentional vocalizations in prelinguistic infants.* Paper presented at the Biennial Meeting of the Society for Research in Child Development, New Orleans, April 1977.

Harmon, R. J., Suwalsky, J. D., & Klein, R. P. Infants' preferential response for mother versus an unfamiliar adult: Relationship to attachment. *Journal of the American Academy of Child Psychiatry* (in press).

Harnad, S., Steklis, H., and Lancaster, T. (Eds.), *Origins of language and speech.* New York: New York Academy of Sciences, 1977.

Hewes, G. W. An explicit formulation of the relation between tool using and early language emergence. *Visible Language,* 1973, 7(2), 101–127.

Hinde, R. A. *Animal behavior.* New York: McGraw-Hill, 1966.

Hinde, R. A., and Stevenson-Hinde, J. *Constraints on learning.* New York: Academic Press, 1973.

Hock, E. *Alternative approaches to child rearing and their effects on the mother–infant relationship.* Final Report to the Office of Child Development, 1976.

Hockett, C. F. The origin of speech. *Scientific American,* 1960, *203,* 89–96.

Holzman, M. *Where is 'under'? The development from pragmatic to semantic meaning.* Paper presented at the Biennial Meeting of the Society for Research in Child Development, New Orleans, March 1977.

Horgan, D. *Individual differences in the rate of language acquisition.* Paper presented at the Boston Child Language Conference, Boston, October 1977.

Huttenlocher, J. Origins of language comprehension. In R. Solso (Ed.), *Theories in cognitive psychology: The Loyola Symposium.* Potomac, Md.: Lawrence Erlbaum Associates, 1974.

Ingram, D. *Language development in the sensorimotor period.* Paper presented at the Third International Child Language Symposium, London, September 1975.

Inhelder, B. Cognitive development and its contribution to the diagnosis of some phenomena of mental deficiency. *Merrill-Palmer Quarterly,* 1966, *12,* 299–316.

Inhelder, B., Lezine, I., Sinclair, H., and Stambak, W. Les débuts de la fonction symbolique. *Archives de Psychologie,* 1971, *41,* 187–243.

Johnston, T. R., and Ramstad, V. *Cognitive development in children with language disorders.* Paper presented at the Annual Convention of the American Speech and Hearing Association, Chicago, 1977.

Jolly, A. *The evolution of primate behavior.* New York: Macmillan, 1972.

Kagan, T. Emergent themes in human development. *American Scientist,* 1976, *64,* 186–196.

Kagan, J., and Moss, H. *Birth to maturity.* New York: Wiley, 1962.

Katz, J. J., and Bever, T. G. The fall and rise of empiricism. In T. G. Bever, J. J. Katz, and T. Langendoen (Eds.), *An integrated theory of linguistic ability.* New York: Thomas Y. Crowell, 1976.

Kawai, M. Newly acquired pre-cultural behavior of the natural troop of Japanese monkeys on Foshima Islet. *Primates,* 1965, *6*(1), 1–30.

Kaye, K. *Maternal participation in the infant's acquisition of a skill.* Unpublished doctoral dissertation, Harvard University, 1970.

Kaye, K. Toward the origin of dialogue. In H. R. Schaffer (Ed.), *Studies in mother–infant interaction.* New York: Academic Press, 1977.

Keenan, E. O. Making it last: The role of repetition in discourse. In C. Mitchell-Kernan and S. Eervin-Tripp (Eds.), *Child Discourse.* New York: Academic Press, 1977.

Kellogg, W. M., and Kellogg, L. A. *The ape and the child: A study of environmental influence upon early behavior.* New York: McGraw-Hill, 1933.

Kemp, J. C., and Dale, P. S. *Spontaneous imitation and free speech: A grammatical comparison.* Paper presented at the Biennial Meeting of the Society for Research in Child Development, Philadelphia, March 1973.

Kempler, D. *The function of automatic speech.* Honors thesis, University of California at Berkeley, Spring 1977.

Kernberg, O. *Object–relations theory and clinical psychoanalysis.* New York: Jason Aronson, 1976.

Killen, M., and Uzgiris, I. *Imitation of actions with objects: The role of social meaning.* Paper presented at the International Conference on Infant Studies, Providence, Rhode Island, March 1978.

King, M. C., and Wilson, A. C. Evolution at two levels in humans and chimpanzees. *Science,* 1975, *188,* 107–116.

Klahr, D., and Wallace, Jr., G. *Cognitive development: An information processing view.* Hillsdale, N.J.: Lawrence Erlbaum Associates, 1976.

Koestler, A. and Smythises, J. R. (Eds.), *Beyond reductionism: New perspectives in the life sciences.* New York: Macmillan, 1970.

Köhler, W. *The mentality of apes.* New York: Harcourt, 1927.

Kohts, N. *Infant ape and human child:* Scientific memoirs of the Museum Darwinianum in Moscow, 1935.

Lakoff, G. *Linguistic Gestalt.* Invited address to the Chicago Linguistic Society, April 1977.

Langer, S. *Philosophy in a new key.* Cambridge: Harvard University Press, 1962.

Laughlin, C. D., and d'Aquili, E. G. *Biogenetic structuralism.* New York: Columbia University Press, 1974.

Lenneberg, E. H. *The biological foundations of language.* New York: Wiley, 1967.

Leonard, L. B. On differentiating syntactic and semantic features in emerging grammars: Evidence from empty form usage. *Journal of Psycholinguistic Research,* 1975, *4,* 357–363.

Leonard, L. B. The nature of congenital aphasia. *Merrill-Palmer Quarterly,* in press.

Leopold, W. F. *Speech development of a bilingual child: A linguist's record.* Evanston, Ill.: Northwestern University Press, 1939–1949.

Lewis, M., and Rosenblum, L. A. *Interaction, conversation, and the development of language.* New York: Wiley, 1977.

Lock, A. Acts not sentences. In W. von Raffler-Engel and Y. Lebrun (Eds.), *Baby talk and infant speech.* Holland: Swets and Aeitlinger V. B. V., 1976.

Lorenz, K. Der Kumpan in der Umwelt des Vogels. *Ornith,* 1935, *83,* 137–213, 289–413.

MacNamara, J. The cognitive basis of language learning in infants. *Psychological Review,* 1972, *79,* 1–13.

MacNamara, J. (Ed.). *Language, learning, and thought.* New York: Academic Press, 1977.

Main, M. *Exploration, play, and cognitive functioning as related to child–mother attachment.* Unpublished doctoral dissertation. The John Hopkins University, 1973.

Main, M. Security and knowledge. In K. E. G. Grossman (Ed.), *Soziale Grundlagen des Lernens.* Munchen: Kinderverlag, 1976.

Matas, L., Arend, R. A., and Sroufe, L. A. Continuity of adaptation in the second year: The relationship between attachment and later competence. *Child Development,* 1978, 547–556.

Mayer, J., and Valian, V. *When do children imitate? When necessary.* Paper presented to the Boston Child Language Conference, Boston, October 1977.

McNeill, D. The creation of language by children. In J. Lyons and R. Wales (Eds.), *Psycholinguistic papers.* Edinburgh: University of Edinburgh Press, 1966.

Mead, G. H. *Mind, self, and society.* Chicago: University of Chicago Press, 1934.

Meltzoff, A. N., and Moore, K. Imitation of facial and manual gestures by human neonates. *Science,* 1977, *198,* 75–78.

Michotte, A. *The perception of causality.* London: Methuen, 1963.

Miller, W., and Ervin-Tripp, S. The development of grammar in child language. In R. Brown and U. Bellugi (Eds.), The acquisition of language. *Monographs of the Society for Research in Child Development,* 1964, *29,* serial 92.

Moore, K., Clark, D., Mael, M., Dawson-Myers, G., Rajotte, P., and Stoel-Gammon, C. *The relationship between language and object permanence development: A study of Down's syndrome infants and children.* Paper presented to the Society for Research in Child Development, New Orleans, April 1977.

Moore, M. K., and Meltzoff, A. N. Imitation, object permanence, and language development in infancy: Toward a neo-Piagetian perspective on communicative and cognitive development. In F. D. Minifie and L. L. Hoyd (Eds.), *Communicative and cognitive abilities—early behavioral assessment.* Baltimore: University Park Press, 1978.

Moore, T., and Harris, A. Language and thought in Piagetian theory. In L. Siegeland and C. Brainerd (Eds.), *Alternatives to Piaget: Critical essays on the theory.* New York: Academic Press, 1977.

Morehead, D., and Ingram, D. *Early grammatic and semantic relations: Some implications for a general representation deficit in linguistically deviant children.* Paper presented to the American Speech and Hearing Association, 1973.

Morehead, D. M., and Morehead, A. E. (Eds.). *Normal and deficient child language.* Baltimore: University Park Press, 1976.

Morgan, E. *The descent of woman.* New York: Bantam, 1972.

Morgan, J. *The types of convention in indirect speech acts.* Unpublished manuscript, University of Illinois, 1977.

Morris, D. (Ed.). *Primate ethology.* Chicago: Aldine, 1975.

Nelson, K. *Lexical acquisition.* Paper presented to the Society for Research in Child Development, New Orleans, April 1977. (a)

Nelson, K. *How young children represent knowledge of their world in and out of language: A preliminary report.* Paper presented at the 13th Annual Carnegie Symposium on Cognition, Carnegie-Mellon University, May 1977. (b)

Nelson, K. Explorations in the development of a functional semantic system. In W. A. Collins (Ed.), *The 12th Minnesota symposium on child psychology.* Hillsdale, New Jersey: Lawrence Erlbaum Associates, in press.

Nelson, K., Benedict, H., Gruendel, J., and Rescorla, L. *Lessons from early lexicons.* Paper presented to the Society for Research in Child Development, New Orleans, April 1977.

Newport, E., and Ashbrook, E. J. The emergence of semantic relations in A.S.L. *Papers and Reports in Child Language,* 1977, *13,* 16–21.

Newport, E., Gleitman, L, and Gleitiman, H. Mother I'd rather do it myself: some effects and non-effects of motherese. In C. Ferguson and C. Snow (Eds.), *Talking to children.* London: Cambridge University Press, 1977.

Nicolich, L. *A longitudinal study of representational play in relation to spontaneous imitation and development of multiword utterances: Final report.* ERIC Document–PS007 854, 1975.

Odom, R. D. *The decalage from the perspective of a perceptual salience account of developmental change.* Paper presented at the Biennial Meeting of the Society for Research in Child Development, New Orleans, March 1977.

Palmer, S. E. Fundamental aspects of cognitive representation. In E. Rosch and B. B. Lloyd (Eds.), *Cognition and categorization.* Hillsdale, N.J.: Lawrence Erlbaum Associates, 1978.

Parker, S. T. Piaget's sensorimotor series in an infant macaque: A model for comparing unstereotyped behavior and intelligence in human and nonhuman primates. In S. Chevalier-Skolnikoff and F. Poirier (Eds.), *Primate bio-social development: Biological, social, and ecological determinants.* New York: Garland, 1977.

Parker, S. T., and Gibson, K. Object manipulation, tool use, and sensorimotor intelligence as feeding adaptations in cebus monkeys and great apes. *Journal of Human Evolution,* 1977, *6,* 623–641.

Pascual-Leone, J. *A theory of constructive operators, a neo-Piagetian model of conservation, and the problem of horizontal decalages.* Paper presented at the meeting of the Canadian Psychological Association, 1972.

Peirce, C. S. *Collected papers.* C. Jartshorne and P. Weiss (Eds.), Cambridge, Mass.: Harvard University Press, 1932.

Pelkwijk, J. J. ter, and Tinbergen, N. Eine reizbiologische Analyse einiger Verhaltensweisen von *Gasterosteous aculeatus, Zeitschrift fur Tierpsychologie,* 1937, *1,* 193–200.

Pentz, T. *Facilitation of language acquisition: The role of the mother.* Unpublished doctoral dissertation, The John Hopkins University, 1975.

Piaget, J. *The origins of intelligence in children.* New York: International Universities Press, 1952.

Piaget, J. *The construction of reality in the child.* New York: Ballantine, 1954.

Piaget, J. *Play, dreams, and imitation in childhood.* New York: W. W. Norton, 1962.

Piaget, J. *Genetic epistemology.* New York: W. W. Norton, 1970.

Piaget, J. *Structuralism.* New York: Harper & Row, 1971.

Premack, D. Symbols inside and outside of language. In J. Kavanagh and J. E. Cutting (Eds.), *The role of speech in language.* Cambridge, Mass: MIT Press, 1975.

Premack, D. *Intelligence in ape and man.* Hillsdale, N.J.: Lawrence Erlbaum Associates, 1977.

Ramer, A. Syntactic styles in emerging language. *Journal of Child Language,* 1976, *3*(1), 49–62.

Rensch, B. *Homo sapiens: From man to demi-god.* New York: Columbia University Press, 1972.

Rosch, E. Principles of categorization. In E. Rosch and B. B. Lloyd (Eds.), *Cognition and categorization.* Hillsdale, New Jersey: Lawrence Erlbaum Associates, 1978.

Rosch, E., and Mervis, C. B. Family resemblances: Studies in the internal structure of categories. *Cognitive Psychology,* 1975, *7,* 573–605.

Rosenblatt, D. *Learning how to mean: The development of representation in play and language.* Paper presented at the conference on the Biology of Play, Farnham, England, June 1975.

Rumbaugh, D. M., and Gill, T. Language and language-type communication: Studies with a chimpanzee. In M. Lewis and L. Rosenblum (Eds.), *Interaction, conversation, and the development of language.* New York: John Wiley and Sons, 1977.

Ryan, J. Early language development. In M. P. M. Eichards (Ed.), *The integration of the child into a social world.* Cambridge: Cambridge Press, 1974.

Sachs, J., and Truswell, L. Comprehension of two-word instructions by children in the one-word stage. *Journal of Child Language,* 1978, *5,* 17–24.

Sadock, J. *Toward a linguistic theory of speech acts.* New York: Academic Press, 1974.

Sander, L. W. The regulation of exchange in the infant-caregiver system and some aspects of the context–content relationship. In M. Lewis and L. A. Rosenblum (Eds.), *Interaction, conversation, and the development of language.* New York: Wiley, 1977.

Schaffer, H. R. (Ed.). *Studies in mother–infant interaction.* London: Academic Press, 1977.

Schaffer, H. R., and Emerson, P. E. The development of social attachments in infancy. *Monographs of the Society for Research in Child Development,* 1964, *29,* serial 94.

Schank, R. C., and Abelson, R. P. *Scripts, plans, and knowledge.* Paper presented at the 4th International Joint Conference on Artificial Intelligence, 1975.

Schiller, P. H. Innate motor action as a basis of learning. In C. H. Schiller (Ed.), *Instinctive behavior.* New York: International Universities Press, 1957.

Schlesinger, I. M. Relational concepts underlying language. In R. Schiefelbusch and L. Lloyd (Eds.), *Language perspectives: Acquisition, retardation and intervention.* Baltimore: University Park Press, 1974.

Schwartz, B. *Animal learning.* New York: W. W. Norton, 1978.

Searle, J. Speech acts and recent linguistics. In D. Aaronson and R. Rieber (Eds.), *Developmental psycholinguistics and communication disorders.* New York: New York Academy of Sciences, 1975.

Seligman, M., and Hager, J. *Biological boundaries of learning.* Englewood Cliffs, N.J.: Prentice Hall, 1972.

Shatz, M. On mechanisms of development in communication-based theories of language acquisition. In L. Gleitman (Ed.), *Proceedings of the Conference on Language Acquisition: The state of the art.* Cambridge: Harvard University Press, in press.

Shettleworth, S. J. Constraints on learning. In D. S. Lehrman, R. A. Hinde, and E. Shaw (Eds.), *Advances in the study of behavior.* New York: Academic Press, 1972.

Shotwell, J., Wolf, D., and Gardner, H. Exploring early symbolization: Styles of achievement. In B. Sutton-Smith (Ed.), *Symposium on play,* in preparation.

Sinclair, H. The transition from sensorimotor behavior to symbolic activity. *Interchange,* 1970, *1,* 119–125.

Sinclair, H. Sensorimotor action patterns as a condition for the acquisition of syntax. In R. Huxley and E. Ingram (Eds.), *Language acquisition: Models and methods.* New York: Academic Press, 1972.

Slobin, D. Cognitive prerequisites for grammar. In C. Ferguson and D. Slobin (Eds.), *Studies in child language development.* New York: Holt, Rinehart and Winston, 1973.

Slobin, D. The more it changes . . . In J. MacNamara (Ed.), *Language learning and thought.* New York: Academic Press, 1977.

Slobin, D., and Welsh, C. Elicited imitation as a research tool in developmental psycholinguistics. In C. Ferguson and D. Slobin (Eds.), *Studies in child language development.* New York: Holt, Rinehart and Winston, 1973.

Smith, C. An experimental approach to children's linguistic competence. In J. R. Hayes (Ed.), *Cognition and the development of language.* New York: John Wiley and Sons, 1970.

Snow, C., and Ferguson, C. *Talking to children: Language input and acquisition.* London: Cambridge University Press, 1977.

Snyder, L. *Pragmatics in language-deficient children: Prelinguistic and early verbal performatives and presuppositions.* Unpublished doctoral dissertation, University of Colorado, 1975.

Snyder, L., Carlson, V., Bretherton, I., and Bates, E. *Communicative and cognitive abilities in nonverbal autistic children.* Paper presented at the 10th Annual Stanford Child Language Research Conference, April 1978.

Snyder, L., and Woods, L. *Levels of pragmatic and sensorimotor performance in very young children with Down's syndrome.* Manuscript.

Spitz, E. A. *The first year of life*. New York: International Universities Press, 1965.

Starr, S. The relationship of single words to two-word sentences. *Child Development*, 1975, *46*, 701–708.

Stern, C., and Stern, W. *Die Kindersprache: Eine psychologische und sprachtheoretische untersuchung*. Leipzig: Berth, 1907.

Stern, D. N., Beebe, D., Jaffe, J., and Bennett, S. L. The infant's stimulus world during social interaction. In H. R. Schaffer (Ed.), *Studies in mother–infant interaction*. New York: Academic Press, 1977.

Stern, D. N., and Gibbon, J. Temporal expectancies of social behaviors in mother–infant play. In E. Thoman (Ed.), *The origins of the infant's responsiveness*. Hillsdale, N.J.: Lawrence Erlbaum Associates, 1977.

Stross, B. *The origin and evolution of language*. Dubuque, Iowa: W. C. Brown Co., 1976.

Sugarman, S. A description of communicative development in the prelanguage child. In I. Markova (Ed.), *The social context of language*. London: John Wiley and Sons, 1977.

Tanz, C. *Studies in the acquisition of deictic expression*. Cambridge: Cambridge University Press, 1978.

Thompson, D'Arcy. *On growth and form*. Cambridge: Cambridge University Press, 1917.

Thomson, J. R., and Chpman, R. S. Who is 'daddy' (revisited)? The status of two-year-olds' overextended words in use and comprehension. *Papers and Reports on Child Language Development*, Stanford University Committee on Linguistics, 1975, *10*, 59–60.

Tolman, E. C. *Purposive behavior of animals and men*. New York: Century, 1932.

Tversky, A. Features of similarity. *Psychological Review*, 1977, *84*, 327–352.

Uzgiris, I., and Hunt, J. McV. *Assessment in infancy: Ordinal scales of psychological development*. Urbana, Ill.: University of Illinois Press, 1975.

Van Lancker, D. *Heterogeneity in language and speech: Neurolinguistic studies*. Unpublished Ph.D. dissertation, University of California at Los Angeles, 1975. (Available as UCLA Working Papers in Phonetics #29.)

Volterra, V., Camaioni, L., and Bates, E. *Le prime parole: Dagli schemi sensomotori agli schemi representivi*. Unpublished manuscript. Rome: Consiglio Nazionale delle Ricerche, Instituto de Psicologia, 1975.

von Baer, K. E. *Entwicklungsgeschichte der Thiere: Beobachtung und Reflexion*. Konigsberg: Borntrager, 1828.

Vygotsky, L. S. *Thought and language*. Cambridge, Mass.: MIT Press, 1962.

Washburn, S. O. Tools and human evolution. *Scientific American*, 1960, *203*, 3–15.

Waters, E. The reliability and stability of individual differences in infant–mother attachment. *Child Development*, 1978, *49*, 483–494.

Wepman, J. M. Aphasia: Language without thought or thought without language? *ASHA*, March 1977, *18*, 131–138.

Werner, H., and Kaplan, B. *Symbol formation*. New York: John Wiley and Sons, 1963.

White, R. W. Motivation reconsidered: The concept of competence. *Psychological Review*, 1959, *66*, 267–333.

Witkin, H., Goodenough, D., and Karp, S. Stability of cognitive style from childhood to young adulthood. *Journal of Personality and Social Psychology*, 1967, 7, 291–300.

Wittgenstein, L. *The blue and the brown books*. New York: Harper and Row, 1958.

Wolf, D. Personal communication, June 1978.

Wolf, D., and Gardner, H. Style and sequence in symbolic play. In M. Franklin and N. Smith (Eds.), *Early symbolization*. Hillsdale, N.J.: Lawrence Erlbaum Associates, 1979.

INDEX